God's Message,
Your Sermon

In memory of Arthur B. Whiting,
whose expository preaching method inspired this book
and produced generations of expository preachers

And to
Dr. Robert A. Williams, Jr., Dr. Larry L. Harris, Sr. (deceased),
and Dr. George Waddles, Sr., who have carried on
this tradition in WHW Ministries.

Contents

Part IV
Demonstrating the Discovery, Development, and Delivery of What God Meant by What He Said

Foreword

Scripture gives no set liturgy for public church services and no detailed manual on church polity. But whenever the Bible does deal with either corporate worship or the duties of church leaders, it always stresses the vital importance of Biblical preaching and teaching.

To qualify for service as an elder in the church, for example, a man must be "able to teach" (1 Timothy 3:2), because his primary duty as an elder and teacher is "holding fast the faithful word as he has been taught, that he may be able, by sound doctrine, both to exhort and convict those who contradict" (Titus 1:9).

Thus when Paul told Timothy, "Preach the word!" (2 Timothy 4:2), he was summarizing and emphatically declaring the heart of the agenda for both corporate worship and the leadership and oversight of the church. Likewise, when Paul gave his charge to the elders of the church at Ephesus and told them "to *shepherd* the church of God" (Acts 20:28), this is precisely what he had first and foremost in his mind: leading and feeding the flock through the ministry of God's Word.

That agenda does not change to suit whatever is fashionable in any given generation. As a matter of fact, Paul's instructions to Timothy plainly stipulated that a time would come when people "will not endure sound doctrine, but . . . they will heap up for themselves teachers; and they will turn their ears away from the truth, and be turned aside to fables" (2 Timothy 4:3-4). In times and cultures such as those (which would certainly include the shallow age in which we now live) every pastor's duty remains fixed and crystal-clear: "Preach the word . . . *in season and out of season.*"

Years ago, when I originally sensed God's calling to pastoral ministry, my father (who was himself a preacher and the son of a preacher) gave me a Bible which he had inscribed with that simple text: "Preach the Word!" It was a simple reminder of every pastor's most crucial task, and that brief command from 2 Timothy 4 has remained a singular focus for me. I have never once thought to deviate from it.

Pastors nowadays are presented with an endless parade of fads and diversions—all claiming to be better means than biblical preaching for stimulating church growth or attracting people. Pollsters, church-growth experts, and even some seminary professors are solemnly warning us that preaching is truly out of season. The church is overrun, it seems, with self-styled experts telling church leaders how to be timely, trendy, and innovative. Biblical preaching is invariably their first target. They counsel pastors to preach shorter sermons with less biblical and doctrinal content and more cultural references. Many pastors today therefore devote inordinate amounts of time and energy to immersing themselves in pop culture and trying to keep up with the latest fads. (One young pastor told me with a straight face that he regarded going to the cinema as "sermon preparation," because he based so many of his messages on themes from hit movies.) Meanwhile, the study and proclamation of God's Word is in serious decline, even in some seminaries and historic churches that were once thought of as strong precisely because of their devotion to biblical preaching.

Blessed is the man who keeps preaching the Word, even when such preaching is supposedly out of season.

Like Wayne House and Dan Garland, I am convinced that the best method of preaching is expository. In other words, it is the kind of preaching that aims to draw the meaning and message *from the biblical text* and proclaim that truth with authority and passion—as opposed to merely using a phrase of Scripture for a sermon title; making a verse of God's Word into a jumping-off point for a topical treatment of something; or borrowing an idea or a story from the Bible as incidental illustrative material for a motivational talk.

Drs. House and Garland carefully outline one very effective method of expository preaching, and they show in thorough detail how to do it and do it well. Their explanation is replete with much valuable and practical help for how to understand the biblical text, how to think it through thoroughly, how to organize a sermon, and how to deliver it clearly and effectively. This is a welcome addition to the expository preacher's library, one of the finest new resources I have seen in years.

I love Dr. House's and Dr. Garland's passion for biblical exposition, their careful attention to the text of Scripture, and (above all) their devotion to the truth of Scripture. Those standout qualities—combined with remarkable giftedness as a teachers and the ability to make almost any concept clear—are the main features that make this book so wonderfully valuable. The authors' commitment to expository preaching is contagious, too. That's why I'm delighted to see this book in print, and I hope it will find a large audience among pastors, young men still training for ministry, and even lay people with teaching duties in the church. If you are in such a role and are looking for help to make your ministry more effective, this could well be the most valuable book you will read all year.

JOHN MACARTHUR
Pastor-teacher of Grace Community
Church in Sun Valley, California,
and president of the Master's College and Seminary

Preface

"Preach the Word!" was Paul's straightforward charge to his young assistant Timothy (2 Tim 4:1–2), and this call has gone out to thousands of ministers of the Word of God since the original command was written. There can be no higher calling given to a servant of Christ than what Paul gave to Timothy.

The calling is honorable, though not all those who have received the call have honored the position. Failure has occurred notoriously in homes and communities when preachers have not been godly leaders. These are tragic shortcomings that are indicative of the on-going struggle with the flesh, the world, and the devil. What has often been passed over, however, is the failure of the man of God when standing in the pulpit, standing before the people of God, with the Word of God. Dealing unfaithfully with the biblical text is no less serious an ethical failure than any lapse into immorality. Those who are to be elders (bishops, overseers, pastors) in Christ's church must meet the high standards of character, given in 1 Timothy 3:1–7 and Titus 1:5–9, precisely because God has commissioned them to proclaim doctrine and give reproof, correction, and instruction in righteousness from the sacred text (2 Tim 4:2; cf 2 Tim 3:16–17). Failure to communicate the timeless truths of God's Word compromises the very purpose for which godly character is demanded of preachers.

In the west there is an abundance of Bibles available to most families, but few of these Bibles are being carefully studied. There are thousands of preachers in the pulpits, but there is a dearth of the proclamation of the words of God. Much of this is due to topical or applicational preaching that gives little consideration to the contextual meaning of the words of God found in the Bible. In our day, the tendency is to use Bible verses as a point of departure for a topic the preacher wants to communicate to his congregation, without ever explaining the author's intent. Application often does not come from the text being preached but from whatever practices the preacher desires for his congregants to follow. Of course, most preachers who follow this approach are well-intentioned but were never taught the importance of expositing the text of Scripture. It is our belief that the minister of Christ is obligated to explain the words of God to those under his care, and to derive the meaning of the sermon directly from biblical text.

God's Message, Your Sermon sets forth in a careful and progressive manner the procedure for preparing and delivering expositional sermons. Chapter by chapter, the building blocks of biblical expositional preaching are provided and illustrated by graphics and charts. The chapters on sermon preparation and delivery use one sermon to show development throughout the book, but then also provide other sermon examples. The appendices give additional examples of sermons showing the application of the procedure to the variety of literature found in Scripture. Those who have limited knowledge of the Hebrew and Greek languages will be able to apply almost all of the techniques of sermon preparation, but there is additional help for those who can use the original languages of Scripture. God is pleased to honor His words when His imperfect but qualified servants are equipped and willing to communicate their true meaning. So "Preach the Word!"

Acknowledgments

Many people have input into the production of a book at its various stages. We must first of all acknowledge Arthur B. Whiting from whose method of, and passion for, preaching we have greatly benefited, though neither of us ever knew him personally. Next, we must express our appreciation for Milton Jones who was the instructor in homiletics at Western Seminary from whom we learned the Whiting Method. We also thank Dr. Dennis Wretlind for the use of his material on integrating exegesis into the Whiting Method.

Daniel Garland thanks the professors of Faith Evangelical Seminary, and its President, Michael Adams, under whom he earned the degree of Doctor of Ministry in Expository Communication, especially H. Wayne House under whom he wrote his dissertation on the Whiting Method of exposition. He is also indebted to his brother Hubert and V. Deane Keller for providing early examples of solid expositional preaching, and especially to his wife, Kathy, without whose faithful love, encouragement and support his contribution to the book would not have been made.

Both of us greatly appreciate Wayne R. Kinde, formerly V.P. and Publisher of Reference and Electronic at Thomas Nelson Publishers, for his encouragement to write this book. Others at Nelson have been involved in its production, especially Michael Stephens, Senior Editor of Bible and Reference at Nelson who has worked very closely with us through the entire process. Additional thanks to Robert Sanford, V.P. and Publisher of Bibles, Mark McGarry, designer at Texas Type & Book Works, and Renee Chavez, copyeditor, for their assistance in the publication of the book.

God's Message,
Your Sermon

CHAPTER 1

The Question: Why Expository Preaching?

WELCOME to a consideration of what is arguably the highest privilege of all earthly endeavors—the solemn, authoritative proclamation of the Word of God.

Someone has said, "If God calls you to be a missionary, don't stoop to be a king."[1] The same advice applies to all who serve as God's ambassadors. But with great privileges—like speaking for God—come great responsibilities, among them, being as well prepared as possible.

THE URGENT NEED FOR A SYSTEMATIC APPROACH TO PREACHING BIBLICAL TEXTS

Speaking for God

Few evangelical Christians would deny the urgency of proclaiming the message of God's Word, the Bible. If its very words are God-breathed and "profitable" (2 Tim. 3:16–17 NKJV), then the value of communicating its timeless truth cannot be overestimated. Hearing the biblical text and understanding its meaning and relevant implications for life-change is the basis for faith (see Romans 10:16–17). And without faith, it is impossible to please God (Heb. 11:6). It is no wonder, then, that the apostle Paul addressed his understudy Timothy with this pressing imperative, which likewise commands all who would be God's spokespeople: "I charge you therefore before God and the Lord Jesus Christ, who will judge the living and the dead at His appearing and His kingdom: Preach the word! Be ready in season and out of season. Convince, rebuke, exhort, with all longsuffering and teaching" (2 Tim. 4:1–2 NKJV).

The problem is that sermons do not ring with God's *authority* simply because the preacher uses God's *Word*.[2] To ensure that *you* serve the Word, and not vice versa, you need an approach to sermon development and delivery that truly allows a text to speak for itself.

Adequate Methodology

Even those who praise biblical exposition as the indispensable means of faithfully communicating God's Word, do not always practice it. One reason that sermons that effectively communicate God's message are so scarce is ignorance of how to prepare and deliver them—especially in developing countries. Without a practical method for developing sermons from within a given Scripture text, preachers tend to speak on topics for which scriptural support is either out of context, incomplete, or missing altogether. As a result, people hear *human* reasoning instead of biblical truth. Not only does this disserve humanity by failing to meet real human needs, for which God's Word is uniquely adequate (see 2 Timothy 3:17), but it also dishonors God by misrepresenting Him.

The Whiting Method

To meet the urgent need for a systematic approach to preaching biblical texts, a British-born preacher and scholar named Arthur B. Whiting initiated a technique that came to be called the *Whiting Method*. This approach develops a text's theme from principles formulated on the basis of word studies. Though the original system was never published, a variety of professors, including Milton William Jones and Dennis O. Wretlind, have taught and made valuable modifications to it. (Their contributions will be discussed in Chapter 4.) In keeping with this refining process, this book will demonstrate that when the Whiting

Method is used with all relevant contextual data, it is a valuable tool in helping preachers rightly interpret and proclaim the intended meaning of Bible texts. *God's Message, Your Sermon* will help expositors develop and deliver the truth they discover, within the boundaries of the literary unit of Scripture under study.

Is Preaching Different from Teaching?

When Paul concluded his charge to Timothy to "preach the word" with the phrase "with . . . teaching" (2 Tim. 4:2), he raised for us an important question: What is the difference, if any, between expository *preaching* and *teaching*?

EXPOSITION, THE COMMON BOND
OF BIBLICAL PREACHING AND TEACHING

In his book *Biblical Preaching,* Haddon Robinson offers a definition of expository preaching that is consistent with a conservative view of Scripture and a commitment to interpretation that is faithful to the biblical text: "*Expository preaching*—the communication of a biblical concept, derived from and transmitted through a historical, grammatical, literary study of a passage in its context, which the Holy Spirit first applies to the personality and experience of the preacher, then through him to his hearers."[3] This definition (as well as that of Lawrence O. Richards and Gary J. Bredfelt, in their book, *Creative Bible Teaching*[4]) hardly distinguishes preaching from expository teaching. From the time of the New Testament's completion, preachers and teachers are essentially indistinguishable. Both are responsible for conveying the meaning and implications of God's written revelation (2 Tim. 4:2; 1 Tim. 4:11, 13). Preaching includes the same explanation of biblical truth for life-change that is normally associated with teaching or instruction. By the same token, the teacher's lesson plan, just as the preacher's sermon, should be structured to achieve the effect that the text was meant to have on the listener's mind, attitude, and behavior.[5] What *distinguishes* preaching from teaching is its authoritative appeal to the will in the context of corporate worship.[6] One might say that all preaching faithful to the text is expositional, but not all exposition is necessarily preaching.

The Distinctive Role of Expository Preaching[7]

Sermons are structured literary units crafted to impact listeners with what God has to say to them in the context of their meeting in His presence.[8] Reminding people of their responsibilities and solemnly charging them in the presence of God, the speaker worships God by letting Him speak (see 2 Timothy 2:14). With His solemn authority, preachers reprove, rebuke, encourage, correct, persuade, and comfort, as well as inform, explain, and motivate. (See Titus 2:15 and 1 Thessalonians 2:9–12.) Those present, then, worship God by giving attention to His message. (See 1 Thessalonians 2:13–16.) But who is adequate to fulfill the responsibilities of the high and holy privilege of ministering to these hearers? (See 2 Corinthians 2:15–16; 3:5–6.)

Are Preachers Born or Made?

Bible scholar R. E. O. White once commented, "Good preachers are born, not made."[9] He then explained by adding, "Technique and teaching will never impart the gift." White balances these remarks, however, by stating, "Without guidance, the most earnest preacher of the gospel hacks away with a blunt knife at the most delicate of operations, his labour vastly increased, his effectiveness sadly decreased, by his lack of a method." If White is correct, books and courses on preaching can provide *part* of the guidance necessary for the development and effective use of God's gifts. But competent preachers are first *born* with *natural* abilities that training can't add. When they are later born from above (see John 3:3 NET), they receive *spiritual* gifts that training can't add (see Galatians 1:15–24). Finally, they develop their natural abilities and spiritual gifts *through* training, without which these gifts and abilities would remain underdeveloped at best.

Is One Method of Sermon Preparation and Delivery Worthy of Universal Adoption?

Methods Are Variable

That this book presents an adaptation of the Whiting Method of homiletics is a testimony to the fact that methods are always various and variable. Richards and Bredfeldt wrote, "Methods are not an end. They are a means to an end."[10] Therefore, preachers should be flexible in their adoption and use of methods.

When the "end" is preaching the Word of God, to His glory, the best methods are likely to have a great deal in common. While no method should ever be used with slavish devotion, or touted as *the* method, what commends the Whiting Method is its step-by-step approach, which can be easily understood, remembered, and taught. It is built on respect for both the Scriptures' authority and the important role of the communicator. It is adaptable and transferable. It focuses on the biblical text from beginning to end, with no introduction of extraneous matter; thus it is exegetical[11] rather than eisegetical.[12]

The value of any systematic approach to preaching is demonstrated not by the greatest public speakers and scholars but by its ability to sustain even those of modest skill in faithful ministries over time. For more than thirty years, the writers have used the Whiting Method and found it beneficial as a means to the end of communicating God's message in the power of the Holy Spirit.

Does One Have to Know Greek and Hebrew to Preach the Word or Use This Method?

The biblical doctrine of the inspiration of Scripture is based on 2 Timothy 3:16 and means that the whole of Scripture is God-breathed and without error *in the original autographs.*[13] The Bible's authority extends equally to all parts and every word. So the ability to read and work in the original scriptural languages is not only advantageous to the preacher and teacher, but necessary in order to preach and teach with maximum confidence and command. But for those lacking formal training in Hebrew and Greek, there are many helpful tools today to assist in gaining much of the knowledge traditionally reserved for the person who reads the original languages.[14] Those who use these tools along with the English translation of the Bible may implement the Whiting Method and greatly benefit both themselves and their listeners.

PART I

Discovering What God Meant
by What He Said

❋

Part I of *God's Message, Your Sermon* surveys certain assumptions and biblical principles on which we base our adaptation of the Whiting Method of homiletics.

Chapter 2, "The Charge: Speaking for God to a Contemporary Audience," explores the preacher's responsibilities. It presupposes that God exists, that the Bible is His word in His very words, and that God uses people to bridge the communication gap between the ancient text of Scripture and contemporary listeners.

Chapter 3, "The Channel: Representing God as His Mouthpiece," probes the preacher's roles and relationships. It presumes that God's message is always conveyed to people through the personalities of unique individuals that He has chosen and prepared.

Chapter 4, "The Challenge: Bridging the Communication Gap," explains how the Arthur B. Whiting Method of homiletics may be adapted and used to build a functional bridge for communicating God's message to listeners.

CHAPTER 2

The Charge: Speaking for God to a Contemporary Audience

SUPPOSE you are to prepare and preach a sermon from 1 John 2:1–2.[1] Your text, from the New King James Version, reads, "My little children, these things I write to you, so that you may not sin. And if anyone sins, we have an Advocate with the Father, Jesus Christ the righteous. And He Himself is the propitiation for our sins, and not for ours only but also for the whole world."

It doesn't take a theological education to notice that these are not your words to your audience. They were written rather than spoken, by an apostle, not by a modern preacher or teacher. The apostle and his readers were of a different nationality. They lived far away and long ago. Yet believing the passage to be the Word of God gives you confidence that its message is still relevant to you and your listeners. It also means that you will stand between God and your contemporaries as His spokesperson. But how can you and those you teach be sure that your sermon communicates God's message? Before embracing any method of sermon development or launching into the actual work of preparing a message, it is important to size up the multifaceted communication gap your sermon must bridge. This involves the issues of *authority, antiquity, relevance, meaning, delivery,* and *connecting.*

THE AUTHORITY OF SCRIPTURE, IT'S NOT OUR OWN

God Has Made Himself Known to Man

Anyone who would write or speak for God assumes an awesome responsibility (see James 3:1). To do so on one's own authority would be the height of presumption (see 1 Peter 4:10–11). But if God exists, and the Bible is His Word, then faithful communication of truth is not only possible, but is commanded, is desperately needed, and is the pinnacle of privilege (see John 17:17; 2 Timothy 4:2; and Proverbs 29:18). The urgency of proclaiming God's Word is indicated by its very purpose. According to authors Lawrence Richards and Gary Bredfeldt, the Bible is meant to reveal the personal being of God, who transcends His creation but still chooses to be in close relation to it.[2] If this is true, then the importance of its message cannot be overstated. The words of J. I. Packer serve well: "What were we made for? To know God. What aim should we set ourselves in life? To know God. What is the 'eternal life' that Jesus gives? Knowledge of God . . . (John 17:3). What is the best thing in life, bringing more joy, delight and contentment than anything else? Knowledge of God."[3]

According to Scripture, things can be known about God by what He has created (Rom. 1:18–20), as things can be known about an artist by looking at his paintings.[4] But only through God's Son (Heb. 1:1–4; John 20:30–31), the Word in human form (see John 1:1, 14, and 18), and through the Bible, His Word in written human language (2 Tim. 3:16), may He be known in personal relationship.[5] Anything less than the authoritative declaration and accurate explanation of His own self-disclosure is powerless to bring sinful people into the intimacy of a right relationship with their Creator, and to bring immature saints to maturity in Christ.[6]

God's Word Meets Real Human Needs

Real human needs stem from the willful rejection of the knowledge of God (see Romans 1:18–20 and John 17:3). The Bible is God-given information about Him, for the purpose of meeting people's need to truly know Him as He is.[7] The Word of God is described as "living and active" because it expresses the discerning mind of the living God (Heb. 4:12 NASU). The apostle Paul commanded Timothy to "preach the word" (2 Tim. 4:2 NKJV). Adequately equipping God's people for every good work depends on the human ministries of teaching, reproof, correction, and training in righteousness, for which the God-breathed Scripture as a whole is profitable (2 Tim. 3:16).[8] Second Peter 1:21 says, "Men moved by the Holy Spirit spoke from God" (NASU) (cp. Acts 4:25). It is precisely because He has put His words into the mouths of men that they need not (and dare not) put *their* words into the mouth of God!

Too often, however, Christian communicators forfeit God's authority by conveying their own messages rather than His, for at least three reasons: popularity, the precepts of men, and perversion of biblical texts. The remedy in every case is to remember that the source of one's sermon is the Scripture.

Popularity

The lure of popularity is a common pitfall, tempting both the compassionate preacher and the unconscionable one. It often results in attending to the felt needs of listeners. An extreme illustration is found in 1 Kings 22.

The question was whether Jehoshaphat, king of Judah, and Ahab, king of Israel, should go to battle against the Arameans at Ramoth-gilead. Some four hundred prophets agreed to tell King Ahab what they knew he wanted to hear: *Go to war! You'll win!* Their popularity with the king ranked higher than integrity before God.

But Micaiah was summoned for a second opinion. Under great pressure to maintain uniformity with the prophets who spoke favorably, "Micaiah said 'As the LORD lives, whatever the LORD says to me, that I will speak'" (v. 14 NKJV). In contrast to what his audience wanted to hear, Micaiah accurately predicted the defeat and death of Ahab. He also revealed that a deceiving spirit had been sent into the mouths of all the other prophets. The account shows that the real needs of people are met by the faithful proclamation of the Word of God, not by tickling their itching ears, which Paul condemned in 2 Timothy 4:3–4: "For the time will come when they will not endure sound doctrine, but according to their own desires, because they have itching ears, they will heap up for themselves teachers; and they will turn their ears away from the truth, and be turned aside to fables" (NKJV).

Precepts of Men

If popularity can pull preachers away from their calling and place them on their own authority, so can the precepts of men. But man's creation in God's likeness means that he has the ability to exercise judgment. Yet every individual has his own ideas of what is true, right, good, important, timely, moral, and appropriate (Isa. 53:6; Prov. 14:12; 16:25), and speaks out of what fills his heart (Matt. 12:34). Being spiritually dead (Eph. 2:1–2) as a result of his sin in Adam (Rom. 5:12), the natural man is neither willing nor able to respond positively to the things of God (1 Cor. 2:14). While this affects every aspect of man's being, it does not remove his ability to make decisions with accountability to God. Neither does regeneration guarantee that a believer will always speak and behave as a spiritual child of God. Because of sin, no one can be trusted, nor trust in himself, to speak for God as an independent agent (Jer. 17:5, 9). Not even Jesus, the sinless Son and Word of God in human form, spoke on His own initiative (see John 5:30; 8:28; 10:18; 12:49; and 14:10). At the conclusion of the Sermon on the Mount in the Gospel of Matthew, we read, "And so it was, when Jesus had ended these sayings, that the people were astonished at His teaching, for He taught them as one having authority, and not as the scribes" (7:28–29 NKJV; cf. Mark 1:22). According to Matthew 15:9, the scribes taught "AS DOCTRINES THE PRECEPTS OF MEN" (NASU).

Perversion of Biblical Texts

In addition to the pressures of popularity and human precepts is the tendency of preachers and teachers to pervert the meaning of Bible texts when they are used to teach something other than what the biblical writer intended.[9] A 1993 article in *Christian Education Journal* warns readers of "an authority crisis" in Bible teaching and Bible-based curricula: "If the Bible is used only as a jump-off point for one's own objectives, the Bible's authority is being bypassed, because if a passage is not being used to teach what the Bible is teaching, the teacher stands only in his/her own authority. Too much of today's modern curriculum teaches only with human authority rather than with the authority of God. This then is the authority crisis in curriculum."[10]

Even teaching a truth from a Scripture that does *not* teach that truth is a form of false teaching! Author and exegetist Walter Kaiser gives practical advice to those who would avoid this common error: "If the particular truth in which we are interested is indeed taught somewhere else in the Bible, then we must proceed immediately to that context for the message."[11]

Speaking for God, with His authority, means that we preach God's message, not our own. It requires the preacher to be willing to tell people what they need to hear rather than being swayed by popularity, human precepts, or perversions of the author's intended meaning.

In contrast with these three improper approaches, there is also a tendency on the part of some to wrongly think that biblical texts are ready-made sermons.

THE SOURCE OF ONE'S SERMON

The text of Scripture provides the material from which a sermon is made, not the sermon itself.[12] First John 2:1–2, for example, is neither a sermon nor the outline of a sermon. If the charge to preach the Word to a contemporary audience meant simply to read or recite the text with good oral interpretation (or even running commentary), then this book would be both misleading and unnecessary. There is certainly value in the audible reading of God's Word as part of public worship,[13] and there are edifying ministries of the Word other than expository preaching and teaching.[14] Such ministries may even avoid the danger of putting human words into God's mouth. But sermons *are* human creations for communicating divine messages given in one setting to learners who live in a different setting. So for you to speak "as the oracles of God" (1 Pet. 4:11), you must recognize and do your part to bridge the contextual divide between the original audience and your own.

THE ANTIQUITY OF SCRIPTURE, THE COMMUNICATION GAP

The Bible was written long ago, in distant lands, to people of different languages, cultures, and history, whose specific responsibilities toward God are different from those to whom the modern teacher and preacher communicates.[15] In short, not a word of Scripture was addressed to the contemporary preacher or audience. Paul's imperative to "preach the word" requires that the herald first understand the author's intended meaning, in his setting and that of his addressees.[16] Only then can the timeless truth be extracted from its original situation and extended without distortion into the new and different situations of people living today. Those now sitting under the preaching of God's Word cannot help but regard the content of Scripture as ancient, foreign, distant, and difficult, as well as supernatural. If they are to hear what God has to say to them in terms that are current, familiar, near, understandable, and life changing, you must do all you can to bridge the communication gap.[17] (See figure 2-1.)

It is not enough that the speaker of biblical principles be personally convinced of their relevance. The successful minister must also help the audience overcome the natural bias against all that seems archaic and irrelevant in favor of the latest scientific discoveries and pop culture. It is good to remember the Bible's own claim to timeless relevance. Ezra the priest declared, "Forever, O LORD, Your word is settled

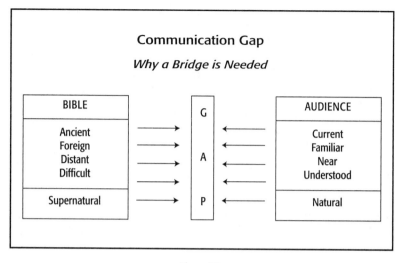

Figure 2.1

in heaven" (Ps. 119:89 NKJV). The modern student of Scripture can learn to appreciate the unchanging truth and universal applicability of the Bible as Jesus and His apostles regarded the Hebrew Scriptures (see 2 Timothy 3:16–17).[18] Communicators of God's plan of the ages can also draw the attention of their listeners to archaeological discoveries that confirm the ancient record.[19] In the hands of the modern preacher, like you, the antiquity of biblical texts can give listeners a fixed point of reference for their personal navigation in a world of constant change. But their natural skepticism and need to be convinced are part of the communication gulf that you are charged to span. In the next chapter, we will consider the importance of the preacher as God's representative. Nothing is more convincing of the Bible's relevance and power to change lives than the changed life of God's spokespeople.[20]

In addition to being ancient, foreign, and distant, the Bible is uniquely difficult. Its sheer length, variety of literary styles,[21] and complexity set it apart. It is comprised of sixty-six books written in three foreign languages. It covers the span of time itself. It presupposes unseen and prehistoric realities that require faith (see Hebrews 11:3, 6). Most important, the Bible is of a supernatural character that necessitates spiritual understanding. "For prophecy never came by the will of man, but holy men of God spoke as they were moved by the Holy Spirit" (2 Pet. 1:21 NKJV). The faithful minister of the Word will take this aspect of the communication gap into account, prayerfully depending on the Holy Spirit for illumination and understanding of God's Word. The preacher will also anticipate that at least some listeners may be utterly insensitive to God, "dead in trespasses and sins" (see Ephesians 2:1–3 NKJV). Until the hearers are born from above[22] and receive the Spirit of truth (see John 14:17; 15:26; and 16:13; and 1 John 4:6), a speaker's accomplishments through relational and verbal bridge building will be limited. And until God changes the listeners' hearts, His message will be met with resistance, indifference, or rejection. (See Matthew 10:24–25 and Romans 3:10–18.) God's representatives must not seek to bridge this gap between spiritual life and spiritual death with the man-made solutions of the social sciences, personal charm, or entertainment.[23] Neither will they fail to craft their sermons as the best possible packages in which to deliver God's message to those whose hearts may be opened to receive it. (See Acts 16:14.)

When considering the Grand Canyon–size rift between the Scripture writers and the hearers of sermons, remember that even re-generate listeners (and speakers) have an enemy, against whose schemes they must be armed and stand firm (see Matthew 13:39; Ephesians 6:10–17; and 1 Peter 5:8). Possessing "ears to hear" (Matt. 13:9 NKJV) is the responsibility of the listener to God's message. Having hearts like soil that is well prepared to receive the broadcast Word of God is a spiritual condition, granted by God. Not even the Son of man produced receptivity in His listeners simply by the content or delivery of His message (see verses 11–12, 23). There are aspects of the commu-nication gap between God's Word and the congregation that only God can bridge. Therefore, you, as God's spokesperson, must carefully de-vote all available energy to the aspects of bridge building for which you are responsible to God: namely, diligent study of God's Word with de-pendence upon His Spirit. Your preaching may be the means God uses to open hearts, since "faith comes by hearing, and hearing by the word of God" (Rom. 10:17 NKJV).

Even at the time of writing, merely understanding the language, knowing the culture, and recognizing the genre did not ensure that the original readers, any more than contemporary readers, would grasp the meaning and application of the text.[24] Spiritual discernment was needed.

Character of Scripture, Written for Us but Not to Us

At least four characteristics of Scripture explain why spiritual discernment (1 Cor. 2:14–15) and diligent study (2 Tim. 2:15) are required of students of the Word: (1) the supernatural quality of Scripture; (2) the progress of revelation; (3) the distinction between the redemptive and kingdom programs of God; and (4) the fact that truth must be derived from what was revealed to others, in circumstances different from those of the contemporary preacher and congregation.

The Supernatural Quality of Scripture

The Bible is the result of the Spirit's revealing the mind of God to humanity (1 Cor. 2:10–13). Its supernatural quality is such that the unaided human mind cannot understand or accept it (vv. 12–14).[25] A person deprived of spiritual understanding, whether as a result of judgment, apostasy, or remaining spiritually dead in trespasses and sins, is walking in darkness. (See Isaiah 9:1; Lamentations 3:2; Luke 11:34–36; Ephesians 2:1–3; 1 Thessalonians 5:4–5; and 1 John 1:6–7.) With the illuminating work of the Holy Spirit, however, the believer is able to understand spiritual truth (1 Cor. 2:13, 15–16). The Bible then becomes a lamp to his feet and a light on his path (Ps. 119:105; 2 Pet. 1:19). This is why the apostle John denied the need of any other source of instruction than the Holy Spirit's anointing, which every believer has from the moment he or she believes (1 Jn. 2:27).

The Progress of Revelation

Written revelation was given step-by-step, as a parent's instruction of a child, giving only information appropriate for each stage of development.[26] Thus, God's Word, says author Robert Traina, "is moving, and moving steadily from the lower to the higher, from the lesser to the greater, from the partial to the total, from the temporary to the final."[27] Therefore, the Old Testament must never be interpreted as if it were the New Testament. The student of Scripture must discover whether a particular standard established in the Old has been abrogated, altered, or affirmed in the New Testament.

The Distinction Between the Redemptive and Kingdom Programs of God

What Stanley A. Ellisen called "the redemptive program"[28] of God, to justify lost sinners,[29] must not to be confused with what he termed "the kingdom program"[30] to restore man's rule on earth through Christ as the last Adam and heir to David's throne (1 Cor. 15:24–28, 45). Accordingly, you must be conscious of changes in the way God administers His earthly kingdom. What He expects from His people as a test of obedience and basis for blessing and reward, changes according to which covenant is in view.[31] God's justification of sinners, on the other hand, has always been by grace through faith in what is revealed about the person and work of Christ (Eph. 2:8–9).[32] This never changes. So truth pertaining to the believer's sanctification and rewards must be faithfully distinguished from truth pertaining to justification.[33]

The Derivation of Truth Revealed to Others

While all Scripture is profitable for the believer's thorough equipping for good works (2 Tim. 3:17), every truth it teaches must be derived from something said to someone else in different circumstances (1 Cor. 10:11). To preach with the authority of firsthand knowledge, there is no substitute for the study of God's Word for the purpose of first knowing and doing His will, then teaching it (see Ezra 7:10). The very passion to communicate is properly derived from changes the speaker is making as a lifelong learner continually growing into the likeness of Christ.

(See Colossians 1:10 and Ephesians 4:15–16.) But first comes the hard work of study.

Adequate preparation for the presentation of God's Word requires strenuous effort. In 2 Timothy 2:15, Paul writes, "Be diligent to present yourself approved to God, a worker who does not need to be ashamed, rightly dividing the word of truth" (NKJV). The word translated "be diligent," means "to take pains." "Rightly dividing," literally means "to cut straight." As a tentmaker, Paul would have had a special apprecia-tion for the importance of accuracy in handling leather and other valu-able fabric so that the pieces cut from it fit together. When a useful finished product was formed without unnecessary waste, the worker himself was approved. Skillful labor was required, not just good inten-tions, the right attitude, or the proper approach.[34]

The Interpretation of Scripture: God Meant Something by What He Said

The Single Meaning of Scripture

Confidence that *your sermon* communicates *God's message* requires an adequate philosophy of meaning. The Arthur B. Whiting Method of sermon development, an adaptation of which is presented in Chapter 4, assumes *literal hermeneutics. Hermeneutics* has been defined as "the science and art of Biblical interpretation."[35] It involves skillful obser-vance of rules within a system that presupposes certain things about authority and the nature of language.[36] Literal hermeneutics assumes the single meaning of Scripture[37] which was fixed by the writer's use of words in their original contexts.[38] Because of its contextual orientation, literal hermeneutics has been called the "historical-grammatical" ap-proach to biblical interpretation.[39] A more complete description would be the "literal-grammatical-historical-cultural-literary-contextual in-terpretation." Though cumbersome, this compound expression reflects the fact that every contextual layer defines the meanings of the words in which they were written. (See figure 2-2.)

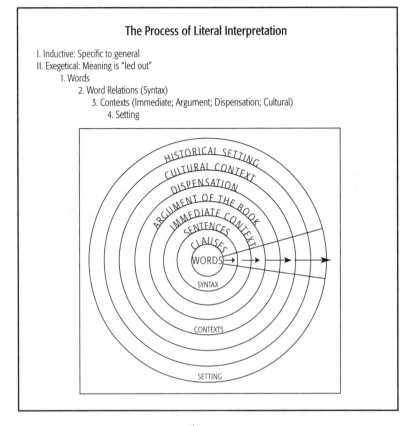

The Process of Literal Interpretation

I. Inductive: Specific to general
II. Exegetical: Meaning is "led out"
    1. Words
        2. Word Relations (Syntax)
            3. Contexts (Immediate; Argument; Dispensation; Cultural)
                4. Setting

Figure 2.2

GUIDING THEOLOGICAL PRINCIPLES

Literal interpretation is guided by at least seven theological convictions about the nature of written revelation, briefly summarized in figure 2-3 and described as follows:[40]

1. *The Principle of Clarity*. This principle holds that God communicated with man for the purpose of being understood. Thus, the single meaning of biblical texts is not only possible, but divinely intended. "By use of scientific philology and the illumination of the Spirit we arrive at the clarity of Scripture, and there is no need to resort to the Church," wrote Baptist theologian Bernard Ramm, explaining the

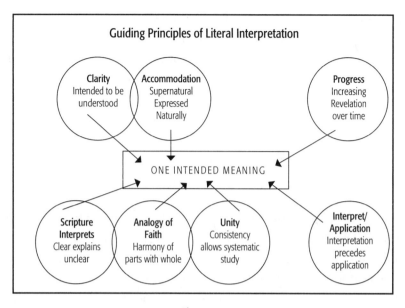

Figure 2.3

Protestant view of clarity in contrast to that of Roman Catholicism.[41] Rather than looking for elaborate systems of codes, symbols, or keys to unlock hidden meanings, the interpreter guided by this principle will expect to discover what God disclosed through "the laws of language."[42] This does not mean that golden nuggets of truth all lie exposed on the surface of Scripture, but that they may be discovered by normal literary "mining" practices when illumined by the Holy Spirit.

2. *The Principle of Accommodation* refers to God's use of words to express supernatural realities in natural terminology so that people can grasp concepts that would otherwise be incomprehensible. Examples include references to God's having eyes (Gen. 6:8), arms (Ps. 44:3), wings (Ps. 91:4), etc. Without God's willingness to condescend to the limits of finite human understanding, there would be no clarity. The close association of these principles is represented in figure 2-3 by the overlapping circles.

3. *The Principle of the Progress of Revelation*, briefly discussed earlier in this chapter, refers to increasing revelation over time. While the

Hebrew Scriptures are no less God-breathed, they are foundational to the New Testament built upon them. This principle is succinctly summarized in the following statement attributed to Saint Augustine (AD 354–430):

> *The New is in the Old contained,*
> *The Old is in the New explained.*
> *The New is in the Old latent.*
> *The Old is in the New patent.*[43]

4. *The "Scripture Interprets Scripture" Principle* refers to the claim of Martin Luther and other reformers that instead of appealing to the magisterium of the Roman Catholic church to provide the meaning of a biblical text, "the entire Holy Scripture is the context and guide for understanding the particular passages of Scripture."[44] In other words, the clearest passages of Scripture on a given topic or doctrine render the meaning of less-clear passages on the same subject.

5. *The Principle of the Analogy of the Faith* is closely related to the previous principle. It means that the correct meaning of a given passage will never contradict the teaching of Scripture as a whole on that point.[45]

6. *The Unity of Scripture Principle* assumes the integrity of revelation as given by one author. In the words of Bernard Ramm, this principle holds that "there is one system of truth or theology contained in Scripture, and therefore all doctrines must cohere or agree with each other."[46] While deductions must never be imposed upon a given text, this principle provides the basis for a systematic study of Scripture in order to discover what "the Bible teaches" on a given topic or doctrine. It also provides a corrective of methods that assert multiple meanings in Scripture.[47]

7. *The Principle of Interpretation and Application* recognizes that, while a text has but one meaning, it may have many applications. Accordingly, the applications of a passage must never be confused with its interpretation, which must always precede its applications in the process of expositing the text of Scripture.[48]

Together, the guiding principles of literal hermeneutics should be appreciated for what they are, without expecting more than they can provide. Simply following them does not impart the skill needed to "play the game," any more than following the rules of tennis makes one a champion. By the same token, skillful play *without* rules is not tennis! This is the conclusion of David Neff's evaluation of I. Howard Marshall's book *Beyond the Bible*. In reference to historic Church councils and creeds, Marshall contends that in moving from revelation to doctrine, more is needed than rules of interpreting Scripture. Neff's conclusion has merit: "The rules for interpreting Scripture can take us only so far, but as Marshall and Vanhoozer demonstrate, we can learn a lot by watching great interpreters playing at their finest."[49]

Literal Interpretation

Literal interpretation stands in contrast to *allegorical interpretation*, which holds that the real, spiritual meaning of Scripture lies hidden beneath the actual words the writer used.[50] The disadvantage and danger of allegorical interpretation is that it provides no objective safeguard against a person's bringing *personal* prejudices and assumptions to the text. It allows the imposition of a theological system upon the text rather than allowing the text to correct the system.[51] William Ames (1576–1633) stated the case against allegorical interpretation with even greater brevity and poignancy: "Anything which does not mean one thing surely means nothing."[52]

Conversely, the great advantage of literal interpretation is its recognition that meaning is grounded in objective fact, thus eliminating the need for speculation and protecting the interpretive process against subjectivity. Literal interpretation is consistent with the inductive method of Bible study, which moves from observation of what the text actually says to a general principle on the basis of specific textual data.[53] Inductive Bible study is, in turn, consistent with the conservative view of Scripture itself, which holds that "God has communicated with us, in just the way we communicate with other people."[54] Respect for the normal, natural use of language recognizes the connotative[55] value of literary figures of speech, such as similes, metaphors, parables, analogies, puns, and even allegories.[56] However, unless there is good reason within a given Scripture passage to regard its language as figurative, words should be taken in their normal, natural sense.

An example of figurative language is found in Galatians 2:9. James, Cephas, and John are described as pillars of the Church in Jerusalem. Pillars physically support buildings. It is obvious that Paul, the writer, did not mean that these three men served the Church by holding up a physical structure. He clearly meant that the Church, as a spiritual structure, depended on these spiritual leaders as a building rests upon foundational posts. So, while the word translated "pillars" is used to picture another reality, this does not give the reader license to read into the word *pillars* a meaning foreign to it. The figurative meaning of language is related to, and governed by, its plain, literal sense.

The text of our model sermon, 1 John 2:1–2, refers to Christ as "an Advocate" (NKJV). Does John use the term *parakletos* in the plain-literal (and more general) sense to denote a person "called to one's side"?[57] The NIV reflects this interpretation, paraphrasing *parakletos*: "one who speaks to the Father in our defense." Rendering the idea behind the word, rather than translating it, makes for easier reading. But did John simply describe a function the Lord serves?

Another possibility is that John used the word as a figure of speech intended to vividly portray the Lord as the believer's defense attorney before the Judge in a court of law. By capitalizing *Advocate*, the translators of the New King James Version; New American Standard Bible; and New American Standard Bible, Updated Edition, indicate their understanding of the term as an official title. This would mean that Jesus' advocacy results from His *being* the believer's representative, which is an outcome of His *being* "Jesus Christ the righteous . . . the propitiation for our sins" (1 Jn. 2:1–2 NKJV).

The point is, literal interpretation calls for an effort to investigate this question on the assumption that words mean something, and that it is the words of Scripture themselves that God breathed (see Matthew

5:18 and Luke 16:17), not the ideas with which people invest them.[58]

The fact that every fulfilled Bible prophecy recorded has been fulfilled *literally* strongly supports literal interpretation. None have been fulfilled in ways that required a spiritual, mystical, or subjective interpretation of the prediction. It has been well said, therefore, that "when the plain sense of Scripture makes sense, seek no other sense, lest it be nonsense."[59]

When literal interpretation is applied to biblical texts in the original language, the process is called *exegesis*.[60] This word comes from two Greek words that mean "to lead out." It describes the process of *leading out* the meaning of a word, phrase, clause, sentence, paragraph, etc., by observing the grammatical construction and ways in which words relate to each other in their various contexts. The opposite of exegesis is *eisegesis*, which refers to reading meanings *into* the text.[61]

The following diagram gives a schematic overview of the process of literal interpretation (see figure 2-4). Notice that the author's intended meaning in the original context is the "interpretation" determined by inductive Bible study. When the meaning is generalized and stated as a timeless truth, it is called a "principle." When the principle is extended into new and different situations without distorting the original meaning, the results are called "applications."[62]

Inductive Bible Study	Interpretation	Principle	Applications
Leading Out the Author's Intended Meaning – Analyzing Contextual Data	The Intended Meaning – In the Historical Setting of the Author and Original Addressees	Universal Truth – Generalized Concept – Applies to all people in all places at all times	Extension of the Principle Into New and Different Situations Without Distorting the Original Meaning

Figure 2.4

EXPOSITORY COMMUNICATION,
THE CONVEYANCE OF GOD'S MESSAGE

Discovering what God meant by what He said is the basis for expository preaching. *Homiletics* is a word used in reference to "the science and art of preparing and delivering the Word of God. It is the framing of the message. It is taking gold and putting a silver frame around it. It is conveying through the spoken word and through life, the words of truth."[63]

The following table shows the distinctions and relationships between hermeneutics, homiletics, and public speaking.[64] (See figure 2-5.)

To remove homiletics from figure 2-5 would imply public speaking of raw biblical data. This would be like serving uncooked agricultural products and calling it a meal. Walter Kaiser's assertion on this point is sure to receive the reader's "amen!":

> Nothing can be more dreary and grind the soul and spirit of the Church more than can a dry, lifeless recounting of Biblical episodes apparently unrelated to the present. The pastor who delivers this type of sermon, reflecting his seminary exegesis class, bombards his bewildered audience with a maze of historical, philological, and critical detail so that the text drops lifeless in front of the listener.[65]

Homiletics without hermeneutics, on the other hand, could be like a very attractive plate of poisonous toadstools—pretty to look at but potentially deadly! And without public speaking, homiletics on the basis of good hermeneutics is like exquisite cuisine that is never brought from the kitchen to the patron of a restaurant. To nourish listeners with presentations of God's Word that are inviting, healthy, and

Hermeneutics	Homiletics	Public Speaking
Interpretation	Preparation	Presentation
Foundation	Building	Exhibition
Argument	Arrangement	Pronouncement
Grasping	Grouping	Giving
Outlook	Outline	Outlet

Figure 2.5

easily digested, the expository communicator cannot neglect the essential bridge-building work of homiletics.

In his book *The Preacher's Portrait*, John Stott compares and contrasts the preacher's various roles and responsibilities according to Scripture. The imagery of a steward, or household manager, emphasizes the preacher as "the trustee and dispenser of another's person's goods."

> So the preacher is a steward of God's mysteries, that is, of the self-revelation which God has entrusted to men and which is now preserved in the Scriptures. The preacher's message, therefore, is derived not directly from the mouth of God, as if he were a prophet or apostle, nor from his own mind, like the false prophets, nor undigested from the minds and mouths of other men, like the babbler, but from the once revealed and now recorded Word of God, of which he is a privileged steward.[66]

Stott observes the various directions in which the preacher, as a steward, is to "be found faithful" (1 Cor. 4:2 NKJV). His trustworthiness is to be "to the householder who has appointed him to the task; . . . to the household who are looking to him for sustenance; and . . . to the deposit which is committed to his trust."[67]

EXPOSITORY COMMUNICATION, CONNECTING WITH CONTEMPORARIES

With respect to the steward's household, the better a speaker and audience know one another, the better the bridge that can be built from the Bible to the listener. In his excellent book *Teaching to Change Lives*, Howard G. Hendricks asserts, "You are not interested simply in inculcating principles; you want to infect people. Therefore, *the way people learn determines how you teach*."[68] Richards and Bredfeldt put the same idea this way: "Teach people, not just lessons. It is people we are called to serve. It is people Christ died to redeem. Be sure that it is the student who is your focus in teaching, not simply the delivery of Bible content."[69]

Though the apostle Paul may not have been well acquainted with anyone in his audience at Athens, his sermon in Acts 17 reflects audience analysis. "He begins in his students' world. He starts with where they live."[70] By referring to his observation of their idol "to an unknown God," Paul gained their attention and stimulated their interest in his declaration of the identity of the true and living God. When Paul addressed Jews, on the other hand, he proclaimed Christ as the one who fulfills the Hebrew Scriptures (Acts 24:14). Richards and Bredfeldt argue convincingly that Jesus knew people's needs and adapted His messages to meet them:

> Jesus geared His teaching to the needs and readiness of His students when He said, "I have much more to say to you, more than you can now bear" (John 16:12). Jesus recognized the basic educational principle that the student's needs, interests, and readiness determines what is to be taught and how it is to be taught. Whether it was with Nicodemus (John 3), the woman at the well (John 4), the woman caught in adultery (John 8), Thomas in his doubt (John 20), or Peter in his guilt (John 21), Jesus understood human need and adjusted His approach accordingly.[71]

Jesus, Paul, and others certainly exemplify the principle of focusing the message to meet their students' needs. It is doubtful that they would take issue with Hendricks's assertion: "Know your students. The more you know of their needs, the better able you are to meet them."[72] But, at the same time, while listeners' needs should certainly determine how the content of revelation is delivered, you cannot allow those needs to dictate the message itself. One who does so fails to serve the householder to whom he or she accounts as a steward, by failing to make the "deposit" of God's entrusted Word.

Ironically, when allowed to rule the roost, seeker sensitivity fails the very household the steward would please! As Richards and Bredfeldt state, "it is important for the creative Bible teacher to remember that basic human needs have not changed significantly over the millennia that have passed since the Scriptures were written."[73] This statement validates the needs theories of social scientists Abraham Maslow and Fredrick Herzberg, who hold that basic human needs (physical safety and relational needs) must be met before higher motivators (such as esteem and achievement) can be effectively addressed. Biblical communicators must distinguish between the *real* needs of people and the *desires* they often refer to as needs.

The constancy of real human needs partly explains why it is entirely possible to develop and deliver an effective sermon to complete strangers, as is often done by speakers at large gatherings and through the mass media. For this to occur, however, the speaker must establish a relational connection of some kind. The Son of God Himself, who alone explains the Father, did not do so from a distance, but came as a human being and tented among us (John 1:18, 14). So Hendricks is on solid theological footing when he says to would-be Bible teachers, "You can impress people from a distance. But you can impact them only up close"[74] If the expository communicator is charged with building a bridge between the "then and there" of Bible times and the "here and now"[75] of his audiences, he must, as Haddon Robinson stated, "know his people as well as his message, and to acquire that knowledge he exegetes both the Scripture and the congregation."[76]

Summary and Conclusion

The Bible is God-given information about God for the purpose of making Him known to people, whose greatest need is to know Him in a life-changing, personal relationship. Granted the privilege of speaking for God to a contemporary audience, expository communicators are responsible for discovering what God meant by what He said. Yielding to the lure of popularity, the precepts of men, and the perversion of what passages actually teach, in part explains why sermons often communicate the preacher's message and authority, rather than God's.

When the source of one's sermon is the Scriptures, the preacher accepts the responsibility for bridging the communication gap created by its antiquity, difficulty, and foreignness to the listeners. The supernatural character of Scripture, the progress of revelation, the distinction between the redemptive and kingdom programs of God, and the derivation of truth revealed to others, call for spiritual discernment and skill.

Literal interpretation seeks the contextual meaning inductively, understanding that every word in the original language is God-breathed. In discovering the single meaning of texts, the interpreter is guided by theological assumptions about the nature of divine revelation. As principles are carefully drawn and extended into new and different situations of listeners, without distorting the original meaning, the preacher realizes the wedding of hermeneutics and public speaking and thus serves as a faithful steward and effective bridge builder.

What kind of messenger does God use to convey what He has to say from His Word to people living today? What is the nature of the messenger's role and relationships? Are *you* personally qualified to be the vehicle in which God is willing to transport what He meant in 1 John 2:1–2, to those willing to hear? These questions express the concerns of Chapter 3.

DISCUSSION QUESTIONS

1. As different kinds of expository communication of Scripture, explain the differences between *preaching* and *teaching*.
2. How have you seen popularity, human precepts, or perversions of the Bible's text detract from a preacher's communication with God's authority? Give examples.
3. In your own words, what is the *communication gap*, and why does it exist?
4. Why is it so important to wed homiletics to hermeneutics?
5. Why do you agree or disagree that you can *impact people only up close*?
6. Explain the following terms:

hermeneutics	homiletics
inductive Bible study	exegesis
interpretation	allegorical interpretation
principle	applications

7. Explain the statement "Expository preachers are authoritative, not authoritarian."

CHAPTER 3

The Channel: Representing God as His Mouthpiece

ARTHUR B. WHITING once said, "Some consider only the message important, but the speaker makes the words of Scripture live. Homiletics is the method and the man, not just the method."[1] In keeping with this assertion, Donald Macleod wrote, "Preaching cannot be discussed apart from the preacher. It is time, then, for us to discover/ rediscover the preacher: Who is he or she? In what are they involved? And why?"[2]

Chapter 2 answered these questions, in part.[3] Preachers build verbal and relational bridges to people far removed from the world and time of the Bible. But who, really, is qualified to speak for God? Is Howard Hendricks correct when he asserts, "What you *are* is far more important than what you say or do"?[4] If so, what kind of person can and does God use to articulate His message in a given generation? Let us begin by acknowledging His use of people—not only to speak for Him, but to be individual incarnations of His revelation.

GOD USES PEOPLE

According to Scripture, God has chosen to *use* people, as His spokespersons, or mouthpieces, to *reach* people. The writer of Hebrews began his epistle, "God, who at various times and in various ways spoke in time past to the fathers by the prophets, has in these last days spoken to us by

His Son" (1:1–2 NKJV). Referring to His apostles (sent ones), Jesus prayed to the Father, "As You sent Me into the world, I also have sent them into the world" (John 17:18 NKJV). And in Romans 10:14–15, Paul asks, "How then shall they call on Him in whom they have not believed? And how shall they believe in Him of whom they have not heard? And how shall they hear without a preacher? And how shall they preach unless they are sent? As it is written: 'How beautiful are the feet of those who preach the gospel of peace, who bring glad tidings of good things!'" (NKJV).

Preachers are bearers of the message God sent them to communicate to others on His behalf. The human factor is not just the mechanism for sowing the Word like seed (see Matthew 13:3, 19); it is also the medium through which the Word is sent and received. As Hendricks noted, "God's method is always incarnational. He loves to take the truth and wrap it in a person."[5] With the exception of the apostles and prophets of the first-century Church, preachers convey God's message already inscripturated through the personalities of those chosen to write it. Again, it is the writer of Hebrews who asks, "How shall we escape if we neglect so great a salvation, which at the first began to be spoken by the Lord, and was confirmed to us by those who heard Him, God also bearing witness both with signs and wonders, with various miracles, and gifts of the Holy Spirit, according to His own will?" (2:3–4 NKJV).

To declare the meaning of a passage such as 1 John 2:1–2, then, is to relate revelation recorded by the apostle John. He was impacted as an eyewitness of the incarnate Son of God as well as guided infallibly by the Spirit of God. (See 2 Peter 1:21.) By the time the message is communicated to the contemporary audience, it will be filtered through one more personality, that of the preacher. (See figure 3-1.)

When Hendricks goes on to describe this process, he says of God, "He takes a clean individual and drops him or her in the midst of a corrupt society, and that person—because of what he knows, feels, and does—convincingly demonstrates the power of God's grace."[6] Assuming this is

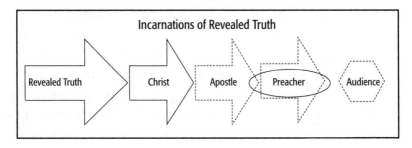

Figure 3.1

true, how *clean* must a person be? Exactly what kind of person can and does God use to articulate the truths of Scripture?

GOD USES IMPERFECT PEOPLE

According to Scripture, God uses whom He will to speak His word. He used Jonah—not just *despite* his uncooperative attitude, but partly *because of* it.[7] Long before that, the Lord used Balaam's donkey to speak for Him! (See Numbers 22.) In Luke 19:40, Jesus declared that if those celebrating His triumphal entry into Jerusalem remained silent, the rocks would cry out. His point was that while God has chosen to speak through people, He is not limited to human agencies, let alone clean ones. In Philippians 1:18, Paul rejoiced that, whether in pretense or in truth, Christ was being proclaimed. Whether people preach out of selfish ambition or pure motives affects their reward, but not God's ability to use them.

Balaam was a false prophet, hired by Moab's king, Balak, to curse the Israelites (see Numbers 22–24). In his willingness to receive a diviner's fee, Balaam became a symbol of mercenary motivation in ministry (see 2 Peter 2:15). Yet despite Balaam's every intention and effort to curse God's people, Yahweh used him to bless His people instead. To this day, the Oracles of Balaam[8] stand as a testimony of God's ability to give His pure words through an impure vessel. Even the sinless Son of

God became man by being conceived and born of a woman who confessed her need of a Savior (Lk. 1:47). So God is not dependent upon human perfection in those who represent Him verbally.

Neither does one's credibility with students depend upon perfection. Hendricks says, "Kids aren't looking for a perfect teacher, just an honest one, and a growing one."[9] In fact, the teacher, he states, is "primarily a learner, a student among students."[10] If, as Hendricks also states, "failure is a necessary part of the learning process," then God can weave your past, forgiven sins into the fabric of your testimony to strengthen your credibility. David could not have penned either Psalm 32 or Psalm 51 without the pathos of a forgiven sinner.

Understand that these observations do not advocate or make light of sin in any way. The answer to Paul's question in Romans 6:1, "Shall we continue in sin that grace may abound?" (NKJV), is "Certainly not! How shall we who died to sin live any longer in it?" (v. 2 NKJV). Paul describes his own self-discipline in terms of a boxer who delivers eye-blackening blows to his own body: "I discipline my body and bring it into subjection, lest, when I have preached to others, I myself should become disqualified" (1 Cor. 9:27 NKJV).

God's spokespeople are naturally unnecessary, unworthy, inadequate, and unprofitable. They are unnecessary because, as we have seen, God can work apart from them. They are unworthy because they owe their existence, usefulness, and calling to God. In 1 Timothy 1:12–13, the apostle Paul stated, "I thank Christ Jesus our Lord who has enabled me, because He counted me faithful, putting me into the ministry, although I was formerly a blasphemer, a persecutor, and an insolent man; but I obtained mercy because I did it ignorantly in unbelief" (NKJV).

And God's spokespersons are naturally inadequate. Paul was quick to remind the Corinthians that neither he nor his coministers could boast of self-sufficiency: "Not that we are adequate in ourselves to consider anything as coming from ourselves," he said, "but our adequacy is from God" (2 Cor. 3:5 NASU).

As finite mortals in unredeemed bodies, all preachers are unequal to their task apart from the adequacy that comes from God. They are unprofitable because their service never exceeds their duty. They can never repay their debt of love.

Still, those who speak *for* God are created, chosen, called, cleansed, and commissioned *by* God. Like the prophet Jeremiah and the apostle Paul, each of God's spokesmen has been formed in the womb for the task he would be given. In Jeremiah, the prophet quotes the words of Yahweh in describing his call to speak for God:

> Then the word of the LORD came to me, saying: "Before I formed you in the womb I knew you; before you were born I sanctified you; I ordained you a prophet to the nations." Then said I: "Ah, Lord GOD! Behold, I cannot speak, for I *am* a youth." But the LORD said to me: "Do not say, 'I am a youth,' for you shall go to all to whom I send you, and whatever I command you, you shall speak. Do not be afraid of their faces, for I am with you to deliver you," says the LORD. Then the LORD put forth His hand and touched my mouth, and the LORD said to me: "Behold, I have put My words in your mouth. See, I have this day set you over the nations and over the kingdoms, to root out and to pull down, to destroy and to throw down, to build and to plant." (1:4–10 NKJV)

Similarly, Paul said, "But when it pleased God, who separated me from my mother's womb and called me through His grace, to reveal His Son in me, that I might preach Him among the Gentiles, I did not immediately confer with flesh and blood, nor did I go up to Jerusalem to those who were apostles before me; but I went to Arabia, and returned again to Damascus" (Gal. 1:15–17 NKJV).

Luke refers to John the Baptist as "finishing his course" (Acts 13:25 NKJV). Paul told Timothy, "Fulfill your ministry" (2 Tim. 4:5 NKJV). In his epistle to the Ephesians, Paul speaks of believers as God's "workmanship created in Christ Jesus for good works, which God prepared beforehand that we should walk in them" (2:10 NKJV). And author

Andrew Blackwood once commented, "The preacher himself is God's 'poem' (another translation of the Greek *poiema, workmanship,* Eph. 2:10)."[11] So, as a minister of God's Word, before taking up the task of fashioning a sermon, recognize first that you are a "piece of work," God's creative composition. Your content and delivery should bear your signature, just as the writings of David, Peter, John, and Paul incorporate their unique personalities.

In addition to God's sovereign work of cleansing imperfect human beings and using them as His representatives, He also places them in the body of Christ according to His will (1 Cor. 12:4–11, 18).

GOD GIFTS THE IMPERFECT PEOPLE HE USES

Assuming that one is among those given to Christ by the Father (see John 6:37; 10:16; 17:6, 24), he or she must also be given to the Church (Eph. 4:11) by Christ and/or be gifted to speak (see 1 Peter 4:11 and Romans 12:6–8). Those with the nonspeaking gifts, such as serving, giving, mercy, ruling, etc., are to specialize in the capacity of their spiritual gifts.[12] Those with speaking gifts, such as prophecy, exhortation, and teaching, as well as those given to the Church to equip the saints for service, including evangelists, pastors, and teachers, may or may not function in one of the two local church offices of elder/overseer and deacon (see 1 Timothy 3:1–13 and Titus 1:5–9). As illustrated in the following diagram, these designations result in a variety of speaking orientations, A through C-3.[13] (See figure 3-2.)

Depending on where an individual fits at a given time, his or her speaking ministry will be affected. Preaching elders may reprove, rebuke, and exhort with authority not exercised in the same way by a Sunday school teacher or street evangelist (see Titus 2:15). (We encourage you to explore for yourself the relation between the kinds of ministers Christ gives to the Church, the nature of the speaking gifts, and implications of church offices. Such exploration is beyond the scope of this book.) But no matter how one's speaking gift can be described, when an imperfect but regenerate human is gifted to speak, the issue of character is paramount.

Figure 3.2

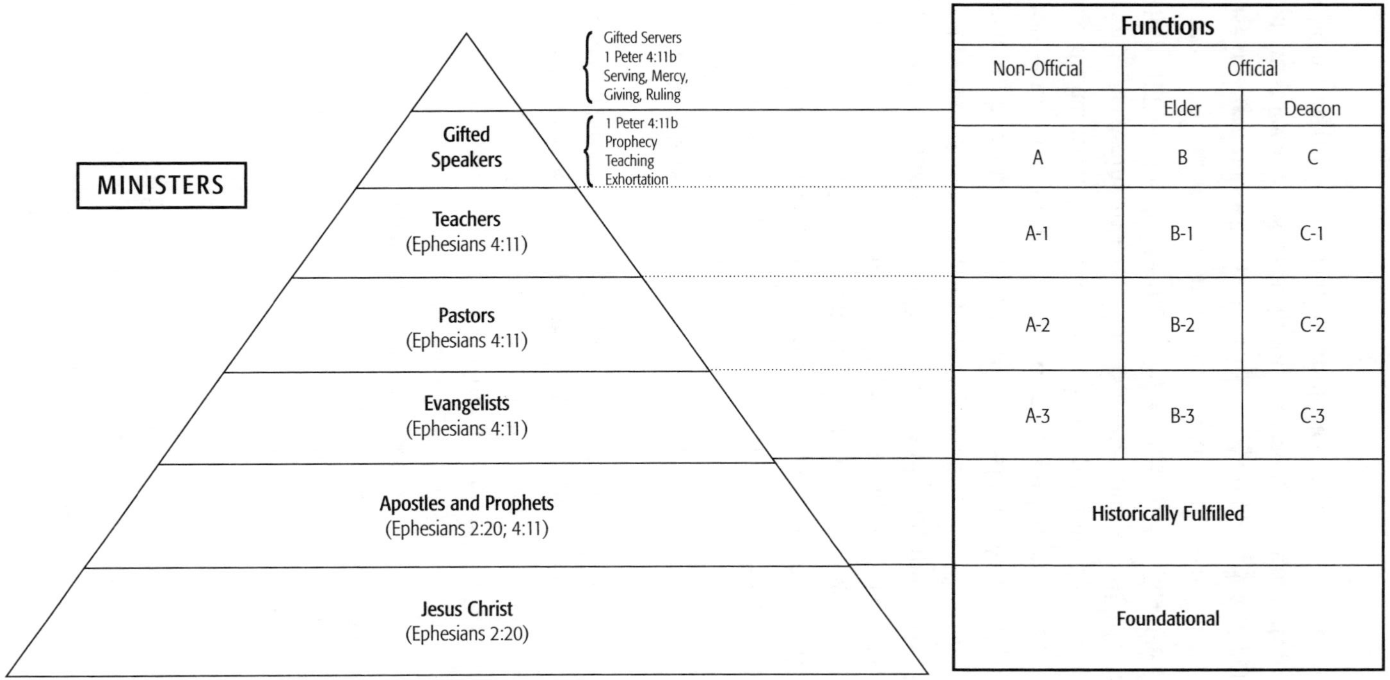

MINISTERS

Gifted Speakers
{ Gifted Servers
1 Peter 4:11b
Serving, Mercy, Giving, Ruling

{ 1 Peter 4:11b
Prophecy
Teaching
Exhortation

Teachers
(Ephesians 4:11)

Pastors
(Ephesians 4:11)

Evangelists
(Ephesians 4:11)

Apostles and Prophets
(Ephesians 2:20; 4:11)

Jesus Christ
(Ephesians 2:20)

	Functions		
	Non-Official	Official	
		Elder	Deacon
	A	B	C
	A-1	B-1	C-1
	A-2	B-2	C-2
	A-3	B-3	C-3
Historically Fulfilled			
Foundational			

Figure 3.2

GOD DESERVES THE HONOR OF GODLY CHARACTER IN THE IMPERFECT PEOPLE HE GIFTS AND USES[14]

Credibility is crucial to effective communication. Remo Fausti and Edward McGlone, in their book entitled *Understanding Oral Communication*, state:

> Many studies of source credibility have been conducted. They have identified three factors as the major determinants of the credibility of a public speaker: his perceived trustworthiness, his perceived expertness, and his general ability as a public speaker.

> Perceived trustworthiness refers to those personality traits which listeners associate with a speaker who has their best interests in mind. Whatever a speaker can do to create a friendly, helpful, ethical, generous, just and unselfish image should increase his credibility.[15]

In a word, the persuasive element they just described is *character*. From the standpoints of social science and philosophy, character may be thought of as part of nonverbal communication which either harmonizes with the words that are spoken, or creates dissonance resulting in distraction, distrust, and confusion. John Milton Gregory's question applies to preachers perhaps more than to anyone else. He asks, "How can the teacher's manner fail to be earnest and inspiring when his subject matter is so rich in radiant reality?"[16]

Ancient philosopher Socrates summarized the essence of communication with the concepts he called *ethos, pathos,* and *logos.* "*Ethos* embraced character. *Pathos* embraced compassion. *Logos* embraced content."[17] According to Hendricks, Socrates thought of *ethos* as "establishing the credibility of the teacher—his credentials. He understood that who you are is far more important than what you say or do, because it *determines* what you say or do. Who you are as a person is your greatest leverage as a speaker, a persuader, a communicator. You must be attractive to those who would learn from you. They must trust you, and the more they trust you, the more you communicate to them."[18]

If it is true that "credibility always precedes communication,"[19] then part of earning the right to be heard involves your willingness to be vulnerable, to let people know your background, experiences, and struggles. Hendricks says, "Great teachers . . . communicate *as* total persons, and they communicate *to* the total person of their hearers."[20] He is not exhorting speakers to add new dimensions to their speeches. Essentially, he is saying that great speakers recognize that "words account for only 7 percent of everything we communicate to others,"[21] but listeners are attentive to the *other* 93 percent! So, though "content counts," say Richards and Bredfeldt, "[creative Bible teachers] know that . . . it is students that they teach."[22] Knowing one's audience is critical. Perhaps this explains why Paul described his ministry with the church at Thessalonica as he did:

> So, affectionately longing for you, we were well pleased to impart to you not only the gospel of God, but also our own lives, because you had become dear to us. For you remember, brethren, our labor and toil; for laboring night and day, that we might not be a burden to any of you, we preached to you the gospel of God. You are witnesses, and God also, how devoutly and justly and blamelessly we behaved ourselves among you who believe; as you know how we exhorted, and comforted, and charged every one of you, as a father does his own children, that you would walk worthy of God who calls you into His own kingdom and glory. For this reason we also thank God without ceasing, because when you received the word of God which you heard from us, you welcomed it not as the word of men, but as it is in truth, the word of God, which also effectively works in you who believe. (1 Thess. 2:8–13 NKJV)

The persuasive ability of any kind of interpersonal communication is enhanced when listeners perceive that the speaker can be trusted. So, your character is important in expository communication of Scripture, because you, the preacher, represent God to people. When your sermon fully communicates God's message, you are demonstrating the attributes of God that mortals can reflect.[23] But to the extent that your message is God's, but your character is ungodly, you misrepresent the one whose mission you are to fulfill. You fail to be the ambassador that Paul and his companions were (Eph. 6:20; 2 Cor. 5:20). Listeners leave with unworthy thoughts of God when those who speak for Him portray Him as other than He is. That this can be done through one's life as well as through one's language accounts for such clichés as "Practice what you preach," "Walk the talk," "Your actions speak so loudly that I can't hear your words," "People don't care how much you know until they know how much you care," etc.

From the standpoint of Scripture and theology, godly character is essential to an effective testimony, and an inseparable part of what it means to glorify God (1 Cor. 10:31–33). Speakers stand before their audiences as examples to be followed. Paul exhorted the Corinthians to imitate him as he also imitated Christ, and as children imitate their father (1 Cor. 4:14–16; 11:1). In Ephesians 5:1, he told his readers: "Be imitators of God as dear children" (NKJV). A comparison of these statements leads to the conclusion that to pattern one's life after Paul's was to be like Christ and God. Preachers of such exemplary character motivate teachable listeners to learn.

Demonstrating God's character in your behavior displays His attributes. This is what it means to glorify God, which is the chief end of man, according to the Westminster Confession of Faith.[24] As a creature made in God's likeness and saved by His grace, every believer owes it to God to present his or her body as a living sacrifice that is holy and acceptable, and to work toward achieving the life transformation that results from a mind constantly in the process of renewal (Rom. 12:1–2). How much more must this be true of the one seeking through the spoken word to present every man complete in Christ (Col. 1:28)! Because it is God who is at work in the believer, both to will and do His good pleasure (Phil. 2:13), the expository preacher has every reason to be a person of godly character, willing even to endure hardship (1 Tim. 4:6–16; 6:11; 2 Tim. 3:14; 4:5). But such character is not the result of personal determination alone. It is the fruit produced by the indwelling Holy Spirit when the believer yields to His control.

God Produces Godly Character in the People He Uses

The Holy Spirit's indwelling of the believer's body results from having once been baptized (placed) into the body of Christ as a member (1 Cor. 12:13; Rom. 12:1–5). Without His presence, a person cannot be "in the Spirit," or even belong to God (Rom. 8:9). This baptism in the Holy Spirit occurs at the moment one believes on the Lord Jesus Christ and is justified.[25] It is properly evidenced by baptism with water as soon after as possible. (See Acts 2:41; 9:18; 10:47–48; 16:15, 33.)

As an expository preacher, you must not only be "spiritual" in this sense of having Christ in your life (Col. 1:27), but you must also be "spiritual" by continually being filled with (or controlled by) the Holy Spirit" (Eph. 5:18). The present passive imperative of the verb πληρόω (pronounced *play-ra-oh*), "to fill," indicates the believer's responsibility to obey this command—continually—while depending upon the Holy Spirit, who exercises the control and produces His fruit (see Galatians 5:22–23).

Spirit-filled preaching, then, occurs when you, a regenerate individual, proclaim the Word of God, under His control. It is *anointed* in that the Holy Spirit in your life *is* God's anointing (see 1 John 2:27). This does not nullify your unique personality and style, nor does it render unnecessary your diligence as a student or your responsibility to maintain your "walk in the Spirit" (see Galatians 5:16, 25). On the contrary, a person is never more his true self than when he is fulfilling the purpose for which God created and called him.[26]

Personal growth that is Christlike integrates the physical, social, intellectual, and emotional aspects of one's personality by obedience to God's Word (1 Thess. 5:23). In Luke 2:52 we are told, "And Jesus kept

increasing in wisdom and stature, and in favor with God and men"
(NASU). Hendricks asserts that proper growth in any of these areas cannot be isolated from appropriate growth in all of them.[27] The Spirit-
filled preacher never stops learning, growing and changing in greater
conformity to Christ.[28] This accounts for the passion to communicate.[29] It also requires some kind of education.

SPIRIT-FILLED PREACHERS MAKE GOOD
USE OF NATURAL ABILITIES

It has been said that "there are three kinds of preachers: those who you
cannot listen to—they turn you off; those who you can listen to—they
can be tolerated; and those who you must listen to—they demand attention."[30] The difference is not always a matter of spirituality. You also
need to possess and develop natural abilities, including the capacities
to think clearly and speak frankly and forcefully. A good speaker does
not mumble, but enunciates every word. We will discuss these and
other aspects of sermon delivery in further detail in Chapter 8.

The goal of any ongoing education, formal or informal, should be to
enable you to understand and evaluate the contextual data of Scripture.
This includes geographical, historical, dispensational, cultural, literary,
grammatical, and syntactical information. Your ability to read and analyze the text in its original language shows respect for the fact that the
very words of Scripture are inspired. Facility in Hebrew and Greek exegesis reduces dependence upon the expertise of others and enhances
your ability to speak with the authority of firsthand information.

SUMMARY AND CONCLUSION

God has chosen to use imperfect people, whom He redeems, gifts, and
places in the Church to be His spokespersons. The Holy Spirit produces His fruit in the life of these believers who, having been baptized
in the Spirit at conversion, yield to His control through moment-by-
moment obedience to His Word. As the Spirit works to conform them

to the likeness of Christ, they will grow in every aspect of their personalities. Godly character enhances their credibility as preachers, makes their testimonies effective, and glorifies God by displaying His attributes. But in order to speak with skill and with the authority of an exegetical theologian, every preacher must be trained. The following diagram illustrates the qualified preacher. (See figure 3-3.)

DISCUSSION QUESTIONS

1. How would you explain, biblically, the apparent effectiveness of preachers who are later discovered to have been leading a double life of immorality?
2. How would you explain, biblically, the apparent ineffectiveness of preachers whose service appears to be faithful with respect to character?
3. Differentiate between baptism in the Holy Spirit, the filling of the Holy Spirit, and anointed preaching.

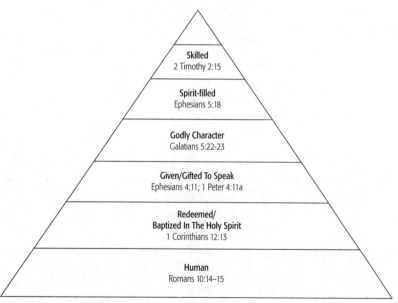

The Qualified Preacher

Skilled
2 Timothy 2:15

Spirit-filled
Ephesians 5:18

Godly Character
Galatians 5:22-23

Given/Gifted To Speak
Ephesians 4:11; 1 Peter 4:11a

Redeemed/
Baptized In The Holy Spirit
1 Corinthians 12:13

Human
Romans 10:14–15

Figure 3.3

4. List the benefits of godly character in a minister of God's Word.

5. Describe how preaching can be affected by the type of minister one is, the spiritual gift a person possesses, and his or her relation to church office.

6. Evaluate the importance of a theological education for preachers, including study of the original languages.

CHAPTER 4

The Challenge:
Bridging the Communication Gap

IN CHAPTER 2, we demonstrated that bridging the communication gap requires discovering Scripture's intended meaning and then preparing for its delivery in terms of listeners' real needs. Chapter 3 emphasized the preacher as the channel through whom God makes Himself known to others. With this dual assignment of communicating God's message through your preachment and personality, you now need a good method by which to provide its package.

This chapter will demonstrate the usefulness of the Whiting Method of homiletics in helping you meet the *challenge*. As professor Milton Jones once said, "There are other systems of homiletics and other good preachers. The strengths of the Whiting System are its combination of exegesis and homiletics, and that its effectiveness has been proven over time."[1] Before introducing the method, some information about its namesake may be helpful.

A BRIEF BIOGRAPHY OF ARTHUR B. WHITING

Arthur B. Whiting was born in England and educated at Cambridge, then at Cliff College. There, he met and studied under Samuel Chadwick, a famous English preacher and professor of exegesis and homiletics.[2] Whiting later came to the U.S. and attended Moody Bible Institute, Pittsburgh Xenia Seminary, and Dallas Theological Seminary, where he studied under Lewis Sperry Chafer. Whiting taught at the Philadelphia

Bible Institute and served First Baptist Church, New York, before proceeding to Biola College; Talbot Seminary; and Western Conservative Baptist Seminary in Portland, Oregon. While at Western Seminary, Whiting reoriented the curriculum to incorporate preaching with an exegetical emphasis.

In 1965, Milton William Jones presented a master of theology thesis at Western Conservative Baptist Seminary, entitled "An Investigation and Explanation of the Whiting System of Homiletics as a Practical Approach to Preaching." In his thesis, Jones stated, "The Method referred to in the thesis as the Whiting method, has come to the author from personal hours of instruction and involvement in homiletics from the homiletician, Dr. Arthur B. Whiting."[3] Milton Jones later became a professor of homiletics at Western Conservative Baptist Seminary and one of the lecturers under whose instruction we learned the system.[4]

SOURCE OF THE WHITING METHOD

As a preacher, Chadwick discovered that to truly understand a passage of Scripture, he needed a solid study of the intricate parts of a passage, but "found that it was pedantic and boring. (Dry as ice and just as

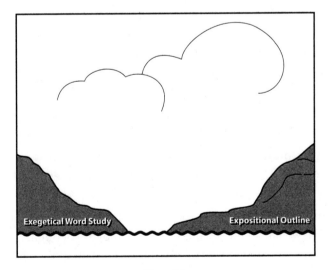

Figure 4.1

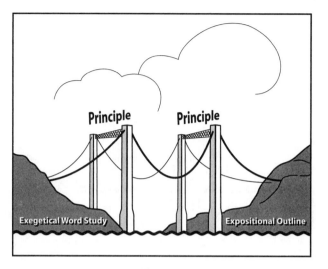

Figure 4.2

cold)."[5] He also recognized the need to bridge the gap between exegetical word studies and the expositional outline. Figure 4-1 represents an early depiction of his conception.

Whiting found that the principles of a passage provide the basis for the connecting link between exegesis and exposition. At the same time, he realized that principles alone did not provide a "roadway" to travel from one side to the other. (See figure 4-2.)

Whiting eventually discovered that a perfect roadway was provided by a statement of the principles in a single sentence called a "theme." (See figure 4-3.)

AN OVERVIEW OF THE METHOD

The Whiting Method of homiletics may be described as a technique for producing an expository outline that develops a text's theme based on principles drawn from word studies. An hourglass is used to illustrate how exegetical data, including word studies, are summarized as principles before they are funneled into a theme, which is then broken down into an outline. (See figure 4-4.)

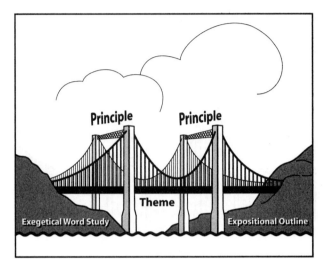

Figure 4.3

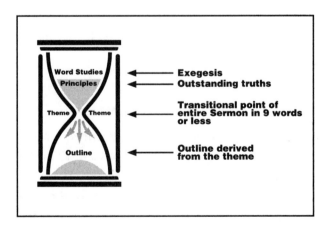

Figure 4.4

The Two Aspects of Sermon Preparation[6]

(See figure 4-5.)

The Elements of the Whiting Method

The *analysis* of a text begins with a determination of the text itself. Where does the author's unit of thought begin and end?[7] When these text boundaries are identified, the unit is called a *pericope*. Studying the words of the text within their contexts[8] is a process of taking apart what

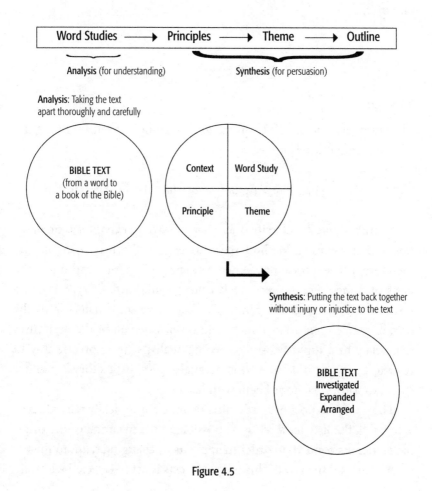

Figure 4.5

the Spirit of God superintended the writer to compose to express what He meant. The goal of textual analysis is to understand both the particles of meaning and the way they were assembled to form the whole thought of the writer. With this insight, the parts are then reassembled through a process called *synthesis* to produce statements of truth called *principles.* The principles are summarized in a single, epitomized principle called the *theme.* When the theme of a passage is divided into bite-size portions, the result is an *outline.* The outline traces the development of the theme from the text so that a sermon hearer can see from his own Bible what God's message is, and how he may be certain of it.

ANALYSIS

The Text

The word *text* is from the Latin *textum*, meaning "woven." Whiting defined a sermon text as follows:

"A text is that portion of Scripture out of which the message is woven."[9]

Sermons may be classified as *topical, textual, expository,* or *devotional.* The Whiting Method seeks to expose the text of Scripture; therefore, it is expositional. When a single passage of Scripture is the basis of a message, the sermon is called *textual-expository.*[10] When a sermon is developed independent of the order and materials of the text, it is called *topical-expository.* However, when all of the Scriptures that relate to a topic are studied contextually, a more precise way to refer to the sermon developed is "textual-topical expository." In either case, expository sermons begin with texts.

The goal of expository preaching of a text, or topically related texts, is to bring the listener as close as possible to the meaning of the original text, in its context, in order to apply its unchanging truth to the listener's context. In view of this purpose, texts must be selected with care to include a complete thought. This unit of thought, or pericope, may consist of a single word, phrase, verse, paragraph, chapter, section, book, or group of books.[11]

A sermon could be preached on the *single word* "repent," in Matthew 3:2. Development might include a description of the original setting, the meaning of the original word, and the application of the principle. Paul's *phrase* describing Tychicus as "a beloved brother and faithful minister in the Lord," found in Ephesians 6:21 (NKJV), could be developed in connection with his relationship, service, and sphere. More commonly, a *verse* of Scripture, such as Luke 19:10, expresses a presentable thought: "For the Son of Man has come to seek and to save that which was lost" (NKJV). Usually, a *paragraph*, such as 1 John 2:1–2, will suggest itself as an appropriate sermon text. First Corinthians 13 is a good example of an entire *chapter* that lends itself to development in one sermon. A *section*, such as 2 Corinthians 8–9, has been surveyed under the heading "Holy Living Produces Holy Giving."[12] Entire books, such as Obadiah or Philemon, can be exposited as texts. It is even possible to proclaim the overall thrust of *groups of books*, such as the Pentateuch, synoptic Gospels, or the Epistles of John.[13]

Textual sermons are, by definition, limited to parameters within which a preacher finds it easier to focus the message and avoid wandering or speaking too broadly. Because textual sermons grow out of the structured thought that God Himself disclosed, they have the advantage of being more authoritative than purely topical sermons. This has the effect of stimulating the appetites of those who are genuinely interested in understanding what God has revealed rather than what a speaker may think. The sheer diversity of biblical literature and subjects provides the preacher of textual sermons with built-in variety and virility. Listeners are also able to remember and retrieve the points of sermons that were demonstrated from a text.

As a preacher, make sure that you carefully rely on the Holy Spirit when selecting texts. Develop the discipline of reading daily from the Bible and other Christian literature, and ideas for texts will come. It is also critical that you be intimately acquainted with your audience to determine when particular texts are most appropriate. Other determinants of text selection include preaching through books according to a long-term plan, seasonal days, personal experiences, natural disasters, world events, and the need for periodic preaching of classical passages.

TEXTUAL ANALYSIS

Translation

Once you have selected a text, the process of textual analysis begins by translating it from the original language, or evaluating existing translations, depending on your abilities. This leads to the study of words in their various uses, relationships, and contexts.

Start by selecting and comparing translations classified as "essentially literal,"[14] such as the New King James Version (NKJV), New American Standard Bible, Updated Edition (NASU), and the English Standard Version (ESV). Note any differences between them that may suggest the need for further study. (See figure 4-6.)

DIAGRAM, OR MECHANICAL LAYOUT[15]

Next, note the role of the word *advocate* in the sentence by diagramming the sentence, or making a mechanical layout. (See figures 4-7 and 4-8.)

My little children, these things I write to you, so that you may not sin. And if anyone sins, we have <u>an Advocate</u> with the Father, Jesus Christ the righteous. (1 John 2:1 NKJV)

My little children, I am writing these things to you so that you may not sin. And if anyone sins, we have <u>an Advocate</u> with the Father, Jesus Christ the righteous. (1 John 2:1 NASU)

My little children, I am writing these things to you so that you may not sin. But if anyone does sin, we have <u>an advocate</u> with the Father, Jesus Christ the righteous. (1 John 2:1 ESV)

Notes:
1. These things I write (NKJV)   I am writing these things (NASU, ESV)
2. And if (NKJV, NASU)   But if (ESV)
3. Advocate (NKJV, NASU)   advocate (ESV)

Figure 4.6

Word Studies

A word study, as referred to in the Whiting Method, is the analysis of a word selected either because it (1) recurs in the text,[16] (2) is an unusual word (seldom if ever used in the Bible outside the text under study), or (3) is a difficult word that poses some kind of problem in grammatical construction or meaning. In 1 John 2:1, the words translated "advo-

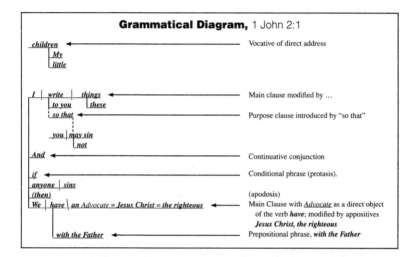

Figure 4.7

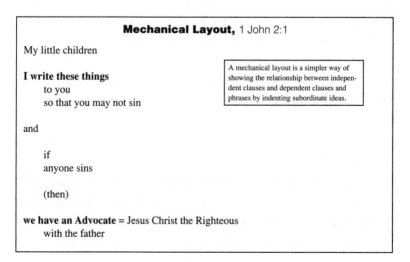

Figure 4.8

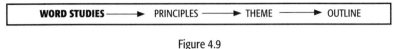

Figure 4.9

cate," and "propitiation," require the kind of understanding and explanation that word studies can provide. (See figure 4-9.)

Tools

Word studies involve the use of various "tools," including lexicons, con-
cordances, grammars, and theological dictionaries, for the purpose of
grammatical analysis and determining the range of meanings.[17] Many
of the tools needed to build a good theological library are available on
Bible software such as the Logos Digital Library System in Libronix.[18]

RANGE OF MEANING

Grammatical analysis generally includes identification of the form,
function, and syntax of the word under study. In contrast, the range of
meaning for a New Testament word refers to the word's root meaning,
its usage in Classical Greek, its treatment in the Septuagint, its use in
the New Testament, and the meaning derived from these considerations. Such studies can be undertaken by non-language users (NLU),
whose ability to study the text is limited to English, as well as those who
are able to work in the original languages (LU).[19] However, the study of
selected words from a passage provides only a small part of the data
that is available only to the exegete.[20]

Advantages of Word Studies

The first and most obvious value of conducting word studies is that
they help the student of Scripture understand the text, because a word's
meaning is determined by its usage in context. Second, the information
discovered often provides helpful illustrative material as well. A study

Advocate	Form
	Masculine accusative singular noun
	Function
	Direct object of the verb "have," in the independent clause of 1 John 2:1a, joined to the first independent clause by "and," and therefore related to 1 John 2:1a.
	Meaning (English word)
	The World Book Dictionary, 32.
	"A person who speaks in favor; one who pleads or argues publicly for something, such as a proposal, belief, or theory; supporter." [<Old French *avocet*, learned borrowing from Latin advocatus, (originally) past participle of advocare summon , ad- to + vocare call]
	(Greek word) James Strong's *Exhaustive Concordance of The Bible*, 19.
	#3875. παράκλητος par-ak'-lay-tos; an intercessor, console:--advocate, comforter, from #3874 παράκληοις , comfort, consolation, exhortation, entreaty, from #3870 παρακαλέω, beseech, call for, exhort, entreat, pray, from #3844 παρα, near, beside; and #2564 καλέω call,
	W. E. Vine's *Expository Dictionary of New Testament Words*, 35; 208. "For 'Advocate' see 'Comforter.'"
	5. PARAKLETOS (παράκλητος), lit., called to one's side, i.e., to one's aid, is primarily a verbal adjective, and suggests the capability or adaptability for giving aid. It was used in a court of justice to denote a legal assistant, counsel for the defense, an advocate; then, generally, one who pleads another's cause, an intercessor, advocate, as in I John 2:1, of the Lord Jesus. In the widest sense, it signifies a succourer, comforter.

Figure 4.10

of the word translated "Advocate" in 1 John 2:1, for example, opens the door to a courtroom, where a defense attorney represents the accused before a judge (see figures 4-10 and 4-11). Third, word studies build confidence in God's Word as listeners see that the very words He breathed were given intentionally, structured purposefully, and that their meaning can be established objectively.

[Note: The following material, marked LU (Language User), has some value for the non-language user (NLU) as well. Those who find the content too technical, however, are welcome to proceed to page 63.]

Colin Brown: *The New International Dictionary of New Testament Theology*, vol. I, 88ff. (excerpts follow)

Advocate, Paraclete, Helper

| παράκλητος | παράκλητος (*parakletos*), helper, intercessor, advocate, paraklete. |

"The noun *parakletos* is derived from the verbal adj. and means called [to one's aid]. It is first found in a legal context in the court of justice, meaning legal assistant, advocate (Demosthenes, 19, 1; cf. Lycurgus, Frag. 102)."

OT "Job's 'comforters' are called parakletores (plur. in Job 16:2 LXX; Acquila and Theodotion have parakletoi). The Heb. Is *mᵉnaᵃmim*.It is significantly the only instance of the word in the LXX."

NT "1 Jn. 2:1 f. gives the term a soteriological character in calling 'Jesus Christ the righteous' our 'advocate' (parakletos) and 'propitiation' (hilasmos) "for the sins of the whole world . . .

"This restriction of the title to Jesus and the Spirit requires a theological interpretation of the term which is at the same time polemical.

"It is striking that the term parakletos is only found in the Johannine writings, and apart from 1 Jn. 2:1 it occurs only in the discourses (Jn. 14:16, 26; 15:26; 16:7; cf. 16:12ff)."

Meaning in Context

Advocate is a title belonging to "Jesus Christ" which name is in apposition to it. He not only comes to the aid of believers who sin, but is uniquely sent to fill this role as the believer's defense attorney before God the Father, as in a court of law.

Application and Contrasts

If the believer who sins did not have Jesus Christ as his counsel for the defense; or, if He were not Himself the righteous propitiation for his sins, a single sin would result in defeat and hopeless despair. With Him, however, there is every inducement never to sin, nor to give up when he does sin.

Figure 4.11

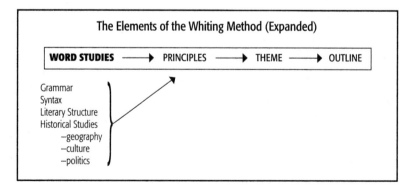

Figure 4.12

LU

THE INTEGRATION OF EXEGESIS
AND THE WHITING METHOD

(See figure 4-12.)

The Whiting Method, as developed and taught by Milton Jones at Western Conservative Baptist Seminary, Portland, Oregon, was found to have a deficiency, which he addressed in a supplementary review sheet, dated September 21, 1972. The method of producing an expository outline that developed the theme of a text based on principles drawn from word studies was lauded for its value as far as it went. But, since there is far more to exegesis than word studies, a question arose as to the relation between exegesis and homiletics.

Jones described the relation of exegesis to homiletics as analogous to the lumber used to build a house. The value of lumber is very real but limited to its owner. When lumber is used to construct a home, however, it benefits all who enjoy the dwelling. In a similar way, the value of exegetical material is limited to the exegete until it has been used in the construction of a well-built sermon. Then it blesses all who hear it.[21] Jones's point was that the disciplines of exegesis and homiletics are not at odds with each other but complementary when properly joined.

Let's take Jones's analogy a step farther. Just as homeowners typically do not attempt to display all of the lumber used to construct their homes, preachers should not display the exegetical resources used in a sermon's construction. With few exceptions, their listeners should be as unaware of the "nuts and bolts" of the sermon, as dinner guests are unaware of the floor joists and rafters of the dining room.

Jones goes on to extol the virtues of exegeting the text of an entire book before beginning a series of messages through the book. After noting the difficulty, in a three-year seminary curriculum, of training exegetical preachers at the same time that they are learning exegesis, Jones recommends that the student preacher learn the system by working within portions of Scripture "no smaller than a sentence and usually no larger (at this point) than a section" (i.e., from a chapter to a book in length).[22]

The next year, Dennis O. Wretlind presented a paper to Dr. W. Robert Cook, (of WCBS), in which the same issue was further addressed with an emphasis on the *preacher's preparation.* Wretlind offered practical suggestions for how a busy pastor could both prepare expository sermons based on solid exegesis of the original text and meet the time-consuming demands of other aspects of ministry.

In agreement with Jones's comments, Wretlind observed that the seminary student learns to write sermons *before* finishing formal training in Hebrew and Greek exegesis. As a result, "the beginning point" of the Whiting Method is necessarily adapted to the abilities of beginning students.[23] Integral to the Whiting System of homiletics, however, is the assumption that "a sermon which speaks God's Word must be based primarily on the meaning of that Word in the original tongue in which it was inspired."[24]

Another problem Wretlind noted is that a preacher's personal passion for his message, and thus his ability to move others as he has been moved, is related to his direct contact with the original text, the joy of discovery, and independent work. If exegesis is defined as "the application of the laws of hermeneutics to the original text of Scripture with a view to declaring its meaning,"[25] then the goal must be to work as independently of secondary sources as possible. So you, the exegetical preacher, are responsible to sift the raw material of the text in order to (a) discern the adequacies and inadequacies of the different translations; (b) understand for yourself the meaning of the text, without being carried away by the opinions of others, which may or may not be correct, and (c) declare your message with the authority of God.[26]

BASIC STEPS OF EXEGESIS[27]

1. Read the text of the book or passage in the original Hebrew, Aramaic, or Greek in order to have the context of the language before [you] throughout the exegetical process.

2. <u>Study</u> the historical, geographical, [and] cultural contexts of the passage.

3. <u>Analyze</u> all the data in the text: literary genre and structure, words, quotations, figures of speech, parallel passages, grammatical observations, etc.

4. <u>Record</u> all information gained through the procedures of 1–3 above as it is gained. [See figures 4-13, 4-14, and 4-15a-b.]

COMPARISON OF EXEGESIS WITH THE WHITING METHOD[28]

(See figure 4-13.)

Example of a Grammatical Diagram from 1 John 2:1

(See figure 4-14.)

Example of a Word Study of παράκλητος, Advocate

(See figures 4-15a and b.)

Discussion of Select Exegetical Data That Contribute to the Formation of Principles

Only by reading the passage in the original language can you have a firsthand impression of John's fatherly tone indicated by the diminu-

Exegesis	Whiting Method
Exegesis calls for the study of *every* word according to the *selection* of which exegetical steps are appropriate.	The Whiting Method *selects* words for study on the basis of whether they are recurring, unusual, or difficult.
The *essentials* of exegesis and the Whiting Method are the same.	While the Whiting Method does not *emphasize* the historical study that is part of exegesis, study of the historical contexts is *implied* in the Whiting Method's basis upon literal interpretation.
Supplementing the Whiting Method with full and complete exegesis strengthens its integrity as a system.	

Figure 4.13

Τεκνία μου, ταῦτα γράφω ὑμῖν ἵνα μὴ ἁμάρτητε καὶ ἐάν τις ἁμάρτῃ, παράκλητον ἔχομεν πρὸς τὸν πατέρα Ἰησοῦν Χριστὸν δίκαιον· 2 καὶ αὐτὸς ἱλασμός ἐστιν περὶ τῶν ἁμαρτιῶν ἡμῶν, οὐ περὶ τῶν ἡμετέρων δὲ μόνον ἀλλὰ καὶ περὶ ὅλου τοῦ κόσμου

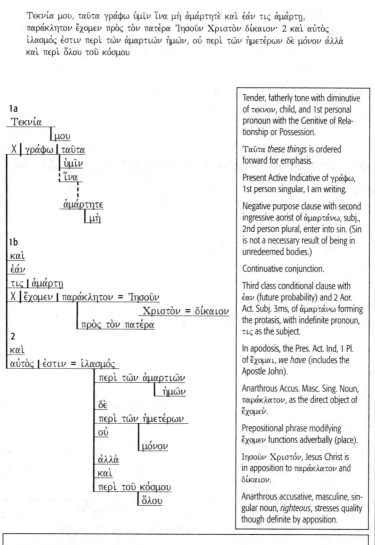

1a

Τεκνία
 └ μου
Χ | γράφω | ταῦτα
 │ ὑμῖν
 ┊ ἵνα
 ┊
 ἁμάρτητε
 └ μὴ

1b

καὶ
ἐάν
τις | ἁμάρτῃ
Χ | ἔχομεν | παράκλητον = Ἰησοῦν
 Χριστὸν = δίκαιον
 πρὸς τὸν πατέρα

2

καὶ
αὐτὸς | ἐστιν = ἱλασμός
 περὶ τῶν ἁμαρτιῶν
 └ ἡμῶν
 δὲ
 περὶ τῶν ἡμετέρων
 οὐ
 └ μόνον
 ἀλλὰ
 καὶ
 περὶ τοῦ κόσμου
 └ ὅλου

Tender, fatherly tone with diminutive of τεκνον, child, and 1st personal pronoun with the Genitive of Relationship or Possession.

Ταῦτα *these things* is ordered forward for emphasis.

Present Active Indicative of γράφω, 1st person singular, I am writing.

Negative purpose clause with second ingressive aorist of ἁμαρτάνω, subj., 2nd person plural, enter into sin. (Sin is not a necessary result of being in unredeemed bodies.)

Continuative conjunction.

Third class conditional clause with ἐάν (future probability) and 2 Aor. Act. Subj. 3ms, of ἁμαρτάνω forming the protasis, with indefinite pronoun, τις as the subject.

In apodosis, the Pres. Act. Ind, 1 Pl. of ἔχομαι, *we have* (includes the Apostle John).

Anarthrous Accus. Masc. Sing. Noun, παράκλατον, as the direct object of ἔχομέν.

Prepositional phrase modifying ἔχομεν functions adverbally (place).

Ιησοῦν Χριστόν, Jesus Christ is in apposition to παράκλατον and δίκαιον.

Anarthrous accusative, masculine, singular noun, *righteous*, stresses quality though definite by apposition.

Personal Translation

My little children, these things I am writing to so that you might not ever sin; and if anyone should sin, we have an Advocate with the Father, Jesus Christ the righteous. And He is the satisfactory payment for our sins, and not for ours only, but also for the whole world.

Figure 4.14

Advocate
παράκλητος

Form

Masculine, accusative, singular noun

Function

Accusative of Direct Object, receiving the action of, or completing the meaning of, the verb ἔχομεν we have (Dana and Mantey, 92).

Root Meaning

From παρακαλέω "called to one's aid" in a judicial sense, hence, most frequently as a substantive, an advocate, pleader, intercessor, "a friend of the accused person called to speak in his character, or otherwise enlist sympathy in his favor (Abbott/Smith, 340–41).

Classical Usage

"Called to one's aid." In Latin, translated by the word *advocatus*. As a Substantive, used of "a legal assistant, advocate" (Liddell & Scott, 597).

Usage in the Septuagint

Used only once, in plural form, παρακλήτορες , in Job 16:2, where Job describes his friends as poor "comforters" (Septuagint, 677).
 Found in Acquila and Theodotian as παρακλητοι (Hatch/Redpath, 1061; Colin Brown, Vol I, 88ff).
Translates Hebrew מְנַחֲמֵי , Piel ptc. m. pl. cs., from נחם ,
be sorry, repent, regret, be comforted, comfort (Bible Works).

Koine Usage

Originally, "one called in" to support, hence "advocate," "pleader," "a friend of the accused person, called to speak to his character, or otherwise enlist the sympathy of the judges" (Moulton and Milligan, 485).

New Testament Usage

Used in John 14:16 of the Holy Spirit as another παράκλητος , implying Jesus (who is speaking) as a παράκλητος. Also used of the Holy Spirit in John 14:26; 15:26; 16:7; and of Christ in 1 John 2:1 (Moulton and Geden, 758).

Originally meant in the passive sense, of being asked. The word came to mean "one who is called to someone's aid;" "one who appears in another's behalf, mediator, intercessor, helper" (Bauer, Arndt, and Gingrich, 623).

παράκλητος (*parakleetos*) meant in classical Greek merely *called to one's aid, assisting*, especially in a court of justice. Hence a *legal advisor or helper*. "But this falls short of the meaning it afterwards obtained: *viz.*, not only of helping another to do something, but to help him *by doing it for him*. It is used only in John of the Holy Spirit's help (by Christ) in xiv. 16, 26; xv. 26; xvi. 7. And of Christ's help (by the Holy Spirit) in 1 John ii. 1" (Bullinger, 854).

Figure 4.15a

PARAKLETOS (παράκλητος), lit., called to one's side, i.e., to one's aid, is primarily a verbal adjective, and suggests the capability or adaptability for giving aid. It was used in a court of justice to denote a legal assistant, counsel for the defence, an advocate; then, generally, one who pleads another's cause, an intercessor, advocate, as in I John 2:1, of the Lord Jesus. In the widest sense, it signifies a succourer, comforter (W. E. *Vine's Expository Dictionary of New Testament Words*, 35, 208).

NT "1 Jn. 2:1 f. gives the term a soteriological character in calling 'Jesus Christ the righteous' our 'advocate' (*parakletos*) and 'propitiation' (*hilasmos*) for the sins of the whole world . . . This restriction of the title to Jesus and the Spirit requires a theological interpretation of the term which is at the same time polemical" (Colin Brown: *The New International Dictionary of New Testament Theology*, vol. I, 88ff).

Meaning in Context
Advocate is a title belonging to "Jesus Christ" which name is in apposition to it. He not only comes to the aid of believers who sin, but is uniquely sent to fill this role as the believer's defense attorney before God the Father, as in a court of law. His representation of the believer is not separated contextually either from His righteous character or His personal payment of the believer's debt, by which He satisfied the Father's just demand.

Application and Contrasts
If the believer who sins did not have Jesus Christ as his or her counsel for the defense; or, if Christ were not Himself *the righteous propitiation* for our sins, a single sin would result in defeat and hopeless despair. With Him, however, there is every inducement never to sin, nor to give up when one does sin. The believer has, in his or her favor, the solution referred to in the apodasis of the conditional clause in answer to the protasis, "If anyone sins."

Figure 4.15b

tive word for *child* and the first personal pronoun in the genitive (of relationship or possession) case. Tone is important in talking to people about sin.

Making a personal translation also enables you to see why the New King James Version retained the slightly rougher word order in English, "These things I write," rather than the smoother "I write these things," as in the other versions we examined. By moving *tauta* forward in the sentence, John is stressing the content of his letter as that which calls for the explanation he is giving. For an example of exegetical notations, see figure 4-16.

In 1 John 1, the Apostle has addressed those who deny a principle of sin within them (1:8). According to 1:10, some deny ever having committed a sin. Having referred to the universality of sin, John begins the second chapter with further explanation of the relationship between Christians and sin. His purpose in writing, that they never commit a single sin, is expressed with the ingressive aorist in the negative purpose-clause introduced with ἵνα.

Contrary to the apparent belief on the part of Gnostics influencing his readers, the Docetic faction of which made light of sin, John does not excuse sin on the part of believers as a human necessity. On the other hand, the third-class conditional statement in the protasis, if anyone sins, reassures those who will in all probability sin, of the secure standing they possess by the gift of Jesus as their righteous Advocate before the throne of God the Father. Not only does He stand in the unique position of their defense attorney at law, but the offering of himself as a satisfactory sacrifice (from a word study of ἱλασμος, propitiation) for sin gives a righteous standing to all for whom His self-sacrifice is efficacious, because He is qualitatively righteous [a nuance apparent only to those who are able to see that δίκαιος is anarthrous (without the article ὁ)].

If the ongoing work of Christ in heaven is the basis for the believer's assurance, His past cross-work on earth provided the basis of forgiveness for all in the world who will believe, and the basis of judgment for all who will not repent.

Figure 4.16

| WORD STUDIES | **PRINCIPLES** | THEME | OUTLINE |

Figure 4.17

Synthesis

The Formation of Principles

The Elements of the Whiting Method
(See figure 4-17.)

According to the Whiting Method:[29]

> "A principle is an outstanding and abiding truth that is not limited to a moment in time."

Outstanding

"Outstanding" describes a truth that is evidently prominent in importance from the perspective of the writer and his addressees. This calls for discernment. Except when quoting the devil or wicked people, everything the Bible says is assumed to be true. But not every true statement is equally germane to the argument of the book or purpose of the writer. While in no place to dismiss a scriptural truth as unimportant, you still can and must develop the art and skill of drawing principles that reflect author intent and support the thrust of the passage.[30] An outstanding truth in a passage is like a bearing wall in a building. It literally carries more weight than a nonbearing wall, though the latter is not unimportant.

Abiding

"Abiding," in the preceding definition refers to what Josh McDowell has called "absolute truth," which he defines as "that which is true for all people, for all times, for all places."[31] This is made explicit in the second half of the definition: "that is not limited to a moment in time." For these reasons, the statement of a "principle" should not employ proper nouns, which identify specific places or persons (other than those of God). Neither should it be stated in terms that date or otherwise restrict its universal application.

Prerequisites

Prerequisites for extracting a principle include (1) complete familiarity with the text under study; (2) careful, well-done analysis of grammar and meanings; and (3) compelling ability to think with the whole text in mind without arriving at vague generalities.[32] A useful technique for sifting the relevance of a text is to ask and answer questions on what has been called a *truth sheet.*

USE OF TRUTH SHEETS[33]

Asking and answering the questions *who, what, when, where, why,* and *how* in relation to a passage of Scripture is a simple and orderly way to be sure you have "covered all the bases" in the discovery of facts.

Truth Sheets refer to the application of the six interrogatives to the text under study to produce statements of fact leading to principles.

The use of truth sheets simply formalizes a mental process that would otherwise tend to occur unconsciously, randomly, and incompletely. Truth sheets are comparable to a filter through which the text is poured to sift the hard facts as raw materials with which to construct principles.

Answering the question, *who?* provides the *identification of persons*. Answering the question, *what?* discovers the *transaction* of any *performance*. "When" describes the *duration* of the *period* of time involved in the passage. By asking *where?* the *location* becomes the focus. The *causation of production* is discovered in answer to the question, *why?* Finally, answering the question, *how?* divulges the *function* of any *procedure* that may be described in the text. (See figures 4-18 and 4-19.)

Completing a Truth Sheet for 1 John 2:1–2.[34] (See figure 4-19.)

From Basic Facts to Principles[35]

The basic facts written on the truth sheet form the basis for recording truths. Each truth should be recorded as a separate declaration, without any judgment regarding its importance or usefulness. Figure 4-20 shows examples from the truth sheet for 1 John 2:1–2.

Next, truths of the same vein are combined in a single, simple sentence. At this stage in the process, the focus should be on words of obvious, outstanding importance. (See figure 4-21.)

Minor, repetitive, subordinate, or implied truths not germane to the thrust of the passage should now be eliminated by crossing them out. The goal is to reword the statements of truth in two to six simple, clear statements. (See figure 4-22.)

Two to six principles should now be stated as positive certainties of universal truth. Before demonstrating how to state a principle positively, the following guidelines are offered to help the preacher avoid common pitfalls.

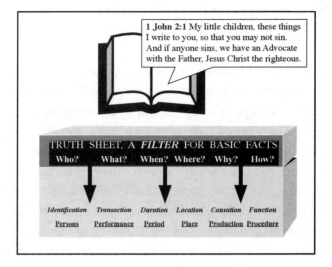

Figure 4.18

How Not to State a Principle [36]

A principle should not be stated:

1. as a question, such as *"Is there a solution to the problem of Christians sinning?"*
2. in the negative, such as *"Believers are not without advocacy when they sin."*
3. using proper nouns (names of people or places), unless they are everlasting. For example, *"The apostle John wrote to encourage believers when they sin."*
4. using personal pronouns, such as *"In Christ, you (or I) have an advocate with God the Father.*
5. using compound sentences or complex sentence structure, such as *"Christ is a righteous advocate for believers who sin and paid the penalty for the sins of the world."*
6. using unnecessarily difficult or many words, such as *"Christ is qualified to be the believer's advocate by virtue of His shed blood, which propitiated the sins of the world, including those of believers."*

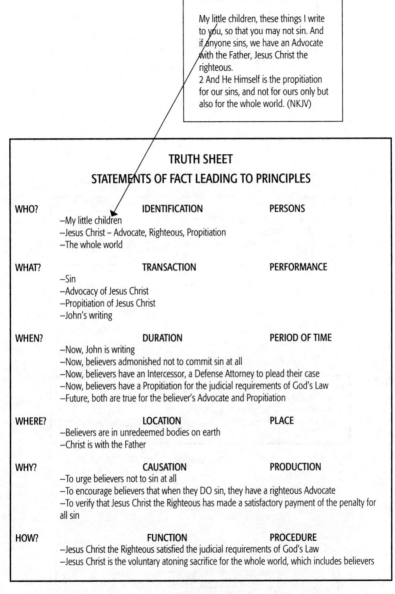

My little children, these things I write to you, so that you may not sin. And if anyone sins, we have an Advocate with the Father, Jesus Christ the righteous.
2 And He Himself is the propitiation for our sins, and not for ours only but also for the whole world. (NKJV)

TRUTH SHEET
STATEMENTS OF FACT LEADING TO PRINCIPLES

WHO?   **IDENTIFICATION**   **PERSONS**
—My little children
—Jesus Christ – Advocate, Righteous, Propitiation
—The whole world

WHAT?   **TRANSACTION**   **PERFORMANCE**
—Sin
—Advocacy of Jesus Christ
—Propitiation of Jesus Christ
—John's writing

WHEN?   **DURATION**   **PERIOD OF TIME**
—Now, John is writing
—Now, believers admonished not to commit sin at all
—Now, believers have an Intercessor, a Defense Attorney to plead their case
—Now, believers have a Propitiation for the judicial requirements of God's Law
—Future, both are true for the believer's Advocate and Propitiation

WHERE?   **LOCATION**   **PLACE**
—Believers are in unredeemed bodies on earth
—Christ is with the Father

WHY?   **CAUSATION**   **PRODUCTION**
—To urge believers not to sin at all
—To encourage believers that when they DO sin, they have a righteous Advocate
—To verify that Jesus Christ the Righteous has made a satisfactory payment of the penalty for all sin

HOW?   **FUNCTION**   **PROCEDURE**
—Jesus Christ the Righteous satisfied the judicial requirements of God's Law
—Jesus Christ is the voluntary atoning sacrifice for the whole world, which includes believers

Figure 4.19

- Believers need not sin.
- Believers sin.
- Christ is the answer to believers' sin problem.
- Christ is righteous.
- Christ is the believer's Advocate.
- Christ paid the penalty for the sins of the world.

Figure 4.20

- <u>Believers</u> need not <u>sin</u>, but do.
- Christ is the <u>believer's righteous advocate.</u>
- Christ <u>paid</u> the penalty for the sins of the <u>world</u>, including believers.

Figure 4.21

- Believers ~~need not~~ sin, ~~but do~~.
- ~~Christ is~~ the believer's righteous advocate.
- Christ paid the penalty for the sins of the world, ~~including believers~~.

Figure 4.22

- Believers sin, though they have the power to avoid sinning.
- Christ is a righteous Advocate for believers who sin.
- Christ paid for the sins of the world.

Figure 4.23

How to State a Principle

Principles should be stated as positive certainties of universal truth (see figure 4-23):

From the Principles of a Passage to a Statement of Its Theme[37]

"The theme is the central truth of the passage expressed in a simple sentence."

Wording the Theme

In the Whiting Method, "the theme is the central truth of the passage expressed in a simple sentence." It states what Haddon Robinson calls "the big idea."[38] In the terminology of Richards and Bredfeldt, the theme is the "generalization" that tells the listener both what the author is talking about, and what he is *saying* about what he is talking about.[39] The theme is the condensation of all of the principles into a single sentence. But it is not to be worded in the abstract language of exegesis. Rather, the theme should be stated in the contemporary language of application. In this way, it fulfills the bridging role of Richards and Bredfeldt's "pedagogical idea."[40] An example from Philippians 2:3–8 follows. (See figure 4-24.)

The Nature of an Effective Theme

As developed in the Whiting Method, the theme is a positive declaration, not a possibility, suggestion, or guess. It is the sermon in a nutshell. The theme is typically no more than nine words and is usually not alliterated. Themes should not consist of clichés, such as "The family that prays together stays together," or "God helps those who help themselves." A good theme will help you avoid extraneous material by expressing the single thought of the central thrust. This gives the mes-

---

Stating the Theme in the Contemporary Language of Application

Example from Philippians 2:3–8 ESV

³Do nothing from rivalry or conceit, but in humility count others more significant than yourselves. ⁴Let each of you look not only to his own interests, but also to the interests of others. ⁵Have this mind among yourselves, which is yours in Christ Jesus, ⁶who, though he was in the form of God, did not count equality with God a thing to be grasped, ⁷but made himself nothing, taking the form of a servant, being born in the likeness of men. And being found in human form, ⁸he humbled himself by becoming obedient to the point of death, even death on a cross.

Rather than stating the theme

*"The Incarnation and death of Christ
demonstrated His humility,"*

a more *applicable* statement of the theme might be,

"Christ is the example of selfless service to others."

Figure 4.24

sage its greatest potential for impacting the listener's mind, will, and emotions. It also makes it easier for the listener to remember, providing a handle by which to recall the major points of the outline. Look at this example of a theme from 1 John 2:1–2 (see figure 4-25):

FROM THEME TO OUTLINE[41]

Main Headings

A good theme produces a good outline. It includes all the headings, but develops only the *main* headings of the outline (I, II, III, etc.), not the subheadings (A, B, C, etc.). An example from 1 John 2:1–2 follows. (See figure 4-26.)

Subheadings

In the following example, notice that the main headings and subheadings of an outline are referenced to verses (1, 2, etc.), and even parts of verses (1a, 1b, etc.). The small-case letters *a* and *b* refer to the subdivisions of a verse—usually according to clauses. This is to help the listener identify the specific portion of the text that supports a given point in the outline. In this way, the sermon is shown to be rooted in or growing out of the biblical text, not the preacher's imagination! By "clicking down" the (bolded) subheadings, A, B, C, etc., the listener is able to see a visual summary of what every portion of the text teaches *and* how it supports the main headings on which the theme rests. (See figure 4-27.)

Transition

Notice that a well-stated theme makes a good transitional sentence that gives continuity to the outline. (See figure 4-28.) The outline develops the theme, because the theme is limited to the text from which it was woven, and expresses a progression of thought, taking the listener from one "place" to another.

Theme of 1 John 2:1–2

When believers sin,
Christ is their righteous Advocate.

Figure 4.25

When Believers Sin,
Christ Is Their Righteous Advocate

When Believers Sin . . .
    → I. The Problem of Sinning Christians

. . . Christ Is Their Righteous Advocate
    → II. The Solution of Christ's Advocacy

Figure 4.26

Summary and Conclusion

The Whiting Method, while not the only strategy for sermon development, is commended for its wedding of exegesis and homiletics. Influenced by Samuel Chadwick, developed by Arthur B. Whiting, and further refined by Milton William Jones and Dennis Wretlind, this system is most effective when principles are based on all of the exegetical data from textual analysis, rather than selected word studies alone. Therefore, the benefits of the system are most fully realized by language users (LU). However, by using the research tools available in a quality theological library or computer software program, non-language users (NLU) can also make good use of the method. This is especially true if the passage is read in several reliable translations, if the text is diagrammed and/or laid out mechanically to note the way the words relate to each other (syntax), and if the historical setting is studied thoroughly.

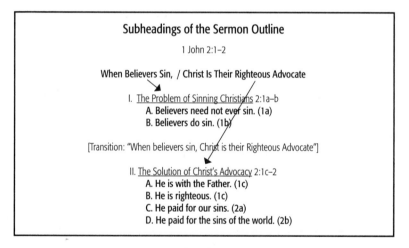

Subheadings of the Sermon Outline

1 John 2:1–2

When Believers Sin, / Christ Is Their Righteous Advocate

I. The Problem of Sinning Christians 2:1a–b
 A. Believers need not ever sin. (1a)
 B. Believers do sin. (1b)

[Transition: "When believers sin, Christ is their Righteous Advocate"]

II. The Solution of Christ's Advocacy 2:1c–2
 A. He is with the Father. (1c)
 B. He is righteous. (1c)
 C. He paid for our sins. (2a)
 D. He paid for the sins of the world. (2b)

Figure 4.27

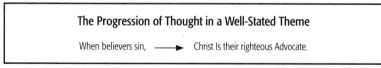

The Progression of Thought in a Well-Stated Theme

When believers sin, ⟶ Christ Is their righteous Advocate.

Figure 4.28

Whether evaluating existing translations (NLUs), or translating personally (LUs), use a *truth sheet* to sift relevant information. Compose three to six statements of timeless truths, called principles, by answering the six interrogatives (*who, what, when, where, why, how*). State the epitome of the principles, called the *theme*, by eliminating repetitious ideas and those of less importance. (The theme should be a single, positive, generalized sentence of no more than nine words.)

When worded in the language of the listeners, this encapsulated message enhances impact. Producing the main points of a good outline gives the listener a memorable handle by which to recall your sermon. When these are broken down into subheadings, indexed to the verses or portion of verses out of which they "grow," a listener is able to see that the message is God's, though the sermon is yours.

A well-stated theme provides an effective transitional statement. This helps the listener grasp the unity of the message. When the timeless truth is thus communicated, understood, applied, and implemented in the listener's life, you have used the Whiting Method to bridge the communication gap between the self-revealing God and those who desperately need to know Him intimately. In short, you have engaged in *delivering God's message in your sermon*.

DISCUSSION QUESTIONS

1. What are the two aspects of sermon preparation under which the elements of the Whiting Method may be arranged?
2. Define the following terms and describe their use or purpose.
   a. Text
   b. Word Study
   c. Truth Sheet
   d. Principle
   e. Theme
   f. Outline
3. List several ways a principle should *not* be stated.

4. Describe the attributes of a well-stated theme.

5. For LU only: List some of the advantages of being able to use the biblical languages.

6. What did you find most helpful in this overview of the Whiting Method of homiletics?

7. List at least three questions that this introduction to the Whiting Method has raised for you.

PART II

Developing the Discovery

❋

Part I of *God's Message, Your Sermon* introduced an adaptation of the Whiting Method as a means of bridging the communication gap that exists between the text of Scripture and the contemporary audience of an expository preacher. Having discovered the meaning of the text in its context, and designed its packaging for delivery, you are ready to develop the actual content. Part II will address ways to assemble the components of the verbal bridge.

Chapter 5, "The Components of an Expository Sermon," deals with elements inherent to every presentation of God's Word. Regardless of your unique style and emphasis, certain factors enhance the effectiveness of any sermon introduction, body, illustration, conclusion, application, and invitation.

Chapter 6, "The Classifications of an Expository Sermon," explores the kinds of expository sermons called for by the variety of biblical literature to be proclaimed. *Paragraph, chapter, book, doctrinal, biographical, parable, gospel,* and *typical* sermons all have their place in a balanced pulpit ministry.

CHAPTER 5

The Components of an Expository Sermon

WELL-ORGANIZED building materials, a good blueprint, and a competent builder are all parts that are necessary to construct a bridge that can effectively connect parties on opposite banks of a great divide. Yet these alone are not sufficient to build the bridge. Actual *work* must be done to assemble the parts so that they all fit together in a unified whole that is straight, strong, and inviting. The same is true of communicating ideas. This chapter concerns the purposes of the parts and how they are joined. Just as a physical bridge must be properly put together to serve its purpose, so must sermons.

Richards and Bredfeldt wisely observe that good planning does not displace Spirit-filled spontaneity; rather, it makes it meaningful:

> It is God's nature to plan . . . God designed His world by very exacting plans. He orders events by a master plan. And we as human beings made in His image have an innate tendency to make plans as well. We plan our days. We plan events. We plan travel. We plan our work. We plan our homes. We plan our lives. We plan worship services. We even try to plan our families. Should we not develop plans for teaching the Word of God as well?[1]

PLANNING FOR SUCCESS

Bridges vary in design to meet the needs and conditions of each span. Likewise, every sermon should be structured to reflect the literary genre and tone of the text. It should relate to the real needs of the particular people addressed. The truth must be communicated in a way that is natural to the speaker and responsive to the various learning styles of the listeners. The goal of every sermon should be to change the thinking, attitudes, and behavior of listeners to obedience to the revelation of God. This does not happen automatically, by accident, or in spite of poor planning. It has been said, "If you fail to plan, you plan to fail" and "If you aim at nothing, you hit it every time."

Even with planning, there are certain perils. When style is emphasized at the expense of substance, for example, the sermon becomes like the original Narrows Bridge in Tacoma, Washington. (See figures 5-1a and b.) Built in 1940 to span Puget Sound, the bridge was celebrated as the world's third-longest suspension bridge. It was slender, elegant, and graceful. Yet just four months after it opened, the bridge collapsed in a windstorm, earning the name "Galloping Gertie."[2] Replaced in 1950, the new bridge, built to carry 60,000 cars per day, regularly handles 90,000![3]

In a similar way, sermons that deliver sound content are better than those that are overly ambitious or structurally weak. When organization

Figure 5.1a

becomes an end in itself, the result can be too mechanical. For example, forced alliteration of an outline produces statements that are contrived or trite. Dazzling illustrations and excessive humor often detract from the thrust of God's message by "stealing the show." The desire to be profound or to impress people can tempt a preacher to use big words, complex sentence structure, and awkward or archaic expressions.

Good planning narrows the scope of the message, allowing the preacher to have a better grasp of a limited subject. It orders the presentation to accomplish strategic objectives without rambling. To hit a long-ranged target, a marksman uses a rifle rather than a shotgun. Similarly, the points of the message should be kept in proper proportion to the text, and ultimately contribute to a single goal. This gives the message integrity. Like a magnificent bridge, a well-structured sermon is more than a work of art; but it is not less!

Think of the listener as a lost traveler depending on the sermon for directions. Good organization causes the material to flow and makes it easier to follow, understand, and remember. Clear cognitive, affective, and behavioral lesson aims make the message more persuasive.

Parts of a sermon include the *introduction, body, conclusion,*

Figure 5.1b

application, and *invitation.* These must be assembled with care. Though sermons begin with introductions, they are last to be prepared. According to Richards and Bredfeldt, one attribute of what they call "a good hook," is that it leads the student into the Word.[4] Until you know what you will communicate in the body of the sermon, you cannot effectively plan the best way to get people's attention or surface the need to which your text provides God's answer. So structuring begins with organization of the sermon's body.

THE BODY OF THE MESSAGE

The *body* is the main portion of the sermon. It is in the body that you will present the analysis of a passage for instruction, and the synthesis of its principles for persuasion. The body corresponds to the *book* part of Richards and Bredfeldt's *hook, book, look, took* (HBLT).[5] According to Haddon Robinson, the material may be arranged as it is developed *deductively,* beginning with the idea that the text supports; or *inductively,* building up to the idea on the basis of the textual data.[6] In either case, this is the portion of the sermon in which ideas are explained, propositions are proved, principles are applied, the story is told, and the subject is completed.[7] Because of its bulk and central purpose, the content of the sermon's body must be *adapted, divided, styled, ordered,* and *developed.*

Adapted

Adaptation is like shopping for clothing that fits both the person and the occasion. It reflects the style and substance of the text from which it is woven. It suits the preacher's gifts and abilities, *and* the nature of the audience. For example, the text of 1 John 2:1–2 was written by the apostle John when he was elderly. When he begins the second chapter, "My little children" (NKJV), the tone is fatherly. He firmly asserts that sin is darkness, the antithesis of the light in which a believer can and must walk in order to enjoy fellowship with God, who *is* light (1 John

1:5). The "blood of Jesus Christ His Son," John tells his readers, "cleanses us from all sin" (v. 7 NKJV). John is both firm and familial as he switches from writing in first-person singular, "My little children, these things *I* write to you" to first-person plural, "*we* have an Advocate with the Father" (1 John 2:1 NKJV, emphasis added). When he refers to "our sins," in verse 2, and for those of "the whole world" (NKJV), John includes himself. For a sermon to communicate God's message, you must also take the tone of John, who balances his emphasis on the gravity of sin with an emphasis on the marvelous grace of salvation.

Divided

Dividing the body of the sermon is necessary for adequate understanding and to carefully distinguish the vital force of the sections. In 1 John 2:1–2, for example, part of the text identifies the problem of sinning Christians. This builds the listener's sense of need for the solution of Christ's advocacy, given in the balance of the text. When given meaningful headings, the transition from one division of the sermon's body to another is clarified. In our sample sermon, the word *problem* in the first major division ("The Problem of Sinning Christians") anticipates the word *solution* in the second major division ("The Solution of Christ's Advocacy").

Styled

The body of the sermon is also *styled* for maximum impact, absorption, and memory. The use of words that start with the same letter is called *alliteration*.[8] The following sermon illustrates the use of an alliterated outline, with partially alliterated subpoints. (See figure 5-2.)

Another device is called *tautophony*, or *assonance*. This is "the repetition of vowel sounds within a short passage of verse or prose."[9] Notice the use of assonance in the following sermon outline. (See figure 5-3.)

Good headings are not just isolated labels or titles but statements

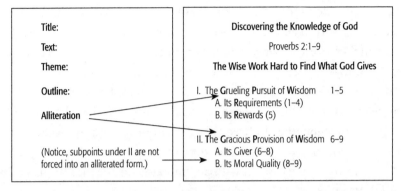

Figure 5.2

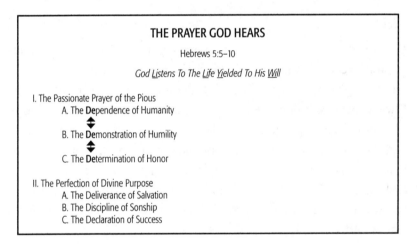

Figure 5.3

with clear meaning. The use of questions in division headings can be distracting if it causes people to try to fill in the blanks rather than listen.

The following outline of the book of Jonah illustrates the importance of symmetry in stating the divisional headings of an outline. Note the consistent use of nouns on the right-hand side of the figure in contrast to the mixture of nouns and verbs on the left-hand side. (See figure 5-4.)

Poor Grammatical Balance	Good Grammatical Balance
I. Yahweh's Offer of Mercy to Sinners (phrase with noun)	I. Yahweh's Determination to Offer His Mercy to Sinners
II. God Delivers Repentant Pagans (clause with verb)	II. Yahweh's Deliverance of Repentant Pagans
III. The Compassionate LORD (phrase with adjective)	III. Yahweh's Demonstration of Compassion

Figure 5.4

Ordered

Ordering the body of the sermon will make it easier for you to remember what you have planned to say. It also makes it easier for the listener to follow. The order should be natural, flowing, moving, and varied. *Natural* order means that it corresponds to the text itself, or the logic of its progression is evident.[10] When one point of a sermon builds anticipation for the next, without sudden breaks, it is described as *flowing*. *Movement* toward a goal or conclusion is another important aspect of well-ordered material in the body of a sermon. *Varied* use of words to avoid repetition helps keep the listener engaged.

Developed

Every heading should have at least two subheadings, if it has any, says Jones.[11] "If a heading stands alone, then it should be included in the main heading from which it originates."[12]

The following outline (figure 5-5) is a model for structuring the body of the sermon.

ILLUSTRATIONS

Just because something is true, does not mean that it is clear. An *illustration* is a story, example, diagram, picture, object, or figure of speech that clarifies a concept by demonstrating what it is, how it works, or why it is important.

When Believers Sin, Christ Is Their Righteous Advocate

I. The Problem of Sinning Christians 2:1a–b
    A. Believers need not ever sin (1a)
    B. Believers do sin (1b)

II. The Solution of Christ's Advocacy 2:1c–2
    A. He is with the Father (1c)
    B. He is righteous (1c)
    C. He paid for our sins (2a)
    D. He paid for the sins of the world (2b)

Figure 5.5

For example, in John 17:20–21, Jesus prays for His disciples, "I do not pray for these alone, but also for those who will believe in Me through their word; that they all may be one, as You, Father, are in Me, and I in You; that they also may be one in Us, that the world may believe that You sent Me" (NKJV). The analogy of the unity of the Father and the Son to the unity of believers is difficult to conceptualize. Some sort of diagram or word picture may help people grasp the idea. For instance, children are in their father's family tree, and their father's genes are in them. Genetically, then, there is a sense in which a father and his children are *in* one another. Similarly, you can be in water, yet also have water in you, as when you are in a swimming pool while also having some of the "pool" in you (water is in your mouth).

Illustrations have been compared to windows, which allow light to fill every room and make visible what would otherwise be unseen or shadowy. The use of the family tree and pool illustrations shed light on the concept of unity. Just as the use of color adds realism to media presentations, illustrations enhance sermons. At their best, they stimulate curiosity, imagination, and thought. Sometimes they are like the flashing lights of an alarm system that get people's attention. A good story or analogy can turn the ears of listeners into eyes with which to visualize the truth they hear. When they serve their purpose in clarifying God's message, they always point away from themselves to the object they illumine.[13]

But every analogy breaks down, and part of the skill of using illustrations is knowing their limitations and not overpressing them.[14] As
someone has said, "Illustrations were not made to walk on all fours."
Like any good thing, they can be abused. This occurs when they domi-
nate the truth. Windows too large, or too many, can structurally
weaken a building. Likewise, illustrations that are too extensive, elaborate, entertaining, or memorable can weaken a sermon.

Skits and multimedia presentations are types of illustrations. In
Matthew 18:1–5, Jesus stood a child before His disciples to demonstrate the kind of humble dependence upon God that is required for a
person to enter the kingdom. To emphasize the importance of every
member of the kingdom, He compared him to one lost sheep out of a
hundred (vv. 12–14).

Illustrations help the listener consider a truth more objectively. In 2
Samuel 12:1–7, when the prophet Nathan told the story of a rich man
who took a poor man's only ewe lamb, it caused David to judge his own
sin against Uriah.

When illustrations actually illumine the truth of an otherwise abstract concept, they give you an opportunity to reinforce that truth by
stating it differently. An example of this is the use of a *descriptive word*,
such as Jesus' use of the word *sword*, in Matthew 10:34, to depict the divisive nature of the truth He brought to the earth. Literary *figures of
speech* are another category of illustration, such as the shepherd/sheep
imagery of Psalm 23 and John 10. Fifty-three figures of speech can be
identified in the Sermon on the Mount in Matthew 5–7.[15] *Similes* and
metaphors provide formal or implied comparisons to add emphasis, in-
tensify feeling, or reveal the unknown by what is familiar.

Other forms of illustration include *analogies*, in which one thing is
described by its similarity to another. *Anecdotes* are brief stories of an
interesting, amusing, or biographical incident, used to make a point.
Stories and poetry, whether fictitious or true, can effectively clarify
ideas that would otherwise remain enigmatic or opaque.

Among the many sources of illustrations, the Bible is the most authoritative. A good example is the story of Joseph in Genesis 39:13 used

to illustrate what Paul meant in 2 Timothy 2:22, by his command to "flee . . . youthful lusts" (NKJV). The disadvantage of biblical illustrations is that their use may require explanation for those in the audience who are not familiar with them.

Personal observation of human nature and current events is one of the best sources of sermon illustrations, because it is fresh and personal. Its disadvantage is seen if "you had to be there" to appreciate the significance of the observation. Media reports of events and human interest stories can also be sources of illustrations. Biographies of people who exemplify good or evil can be very useful as long as they do not require too much time to explain. When gleaning illustrations from sports, songs, movies, and novels, make sure to avoid references to unwholesome sources.

Historical lessons, theological issues, the church hymnal, and developments in the arts and sciences can be used to good advantage. Books and Web sites that provide illustrations and humor can also be helpful, but personal discoveries are usually far more natural and effective.

The most important guideline for the use of illustrations in sermon development is that they actually shed light on important truth that would otherwise remain shadowy. They should not simply entertain, illustrate the obvious, or be too long or numerous. They should be simple (like clear glass, not stained glass!) and accurate (not "evang-elastically" exaggerated or carelessly taken out of context). Statistical data has its place, but listeners may question how it was gathered and whether it is current or out-of-date.

Recording illustrations in the backs of books the preacher reads; on notepads kept in one's pocket, car, or nightstand; or in a PDA, makes it possible to file them by subject and biblical text at a later date. The parables of Jesus indicate His attention to illustrative details as He observed life. The development of a hunter/gatherer's attitude regarding potential illustrations is a delight as well as a discipline for the expository preacher of God's Word.

Conclusion

The *conclusion* of a message follows the presentation and provides a résumé, succinctly gathering together everything said and drawing the message to a clear end. While a conclusion does provide the summary that ends a message, it should never consist of a statement that indicates that you're finished—especially if you're not! Rather, it adds the finishing touch that leaves a lasting impression and prepares the listener to decide what he or she is going to do in response. Sometimes simply repeating the theme of the sermon serves as an effective conclusion. The Whiting Method has identified several kinds of conclusions:

Formal

Formal conclusions actually restate the points and headings.[16] This tends to call undue attention to the mechanics of the presentation. If the outline is to be recapped, it can be paraphrased, reduced to a series of single words, restated in the vernacular of the day, stated in terms of inspirational ideals, or balanced with statements that convey a contrasting truth. For example, a message that has emphasized sin could be summarized with a reminder of God's forgiveness.

Informal

It is often best to conclude a sermon with an illustration. Other informal techniques include a personal testimony; an appropriate quotation; or a poem, prayer, challenge, rhetorical question, or song chosen for the purpose.

Effective conclusions have six features: they are *streamlined, simple, strong, short, skillful,* and they provide a *summary.* Conclusions must move without detours or stop signs. They are closure oriented and efficient in encapsulating the message. They consist of clear statements without big words. Good conclusions are stated with passion and conviction. Their wording is vivid, alive, energetic, and motivational. Since they should take no longer than two or three minutes to communicate, you must be skillful in preparing and delivering a summary that recalls the main points of sermon *without* introducing new ideas, arguments, or Scripture references.

APPLICATION

Application of the sermon refers to the threads of relevance that run throughout the sermon but are finally drawn together for personal appeal and action for both preacher and people. In terms of Richards and Bredfeldt's well-known *hook, book, look, took* (HBLT), application logically follows the *hook* (introduction), and *book* (body), with a *look* to the "*took*" (implementation) of the truth.[17] Richards and Bredfeldt distinguish between *self-guided application*, in which the listener is on his own to perceive the text's implications, and the far preferable *guided self-application*, in which the hearer is led "to discover and grasp the relationship of the truth just studied to daily living."[18] These authors describe application as the navigational process in which a pilot lines up with the runway in order to land the plane at its destination. It clearly identifies the target, goal or objective.[19] From the standpoint of time, the application (*look*) marks a return from the past consideration of ancient revelation (*book*) to the present time, from which the introduction (*hook*) launched the message. Its implementation (*took*) will take place in the future. The following diagram illustrates what the authors refer to as "a trip through time."[20] (See figure 5-6.)

Expository preaching aims at changed lives on the part of people willing to respond mentally, affectively, and behaviorally to the revealed knowledge of God. Attributes of appropriate application have been described with the words *factual, fleshed-out, focused, fresh,* and *forceful.*

Factual

Applications must accurately represent the actual claims of Scripture upon the individual. Just as you must vigilantly avoid reading meanings into the text of Scripture, you must also avoid the temptation to let

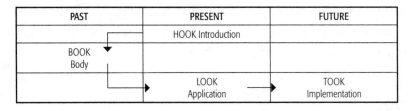

Figure 5.6[21]

applications be contorted by pressure from contemporary culture or sabotaged by your own hidden agenda. Many times exhortations on the basis of related principles taught elsewhere in Scripture will suggest themselves. But good application reinserts the very principle led out of its ancient context into the contemporary context without distorting its meaning. Put another way, good applications are those which the author would have made if he were writing today. For example, the requirement that elders be "blameless" in 1 Timothy 3:2 (NKJV) is explained by the list of character qualities that follows in the text. In applying the word *blameless* today, you will need to evaluate behaviors that were not moral issues at the time Paul wrote. Yet in doing so, you must be careful to avoid subjective judgments that reflect your own cultural biases. For example, ongoing addictions to illegal substances or Internet pornography clearly disqualify a man from the office requiring that he be *blameless,* while other less clear actions, such as body piercing or lottery gambling, may be debatable.

Fleshed-out

This attribute of good application is incarnational.[22] It looks to implement the principle in daily practice. It informs the listener's commitment to think, feel, and behave differently.

Focused

When an application zeroes in on particular issues of thought, attitude, and action, it is like the burning-hot concentration of sunlight as it passes through a magnifying glass held the right distance from an object. It is specific, pointed, and related to real needs; not diffuse, vague, or frivolous. As a result, it ignites change.

Fresh

Applications should avoid repeating tired, worn-out phrases and clichés. It may seem that virtually every sermon could be reduced to "trust and obey," or "read your Bible and pray," or "God is sovereign, but man is responsible." But this is not the time to generalize. Applications answer the question, "So what?" in the specific language of the listener's real circumstances.

Forceful

Finally, applications should pack a punch. Like the closing argument of a trial lawyer, a good application calls for the listener to render his or her verdict on the case just presented. It makes a short, pointed, simple appeal to the will. This should not be a high-pressure sales pitch, feisty challenge, or emotional manipulation. Neither does good application flatter or make outlandish promises. It simply guides the listener to accept the challenge of actually doing what he knows is in his own best interest. Forceful application urges him to explore, discover, and *do* what God wants him to do by exposing the contemporary implications of the timeless truth.

In the Whiting Method, guidelines for the development of good applications include their need to be *related* and *relational*. When they are related, they discreetly address specific needs of people as individuals without calling attention to particular individuals. Relational applications are communicated with the compassion of a preacher who is transparent about the impact of the truth on his own life, not that the sermon is *about* the preacher, but that he speaks to his audience as one of them.

INVITATION

An invitation is simply the call for a particular personal response to God in light of His Word. Its purpose is to urge timely implementation of biblical principles while choices are clear. It is not necessarily an "altar call" to physically walk to a place of decision,[23] but an opportunity to decide on a change of thinking, feeling, and/or behaving.[24]

Invitations have been described as addressing the whole person, intellect, emotion, will, and conscience. Commending the argument of the discourse to the mind of the listener appeals to his *intellect*. Communicating the feeling of urgency to respond to the heart of God addresses the *emotions*. Calling for a conscious personal decision that is clear and specific, addresses the *will*. Appealing to the listener's heightened sense of right and wrong addresses his *conscience*.

INTRODUCTION

The introduction of a message precedes the theme and proof of the text. In Richards and Bredfeldt's comparison of a Bible lesson to a plane flight, the goal of the introduction, or "hook," is to achieve liftoff with all passengers on board and en route to a safe landing at the desired destination.[25]

It has been said, "You only get one chance to make a first impression." This indicates the importance of the sermon introduction. Once the rest of the sermon has been prepared, you know the destination of the flight. The next task is to decide how best to sell tickets to prospective passengers. One of several dangers to avoid is overselling. This can easily result from preparing the introduction first. Jones has dubbed this problem as giving "a *Cadillac*-introduction to a *Ford*-body and conclusion."[26] Another problem is the tendency to preach your introduction rather than your sermon!

The introduction has been compared to the porch of a building, a stepping-stone, and a driveway.[27] It is only the entrance and should not be made so attractive that people won't move past it! Introductions are meant to prepare people to listen by getting and holding their attention. French general Napoleon once reportedly re-marked, "The first five minutes of battle are decisive ones." It is during these early moments that a connection must be established between you and the people. The audience is deciding whether the message will be worth listening to based on what they perceive *you* to be. Introductions also let the audience in on what the sermon is about and awaken their interest in the subject.

Sometimes planes take off in the opposite direction of their desti-nation due to weather conditions or airway traffic. Sermons, generally, should not. The best introductions are directly in line with the theme of the text.

A brief "introduction" offers a functional entryway to a home. It in-vites people to move, as directly as possible, from the front door to the dinner table. A similar sermon introduction can be described as *sugges-tive, simple,* and *relational*. It is *suggestive* in that it simply whets the ap-petite, as does an hors d'oeuvre, rather than spoiling the meal with too much food. It is *simple* because it only arouses the listener's curiosity, instead of overwhelming him or her with something too ornate or de-tailed. A simple introduction may state the title, give the reason for its choice, and tell its relation to life situations. Effective introductions are *relational* when they invite a warm audience response.

Ideas for introductions may be found in any number of possible sources. You may need to determine if the text is familiar, commonly misunderstood, controversial, or relevant to a current event. From the context, how does the Scripture passage fit the theme or argument of the chapter, book, etc.? What historical, geographical, and cultural set-tings might need to be explained to set up the sermon? On special days, including traditional holidays and anniversaries, seasonal or memorial emphases may suggest appropriate introductions. At Halloween, for example, it may be suitable in some settings to begin a sermon by tem-porarily putting on a mask to depict Satan's tactic of disguising his true identity (see 2 Corinthians 11:14), or the believer's tendency to mas-querade in the mannerisms of the world (see Romans 12:2).

Newspaper and magazine articles can provide ways of taking people from what is presently on their minds to where their attention needs to move. (Media sources should first be checked for accuracy and relevance to the theme of the text.)

Other sources of introduction include the occasion for a guest speaker's invitation to speak. Personal observations of human nature or overheard conversations with one's barber, gas station attendant, fellow travelers, etc. can give the preacher a way to establish common ground. Finally, a variety of published sources of illustrations and humor are often indexed by subject and/or Scripture reference and can provide historical or hysterical "hooks."

Here, the sermon from Proverbs 2:1–9, seen in an earlier example, is introduced with a bit of humor from a published source.[28] This is to get the listener's attention, cause him to chuckle, and start him or her thinking about the difference between human wisdom, which is merely *clever*, and divine wisdom, which is synonymous with *character*. (See figure 5-7.)

Textual introductions refer listeners to the passage under consideration. They set the stage for the message by giving the background for the text. Stories and skits are another type of introduction. (When using these, avoid being overly dramatic.) Another handy way to introduce a sermon is by using the text's topic as a *springboard*. Stating key problems that people face can build interest. Occasionally it is appropriate to simply announce the subject of the sermon, as in a more aca-

---

Discovering the Knowledge of God

Proverbs 2:1–9

John and Dave were hiking when they spotted a mountain lion staring at them. John froze in his tracks, but Dave sat down on a log, tore off his hiking boots, pulled a pair of running shoes from his backpack, and hurriedly began to put them on.
"For crying out loud! You can't outrun a mountain lion!" John hissed.
"I don't have to," said Dave, with a shrug. "I just have to outrun you."

There are many concepts of wisdom. Dave's wisdom was clever; but God's wisdom involves character. The proverbs before us today teach that **the wise work hard to find what God gives.**

Figure 5.7

demic setting. You can also use a striking quotation as an introduction, but be sure to carefully identify the source and quote it accurately. (How many times has a quotation from German Reformation leader Martin Luther been mistakenly attributed to 1960s' Civil Rights leader Martin Luther King Jr.?)

Good introductions sometimes make use of rhetorical, challenging, or provocative questions, with pauses to allow people to ponder issues the sermon will later address. Beginning with a definition of a word, either from a dictionary or from your use of a key term, can also be a suitable introduction.

When comparing contrasting political views or doctrinal stances, do not unnecessarily alienate part of the audience by taking a potentially controversial personal position. By the same token, correcting a doctrinal error in an introduction requires skill to avoid leaving the impression that those believed to be in error are being personally attacked.

Object lessons, references to literature or movies, multimedia presentations, and songs are examples of other ways to introduce the sermon.

Avoid being abrupt in any sermon introduction. This can seem rude to listeners. It is also counterproductive to make excuses for either yourself or your subject. Dogmatism or erroneous facts can close people's minds. You should also avoid developing the introduction with multiple points that form a minisermon in itself. Also, using the same approach too often will certainly blunt its ability to hook the listener.

In composing introductions, determine exactly what you're trying to accomplish. Review the message to make sure the introduction actually *introduces* it! Whether you manuscript the entire message or not, write out the introduction, committing the first sentence of it to memory. Then deliver the introduction with the enthusiasm of one sold on what he is about to say.

INTRODUCING 1 JOHN 2:1–2

Following is one of many ways that the message of 1 John 2:1–2 could be introduced. (See figure 5-8.)

Courtroom drama is a staple of American entertainment. Questions of justice seem to captivate the imaginations of TV viewers. But mention the phrase "defense attorney," and the name that jumps to mind may not be Perry Mason or Matlock, but Johnnie Cochran. Cochran led the so-called dream team that successfully won the acquittal of celebrity O. J. Simpson in 1995. Simpson, a famous football player, sports commentator, and actor, had been charged with murdering two people, including his wife. When the longest jury trial in California history ended, having involved 150 witnesses and costing $15 million, everyone seemed to have a different opinion.

People have a God-given capacity to make judgments. As a result of sin, they are also subject to the judgment of God. For Christians, sin raises tough questions. On one hand, how can those who sin stand before the God of absolute justice? On the other hand, if the blood of Jesus has cleansed them, why should it matter that they sin? The answer to these questions involves a greater courtroom drama than any on earth. You see, **when believers sin, Christ is their righteous Advocate.**

Figure 5.8

Summary and Conclusion

Like a bridge, every expository sermon consists of parts that have to be understood and put together carefully. For structural soundness, good planning is indispensable. The introduction, written last, gets attention and directs thought to the text for the truth that meets the needs it surfaces.

The body of a sermon must be structurally adapted to the preacher, the audience, and their circumstances. Dividing and subdividing the text distinguishes the vital forces that give the text its punch and make the sermon work. When these main points are styled and ordered, the flow of thought is unobstructed. When they are appropriate, illustrations help listeners pay attention and visualize abstract concepts.

Well-crafted conclusions give the audience a way to remember the gist of the sermon. This gives them a more condensed basis for deciding how to respond. Applications bring listeners back to the present from their consideration of timeless truths recorded in the context of the ancient past. They guide hearers in a process of self-application that results in commitment to implement changed thinking, attitudes, and actions in the future. The invitation simply calls individuals to timely action by appealing to their total personalities, minds, wills, emotions, and consciences.

DISCUSSION QUESTIONS

1. What are clear and meaningful differences between a structured sermon and a presentation of God's Word that might be called a running commentary, devotional, exhortation, theological discourse, Bible talk, etc.?

2. Isn't a *good* unstructured presentation of a passage better than a structured homily that isn't as good? Are you convinced that the advantages of a well-built sermon are actually worth the effort it takes to build it? Do you truly believe that the average person who attends a preaching service really needs, wants, appreciates, and responds better to a polished, artistic sermon than to an informal talk?

3. Describe ways that the structural integrity of a sermon may be weakened.

4. List and describe the components of a sermon that must be understood and assembled.

5. Why should the sermon introduction be written last?

6. What are the advantages when the body of the sermon is adapted? divided? styled? ordered? developed?

7. Briefly describe the qualities of an effective conclusion by explaining what is meant by *streamlined, simple, short, summary,* and *skillful.*

8. What is meant by *factual, fleshed-out, focused, fresh,* and *forceful* when describing effective applications?

9. How is an invitation different from an altar call, and why do you agree or disagree that every sermon should have one?

10. Describe a good introduction.

CHAPTER 6

The Classifications of an Expository Sermon

SUSPENSION bridges are only one kind of bridge, and not all of them are alike. The particular need and purpose of a bridge depends on many factors. As can be seen from this picture of the Sundial Bridge over the Sacramento River near Redding, California, the form and style of a bridge also reflect the imagination of the designer. (See figure 6-1.) The same is true of Scripture and should be true of sermons.

Kinds of sermons differ partly because, like the land of the Bible, the literature of the Bible varies dramatically. To treat God's Word as a paved parking lot with uniform spaces, in which answers to man's questions are neatly parked in accessible rows, is not only naive but dishonoring to the artistry of the Author. The infinite God has revealed Himself through the hills, valleys, rivers, cities, and deserts of diverse literature. Narrative, law, poetry, wisdom, and apocalyptic genres comprise a broad spectrum through which God has communicated His dual programs to redeem lost sinners and establish the reign of His Son upon the earth. The Word was written by people, and to people, who represent the full range of personalities, in circumstances that run the gamut of human experience. As a result, several types of sermons are needed in a pulpit ministry committed to declaring the whole purpose of God to all kinds of people. (See Acts 20:27.) They include the *paragraph sermon, chapter sermon, book sermon, doctrinal sermon, biographical sermon, parable sermon, gospel sermon*, and the preaching of *biblical types*.

Figure 6.1

THE PARAGRAPH SERMON[1]

The paragraph sermon is short enough for an intensive exegesis, but long enough for a sermon. It is practical and flexible enough for any situation.

The paragraph is the most frequently used unit for preaching, because a paragraph expresses a single unit of thought. Where it begins and ends is determined by the context. In narrative, paragraphs are often marked by references to time, called *temporal markers*. To determine the natural breaks in narrative, it is often helpful to read the text aloud. The texts of the Greek New Testament are usually more reliable in determining the limits of a paragraph than most English translations, which sometimes impose chapter divisions in the middle of a thought.[2] An example is found in the paragraph of 1 Corinthians 13:1–3, which actually begins with the second half of 12:31.

[Note: Non-language users may benefit from a perusal of figures 6-2 and 6-3 but are welcome to skip to the next section if they so desire.]

Language users will find that grammatical diagrams and/or mechanical layouts can be very helpful in identifying the subject, predicate, object, conclusion, etc., that express a complete idea.[3] (See figures 6-2 and 6-3.)

Paragraphs that deal with concrete subject matter are generally more "preachable" than those whose subjects are abstract or problematic, such as the baptism for the dead, in 1 Corinthians 15:29–34. The content of some paragraphs will suggest themselves for weddings, funerals, holidays, and other special occasions. Just make sure that your

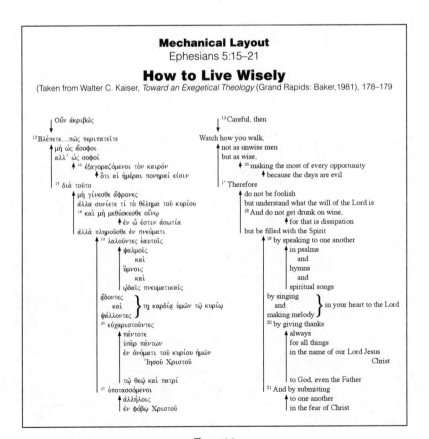

Figure 6.2

Grammatical Diagram,
Ephesians 5:15–21

How to Live Wisely

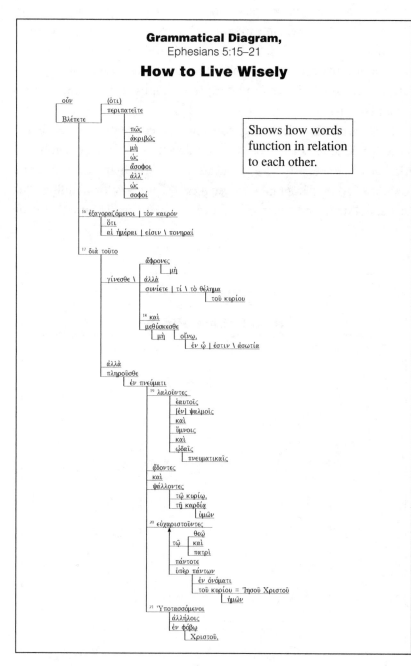

Shows how words function in relation to each other.

Figure 6.3

selections fit your stage of development as an exegete. For example, long or difficult paragraphs, such as 1 Peter 3:13–22, are better tackled when you have gained some experience.[4]

There are eight types of paragraph sermons.[5] *Narrative* paragraphs represent one episode that is part of a longer story, such as Abraham's offering of Isaac (Gen. 22:1–19). The parable of the lost sheep (Luke 15:3–7) is an example of a *discourse*. Isaiah 12:1–6 is a *poetic strophe*, or stanza, like the verse of a song. The apostle Paul's commendation of Epaphroditus, in Philippians 2:25–30, is called a *character sketch*. In 3 John 9, Diotrephes could be developed as a *career character*. An *event* is represented in the account of Jacob's wrestling with the Angel of Yahweh in Genesis 32:22–30. The apostle Paul's discussion of justification by faith, in Romans 3:27–30, is an example of a *doctrinal* paragraph sermon. *Problem paragraphs* include such passages as Matthew 19:3–9, where Jesus responds to a question (whether it is ever permissible to divorce and remarry).

THE CHAPTER SERMON[6]

A chapter sermon is a textual expository message woven from the fabric of an entire chapter of the Bible. Chapter sermons confirm and utilize commonly accepted divisions of Bible books, which are thus easily identifiable and memorable as literary units. They can be developed and presented *on their own*, without being part of an ongoing series through the Bible book in which they are found, or they can be part of a series of great chapters on a topic, like giving (2 Cor. 8–9; Phil. 4, etc.); the rapture of the church (1 Thess. 4; 1 Cor. 15, etc); or rewards (1 Cor. 3; 2 Cor. 5). Several chapters of the Bible have been recognized as *classical* passages.[7] Examples include Genesis 2, "Why We Are What We Are"; Zechariah 4, "The Secret of True Strength"; 1 Corinthians 13, "The Love Chapter," and Hebrews 11, "The Hall of Faith."

Chapters, properly divided, lend themselves as texts for single sermons, especially when they concern a single subject. However, not every chapter is centered around a single person, place, event, or idea.

Acts 16, for example, encompasses five separate accounts: The selection
and circumcision of Timothy, Paul's Macedonian vision, Lydia's conversion, Paul and Silas's imprisonment, and the Philippian jailer's conversion. It is not impossible to preach all five of these accounts in one
sermon, showing how they relate to Paul's second missionary journey,
but chapter sermons usually develop an integrated whole.

Chapter sermons are developed by carefully reading the chapter
and tracing the argument of the book to confirm proper chapter division and understand the context. Next, the key portion of the chapter
must be fully exegeted, noting how every element in the chapter supports the theme. Finally, the chapter must be clearly set in its historical,
literary, and theological contexts. (See figure 6-4.)

THE BOOK SERMON[8]

The text of a *book sermon* is an entire book of the Bible. Though they
are the most difficult of all sermons to prepare, book sermons benefit
both preacher and congregation. According to Jones, "it enables them
to see a whole rather than such concentrated detail that the overall understanding is dissipated."[9] But there are obstacles to overcome in
order to realize the advantages of preaching a whole book at a time.
One is the listeners' predisposition to resist messages that they perceive
as being too long. The very idea of covering even a one-chapter book,
such as 2 John, Philemon, or Obadiah may seem daunting. However,
the panoramic overview of whole books of the Bible is a very impor-

---

Example, Chapter Sermon

1 Corinthians 13

I. Nature of Love	1–3
II. Necessity of Love	4–7
III. Nobility of Love	8–13

Figure 6.4

tant part of a healthy pulpit ministry. It provides the contextual background necessary for interpreting texts within the book, and can be a good way to introduce a series of messages through a book of the Bible that may even be lengthy.

The large amount of text to be analyzed in most book sermons can also intimidate the preacher. It is best to prepare it over a period of several weeks, while working on less demanding sermons. Announcing an upcoming book sermon ahead of time, and encouraging the congregation to read the book several times in advance, can build interest and stimulate questions.

Becoming very familiar with the book's content by reading it several times in various translations (or, for LU, in the original text) will help you see where its natural divisions fall, and what verse or passage might suggest itself as most important to study thoroughly. Revelation 1:19 practically gives an outline for the entire book when it states, "Write the things which you have seen [ch. 1], and the things which are [chs. 2–3], and the things which will take place after this [chs. 4–22]" (NKJV).

When preaching whole books, it is important to major on the author's reason for writing it. As the cast of a film supports the role of the star actor, tracing the thread, or threads, of minor themes is not only a legitimate part of analyzing the text, but is essential to the development of the book's "big idea."

A good way to build up to preaching book sermons is to tackle small ones first. For examples, Dan once preached a series of messages entitled "Postcard Epistles," consisting of sermons on the one-chapter epistles of Philemon, 2 John, 3 John, and Jude. Figure 6-5 is an example of the development of 2 John.

DOCTRINAL SERMON[10]

The word *doctrine* is used here in reference to the collection and arrangement of the entire body of what the Bible teaches about a particular subject. A proper doctrinal sermon communicates the truth of

```
The Truth of Love
2 John
Love Cannot Be Separated from Truth

I. Truth Binds Believers Together in Love                                    1–3
II. Truth Governs Believers' Walk in Love                                    4–6
    A. Walking in Truth Determines Love for One Another
    B. Walking in Obedience Demonstrates Love for One Another
III. Truth Makes Believers' Love Discriminating                              7–13
    A. Deceivers Are on the Loose
    B. Rewards Are on the Line
    C. Fellowship Is Limited by Doctrine
```

Figure 6.5

divine revelation in a clear, cogent, concise manner, to evangelize the lost and edify the regenerate. First John 1:5–2:2, for example, deals with God's provision for the presence of sin.

In preaching doctrinal sermons, understand that they are to be *in*-structive rather than *de*structive; your job is not to attack those who hold opposing views. Doctrinal sermons should develop a single, main idea, building upon elements that are clearly understood before progressing from one to another. The listener should be drawn to doctrinal preaching by the expectation of learning what God reveals about a subject, not the lure of slick titles or clever presentations.

Because doctrinal sermons are essentially textual-topical expository messages, only the Scripture text is more important than the sermon's subject. Therefore, the sermon's title can generate interest and stimulate curiosity—or fail to do so. Titles can also be useful for informing the public and preparing the congregation. Creating innovative titles helps broaden your own thinking about the message. Consider the following titles for their attention-grabbing quality. (See figure 6-6.)

Every sermon should answer one question: "So what?" Since every doctrine answers questions, solves problems, and meets needs, always state the doctrine's purpose in your theme. For example, in Ephesians 5:18, the command to be filled with the Holy Spirit is parallel to the command to understand what the will of the Lord is (v. 17). Both are

Attention-Grabbing Titles of Doctrinal Sermons	
Noun and Phrase:	"Payday Someday!" (R. G. Lee)
The direct or indirect question:	"Why Do Bad Things Happen to God's People?" (Warren Wiersbe)
Heading and a question:	"Man: Why on Earth Was He Made?"
Double Title:	"Israel and the Future"
Direct Address:	"Let the Church Be the Church"
Clarity of sentence:	"Jesus Is a Friend of Sinners"
Using part of a text:	"'Not My Will'"

Figure 6.6

given in the context of conducting one's life wisely in evil days (vv. 15–16). The theme, then, of 5:18–20, could be stated, "*Living wisely in evil days requires the Spirit's control.*"

As noted in Chapter 2, the supernatural origin and spiritual quality of Bible doctrine make it difficult for immature believers to comprehend. (See Hebrews 5:11–14.) Its meaning may seem abstract. Its truth may have been obscured by false teaching or poor presentation in the past. So the clarity of doctrinal sermons is of utmost importance. It has often been said, "A mist in the pulpit is fog in the pew."[11] Since doctrinal sermons tend to be mentally demanding, they should be moderate in length.

Intellectual honesty is crucial to your credibility in preaching all kinds of sermons. It is especially important to avoid exaggeration, generalities, half-truths, inaccurate quotations, and jumping to conclusions when presenting doctrines that are invariably contradicted by opponents. When preaching doctrines of the future, exercise discipline to avoid sensationalism, and refuse to set dates or speculate about symbols. The simple, safe guideline is: never claim more than the Scriptures support.

After determining the topic of a doctrinal sermon, find and study every Scriptural reference to the subject. The goal is to discover how each passage relates to the doctrine. What contribution does it make? Group the verses according to the areas of doctrine and thought.

THE BIOGRAPHICAL SERMON[12]

Biographical sermons are of two kinds. *Objective* biographical sermons deal with the entire life cycle of a biblical character. They are often arranged chronologically so as to demonstrate God's ability to work in the listener's life as He has worked in the character's life. The life of John the Baptist shows God's use and praise of a man whose life seemed to end in defeat.

Subjective biographical sermons develop the story of someone's life according to themes and lessons determined by the preacher independently of explicit statements. For example, the life of Samson can be developed around the idea that he was a tragic hero. Lessons can be drawn from the life and death of Judas Iscariot.

The value of biographical sermons is that they reveal character. For example, in light of David's great sins, God still evaluates David as a man after His own heart (1 Sam. 13:14; Acts 13:22), a description that bears analysis.

Biographies relate the truth of God's Word to the daily lives of listeners who can identify with the characters studied. Whether they leave us in admiration and hope, or rebuked and without excuse, biographies utilize the method of the Holy Spirit to communicate truth through the experiences of real people. (See 1 Corinthians 10:11.)

To prepare for biographical sermons, collect all of the biblical material needed to reconstruct the person's life. (Be careful not to confuse different individuals with the same name.[13]) Then organize the material using some scheme. A chronological analysis of Moses' life reveals three periods of forty years. The life of Peter might be arranged in reference to before and after his critical denials of Christ. Jacob's story can be told on the basis of various experiences that are recorded. Joseph and Daniel might be described in terms of their dramatic changes in status. Outstanding lessons from the stories of characters such as Ruth, Esther, and Job provide another way to arrange the biblical information about them.

In synthesizing (generalizing, or principlizing) the biographical sermon, do not allow a character's reputation to prejudice your attitude.

Lot, for example, must be evaluated on the basis of what Scripture actually says about him. Keep details in perspective so they do not overly influence people's perceptions. Obvious flaws in the good kings of Judah, for example, should not be allowed to obscure their overall character and influence. The life lesson of a character can also be spoiled by spending too much sermon time on a relatively minor point.

Pertinent questions that lead to the discovery of useful information make preparing biographical sermons similar to detective work. What sort of person is the subject? How did the subject come to have this character? What are the results of this individual's manner of life? What is the subject's national and cultural background?

Biographical sermons are an exception to the Whiting Method's rule forbidding the use of proper names in the statement of sermon themes. The following biographical sermon on Apollos is a good example of this application of the Whiting Method. (See figure 6-7.)

THE PARABLE SERMON[14]

The parable sermon requires special consideration of the parable as a literary figure of speech. Zuck defines a parable as "a form of figurative language involving comparisons,"[15] a "true-to-life story to illustrate or illuminate a truth."[16] He adds, "Since parables are true to life, they differ from allegories and fables."[17]

In the New Testament, a parable is a fictitious narrative, true to life, designed for the purpose of teaching[18] a specific kingdom truth to those with receptive hearts, and to conceal them from those whose hearts are unreceptive to the truth presented (see Matthew 13:11–15). Thompson states, "In the context of prophecy a parable reveals something about a specific, crisis situation. Most parables in the Gospels interpret and illumine in some way the crisis situation created by the presence of Jesus."[19] Parables are persuasive in purpose, seeking to evoke a decision by presenting a critical choice. Parables perpetuate the truth by picturing it in such a way that it sticks in the mind, potentially convicting the unreceptive person when recalled at a later date.

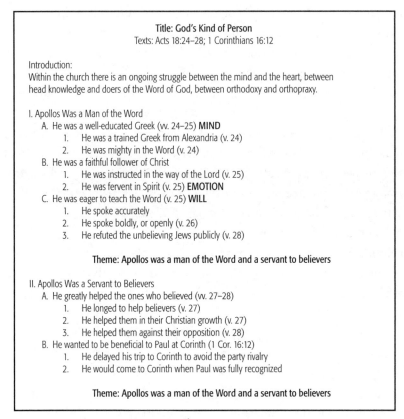

Title: God's Kind of Person
Texts: Acts 18:24–28; 1 Corinthians 16:12

Introduction:
Within the church there is an ongoing struggle between the mind and the heart, between head knowledge and doers of the Word of God, between orthodoxy and orthopraxy.

I. Apollos Was a Man of the Word
   A. He was a well-educated Greek (vv. 24–25) **MIND**
       1.   He was a trained Greek from Alexandria (v. 24)
       2.   He was mighty in the Word (v. 24)
   B. He was a faithful follower of Christ
       1.   He was instructed in the way of the Lord (v. 25)
       2.   He was fervent in Spirit (v. 25) **EMOTION**
   C. He was eager to teach the Word (v. 25) **WILL**
       1.   He spoke accurately
       2.   He spoke boldly, or openly (v. 26)
       3.   He refuted the unbelieving Jews publicly (v. 28)

        Theme: Apollos was a man of the Word and a servant to believers

II. Apollos Was a Servant to Believers
   A. He greatly helped the ones who believed (vv. 27–28)
       1.   He longed to help believers (v. 27)
       2.   He helped them in their Christian growth (v. 27)
       3.   He helped them against their opposition (v. 28)
   B. He wanted to be beneficial to Paul at Corinth (1 Cor. 16:12)
       1.   He delayed his trip to Corinth to avoid the party rivalry
       2.   He would come to Corinth when Paul was fully recognized

        Theme: Apollos was a man of the Word and a servant to believers

Figure 6.7

Parables may be classified in various categories, including *parabolic sayings, similitudes, example-stories,* and *symbolic parables. Parabolic sayings* are short statements that could be expanded into figurative narrative. One example is found in Matthew 15:14, where Jesus said, "Let them alone. They are blind leaders of the blind. And if the blind leads the blind, both will fall into a ditch" (NKJV). Jesus used parabolic sayings mostly during his early ministry.[20]

A *similitude* is the expansion of a germ parable into a generalization. Similitudes describe familiar objects or phenomena for multiple, present application. An example is the parable of the ninety-nine sheep, in Luke 15:4–6. It is based on what any shepherd would do.

Example-stories are typical-case parables. They present a general truth by a specific example from the same realm. The Samaritan epitomized the good neighbor in the parable of Luke 10:30–37. Other examples include the rich fool (Luke 12:16–21), the rich man and Lazarus (Luke 16:19–31), and the Pharisee and the publican as they prayed in the temple (Luke 18:9–14).

Symbolic parables teach truths about relationships by describing things from everyday life. The prodigal son, in Luke 15, and the parable of the tares, in Matthew 13, are examples.

Parables are naturally persuasive, often incorporating facts, specifics, illustration, comparisons, contrasts, and testimony. The parables of Matthew 13, if not all New Testament parables, teach truth needed to properly understand how the Church relates to the kingdom of God during this time between the first and second comings of Christ (see Matthew 3:10–17).[21] As does every good sermon, parables strike for a decision by appealing to the will.

To interpret a parable, the first step is to recover the original setting. To whom was the parable spoken, and under what circumstances? What can be learned from parallel passages, as well as from prologues, epilogues, etc.? What is the problem the parable was given to solve? It is usually stated in the context, but sometimes as far removed as the preceding chapter. What are the principle elements of the narrative? A mechanical layout (illustrated by figure 6-8) can help expose how the parable is structured. Who did what, when, where, how, and why? The goal is to seek the central truth. It is the solution to the problem at hand. Avoid trying to make the parable "walk on all fours." It is not an allegory, in which every detail has a representative meaning, but a story with one point, or a few points, of resemblance. Properly identifying the central truth makes it possible to determine which details actually contribute to the central truth, and which serve as "window dressing" to enhance and embellish it.[22]

The interpretation of a parable should be evaluated for proper perspective and balance. The central truth will never contradict the clear teaching of Scripture elsewhere. For example, interpreting the parable of the prodigal son (Luke 15:11–32) as teaching how a sinner may be justified could lead to the conclusion that a sinner may naturally come to his senses and come to God. This contradicts the doctrine of justification by grace alone, through faith alone, as taught in Romans 3:10 and Ephesians 2:1–10.

An interpretation that is consistent with the rest of Scripture is that the parable of the prodigal son, like the parables of the lost sheep and lost coin, teaches God the Father's concern for heirs of the Abrahamic covenant who are not enjoying its blessings. It answers the question of why Jesus spent so much time with sinners. Jesus had the Father's concern for disenfranchised Israelites. The religious leaders of Israel, like the prodigal's elder brother, did not. The fact that the prodigal was already the son of his father, is, therefore, a detail that contributes to the central truth. That the elder son failed to share his father's joy over the restoration of his wayward brother is another detail that enhances the central truth.

Finally, determine the intended appeal. What is the verdict for which the parable is appealing—not only to the intellect, but also the conscience and will?

The following statement by Ellisen summarizes proper interpretation of parables:

> It is, then, proper to consider the interpretation to be correct and complete if the historical context has not been distorted and the grammatical context has been duly expounded. The central truth will then correspond consistently with the basic elements of the story, and the significant details will enhance and enforce this central thrust. An indictment will usually be found, explicit or implicit, coupled with an appeal relative to the kingdom program. These basic elements will usually be seen, embroidered with details of realism which give the parable its uncontestable argumentative force.[23]

Examples of parables, given in figure 6-8, demonstrate the three essential elements to consider in preparing to preach the parables: the *context*, the *problem*, and the *central truth*.[24]

Essential Elements of Various Parables

(1) **Good and Bad Fruit Trees,** Matthew 7:16–20.
Context: Sermon on the Mount, warning false teachers
Problem: How can you spot a false teacher?
Central Truth: The false teachers are those whose lives do not produce spiritual fruit

(2) **Bridegroom and Fasting,** Matthew 9:14.
Context: Disciples are not fasting
Problem: Why doesn't Jesus promote fasting?
Central Truth: Fasting on the part of the groomsmen is inappropriate as long as the Bridegroom is here!

(3) **New Patch and Old Garment,** Matthew 9:16.
Context: The parable of the Bridegroom's leaving has just been given.
Problem: Why will the Bridegroom be absent?
Central Truth: Israel is beyond repair and must be reformed!

(4) **New Wine in Old Wineskins,** Matthew 9:17
Context: Same
Problem: Same
Central Truth: Israel's history of inflexibility in response to the Holy Spirit has become crystallized.

Figure 6.8

From the parables of Matthew 13, outlined in figure 6-9, a potential series of nine messages is indicated in bold-face type. (Though this figure reflects our theological perspective, the principles of the parables are true even if one holds to another theological perspective.[25])

Preaching the Parables

"The truths of the parables are to be applied to purposes of practical utility for current life situations and spiritual growth," says Ellisen.[26] But he gives three important precautions. First, allegorizing the parables, assigning meaning to insignificant elements, forfeits the power and blessing of the Holy Spirit and leaves the listener uncertain of the intended meaning. Second, preaching fragmented segments of the parables disrespects the unity of the figure and risks missing the central truth. Finally, application must proceed from proper interpretation.[27]

Stated positively, to properly preach the parables, you must observe dispensational distinctions, extract doctrine cautiously, and maintain simplicity.[28]

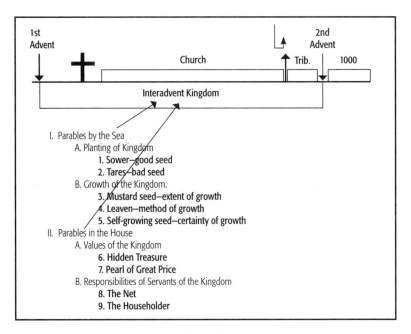

Figure 6.9

Dispensational Distinctions. You do not need to be a *dispensationalist* to appreciate the fact that the New Testament parables, when interpreted contextually, generally teach principles concerned with the responsibilities of believers within the household of faith. They generally do not deal with saving faith or eternal destiny.[29] When the central truth is discovered as the answer to a question or problem found within the context, it should be stated as a generalization. For example, the parable of the sower teaches the principle that God's Word is productive only in the hearts of individuals prepared to receive it.

Doctrine. Like "all Scripture," the New Testament parables are "profitable for doctrine" (2 Tim. 3:16–17 NKJV). However, the doctrine gleaned from a parable must be balanced by the teaching of *every other* relevant passage of Scripture in its context.

Simplicity. The very nature of the parables is such that their meaning is simple, clear, and forthright to the *spiritually receptive.* "The further exposition strays from the natural and obvious meanings and indulges in intricate analogies, the less likely is the original intention served."[30]

THE GOSPEL SERMON[31]

The gospel (or evangelistic) sermon is distinguished by its direct address to those who have not yet believed in the Lord Jesus Christ. It is further described by its intention to bring the listener to conviction of sin and willingness to receive the Bible's good news of forgiveness of sins and eternal life through faith in the Lord Jesus Christ. In light of Romans 1:16, the importance of such sermons can hardly be overstated: "For I am not ashamed of the gospel of Christ, for it is the power of God to salvation for everyone who believes, for the Jew first and also for the Greek" (NKJV). No person has been, or can be, saved apart from the Holy Spirit (Titus 3:5) and, with the exception of Adam and Eve, some human instrument (Rom. 10:14).

As important as evangelistic preaching is, the church primarily gathers for worship, not for evangelism. However, two facts bear consideration when discussing gospel preaching. First, unbelievers, including young children, visitors, and, possibly, those who falsely claim to believe in Christ, are often present at worship services. Second, expository preaching of the gospel occurs on occasions other than the church worship services, including special meetings and outreach activities.

There are distinct advantages to preaching messages designed to present the way of salvation. (See figure 6-10.)

**Advantages of Preaching Messages
Designed to Present the Way of Salvation**

- Teaches the saved how to explain the gospel
- Wins some of the lost
- Clarifies the doctrine of salvation
- Gives insight into people's problems
- Alerts people to opportunities
- Keeps the pulpit *hot*

Figure 6.10

```
┌─────────────────────────────────────────────────────────┐
│                                                         │
│        Areas covered by the gospel sermon include:      │
│                                                         │
│   •  the nature of man, guilt, and the consequences of sin │
│   •  the grace, power, and love of Christ               │
│   •  the nature of salvation                            │
│   •  how to "receive Christ"                            │
│   •  how to escape sin's consequences                   │
│   •  an explanation of the "gospel" (1 Cor. 15:3–4)     │
│                                                         │
└─────────────────────────────────────────────────────────┘
```

Figure 6.11

The following areas should be covered by the gospel sermon. (See figure 6-11.)

The proper gospel message may be either topical-textual expository, or textual expository. *Topical-textual gospel sermons* present man's need of salvation because of sin, and God's provision in Christ. Like an evangelistic tract, they draw principles from a variety of relevant texts within their respective contexts. *Textual expository gospel sermons* develop these principles from the context of a *single* passage. Examples include Isaiah 53:4–6; John 3:16–21; and John 5:24–29.

Gospel sermons are adapted to various situations and circumstances but always address the consciences and wills of lost individuals.[32] They are straightforward, simple, and positively instructive. They are not clever, complex, or argumentative. If theological terminology must be used, it should be clearly explained and well illustrated. Your own testimony should be part of your presentation of the gospel, because it speaks of what you know to be true by personal experience. (See John 3:11; 4:22; Acts 2:32; 3:15–16; 22:3–21; 2 Corinthians 4:13–14; and 1 John 1:1–4.)

PREACHING OLD TESTAMENT TYPES[33]

Zuck defines a type as "an Old Testament person, event, or thing having historical reality and designed by God to prefigure (foreshadow) in a preparatory way a real person, event, or thing so designated in the New Testament and that corresponds to and fulfills (heightens) the type."[34]

Old Testament Types . . .

- Illustrate something future, but are *not* prophecy
- Consist of historical persons, objects or ceremonies, *not* visions or dreams
- Demonstrate divine appointment, *not* human concoction or imagination
- Are fulfilled in the New Testament, *not* the Old Testament
- Are distinguishable from other figures of speech

Figure 6.12

Ellisen describes how a *type* is distinguished from other kinds of revelation as follows (see figure 6-12): [35]

Unlike symbols, which were understood at the time they were given, types are more like pictures taken in the Old Testament and developed in the New.[36] Unlike parables, types are physical, not verbal. They are real, not fictitious. Unlike allegories, again, types are physical, not verbal, and bear only a few points of resemblance.

There are two kinds of Old Testament types: *innate* and *inferred*. *Innate types* are expressly identified as types in the New Testament, including typical people, things, and ceremonies. Examples of *typical people* are Adam (Rom. 5:14; 1 Cor. 15:22), Abel (Heb. 12:24), and Melchizedek (Heb. 5:6–10; 7:1–11). Examples of *typical things* include the sacrificial Lamb (John 1:29; Heb. 9:14), and manna in the wilderness (Ex. 16:14–30; John 6:34, 58). Manna pictured Christ in that it provided daily sustenance from heaven for the people of God in their time of need (Num. 11:8; John 6:51). It came down from heaven, was given by God as a free gift, and resulted in judgment when rejected (Num. 11). *Typical ceremonies* include offerings and feasts, most notably, Passover (Ex. 12; Lev. 23:4–8; 1 Cor. 5:7) and Sabbath (Lev. 23:1–3; Ex. 34:21; Heb. 4).[37]

Inferred types are not explicitly identified in the New Testament, but they parallel some aspect of Christ or New Testament truth with apparent intentionality on the part of the writer. Isaac is an example of an *inferred typical person*. Like Jesus, Isaac was his father's uniquely begotten son (Heb. 11:17; cf., John 3:16). His birth, too, was foretold, and his conception was miraculous. And, like Jesus, Isaac was offered by his father as a sacrifice, and voluntarily yielded to his father's purpose (Gen. 22). In these and other ways, Isaac provides an historic pattern and illustration of what God was determined to do in a greater way through the person of Christ. By the same token, important differences between a type and its fulfillment (antitype) often help to emphasize important truths by contrast. Jesus, for example, was not spared at the last moment, as Isaac was, but was actually slain as an offering for sin.

Joseph prefigured Christ by his father's love (Gen. 37:3), the record of his character without any mention of sin, his unjust suffering, his being hated and rejected by his brethren (Gen. 37:4, 8, 28; 39:17–18; Matt. 21:37–39; 27:19), his exaltation (Gen. 41), his Gentile bride (Gen. 41:45; Eph. 5:23), and his eventual recognition and reception by his brethren (Gen. 45:1–8; Zech. 12:10; Matt. 24:30).

Inferred *typical things* include:

- Noah's ark, resembling Christ as a place of deliverance from judgment (Gen. 6:17–18; Rom. 8:1; Heb. 6:18), having just one door (John 10:9), which God alone could shut (Gen. 7:13; cf., John 10:28; Eph. 1:3); and
- cities of refuge (Num. 35; Heb. 6:8) which resembled Christ in that they were conspicuous and accessible to both Jews and Gentiles as long as the high priest lived (cf., Josh. 20:9; Gal. 3:27–29; Heb. 7:25; Rev. 22:17).

The history of interpreting Old Testament types reveals the problem of excess, finding types in virtually everything![38] This approach substitutes imagination for sound hermeneutical principles. It tarnishes the reputation of typology as a whole, and leads to false teaching. As someone has said, "the blessing does not justify the means." At the other extreme has been the problem of neglect, rejecting typology altogether.[39] This approach denies the artistry of biblical interpretation and ignores the value of "visual aids." Both theological liberalism and neoorthodoxy deny the unity of the Old and New Testaments, and so tend to view types simply as devices used by New Testament writers to illustrate Old Testament truth.

The mediating position recognizes legitimate types and has been thus called "the Golden Mean." Patrick Fairbairn (1805–1874) articulated this view, which was held during the apostolic period.[40] It holds that inferred types are validated by a consistent hermeneutical principle called "manifest analogy." The moderation of Fairbairn and more recent scholars is due to the development of principles that protect against extremes. Before surveying eight guidelines for interpreting types, Ellisen lists five reasons that the study of Old Testament types is valuable.

First, it refines and deepens one's understanding of the New Testament to observe how "the New is in the Old contained, and the Old is in the New explained."[41] Second, it deepens and broadens one's understanding and appreciation for the person and work of Christ throughout the Bible. Third, it serves as a biblical aid in teaching doctrine, especially in Christology and soteriology. Fourth, sound typology also has an apologetic value. It confirms divine inspiration by recognizing the prophetic character of the types. Fifth, principled typology emphasizes the value of the Old Testament for the believer today by demonstrating the unity of the whole Bible as given by a single author.[42]

Ellisen offers eight guidelines for interpreting Old Testament types.[43] First, the local setting of the type must be studied. "This forms the basis of the typical meaning, suggesting the purpose and character of the historical type."[44]

Second, applications must be based on the fulfillment of the type's purpose in history. [45] Third, the areas of resemblance and contrast between the type and antitype must be identified. These are usually found in the character, activity, or purpose of the type, often suggested by the New Testament. For example, while Abraham willingly offered his unique son, Isaac, God the Father actually sacrificed His.[46]

Fourth, this resemblance or contrast must be used to more sharply describe the type's analogy to the New Testament truth it anticipates.

Fifth, the type's quality as a *divine appointment* to prefigure New Testament truth (as opposed to a mere illustration or object lesson) must be emphasized.

Sixth, the analogy is not to be pressed or forced to *say* more than it was meant to from any point of resemblance.

Seventh, doctrines are not to be based on types alone, since, as Ellisen's handout states, "types are illustrations of doctrines taught in non-figurative language elsewhere."[47] Ellisen added that types challenge "the mind to accept or re-think a doctrine explicitly taught elsewhere, by showing how God foreordained and foreshadowed this truth in the times of the Old Testament shadows."[48]

Eighth, the advantage of New Testament hindsight in bringing into sharper focus the person and work of Christ must be recognized.

Preaching Old Testament types moves the student of Scripture in the *affective domain* of the heart, as well as addressing the *cognitive domain* of the head and the *behavioral domain* of the hands. It recognizes the value God Himself has placed on historical figures and word pictures. Types not only provide the mental images that colorfully portray the person and work of Christ, but do so in a way that carefully displays the sovereignty of God in fulfilling His plan of the ages!

The *film* exposed to the light of sanctified scholarship must be fully developed in the *darkroom* of your study, and appropriately displayed in the *gallery* of the congregation. Some of the most vivid pictures of the Lord Jesus Christ can only be seen in the Old Testament from the vantage point of New Testament hindsight.[49] Occasionally preaching a type, or series on the types, can change them from mere *negatives* in the minds of listeners to positive *proofs* that stimulate their desire for more. As preacher and people peer into the face of each portrait, they will revel in the sovereignty of the Artist. The decisions called for will be seen more clearly as part of one's well-reasoned service.

SUMMARY AND CONCLUSION

The rich variety of biblical literature, as well as the broad range of human needs, suggest the kinds of sermons surveyed in this chapter.

Paragraph sermons provide the mainstay, but there are no less than eight kinds! Doctrinal sermons are orderly presentations of what the Bible teaches on particular topics such as Scripture, man, sin, salvation, God, Christ, the Holy Spirit, Israel, the Church, and last things. They present a special challenge because they call for study of every passage of Scripture to determine how it relates to a particular truth.

Chapter sermons must be carefully set in the context of the book. Book sermons help people see the big picture of a writer's theme and purpose, and how his book fits into the Bible as a whole.

Biographical sermons reveal character in ways that help people identify with the person whose life is under consideration.

Preaching the New Testament parables and Old Testament types, are specialties. Their interpretations and applications require careful observance of guidelines that yield rich rewards.

Gospel sermons are needed because there are usually unsaved people present in preaching services, and those who know the Lord need to see good examples of how the Bible's good news of eternal life through faith in Jesus Christ can be presented to those who don't yet know Him.

DISCUSSION QUESTIONS

The following sermon is offered as an example of the Whiting Method. (See figure 6-13.) Answer the questions about this sermon to review the principles and guidelines in chapters 4–5.

1. What kind of sermon is it?
2. How is it styled?
3. Evaluate its use of typology.
4. How would you introduce, illustrate, and conclude such a sermon?

The Proof of Your Faith
Genesis 22:1–19

God Will Prove Your Faith in His Faithfulness to Provide

I. God Proves the Faith of His People (1–10)
    A. God Tested Abraham's Faith
        by Commanding Isaac's Sacrifice (1–2)
    B. Abraham Demonstrated Loyalty to God
        by Complete Obedience (3–10)
    C. God Proved Jesus' Commitment
        to His Word by Testing Him (Matt. 4:1–11)
    D. God Tests the Quality of Our Loyalty to Him
        (Rom. 5:3–4; 12:2; James 1:2–4; 1 Peter 1:6–7)

II. God Provides on the Basis of His Own Faithfulness (11–19)
    A. God Prevented Abraham from Harming Isaac (11–12)
    B. God Presented Abraham with a Substitute Lamb (13–14)
    C. God Promised to Keep His Covenant with Abraham (15–19)
        1. God swore by Himself (16)
        2. God honored Abraham's faith (18)
    D. God Blesses Us Through Our Faith in the Faithfulness
        of Christ (1 Cor. 1:9; Heb. 3:6)

Figure 6.13

PART III

Delivering the Development

✺

Parts I and II were concerned with how to build the verbal bridge that conveys God's message through the unique agency of God's human instrument. Part III involves the assembly of the bridge to effectively transmit the truth.

Chapter 7, "The Characteristics of Effective Expositional Sermons," emphasizes the importance of messages that are authoritative, accurate, unified, organized, and passionate. Several styles of preparation are briefly examined and evaluated.

Chapter 8, "The Characteristics of Effective Expository Communicators," primarily deals with the preacher's need to be godly, relational, and articulate.

The Characteristics of Effective Expositional Sermons

A BRIDGE can be a thing of breathtaking beauty, a photographer's delight, an artist's inspiration. But bridges are built primarily, not to admire, but to facilitate travel across barriers. One can argue that functionality *is* beautiful, but few would celebrate the design or appearance of a structure that didn't actually work. Different kinds of bridges work in different ways, but those that fulfill their purpose share common characteristics. They are structurally sound and well constructed of suitable materials. Despite radical differences in style and dimensions, every worthy bridge fulfills the same goal. A well-conceived design makes them all alike, in a manner of speaking. Similarly, all good sermons are alike in certain ways.

In this chapter we will briefly survey a few general characteristics of effective expositional sermons in conjunction with the Whiting Method of homiletics. Specifically, we will look at the pros and cons of three styles of preparation.

Sermons that do their job of bridging the communication gap all manifest the qualities of *authority, fidelity, order, movement, clarity,* and *passion.*[1] Each attribute contributes to the connection necessary to transmit timeless truth from the ancient world of the Bible to the contemporary world of your audience.

AUTHORITY

Not as the Scribes

Every effective expository preacher speaks with authority because the sermon communicates God's message. Unfortunately, there are many ways to squander and forfeit the effectiveness of divine authority. One way that even the least worthy speaker may steal the Creator's thunder is by relying on personal, human, finite expertise, knowledge, and wisdom. In accounting to the Author of Scripture, more than a few preachers might be asked the question God put to His servant Job: *"Who is this who darkens counsel by words without knowledge?"* (Job 38:2 NKJV).

With Job many speakers might be forced to admit, "You asked, 'Who is this who hides counsel without knowledge?' Therefore I have uttered what I did not understand, things too wonderful for me, which I did not know" (42:3 NKJV).

The effective power of God's Word is decimated by those who add their own puny authority to it, to "give it more oomph." Preachers have been accused of pounding the pulpit the hardest on the points of which they are the least certain. With dogmatism they have undermined their credibility. Or, in an attempt to humanly embellish, explain, defend, or politically correct the scriptural truth, they have diminished its impact.

Preachers also forfeit divine authority when they constantly quote (or plagiarize) the words of others. In these ways, the religious leaders of Israel provided the bland background against which the preaching of Jesus was all the more outstanding. Matthew 7:28–29 says, "And so it was, when Jesus had ended these sayings, that the people were astonished at His teaching, for He taught them as one having authority, and not as the scribes" (NKJV).

Not Authoritarian

To speak for God is to speak with His authority, not your own. As God the Son, Jesus could have spoken on His own authority. But as God the

Son, with the addition of human nature, Jesus always did and said only what the Father initiated (see John 5:30; 8:28; 8:42; 12:49; 14:10). The only weapon He wielded against the devil's onslaught was the same "sword of the Spirit" with which the believer is armed: "the Word of God" (see Matthew 4:4 and Ephesians 6:17).

Authoritative

Jesus and His apostles spoke what they knew by faith to be true. (See John 3:11; 4:22; and 2 Corinthians 4:13.) Accordingly, you should proclaim the things of which you are certain, based on prayerful study. Phrases such as "I think," or "I believe" express doubt or speculation that should be avoided. This is not to say that you should pretend to be sure about something uncertain. In fact, some texts present problems in which intellectual honesty requires the admitting of two or more possible solutions that must be decided on the basis of their merits. For example, one who interprets the days of Creation as literal, twenty-four-hour days would be remiss not to mention the bases on which some conservative scholars believe that the word *day* refers to longer periods of time.

Another example is found in 2 Kings 6:24–25. The sale of dove dung is mentioned in the context of a food shortage when the inhabitants of Jerusalem were under siege. This may or may not imply that dove droppings were eaten out of desperation. Author John Gray suggests that it refers to the use of bird manure for fuel.[2] Another possibility, noted in *Easton's Bible Dictionary*, is that "dove's dung" refers to "the seeds of a kind of millet, or a very inferior kind of pulse, or the root of the ornithogalum, i.e., bird-milk, the star-of-Bethlehem."[3] No matter what the correct interpretation, the point is clear: the besieged people of God were in dire straits! Though it may be impossible to say exactly what the author meant, a goal of the Whiting Method is to proclaim the point of the passage with the greatest possible confidence in the meaning of its supporting details.

FIDELITY

Historical Accuracy

The fruit of faithful study is to "tell it like it is." Luke, the physician-historian and traveling companion of the apostle Paul, begins his Gospel with an emphasis on the historical accuracy of his research.

> Inasmuch as many have taken in hand to set in order a narrative of those things which have been fulfilled among us, just as those who from the beginning were eyewitnesses and ministers of the word delivered them to us, it seemed good to me also, having had perfect understanding of all things from the very first, to write to you an orderly account, most excellent Theophilus, that you may know the certainty of those things in which you were instructed. (1:1–4 NKJV)

The need/desire of listeners to know the certainty of those things declared in expository preaching is met by those who are most effective. Like the book of Luke, the effective expository sermon should be painstakingly factual. When preaching the first eleven verses of Matthew 2, for example, the careful preacher will answer these questions: Were there *really* three magi who visited the Christ child in Bethlehem, or is this assumed because they brought *three* gifts? Were they *kings* ("We three kings of Orient are . . ."), or did the hymn writer *assume* their royalty? Did they arrive at the manger along with the shepherds, or did they visit Jesus in a house more than a year later? When communicating God's Word, be careful to get the details right and explain what the average listener may not know.

For example, the gall given to Jesus on the cross fulfills the prophecy in Psalm 69:21. In Matthew 27:34, He refused to drink it, not because it tasted bad, but because it contained an opiate that would have lessened His pain. He was determined to endure the *full* punishment for sin, in the place of sinners—including the preacher and congregation!

Historically accurate sermon content enhances your ability to speak with God's authority. It also facilitates a single focus by keeping the sermon on track.

Unity

Focus. All effective sermons aim for a specific response, as if using a rifle rather than a shotgun. In the Whiting Method this is accomplished by developing the theme of a passage through the supporting outline that "grows" out of the text itself. An advantage of this approach is that it gives you a basis for emphasizing in the sermon what is emphasized in the text. As a result, the point of the sermon is the point of the biblical writer. This assumes intentionality on the part of the writer and implies your need to sort out what Kaiser calls the "authorial intent."[4] Though everything in the text is important, not everything in a given passage has equal prominence.

Integrity. The concept of unity also implies the connectivity and distillation of principles. In other words, the sermon not only "hangs together" structurally, so that it flows from one thought to the next, from beginning to end, but it has a center, like the nucleus of a cell. This organic unity of a sermon is especially important to its impact as a monologue. In the classroom or group Bible study, dialogue tends to decentralize the consideration of various principles in a passage, without adversely affecting its impact. A given discussion might, in this sense, involve several sermonettes. But when one person is speaking to a listening audience, the communication of a single, central, integrated, whole idea is the hallmark of the greatest effectiveness.

Order

Organization

When a sermon is centered in relation to its main thought, the *theme* of the passage, its organized development is very natural and beneficial. Every thought flows out of the one that precedes it, and the listener finds it easy to follow. A sense of progress toward a goal helps to gain and hold his attention. Regardless of the various learning styles represented in the congregation, an orderly presentation of truth helps listeners adapt the message to the way they learn.

Meaningfulness

In their book *Creative Bible Teaching*, Richards and Bredfeldt assert that "order and structure give meaning to information and ideas." To illustrate the point, they ask:

> Which list of words is easier to remember? Which has more meaning?
> 1. dog, elephant, rabbit, mouse, whale, horse
> 2. mouse, rabbit, dog, horse, elephant, whale[5]

While the first list is random, the second moves from smaller to larger animals. In a similar way, sermon points that follow a logical sequence and are related to life experience are more apt to be understood and remembered.

MOVEMENT

Progress

Closely related to the organization of an effective expository sermon is its movement. People need to feel as if they are getting somewhere. If the concept of *order* is compared to a system of clearly marked surface roads, on-ramps, freeways, and exits, the concept of *movement* is comparable to the actual travel. No matter how desirable the destination, or how well mapped out the itinerary, a potential passenger will have little interest in riding with a driver who goes too slowly, gets stuck in traffic, takes a side trip or two along the way, or simply embarks on too long a journey for one day.

Impediments

External distractions, such as noise from nearby construction, a crying baby, or the persistent coughing of someone in the congregation, hinder a sermon's progress. Internal distractions, like hunger, anxiety, drowsiness, or preoccupation with relational difficulties, do the same.

Whether external or internal, these things are not your responsibility as a preacher, because they are out of your control. Obstacles you *can* remove, however, include an excessive number of sermon points, too many details, unnecessary or ineffective illustrations, or too much time spent on minor issues.[6] In short, harness the power of condensation.

Economy

In her excellent book entitled *Words on Target,* author Sue Nichols emphasizes what she calls "the big three" qualities that emerge in successful writing. They are *economy, energy,* and *subtlety.* "Economy," she says, "means communicating without any unnecessary words. It means saying things quickly, using short words in short paragraphs."[7] The elements to be described or explained should be prioritized. Invariably, good material will be left on the *editing floor* so that what is most needful can be presented uncluttered. The length of time spent on each element of the sermon will be proportional to its importance.

Moderation

Effective expositors *moderate* their emotions so that the congregation is not worn out from too much gravity, levity, or sameness.

CLARITY

Clear Thought

The words of R. E. O. White on the importance of clear thinking are sure to strike a responsive chord with any preacher:

> Usually we speak or write just as clearly as we think. When words dry up, and our writing runs into a tangle or becomes turgid and diffuse, the cure is to sit back and think out clearly what it is we are trying to say. When we have sorted out our muddled thinking, have corrected our preconceptions,

hasty generalizations, hidden assumptions, false analogies, exaggerations and contradictions, then words come readily enough.[8]

Assumptions

Preachers who deliver sermons with impact are those who make it impossible for people *not* to understand the message. Without insulting the intelligence of their audiences, they are careful not to assume that their listeners know their Bibles, understand theological terminology, or have instant recall of statements made earlier in the message. Most important, they do not assume that their audience came to the gathering motivated to learn or even interested in the topic!

Good communicators know that people can't read their minds or always understand their words. They look for opportunities to provide visual aids, whether physical objects, projected images, handouts, body language, or picturesque speech. Without dumbing down God's message, they word their sermons for ease in understanding.

PASSION

All preachers of effective sermons share this vital quality: *passion*, or strong feeling, both in relation to their personal motivation to communicate and their empathy for their listeners.

Compulsion to Communicate

In the introduction to his book *Teaching to Change Lives*, Hendricks says of the seven laws of the teacher, "If you boil them all down, these seven laws essentially call *for a passion to communicate*."[9] Such passion comes from the communicator's own growing edge of a life God is changing as he or she continues to learn, grow, and improve.[10] Paul described the apostles' passion as "the love of Christ [which] compels us" (2 Cor. 5:14 NKJV). Whether that was the apostles' love *for* Christ, or *Christ's* love, or both, the compulsion was affective.

Compassion for People

Not unrelated to the passion to communicate is the speaker's genuine compassion for those hurting and in need. This was the compassion modeled by the Lord Jesus in Mark 6:34: "Jesus . . . saw a great multitude and was moved with compassion for them, because they were like sheep not having a shepherd. So He began to teach them many things" (NKJV). You should certainly demonstrate the relationship every believer has to fellow members of the same body. In 1 Corinthians 12:26, Paul said, "If one member suffers, all the members suffer with it; or if one member is honored, all the members rejoice with it." This describes not mere sympathy, in which one feels sorry for another, but real empathy, in which one feels the pain of another. Caring enough to both weep with them and confront them in love comes from an experiential knowledge of God as one's own Father. (See Psalm 103:13; 1 Thessalonians 2:11; and Colossians 3:12–13.) Moses and Paul felt such compassion for the people of Israel that each expressed his willingness to forfeit his own enjoyment of God's blessings if by doing so he could secure God's blessings for His chosen people. (See Exodus 32:32 and Romans 9:3.)

Godly Zeal

When Jesus cleansed the temple, in John 2:17, He fulfilled the prophecy of Psalm 69:9, being consumed with zeal for Yahweh's house. In a similar way, Stephen was outspoken in his confrontation of those whom he said had always resisted the Holy Spirit (Acts 7:51). Sermons that change lives also demonstrate divine passion in the sense of loving what God loves and hating what He hates.

STYLES OF PREPARATION

Manuscript

Advantages. Sermons written out word for word are *precise*. In the process of composing the script, you are able to work on all of the attributes of effective expository sermons discussed earlier in this chapter. You have time not only to pay careful attention to the unity, order, and movement of your message, but to vary the vocabulary, economize the wording, and polish the delivery by rehearsing it from a fixed script. Once you have the manuscript well enough in mind, you may use it merely as a prompt, glancing at it for the gist of what you have written, with freedom to depart from it.

Disadvantages. Manuscripts take a great deal of time to prepare, and, unless kept from the congregation's view, their appearance can distract the listener, giving the impression that you are presenting a paper or lecture rather than speaking, as Andrew Blackwood put it, "from heart to heart and eye to eye"[11] in the Spirit. Further, in poor lighting or during outdoor occasions (weddings, funerals, camp meetings, etc.), where wind may be a factor, extensive notes can be hard to read and manage. They tend to restrict spontaneity and can even tempt you to read your message, which is fine for radio, but not for the pulpit.

Memorization

Advantages. Memorized messages can be presented with the dramatic style and freedom of movement of a stage performer. They have all of the advantages of a manuscript without the problem of hiding, seeing, or managing extensive notes. Memorizing certain parts of a sermon, such as introductions, illustrations, or conclusions allows precise wording and good eye contact.

Disadvantages. In addition to the obvious time and effort it takes to memorize a sermon of any length is the possibility of forgetting your lines! Unforeseeable interruptions can present a dilemma as to where and how to start again. And, like a manuscript, memorized sermons can seem canned, impersonal, and inflexible.

Extemporaneous

Advantages. Many would agree that extemporaneous preaching provides the preacher with the best of both worlds.[12] With minimal notes to keep you moving through your outline, remind you of your theme and illustrations, etc., you are free to speak as the words come to mind. There are no conspicuous notes in your way or in view of the congregation, and less worry about losing your place. As long as you are thoroughly prepared, your delivery is likely to be more natural and convincing and will allow for flexibility. An excellent way to prepare to preach is to manuscript a sermon, working hard on its wording, but then leave it in the study and take only the outline into the pulpit.

Disadvantages. Forgetting something you planned to include, including something that would have been better left out, and repeating yourself are among the disadvantages of speaking freely within the guidelines of limited notes. Sermons can also run longer—or shorter—than you intended.

Summary and Conclusion

Effective expositional sermons are not the result of following strict rules, but they do exhibit common qualities. They communicate *divine* authority, not yours or someone else's. As a result, they are both factual and faithful to historical reality. Avoiding egotistical sideshows or demagoguery eliminates digressions that cloud your sermon's reflection of the single focus and integrity of the text. As a unit, the sermon is obviously dissectible. Orderly arrangement of your material makes it meaningful to the listener. As it efficiently moves toward a definite goal, the listener feels a sense of progress and accomplishment. Distractions are minimized and emotions are varied and controlled. Rather than assuming the listener's knowledge of, or interest in, the Bible and theology, express your ideas in ways that make misunderstanding practically impossible. With divine compulsion to communicate, you will empathize with the listener and demonstrate zeal for God's glory.

Whether you prepare a manuscript, memorize your sermon, or speak from limited notes will depend on your personal preference and the occasion. There is no biblical right or wrong, and all three styles have been used effectively by expository preachers. After assessing the advantages and disadvantages, however, it seems that most effective expository preachers speak extemporaneously.

DISCUSSION QUESTIONS

1. In what ways did Jesus teach, not as the scribes, but with authority?
2. Without mentioning names, describe how you have witnessed the forfeiture of divine authority on the part of a contemporary preacher.
3. Why is *historical* accuracy so important to a sermon that aims to change people's *hearts*?
4. Why do you agree, or disagree, that organic unity is more important in a sermon than in a classroom discussion?
5. What is meant by "the economy of words"? What happens if concision is taken too far?
6. Using Peter's sermon in Acts 2, Stephen's sermon in chapter 7, and Paul's sermon in chapter 17, identify examples of passion as described in this chapter.
7. What is your chosen style of sermon preparation, and why?

CHAPTER 8

The Characteristics of Effective
Expository Communicators

THE HUMAN component of bridges that effectively span the communication gap is marked by certain qualities. Like the substance of effective sermons, the servants who deliver and model them with impact generally are *godly, relational,* and *articulate.* They recognize that a sermon is not good on its own, but only as it is well communicated. At the same time, godly expositors realize that they are prominent, not preeminent. Their value and importance is directly proportional to the extent that their sermons communicate God's message. A comment by author Donald Demaray on Jonathan Edwards, the persuasive preacher of the Second Great Awakening, will serve as a disclaimer for this chapter:

> Some of Edwards' sermons were over two hours long, which is not so uncommon in a day and age more leisurely than ours. Nonetheless, it is probably true that his delivery was dull at times. His voice was weak and not very commanding. He lacked many pulpit graces. He read his manuscripts; and one author, observing Edwards' nearsightedness, pictures him as clutching his papers in one hand, holding a candle in the other, and staring down the words as he read.[1]

Yet Edwards's weaknesses are mentioned to draw attention to an important fact: "The Holy Spirit overcomes weaknesses and handicaps, and develops the natural abilities of God's servants."[2] (This does not mean that Edwards might not have communicated even more effectively if he had been strong in his areas of weakness.)

GODLY

Godliness describes the life of a God-centered person, whose thoughts, feelings, and actions reflect conscious dependence upon and reverent response to God. Godly thinking precedes godly action (see Romans 12:2). To be godly, you must accept yourself for who God has made you, and then act naturally, speak directly, and be real (see Romans 12:3).[3] But self-acceptance does not mean self-reliance. And godly communicators are not to ask God to empower their own messages for the glory of the preacher. Rather, they rely on the power of the Holy Spirit to deliver *His* message for *His* glory. Consider how Paul requested prayer from the Church at Ephesus: "[Pray] always with all prayer and supplication in the Spirit, being watchful to this end with all perseverance and supplication for all the saints—*and for me, that utterance may be given to me, that I may open my mouth boldly to make known the mystery of the gospel, for which I am an ambassador in chains; that in it I may speak boldly, as I ought to speak*" (Eph. 6:18–20 NKJV, emphasis added).

In view of their dependent role, the people God uses engage in the intellectual discipline of meditating on the Word of God, prayerfully brooding over the implications and significance of principles drawn from the passage (see Colossians 4:2–4). They exercise good judgment in deciding how best to deliver their discovery of what God meant by what He said. They avoid grumbling about the congregation. Being transparent and vulnerable about their own weaknesses and struggles not only keeps them taking God more seriously than themselves, but it also endears them to those able to identify with them. It also disarms potential adversaries.

God-centeredness gives you credibility as a preacher, which Richards and Bredfeldt identify as the first of several characteristics of all great teachers. Citing the research of David W. Johnson and Frank P.

Johnson, they name six factors that influence credibility: *reliability of information, purity of motives, warmth and friendliness, reputation, expertise,* and *passion.*[4]

RELATIONAL

By *relational* we mean that you do not simply preach sermons; you serve people. You establish and nurture a bond of commonality, using your entire personality to impact the entire personality of each of your listeners. Every individual in the audience should feel that you are talking directly to him or her. You accomplish this by getting and holding their attention with a creative introduction and good eye contact. Appropriate smiles, gestures, and a friendly tone all *say* that the message is not just about God, or about you, but about the listeners. The people are not there to observe your performance. Rather, *you* are there so that *they* will better know, love, and serve the true and living God for the rest of their lives. Vivid words, purposeful actions, vocal variety, and visual displays are other ingredients noted by Richards and Bredfeldt, as part of a style that delivers.[5] None of these factors dictates a particular style, but all are incorporated by effective preachers, whether they stand behind an opaque pulpit, rove with a lapel microphone, project visuals onto a screen, or sit on a stool![6]

Relational preachers greet people with genuine interest in the things that are interesting to them. They don't just turn on the charm while standing before others, but take the initiative in getting acquainted and making themselves available for further contact and help.[7]

ARTICULATE

The Voice

According to an old saying, "Many a sip is lost between cup and lip."[8] A drink spilled at the last possible moment before it would have been drunk might as well have not been poured. The same is true of the spoken word. If everything about the sermon is wonderful *except* that people can't hear it, understand it, or stay awake, it is like the original Narrows Bridge to Gig Harbor from Tacoma, Washington, which spilled cars into Puget Sound when it collapsed. Speaking too softly, rapidly, indistinctly, or monotonously can put people to sleep. But when used well, your voice is your best tool. The most effective way of gaining and holding attention is by speaking with appropriate modulation or variety.

Inflection

Deliberate changes or modulations in the speaker's tone of voice are known as *inflection*. Use upward modulation to express a question, indecision, uncertainty, doubt, or suspense. Use downward modulation to suggest firmness, determination, certainty, finality, and confidence. The most effective way to ensure appropriate voice modulation, however, is not by thinking about it, but by genuine enthusiasm for what you have to say. Hendricks says, "If you really believe and feel your message, it will show. You'll use good gestures." He further asserts, "The most effective communication always includes an *emotional* ingredient—the *feeling* factor, the excitement element."[9] This is not a new assertion. Jonathan Edwards's philosophy of preaching emphasized that, within intellectual structure, a strong appeal to the emotions was the key for unlocking a volitional response.[10]

Rate

The rate at which you speak should correspond to the thoughts you are expressing. Weighty matters, such as the theme or application, should be spoken slowly for clarity and emphasis. Short and quick speech, on the other hand, can communicate excitement or surprise. Varying the rate of speech makes it more interesting to listeners.

Pitch

While there are notable exceptions, a voice pitched too high can communicate weakness, irritation, youth, or nervousness. Using the lower range of your voice is generally preferable for communicating assurance, poise, strength, maturity, and confidence.

Movement

Whether it consists of hand and arm gestures, taking a few steps, use of visual aids (such as PowerPoint), pausing momentarily, or simply changing your voice, movement is the primary way to get and *hold* the attention of your audience.

Language

Effective communicators of God's Word not only speak distinctly, but they choose their words carefully and pronounce them with good diction. Avoid slang and "hip" language. Express yourself naturally, without a "preacher's twang." And definitely stay away from coarse jesting, cursing, and all expletives.

SUMMARY AND CONCLUSION

Effective expository communicators are godly, relational, and articulate. Though they are prominent in the pulpit, God is obviously preeminent in their thoughts, words, and behavior. As a result of who they are in relation to God, they care about the people to whom their entire personalities form part of the communicative bridge. Their speech is energized by their passion for God and the message He has given to them. Their compassion for their listeners and genuine interest in their spiritual and eternal well-being is expressed in their appropriate use of the voice, body, and language.

DISCUSSION QUESTIONS

1. Describe the preacher, or preachers, whose sermons have had the greatest impact on your life. How were they like, or unlike, the profile presented in this chapter?

2. Why, biblically, do you agree or disagree that transparency and vulnerability on the part of an expositor of Scripture enhances effective communication?

3. Why, biblically, do you agree or disagree that the most effective communication always includes an emotional element?

4. Why, biblically, do you agree or disagree that, though God can use whomever He will, those who exhibit the characteristics of effective expository communicators could be even more useful as His spokespersons?

PART IV

Demonstrating the Discovery, Development, and Delivery of What God Meant by What He Said

❀

Chapter 9, "Preaching from the Pentateuch," briefly introduces the nature of Hebrew narrative. It surveys the Hebrew Scriptures, Pentateuch, and the book of Exodus. A sample sermon is presented from Exodus 20:1–17, entitled "God's Prescription for Right Relationships."

Chapter 10, "Preaching Historical Narrative," introduces the nature of story, plot, and archetype. To show how a sermon may be structured to match the story, a sample sermon is presented from the book of Ruth, entitled "The Hidden God Who Is in Control."

Chapter 11, "Preaching the Poetic Books," introduces the nature of hymnic literature. A sample sermon is presented from Psalm 113, entitled "Telling the Greatness of God."

Chapter 12, "Preaching Old Testament Prophecy" introduces the nature of biblical prophecy, relating prophecy to the biblical covenants and extending the meaning of a text into new contexts. From Zechariah 4:1–7, a sample sermon is presented, entitled "God's Work, God's Power."

Chapter 13, "Preaching the Gospels and Acts," surveys the nature of the Gospel genre and the book of Acts. The historical background, literary analysis, and theological understanding of each book is summarized. Sample sermons are presented from John 3:10–16, "Why the Son Descended"; Acts 6:1–7, "The Value and Importance of Official Service in the Church"; and Luke 10:25–37, "Action or Apathy?"

Chapter 14, "Preaching the Epistles," surveys the nature of the Epistle genre and twenty-two New Testament Epistles, with attention to their historical background, literary analysis, and theological understanding. A sample sermon is provided, entitled "The Excellence of Love," from 1 Corinthians 13.

Chapter 15, "Preaching the Revelation," undertakes questions of genre, approaches to interpretation, historical background, literary analysis, and theological understanding. A sample sermon from Revelation 1:1–8 is offered, entitled "The Revelation of Jesus Christ."

CHAPTER 9

Preaching from the Pentateuch

THE IMPERATIVE

THE IMPERATIVE to preach the Word of God certainly applies to the first five books of the Bible, since they form its foundation. Rooted in the rich soil of mostly historical narrative grow the major themes of the Bible. And yet the Pentateuch[1] is often neglected in the pulpit ministry of even expository preachers. This may be due to a lack of confidence in the relevance and integrity of the Hebrew Scriptures as a whole, or ignorance of the basic structure and message of the books of Moses in particular. This chapter will demonstrate how to use the Whiting Method of homiletics to develop a sermon from the Pentateuch. In doing so, the historical, cultural, and dispensational rings of context will be emphasized rather than the grammatical analysis emphasized in Chapter 4. To help you understand and appreciate the foundational role of the Pentateuch, the following is a brief overview of the Old Testament as a whole.

OVERVIEW OF THE HEBREW SCRIPTURES

Its Relevance

In his *Survey of Old Testament Introduction,* Gleason Archer notes that the New Testament writers referred to the Old Testament as a single, composite whole, ultimately authored by God Himself.[2] Archer explains his assertion by saying, "The New Testament writers regarded the entire Hebrew Scriptures as a testimony to Jesus Christ, the perfect Man who fulfilled all the Law; the Sacrifice and High Priest of the ritual ordinances; the Prophet, Priest, and King of whom the prophets foretold; and the Lover whom the poetical books described."[3]

As noted in the discussion of types in Chapter 6, events recorded in the Old Testament were seen by New Testament writers as prefiguring New Testament realities. The crossing of the Red Sea foreshadowed Christian baptism (1 Cor. 10:1–2). The conquest of Canaan under Joshua was divinely intended to picture the spiritual rest into which Christians enter by faith (Heb. 3–4). Calling Israel out of Egypt pointed to Jesus' experience recorded in Matthew 2:15. Thus, the New Testament gives convincing evidence that the Hebrew Scriptures constituted a coherent and integrated organism, focused on the dual themes of redeeming lost sinners and reclaiming God's kingdom on earth.

Its Structure

The Hebrew arrangement (referred to in Matthew 5:17; 7:12; etc., as the *Law and the Prophets*) includes the *Law* (of Moses), the *Prophets* (i.e., former prophets: Joshua, Judges, Samuel, Kings; and latter prophets: Isaiah, Jeremiah, Ezekiel, and the Twelve), and the *Writings*. The books referred to as the Writings consist of the Poetic Books of Job, Psalms, and Proverbs; the *Rolls*, including Song of Solomon, Ruth, Ecclesiastes, Esther, and Lamentations; and the *Histories*, including Esther, Daniel, Ezra, Nehemiah, and Chronicles.

When the Hebrew Scriptures were translated into Greek at Alexandria, Egypt, in the third century BC, the books were arranged as they are in modern translations. This first translation became known as the *Septuagint* (LXX, for short) for the seventy-two men involved in making it (LXX being the closest round number). Five books of Law and twelve books of History (totaling seventeen) are followed by the five books of the Major Prophets and twelve books of the Minor

Prophets (totaling seventeen). The five books of Poetry at the center have been thought of as forming the "heart" of the body of the Old Testament. The resulting symmetrical pattern of 17–5–17 is illustrated in figure 9-1.[4] That the Word of God can be so arranged demonstrates something of the order and balance we would expect in the written revelation of the Author of creation and redemption.

GENERAL OVERVIEW

The Hebrew Scriptures reveal God's Plan to redeem lost sinners and reclaim His kingdom on earth through His Son of promise (see Genesis 3:15 and 1 Corinthians 15:24).[5]

The Books of Law and History are mostly narrative of God's work in past events on behalf of one nation, Israel, which Yahweh formed by His sovereign grace. Having called Abram into a covenant relationship with Him, Yahweh began to fulfill His promises to bless Abram and to bless all nations through the nation (Israel) that would come from him. The Pentateuch has been related to Israel as follows.[6] (See figure 9-2.)

Law & History	Poetry	Prophecy
5	5	5
12		12
17		17
Retrospective	Introspective	Prospective

Figure 9.1

The Pentateuch in Relation to the Nation of Israel		
1. Genesis:	Israel *selected*	from idolatry
2. Exodus:	Israel *saved*	from Egypt
3. Leviticus:	Israel *set apart*	from world and flesh
4. Numbers:	Israel disciplined for *service*	from Sinai wanderings
5. Deuteronomy:	Israel's Law *surveyed*	for blessing in Canaan

Figure 9.2

The twelve books of History cover Israel from her conception to the time of the prophet Malachi. The five books of Poetry express the fact that a life of meaning, purpose, skill, and beauty depends on enjoying a right relationship with God. Finally, the seventeen books of Prophecy proclaim God's judgment of sin and future restoration of His covenant people, Israel.[7]

THE PENTATEUCH

Authorship

Critics have theorized that the Pentateuch is a compilation of writings, edited after the Babylonian captivity, by *different* authors recording various stages in the development of Israel's religion.[8] But Jesus referred to Moses as the Lawgiver in John 5:46–47; 7:19–23; and many other places. Also, the books of Moses demonstrate a continuity of content, theme, purpose, and style that is consistent with a single author.[9] The consecutive history found in the Pentateuch is but one of many factors confirming its unity. One book takes up where the other leaves off. Other indications of single authorship include the progressive spiritual development from Genesis through Deuteronomy and smoothness of transition from one book to the next. Finally, the Pentateuch gives evidence of an inverted chiasmus (a symmetrical arrangement of literary units in which the first set is matched by the second set in reverse order, producing a prominent center for emphasis).[10] (See figure 9-3.)

Genesis and Deuteronomy concern the formation of the universe and nation of Israel, while Exodus and Numbers have to do with the

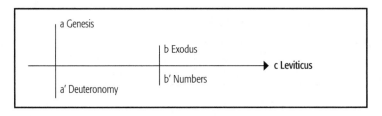

Figure 9.3

ordering of the nation. The prominent center created by this parallel design is the book of Leviticus, which calls upon God's people to reflect His holiness.[11]

Dominant Themes

Gary Derickson, in a lecture demonstrating the importance and contribution of the Pentateuch to Old Testament theology, identified these dominant themes: God's sovereignty, judgment, faithfulness, holiness, and redemption. He further states that, cosmically, the Pentateuch provides the only rational explanation of the origin of the universe. Ethnically, it alone accounts for the diversity of nations. Religiously, the books of Moses document the beginnings of man's sin and redemption, the nation and covenants of Israel, and God's plan of the ages. Historically, Genesis alone covers a greater span of time than all sixty-five other books put together![12] (See figure 9-4.[13])

Covenants

A biblical covenant is a formal agreement in which God promises to do certain things on behalf of humanity.[14] With the exception of the Mosaic covenant (explanation to follow), all of the biblical covenants depend only on the faithfulness of God for their fulfillment.

The Adamic covenant refers to God's promise in Genesis 3:15 to crush the head of the serpent by the heel of the Seed of the woman. It has been called the *protevangelium* because it provides the basis for hope that God would send a human to deliver man from sin and reestablish his rule on earth.

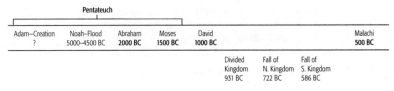

Figure 9.4

The Noahic covenant, in Genesis 9, provides the biblical basis for human government by authorizing the use of deadly force in upholding justice.

God's covenant with Abraham in Genesis 12 (and repeated in chapters 13, 15, 17, 18, and 22) forms the central set of promises. As shown in figure 9-5, the Abrahamic covenant is based on the redemptive and kingdom promises of the Adamic and Noahic covenants.

The promise to Abraham of personal blessing is the basis for the temporary Mosaic covenant. The Mosaic covenant, the heart of which is formed by the Ten Commandments, was replaced by the new covenant of Jeremiah 31, which promised the internalization of God's righteousness in the hearts of God's people. The New Covenant is ratified by the blood of Jesus Christ (compare Jeremiah 31:31 and Matthew 26:28; Mark 14:24; Luke 22:20; and 1 Corinthians 11:25), and obedient believers in Christ are already enjoying its personal, spiritual blessings through the indwelling Holy Spirit (see Galatians 3:27–28).

The land covenant in Deuteronomy 28–30, guarantees Israel the land promised to Abram, and sets forth the conditions of blessing in the land.

The Davidic covenant of 2 Samuel 7:16 is built on the Noahic covenant of human government, and promises the permanent, universal rule of a descendant of David upon his throne.

The following summary of biblical covenants shows the unique

Identification of the Biblical Covenants

1. Adamic, Genesis 3–redemption; rulership
2. Noahic, Genesis 9–governmental
3. Abrahamic, Genesis 12; 13; 15; 17; 18; 22
4. **Mosaic, Exodus 19:24–conditional blessing**
5. Land, Deuteronomy 28–30–land guaranteed
6. Davidic, 2 Samuel 7–Kingship guaranteed forever
7. New Covenant, Jeremiah 31–Replacing the Mosaic

Figure 9.5

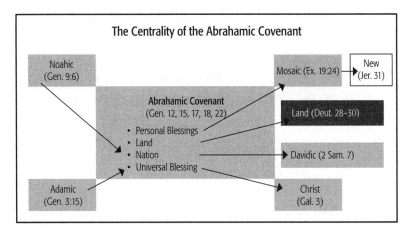

Figure 9.6

conditionality of the Mosaic covenant with regard to the nation of Israel. (See figure 9-5.)

The following graphic, adapted from Stanley Ellisen, shows how the Abrahamic covenant is central to the other covenants of Scripture. (See figure 9-6.)

SUMMARY OF THE PENTATEUCH BY BOOK[15]

Derickson's succinct descriptions of the books of Moses, listed below, provide a basic summary of the Pentateuch.

1. **Genesis:** God's word . . . created a perfect world order and brought judgment and blessing upon its inhabitants, preserving a line through whom blessing would come.
2. **Exodus:** God's preparation of Israel for nationhood . . . is accomplished through His deliverance of the nation to Himself, entrance into a national covenant, and their constructing of a tabernacle.
3. **Leviticus:** The holiness of God . . . demands holy worship and conduct from His people.

4. **Numbers:** Israel's preparation for entering Canaan, under God's leadership . . . involved national organization, discipline, and provision of additional laws amid God's blessings.

5. **Deuteronomy:** Israel's call to covenantal faithfulness . . . results in God's blessing rather than punishment on the basis of His covenant.

PREACHING THE LAW

Establishing the Text

The first step in preparing a sermon from the Pentateuch is to identify where the selected passage fits into the scheme of the Pentateuch as a whole. What is the role of the particular book in which the passage is found? This can be done by making, or referring to, good outlines of the books. For example, the Ten Commandments are found in the book of Exodus. An overview of the Pentateuch indicated that Exodus has to do with the ordering of the nation of Israel. It is based on the formation of the nation in Genesis. It anticipates the climactic emphasis on holiness in Leviticus. Exodus is parallel to the book of Numbers, which deals with the organization of the nation in the Sinai wilderness before entering the land promised to Abraham in Genesis. Before even looking at the text of Exodus 20, then, its placement in the Pentateuch indicates its purpose of establishing the basis for a right relationship with God on the part of a nation He has called to be set apart from the world as an agency of universal blessing.

Where does the passage fit in relation to the argument of the book? An outline of Exodus serves to further pinpoint the Ten Commandments in their context. The word *exodus* is Greek and means "the way out." The book of Exodus concerns Israel's deliverance from bondage in Egypt and development in the wilderness as a nation in a covenant relation with their Creator and Redeemer, Yahweh. Israel's redemption and organization as a theocratic nation establishes principles for the way God deals with believers in the church age of grace (1 Cor. 10:11). In short, the theme of Exodus is "Israel's redemption and organization as a theocratic nation"[16] It may be outlined as follows. (See figure 9-7.)

From the outline of Exodus, it is apparent that the Ten Commandments form the foundational bridge between God's redemption of Israel in chapters 1–19, and Israel's worship of God in chapters 25–40.

The specific text is established by determining the boundaries within which the writer expresses a complete thought. In the case of the Ten Commandments, each command is a paragraph, but the paragraphs are bound by identifiable markers of time, place, or persons, in the text.[17] Observing these indicators is called *establishing the text.*

The Ten Commandments are introduced by the statement "And God spoke all these words, saying . . ." (Ex. 20:1), indicating a change in speaker. In verse 18, the speaker changes again, from God to Moses, who narrates the people's response to all they witnessed. Thus Exodus 20:1–17 is marked by who is speaking.

Identify Points of Emphasis

By listing observations from the text, it is possible to identify the Ten Commandments' chiastic structure.[18] They begin and end by addressing how a person *thinks*. Second, and second to last, is an emphasis upon what a person *says*. This leaves, accentuated in the center, the

Outline of Exodus	
I. Exodus	1–19
God separates the nation to Himself	
II. Law	20–24
God enters into covenant	
III. Tabernacle	25–40
God builds His throne room	
A. Instruction (25–31)	
B. Obstruction [Golden Calf] (32–34)	
C. Construction (35–40)	

Figure 9.7

focus on what a person *does*. Right words and deeds come from right thoughts.

Another observation is that man's relations with God are balanced by man's relations with man. The fact that man's relations with God come first is also significant. Good human relations depend on a proper relation to God. Other observations can be made and should be listed as you develop the truth sheet discussed in chapter 4.[19]

Identify the Literary Genre

Within the text, the kind of literature must be identified. Among the possibilities are prose, historical narrative, wisdom literature, and apocalyptic literature. *Historical narrative* is a type of prose, the genre of stories, in which a variety of *archetypes*[20] (or *plot motifs*) may be represented. *Hebrew poetry* employs parallelism, in which the thought of the second line either repeats, completes, contrasts, or highlights the thought of the first line, for emphasis and emotional appeal. *Wisdom literature* includes poetry, but is distinguishable by its sustained argumentation for conclusions about spiritual, ethical, and moral issues. *Apocalyptic literature* is highly symbolic in depictions of unseen and future events impossible to know apart from divine disclosures to the prophet.

The Ten Commandments are written in prose, the straightforward literature of historical narrative, records, and law. As prose, there are two kinds of law. *Apodictic* law consists of assertions or demands based on grounds.[21] *Causal* law states the consequences of an action as the effect of its cause.[22] The Ten Commandments are primarily *apodictic*, stating what is required of God's people on the basis of His having redeemed them.

The Author's Meaning

The meaning of biblical narrative is determined by the writer, not the reader. Through Moses, God gave the revelation of His holiness in the identifiable form of international treaties between kings (*suzerains*) and their subjects (*vassals*). This observation alone precludes reading the Ten Commandments as a means of justifying sinners. According to their form, the Ten Commands stipulate the basic obligations imposed upon and accepted by a ruler's subjects. At issue is not whether the relationship between the parties exists or continues, but whether those under the authority of their ruler enjoy his blessings or endure his curses. In the case of God and Israel, the question was whether the nation would appropriate or forfeit the blessings of the Abrahamic covenant, prospering in the land of promise and being a blessing to the nations.[23]

Following the pattern of the Hittites in the fourteenth and thirteenth centuries BC, the Mosaic covenant is *dated* in Exodus 19:1–2. Next, the activity of the king, or *suzerain*, is described in terms of His geographical setting. Then Moses, as the mediator of the covenant, is described in terms of his title and activity (19:3–25). The actual covenant is preceded by a *preamble* in 20:1 that emphasizes the majesty and power of the King, God. A *historical prologue* describes previous relations between the king and his subjects, to produce thanksgiving and trust in subjects' hearts. In Exodus 20:2 the people are told, "I am the LORD your God, who brought you out of the land of Egypt, out of the house of bondage" (NKJV). Note that the nation belonged to God not on the basis of *their* performance, but *His*![24]

The Ten Commandments are *stipulations* that state specific, basic conditions for blessing (20:3–17). These are followed by detailed demands and other provisions for placing the record of the treaty on display in the temple for public reading. *Covenant ratification* involved the people's acceptance of the terms of the contract in oral and written form. It was sealed with blood and finalized by participation in a covenant meal (24:11).[25]

To correct the popular misconception that the Law was antithetical to the grace of God, the *Nelson Study Bible* states:

> The Law was benevolent instruction from God Himself. It was God's direction, like an outstretched hand, pointing out the way one should take on the road of life. The Israelites were in an enviable position. God had demonstrated His love for them by saving them. He

had shown His faithfulness to His promises to their parents, Abraham and Sarah. He had formalized His relationship with them in a treaty and promised to make them His special people. Finally He even gave them instructions for how to live. They were at peace with their Creator.[26]

Sermon Development

As noted earlier, the sermon should reflect the structure and tone of its biblical text. With this in mind, the following sermon outline is offered as an example. (See figure 9-8.)

SAMPLE SERMON
Introduction (hook)

In the 1981 movie *Chariots of Fire,* two elderly deans of the University of Cambridge discuss the zeal of one of their student-athletes named Harold

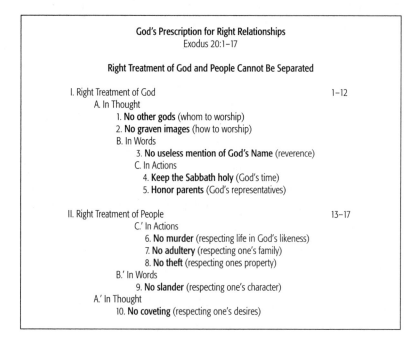

God's Prescription for Right Relationships
Exodus 20:1–17

Right Treatment of God and People Cannot Be Separated

I. Right Treatment of God	1–12
A. In Thought	
1. **No other gods** (whom to worship)	
2. **No graven images** (how to worship)	
B. In Words	
3. **No useless mention of God's Name** (reverence)	
C. In Actions	
4. **Keep the Sabbath holy** (God's time)	
5. **Honor parents** (God's representatives)	
II. Right Treatment of People	13–17
C.' In Actions	
6. **No murder** (respecting life in God's likeness)	
7. **No adultery** (respecting one's family)	
8. **No theft** (respecting ones property)	
B.' In Words	
9. **No slander** (respecting one's character)	
A.' In Thought	
10. **No coveting** (respecting one's desires)	

Figure 9.8

Abrahams. Abrahams, who is Jewish, has just left the room after passionately defending his controversial use of a professional coach in preparation for the 1924 Olympics. Shaking his head, one of the deans expresses his disapproval of Abrahams' perceived arrogance, saying of his Jewish student and his heritage, "A different mountain, a different God."

To many Christians the Ten Commandments represent the harsh Law of Moses received on Mount Sinai, in contrast to the friendly grace of God revealed in Jesus on Mount Calvary! But do the two mountains represent different gods?

Properly understood, Sinai, where Moses received *God's* Law, and Calvary, where Christ was crucified "by the predetermined plan . . . of God" [Acts 2:23 NASU], represent different purposes of the same God. Their purposes are *complementary*, not *competitive*. They are in conflict only when one or the other is misunderstood. Both concern right relationships. Sinai gives the prescription; Calvary fills it!

Body (book)

According to Exodus 19:1, the Law was given "in the third month after the children of Israel had gone out of the land of Egypt." [NKJV] It had taken two months to bring the people to the place where God appeared to Moses and declared Himself to be the "I AM," from the burning bush. At that time, God had also given Moses a sign. According to Exodus 3:12, God would bring Moses and the people of Israel to this location at the base of Mount Sinai, where they would worship Him. What a profound wonder it must have been for Moses to realize the fulfillment of God's promise!

As for the people, they had seen the power of God in operation. After bringing a series of miraculous plagues on Egypt, He had brought them through the Red Sea on dry land, destroyed the pursuing Egyptian army, led them with the cloud and pillar of fire, and miraculously provided food and water. Now they needed to understand the holiness of God.

Having received the Ten Commandments on the mountain, Moses came down to the people and spoke to them, teaching them God's Law.

What is the point of the Law, anyway? One way to state it is that: *Right treatment of God and people cannot be separated.*

The first twelve verses of Exodus 20 are concerned with . . .

I. Right Treatment of God

Notice, in verses 1–2, who initiated the communication of God's Law, and on what basis.

> And God spoke all these words, saying: "I am the Lord your God, who brought you out of the land of Egypt, out of the house of bondage." (NKJV)

In keeping with the known pattern of international treaties by which kings ordered the conduct of their subjects, God identifies Himself. He reminds the Israelites that He delivered them from slavery in Egypt. The people have God to thank for their well-being and very existence. They belong to Him on the basis of what He has done for them. They have every reason to embrace the terms He is about to state for the order and meaning to their already-existing relationship.

The first two commands concern right treatment of God *in thought*. Obedience to these Laws is in the realm of the heart and mind. Having learned idolatry in Egypt, Israel was now given the first stipulation for blessing. It concerned *whom to worship*: *"You shall have no other gods before Me"* [v. 3 NKJV]. This demand is reasonable because He is the only true and living God. The demand is compassionate because every person, place, object, or idea that might be exalted in God's place is false, disappointing, and ultimately disastrous.

The problem with idolatry is unreality, and it is as real today as it was in the days of Moses. If modern Christians were not capable of breaking this commandment, to their own detriment, the apostle John would not have said, at the end of his first epistle, *"Little children, keep yourselves from idols"* [5:21 NKJV].

Most of us do pretty well at avoiding bowing down to carved statues. Yet we still often worship the creations of God in His place: the human body, pleasure, our children, friends—even physical life. God wants to spare us the let-down from promoting such things to the level of their own incompetence.

Having addressed whom Israel was to worship, God next addresses *how to worship*, prohibiting the dishonorable practices they had learned from the Egyptians. Beginning again with verse 4, we read:

> "You shall not make for yourself a carved image—any likeness of anything that is in heaven above, or that is in the earth beneath, or that is

in the water under the earth; you shall not bow down to them nor serve them. For I, the Lord your God, am a jealous God, visiting the iniquity of the fathers on the children to the third and fourth generations of those who hate Me, but showing mercy to thousands, to those who love Me and keep My commandments." [Ex. 20:4–6 NKJV]

What's so bad about setting something before us that represents God and reminds us to worship Him? God is incomparable. Nothing people can make or discover can adequately portray what He is like. Every attempt to do so reduces Him in one's thoughts to someone other than (therefore, less than) He is. Having created us for personal intimacy with Him, no object can take His place.

God did not deliver Israel in order to collect tribute from them, as if He needed something from them, but for the *personal* relationship they needed with Him. God is jealous for His name, because He is worthy of our love and service.

His willingness to deal with people for generations according to their love for Him, or lack of it, demonstrates His long-term commitment to His covenant people for their good. He honors His end of the bargain whether they do or not.

Jesus would later state that a man speaks out of what fills his heart. So, having addressed the heart, God moves to man's treatment of God *in words*. In verse 7, we read:

"You shall not take the name of the Lord your God in vain, for the LORD will not hold him guiltless who takes His name in vain." [NKJV]

A person's *name* in this context is his reputation. It stands for all that is true of him. God revealed Himself in the personal name *Yahweh*, the "I AM" of Exodus 3:14. It speaks of His being eternally the God who depends on no one and nothing outside of Himself for existence. It is the name by which He signs His covenants, binding Himself to the good of His people. To treat His name lightly is to fail to demonstrate reverence for His very being. It hurts His testimony among the unsaved. Invoking the name of God in an attempt to manipulate the outcomes of events reduces it to a charm. Such abuses make a person liable for punishment for the good of the community and preservation of God's honor.

Beginning with verse 8 the movement from thoughts to words is extended to right treatment of God *in deeds*. To *keep the Sabbath holy* as a steward of God's time involves not only resting on the seventh day, as God rested from His creative work on the seventh day, but also working the other six days! The text says:

> "Remember the Sabbath day, to keep it holy. Six days you shall labor and do all your work, but the seventh day is the Sabbath of the Lord your God. In it you shall do no work: you, nor your son, nor your daughter, nor your male servant, nor your female servant, nor your cattle, nor your stranger who is within your gates. For in six days the LORD made the heavens and the earth, the sea, and all that is in them, and rested the seventh day. Therefore the LORD blessed the Sabbath day and hallowed it." [vv. 8–11 NKJV]

God, though He lives beyond the boundaries of time, has acted and rested in time, setting the example that is beneficial for all but obligatory only for Israel under the covenantal relation.

To *honor parents* relates to right treatment of *God* because parents are *God's representatives* to their children. Verse 12 says:

> "Honor your father and your mother, that your days may be long upon the land which the Lord your God is giving you." [NKJV]

To *honor* parents means to treat them with respect. It implies a child's obedience, as Paul applies this principle in Ephesians 6:1. Absolute obedience to parents was not intended, because the other commandments applied to the child as well. So Paul limits his charge for obedience to parents with the phrase "in the Lord" [NKJV.] There are rare instances in which a child may have to disobey a parent in order to obey God. But then it is a "can't," rather than a "won't." The overarching principle is that *right treatment of God and people cannot be separated*.

The sixth commandment begins a new division in which the focus has shifted from right treatment of God to . . .

II. Right Treatment of People

The symmetrical development of these covenantal stipulations is instructive in itself. The vertical responsibilities (people to God) are balanced by the horizontal (people to people), but in the proper order. Unless a person is *godly*, he or she cannot be *neighborly* in the truest sense. In fact, failure to demonstrate compassion toward people in need indicates a problem in a person's relationship with God, as the parable of the good Samaritan shows. By the same token, crimes against humanity, such as David's sin with Bathsheba, are ultimately, as David later confessed, against God, and God only. Another example is young Joseph. When tempted by Potiphar's wife, he answered, "How then can I do this great wickedness, and sin against God?" [Gen. 39:9 NKJV]. *Right treatment of God and people cannot be separated.*

The sixth command, in verse 13, *"You shall not murder"* [NKJV], remains in the category of *actions*. Actions are emphasized in the arrangement of the Ten Commandments as the expression of what is in the heart. God cares about people and property. So be careful to avoid the philosophy that minimizes the importance of *stuff* in its emphasis upon what is considered *spiritual.* Remember that God, who is *Spirit*, made all the *stuff* there is!

The command to not murder does not outlaw killing people in self-defense, national defense, or in the execution of capital criminals. Neither is this command in conflict with Genesis 9:6, which says, *"Whoever sheds man's blood, by man his blood shall be shed; for in the image of God He made man."* Man owes his life to God. This is the most basic biblical argument against abortion and doctor-assisted suicide.

The seventh command, in verse 14, *"You shall not commit adultery"* [NKJV], concerns the boundaries of marriage within which God has safeguarded the act of procreating life in His image. It is a provision respecting one's family. It also honors the marriage covenant as establishing a relationship intended to reflect God's own promise keeping. *Right treatment of God and people cannot be separated.*

The eighth command, in verse 15, is *"You shall not steal"* [NKJV]. Theft disrespects God's ownership of all things. It is the rejection of His providence in meeting people's needs according to His will. More obviously, stealing is failure to treat others the way one would want to be treated. Today, people's "innocence"; intellectual property, or ideas; and identities are often stolen, as well as their wealth.

When God said, *"You shall not bear false witness against your neighbor"* [v. 17 NKJV], He addressed the basis of Israel's legal system. The confirmation of what is true by the testimony of two or three witnesses depends on their truthful reporting. Those who lie on the witness stand undermine justice and can ruin the reputations of those they slander.

This ninth command, forbidding *slander*, is back in the domain of words. It matches the prohibition against abusing God's name, in verse 7. The very ability to express oneself verbally is a godlike quality. With this power, people are able to confess faith in God's revelation, and bless God and others. When this privilege is abused, it reflects badly on the original Communicator, in whose likeness we were made.

The tenth command, recorded in verse 17, returns to the sphere of *thought*. It has to do with a person's mental appetite for what belongs to others.

> "You shall not covet your neighbor's house; you shall not covet your
> neighbor's wife, nor his male servant, nor his female servant, nor his
> ox, nor his donkey, nor anything that is your neighbor's." [NKJV]

Coveting is harboring inordinate selfish desires for things God has not given. It often leads to theft. But even when it doesn't, the spirit of discontent is an affront to the wise providence and generosity of God. In Colossians 3:5, Paul equated greed with idolatry. In Hebrews 13:5–6 the writer says:

> Let your conduct be without covetousness; be content with such things
> as you have. For He Himself has said, "I will never leave you nor for-
> sake you." So we may boldly say: "The Lord is my helper; I will not fear.
> What can man do to me?" [NKJV]

Conclusion

The point of these core commands is that God deserves to have His people reflect what He is like in their relationships with Him and one another. He demands their obedience not only because they owe it to Him, but because it is essential to the life of spiritual prosperity which He graciously offers them. In short, *right treatment of God and people cannot be separated.*

Applications (look)

Throughout the text, the commands address the individual Israelite. National obedience depended on what every man, woman, young person, and child did individually. The same is true of us.

If you have not yet come to Christ, you need to understand four things about the Law. First, no one is saved by keeping it. Salvation from the penalty of sin was never the purpose of the Law. In Romans 3:20, Paul wrote, "Therefore by the deeds of the law no flesh will be justified in His sight, for by the law is the knowledge of sin" [NKJV].

Second, the Law is like God's straightedge, against which even the best of people are shown to be crooked, or sinful. James said, "For whoever shall keep the whole law, and yet stumble in one point, he is guilty of all" [2:10 NKJV].

Third, without the righteousness revealed in God's Law, there is no hope of eternal life, only the certainty of eternal punishment. In Matthew 5:20, Jesus said, "Unless your righteousness exceeds the righteousness of the scribes and Pharisees, you will by no means enter the kingdom of heaven" [NKJV].

Fourth, Christ has fulfilled the righteousness demanded by the Law; and God puts His righteousness to the account of anyone who simply believes in Him. In Romans 3:21–26, Paul writes:

> But now the righteousness of God apart from the law is revealed, being witnessed by the Law and the Prophets, even the righteousness of God, through faith in Jesus Christ, to all and on all who believe. For there is no difference; for all have sinned and fall short of the glory of God, being justified freely by His grace through the redemption that is in Christ Jesus, whom God set forth as a propitiation by His blood, through faith, to demonstrate His righteousness, because in His forbearance God had passed over the sins that were previously committed, to demonstrate at the present time His righteousness, that He might be just and the justifier of the one who has faith in Jesus. [NKJV]

Although the believer in Jesus Christ is not obligated to keep the Ten Commandments as a condition for covenantal blessing, the righteousness of Christ, which is put to the believer's account by faith in Him, fulfills the moral demands of this very law. Until a person comes to faith in the Christ of Mount Calvary, the Law of Mount Sinai is an indispensable tool to make him aware of his need of a Savior. In Galatians 3:24, Paul compares the Law to a child's tutor, whose job it was to bring the child to the point of legal heirship.

Invitation (took)

If God has used His Law to make you aware of your need of the Savior, I urge you to put your trust in Him today. He is God's Son in human form, who died in your place and rose again. The Bible says, "Believe on the Lord Jesus Christ, and you will be saved" [Acts 16:31 NKJV].

If you have already trusted in Jesus as God's payment for the penalty of your sins, I invite you to confess to Him any sins He has brought to your awareness through this consideration of the Ten Commandments. First John 1:9 says, "If we confess our sins, He is faithful and just to forgive us our sins and to cleanse us from all unrighteousness" [NKJV].

Finally, be encouraged to use the Law "lawfully," as Paul put it in 1 Timothy 1:8 [NKJV]. It is not a means of saving grace, but a way of showing people their need of it. In the words of Harold Abrahams' academic advisors, there are indeed two mountains. But the one and only God designed Sinai to prepare His people for Calvary so that through faith in Christ, they might enjoy the blessings of right relationships forever stated in the Ten Commandments. *Right treatment of God and people cannot be separated.*

SUMMARY AND CONCLUSION

The Hebrew Scriptures comprise a unified part of the written revelation of God and rest upon the foundational Books of Moses, the Pentateuch. The unity, order, and symmetry of the Old Testament books and of the Pentateuch reflect God as their ultimate Author. The Books of Moses form a chiasmus that emphasizes the holiness in which God's covenant people must relate to Him.

The biblical covenants are related through the promises God made to Abraham. The Mosaic covenant alone was conditional upon the people's obedience. It is replaced by the new covenant, already ratified by the blood of Jesus Christ. In the Holy Spirit, believers in Christ enjoy the personal blessings promised to Abraham. Israel will participate in other features of the new covenant in the Davidic kingdom to come. The Law, recorded in the book of Exodus, was a gracious provision from God. Its revelation of how Israel was to enjoy true prosperity in the land of promise encodes the right treatment of God and people that is fulfilled in the Christian through the Holy Spirit.

Preaching the Law begins with establishing the text and identifying points of emphasis and literary genre. The author's meaning is discovered by attention to the historical, cultural, and dispensational rings of context, as well as to grammatical analysis of the text.

Discussion Questions

1. In your own words, why should we preach from the Hebrew Scriptures in general, and from the Pentateuch in particular?
2. How would you argue for the single authorship of the Pentateuch, if challenged?
3. Trace the provisions of the Abrahamic covenant from the foundational covenants with Adam and Noah, to the covenants given later.
4. Why is it so important to understand the conditional nature of the Mosaic covenant and its replacement with the new?
5. List three aspects of sermon development by the Whiting Method that you felt were exemplified in the sample sermon on Exodus 20:1–17.
6. List three weaknesses of the sample sermon, in view of your understanding of the Whiting Method.

CHAPTER 10

Preaching Historical Narrative

PEOPLE like stories, because they are *living* a story. Stories about people enrich the lives of listeners and readers, who are able to experience life vicariously through characters who are more or less like themselves. When true stories are told about real people, they are part of history. They provide an instructive pattern for comparison and contrast. When God is the author of true stories about real people, the historical lessons reveal truth about a person's relationship with Him and with other people that could not be communicated as well any other way. In short, stories are personally relational; true stories are historical, and the story of God's relations with people is revelatory.

The Pentateuch tells the origin of the universe, man, sin, and salvation through God's covenant people, Israel. The subsequent books of history (Joshua through Esther) tell the story of how God keeps the promises of His covenants, but does so through the stories of a lot of people with whom we can identify. The various accounts are unified by the plan and purpose of the God who is in control of both the events and their recording. His revelation is conveyed through many stories written by numerous people in the variety of ways in which stories are told and life is experienced. Each pattern of storytelling, then, has a place and purpose in communicating the spiritual truths that are grounded in "His-story" and desperately needed by all kinds of people in all types of circumstances.

In an attempt to explain why Bible stories are so often relegated to children's books and Sunday school and neglected from the pulpit, Steven Mathewson offers four reasons: First, compared to the New Testament Epistles, the stories of Old Testament history seem to pack little significance for the amount of space they take up. Second, those who identify themselves as "New Testament preachers" have a tendency to see the value of Old Testament narrative as merely *illustrative* of New Testament truth rather than *foundational.* Third, the length of Old Testament history and the difficulty of the biblical languages can be overwhelming. And fourth, stories do not naturally lend themselves to the analytical outlines of rigid homiletical systems.[1]

Of particular relevance to the Whiting Method of sermon development is Mathewson's comment "The analytical outline approach presses the story into a mold that often works against it, especially when the outline points are alliterated or parallel."[2]

This chapter highlights some important considerations in developing sermons that reflect the form of the narrative text in the historical books of the Bible. These considerations include a brief overview of the Historical Books not covered in Chapter 10, a survey of some ways in which stories are structured, and a development of a sample sermon on the book of Ruth.

OVERVIEW OF THE HISTORICAL BOOKS

Narrative, the literary genre of stories, is found in other books of the Bible besides the twelve books of history. However, an overview of the biblical books of Joshua through Esther indicates a consistent emphasis, which deserves attention when developing sermons from one of these books, such as the book of Ruth. Bruce Wilkinson and Kenneth Boa introduce the Historical Books with the following summary:

> These books describe the occupation and settlement of Israel in the Promised Land, the transition from judges to the monarchy, the division and decline of the kingdom, the captivities of the northern and southern kingdom, and the return of the Remnant.

The historical books break into three divisions: (1) the theocratic books (Joshua, Judges and Ruth), (2) the monarchical books (Samuel, Kings and Chronicles), and (3) the restoration books (Ezra, Nehemiah, Esther).[3]

This categorical description of the Historical Books provides a helpful way to think through their content in relation to the time period in which the recorded events occurred. According to Wilkinson and Boa, the *Theocratic Books* cover events when God alone ruled His people, prior to the era of the kings, between 1405 and 1043 BC. The *Monarchical Books* deal with the times of the kings, from Saul until the Babylonian captivity, 1043 and 586 BC. The *Restoration Books* pertain to the postexilic events between 605 and 536 BC.[4]

Not only are the history books arranged to cover periods of time in an orderly fashion, but their collective message is that God is faithful to fulfill what Moses recorded in the book of Deuteronomy, particularly chapters 28–30. The history of Israel demonstrates the blessings of obedience to the revelation of God, and the curse of disobedience. The consistency of this theme is apparent in Derickson's message statements, arranged below under the categories and dates of Wilkinson and Boa.[5]

The Theocratic Books, 1405–1043 BC

1. **Joshua:** Israel's conquest and distribution of the land . . . *resulted from following God's lead* through Joshua and from obedience to His commands.

2. **Judges:** The evil not purged from the land when Israel occupied it . . . overcame the people while *God repeatedly raised up deliverers* to combat with evil.

3. **Ruth:** *The sovereign care of God* in Naomi's and Ruth's lives . . . came through both divine agency and the human agency of Boaz.

The Monarchical Books,[6] 1043–586 BC

4. **Samuel:** *God's rule over Israel . . . was mediated* through Samuel, then Saul, and finally through David.
5. **Kings:** *God's blessings and curses upon Judah and Israel . . .* came in accordance with His covenant and as a result of either faith and obedience, or rebellion.
6. **Chronicles:** *God's blessing (with victory and peace) or cursing (with defeat and exile) . . .* resulted from Judah's spiritual commitment or rebellion (reflected in its treatment of the temple).

The Restoration Books, 605–536 BC[7]

7. **Ezra:** *God's blessing in response to obedience and national purity . . .* enabled the people to rebuild His temple and obey His law through the support of both the kings of Persia and princes of Judah.
8. **Nehemiah:** *God's restoration of the nation . . .* was accomplished through the leadership of Nehemiah.
9. **Esther:** *The sovereign care of God in preserving His chosen people . . .* is demonstrated in His working through circumstances and exaltation of key persons in order to nullify the attempt of their enemies to destroy them.

The historical continuity and theological consistency in the overall message of these books are what one would expect from writers who are moved by the Holy Spirit (see 2 Peter 1:21). They give the expository preacher a contextual basis for drawing the principle that a given story was actually intended to teach. By practicing what Walter Kaiser calls the *syntactical-theological method*,[8] the faithful expositor avoids the twofold danger of presenting historical facts without their theological significance[9] and separating the spiritual meaning from its basis in history.[10] For example, the meaning conveyed by the writer of Ruth, and the significance preachers find in that meaning, will fit with the historical facts, the revelation of God to that point in history, and the overall message of the history books.[11] Because stories are told in certain ways, however, the Whiting Method must be applied with particular attention to their structure and shape, and the sermon must be developed in such a way as to reflect that pattern.

THE NATURE OF STORIES

Stories seem easy enough to tell, and even easier to listen to. But to decipher the storyteller's intended meaning is often difficult, though not impossible. In discussing how to identify the overall plan and purpose of biblical books, for example, Walter Kaiser states, "The most difficult pattern of all to determine is in those cases where the major portion of a book, if not its entire text, is made up of narrative materials."[12] According to Kaiser, the interpreter must often "make his decision on the basis of what details were *selected* for inclusion and how they were *arranged* by the writer."[13] Kaiser is not saying that everything excluded from a narrative is unimportant. In fact, the provident hand of God, who isn't mentioned in the book of Esther, is made all the more prominent by His unseen involvement in the outworking of events.

ARCHETYPES

One way to analyze the literature of biblical stories is to identify which of several possible plot patterns, known as *archetypes*, is found in them.[14] The archetype of the overall story is sometimes referred to as the *plot motif*. The archetypes found in various episodes within the story are sometimes called *type scenes*.[15] Among the most prominent archetypes in Scripture are the *hero, epic, tragedy*, and *comedy*.

Hero

According to Leland Ryken, hero stories are the most common archetype in narrative.[16] He describes them as follows: "Hero stories focus on the struggles and triumphs of the protagonist. The central hero or heroine is representative of a whole group and is usually a largely exemplary character, at least by the end of the story. The hero or heroine's destiny is an implied comment about life and reality."[17]

It is important to understand that the stories of Bible heroes include the record of faults and failures to teach a positive ideal by negative example.[18] David's sin with Bathsheba is an obvious case in point. Just because the Bible records something a hero says or does, doesn't stamp his or her behavior with divine approval.[19]

A subclass within the archetype of the hero is the *epic*, described by Ryken as "long narrative, a hero story on a grand scale," which is sufficiently expansive to represent a nation or produce self-awareness on the part of society as a whole.[20] Ryken's examples include the covenant theme of the Pentateuch, the Exodus, the life of David, the book of Revelation, and the Bible as a whole.[21]

Tragedy

Tragedy, says Ryken, "portrays movement from prosperity to catastrophe."[22] He describes the pattern by which such stories unfold as: dilemma/choice/catastrophe/suffering/perception/death."[23] When it involves a prominent figure, such as a king or ruler, he is called a *tragic hero*.[24] Saul and Samson are among the surprisingly few examples of tragedy in the Bible.[25]

Comic Plots

Comedies refer not to stories that are funny but to those having happy endings.[26] The protagonist moves through a series of obstacles to eventual triumph over them. Ryken notes, "In comic stories the protagonist is gradually assimilated into society (in contrast to tragedy, where the hero becomes progressively isolated from society). The typical ending of a comedy is a marriage, feast, reconciliation, or victory over enemies."[27] The plot has been described as "U-shaped,"[28] because the action moves from favorable circumstances through adversity and back to circumstances made even more favorable by the experience of loss or opposition. Most Bible stories fall into this category, including the stories of Job, Ruth, and even Jesus![29]

COMMON ELEMENTS

All stories, according to Steven Mathewson, revolve around four key elements: "plot, characters, setting, and point of view."[30] Discovering the meaning of Old Testament stories requires the exegetical preacher to look at them "through the lens of each element."[31] Such analysis can be incorporated into the development of the truth sheets discussed in Chapter 4. Simply ask and answer such questions as: *Who* are the characters? *What* is the plot? *When* did the events occur? *Where* does the action occur? *Where* is the writer in relation to the events he records? *How* is the story set? *Why* is the story told?

Another important idea to bear in mind in analyzing stories is the way they "combine to form larger narrative structures."[32] Using the story of Samson and Delilah, Thompson explains, "In biblical narrative originally independent stories lose their autonomy and become subordinated and integrated into a larger coherent whole. Consequently, the examination of one small story leads into the larger narrative structure in which it occurs."[33]

Plot

Political pundits, detectives, and reporters sometimes tell us to "follow the money" if we want to understand why things happen the way they do. In a similar way, the key to understanding biblical narrative is to "follow the action." According to Mathewson, "plot refers to action. It consists of a sequence of events that usually hinges on a conflict or crisis. The events in the story move through this conflict or crisis toward some kind of resolution."[34] This organization of information about events tends to take one of several possible forms, which Mathewson

calls *plot shape*.[35] He identifies the flow of action in a plot as progressing through four main stages: (1) exposition, (2) crisis, (3) resolution
and (4) conclusion.[36] While it is not necessary or always possible to
pinpoint the transition from one element of the plot to another, it is
important to follow the general movement.

Exposition refers to the information provided to set the stage. In the
book of Ruth, this information is found in chapter 1.

> Now it came to pass, in the days when the judges ruled, that there was
> a famine in the land. And a certain man of Bethlehem, Judah, went to
> dwell in the country of Moab, he and his wife and his two sons. The
> name of the man was Elimelech, the name of his wife was Naomi, and
> the names of his two sons were Mahlon and Chilion—Ephrathites of
> Bethlehem, Judah. And they went to the country of Moab and re-
> mained there. (vv. 1–2 NKJV)

Understanding the story of Ruth requires that one know something
about the period of the judges. Because of Israel's failure to execute
God's judgment and exterminate the inhabitants of Canaan, the people
were constantly subject to idolatry, anarchy, and harassment by enemies. Israel had not yet taken Jerusalem from the Jebusites (see Judges
1:21) and didn't have a king. Judges 17:6 states, "In those days there was
no king in Israel; everyone did what was right in his own eyes" (NKJV).
God raised up rulers known as *judges* to deliver the people from ruin
when they lapsed into disobedience to the Mosaic covenant and reaped
the promised consequences. When they repented, there was restoration
and rest until the next relapse into sin. Seven such cycles have been
identified. From the vantage point of the first readers of the story, this
would have raised an important question: Without the stability of the
monarchy in Jerusalem, who was looking out for the well-being of individual Israelites?

Due to a famine, Elimelech, whose name means "God is my King,"
leaves Bethlehem ("house of bread"), in the land of God's promises, to
go and live among the people of Moab, who were forbidden to enter

the assembly of Israel and with whom the Israelites were forbidden to intermarry. These facts are the exposition that sets up the story.

Crisis refers to "the complication, the conflict, or the tension"[37] that creates the question to be answered or the problem to be solved in a story. When it reaches its highest level of intensity, the crisis is sometimes called "the climax or peak moment."[38] In Ruth 1:3–5 the picture of moral chaos as a result of bad judgment is further darkened by the deaths of all the husbands: "Then Elimelech, Naomi's husband, died; and she was left, and her two sons. Now they took wives of the women of Moab: the name of the one was Orpah, and the name of the other Ruth. And they dwelt there about ten years. Then both Mahlon and Chilion also died; so the woman survived her two sons and her husband" (NKJV).

As bad as things were going for the bereft women, the husbands' deaths provide the turning point toward conflict resolution.

Resolution is first hinted at by Ruth's unexpected commitment to Naomi to cling to both her and the God Naomi has remembered only for the purpose of complaining about her losses. When the two return to the house of bread in the land of promise, it just *happens* to be the time of barley harvest. Ruth just *happens* to glean in a field owned by a near kinsman who just *happens* to be willing to redeem Ruth by paying Naomi for her land and to forfeit to his son the land he might have inherited.

The *conclusion* of a story often takes the form of an *epilogue*, which sums up the outcome, tying up the loose ends. The story of Ruth concludes with the acknowledgment that Ruth the Moabite is better to Naomi than seven sons. This is an amazing statement from a widow bereaved of her sons in a culture in which sons were highly prized and the Moabites were cursed. The story ends with Naomi caring for the grandson who, from the viewpoint of the storyteller (possibly Samuel), is in the line of King David!

Conclusions often clarify the writer's purpose in writing. Ellisen describes the purpose of Ruth as the portrayal of a pastoral love scene of faithfulness in the midst of a time of sin, idolatry, and infidelity—and *that* involving a woman from Moab! She became one of two Gentile women mentioned in David's genealogy, the other being Rahab the harlot. The story demonstrates Yahweh's concern for the people of the nations that will one day be blessed through the promised Seed of the woman, Israel's Messiah![39] Gregory Trull's summation is more succinct: Ruth is a "story of love and loyalty leading to a Royal Line."[40]

Characters

Old Testament stories, like any other, have a central character known as the *protagonist.*[41] The main adversaries who work against the central character are known as *antagonists.*[42] The characters who accentuate the central character are known as *foils.*[43] Then there are any number of minor characters whose roles are less important. When preparing to preach historical narrative according to the Whiting Method, the *who* question on the truth sheet should be expanded to identify the major *and* minor characters. For example, in the book of Ruth, see figure 10-1.

After analyzing each character's role from a literary standpoint, you can now evaluate them in light of the historical information provided. How are the characters described? (Ruth is a Moabitess. Is this a significant fact?) What does each one do? What is the meaning of each character's name? (Naomi means "pleasant," which explains why she asked people to call her Mara ["bitter"] instead of Naomi upon her return to Bethlehem.) How do the characters converse and interact? (In Ruth 1:14, Orpah *kissed* Naomi, but Ruth *clung* to her and said, "Your God [will be] my God" [v. 16 NKJV].)

Character Classification of Ruth	
Major:	*[Hidden: Yahweh]* Ruth and Boaz – Protagonists Naomi – Foil
Minor:	Elimelech, Mahlon, Chilion, Orpah

Figure 10.1

According to author Ronald Hals, the writer of Ruth mentions the name of God no fewer than twenty-five times in eighty-five verses.[44] Kaiser further observes:

> In nine of these references God's name is used in a prayer asking for blessing on one of the major characters in the book. It is significant that each of the major characters is the object of at least one such prayer. Even more striking is the fact that, without interrupting the flow of the narration, the writer goes on to show by implication that in each case the prayer was answered.
>
> Thus restraint and reticence dominate the author's style in that he does not openly moralize or editorialize on what has (or has not) taken place. This makes the conclusion all the more dramatic and powerful. The major and minor incidents in the life of this family are all under the providential care of God and included in the history of salvation.[45] The "thread of God's plan" is woven directly "into the tapestry of everyday events."[46] That he directs even the smallest details of our lives is a motif which recurs throughout the Book of Ruth.[47]

Setting

As mentioned previously, the setting of the story begins in Moab, where three husbands die, and progresses on to Bethlehem, where Ruth is redeemed and Naomi's hope is restored.

Point of View

To correctly understand the meaning of a story, you must identify the point of view from which it is told. This sometimes shifts. Mathewson describes the storyteller's perspective as *focalization*.[48] If the narration is from the reader's perspective, he calls it *external focalization* because the reader (from outside the story) knows things about the characters that the characters don't know about themselves.[49] If the story is told from the character's point of view, the perspective is that of *internal fo-*

calization, because the reader is at the mercy of what the characters (insiders) reveal about themselves.[50] If the narrator speaks or writes from his own perspective, Mathewson calls it *zero focalization*, because both the outsider/reader and the insider/character depend on the narrator, who is in charge of what he reveals about the characters.[51]

Shifts in focalization are often indicated by verbs of perception, describing what the storyteller sees, hears, or knows.[52] When the narrator reveals his own heart on a matter, there is no doubt that he is in charge of the story.[53] One of the most common indicators of a change in perspective is when the word translated "behold" is used.[54] Sometimes the story is told from the perspective of God, who knows all things.[55] The story of Job, for example, begins with information about Satan's challenge, that only God could know and which is never told to Job.

Sample Sermon

The following sermon notes on the book of Ruth do not represent the usual format of the Whiting Method. It is included here partly to demonstrate your freedom to adapt your sermon within the basic Whiting Method principles. The Whiting Method simply establishes a point of reference from which you can depart, if desired, according to your own preaching style or for variety, but still be confident that the exegetical bases are covered. Approaching the story of Ruth as a play or movie is one way to reflect the way the story is actually told in Scripture. It eliminates points of an analytical outline that might be distracting as well as unnecessary.

Notice that the sermon begins with an introduction and survey of the entire book of Ruth. This can be thought of as a reconnaissance flight at high altitude. Next, from closer range, the sermon is developed around the central character, whose name, Yahweh, is explained. Circling at a lower altitude, the writer refers to the prayers of the characters to show God's faithfulness in answering them. Finally, God's providence in everyday life is acknowledged as the basis for great encouragement to the contemporary audience.

THE HIDDEN GOD WHO IS IN CONTROL[56]
RUTH 1–4
GOD CAN TAKE BAD DECISIONS AND USE THEM FOR GOOD

Introduction:

This book is a story written in the time of David or Solomon about real people and events that occurred about two hundred years before, in the period of the judges. Not everything that happened in the lives of the people in the book is included, so the author of the book of Ruth selected details that developed the theme or idea he wished to teach in the book. Ruth is a theological book, not just a nice story.

Survey of the Book of Ruth:

Introduction	Setting the Scene	1:1–5
Scene I	The Road to Bethlehem	1:6–18
Interlude 1	*Arrival in Bethlehem*	*1:19–22*
Scene II	The Field of Boaz	2:1–17
Interlude 2	*Ruth's Report*	*2:18–23*
Interlude 3	*Naomi's Plan*	*3:1–5*
Scene III	The Threshing Floor of Boaz	3:6–15
Interlude 4	*Ruth's Report*	*3:16–18*
Scene IV	The Gate of Bethlehem	4:1–12
Conclusion	A Son Is Born	4:13–17
Genealogical	Appendix	4:18–22

Development of the Book of Ruth

Major Character: Not Ruth, Naomi, or Boaz, but Yahweh!

Theme: *God can take bad decisions and use them for good.*

Theme Developed:

Names of God in the Book:

Yahweh—Covenant Name of God, "He who is and will be" for His people; cf. Ex. 3:14, the God of faithfulness, used seventeen times.

God—Basic meaning is "He who is great or mighty," refers in this book to the God of Israel three times and to the God of Moab one time.

Almighty—Used in the two verses where Naomi speaks and says that Yahweh came against her.

Direct References to God:

Prayer:

Naomi prays for Ruth to receive kindness from Yahweh and that she may find a home and a husband (1:8–9).

In 2:20, Yahweh's kindness to Ruth is mentioned.

In Boaz she receives the latter request.

The Benediction of Boaz by Naomi (2:19–20) and of Ruth by Boaz (3:10).

Finds fulfillment in story's happy ending.

Prayers for family's prosperity (4:11–12, 14b).

Fulfilled in that couple's great-grandchild.

Became David the king.

Boaz prays that Ruth may find shelter under the wings of Yahweh (2:12).

Fulfilled in Ruth's request for Boaz to do the part of the next of kin (3:9) where "wing," or "skirt," is the same word. Here Boaz became the answer to his own prayers.

God's Actions:

Narrator speaks and has the action of Yahweh, initiating the movement of the story (1:6).

Narrator shows action of Yahweh, bringing the story to a happy ending (4:13).

Naomi mentions God's action against her (1:13, 20–21).

Naomi mentions God's action of favor (2:20).

Women of Bethlehem report God's goodness (4:14).

Indirect References to God:

"Blessed," in 2:19, implies *by Yahweh.*

Ruth "happened to come to the . . . field [of] Boaz" (2:3 NKJV) (even so-called accident attributed to Yahweh).

Scheme of Naomi and actions of Ruth (3:1–13)

Conclusion:

The story speaks to us. In the various events of our lives, we seldom see spectacular acts of deliverance and provision. But God is there, taking care of His world and fulfilling His plan for His children according to His schedule.

SUMMARY AND CONCLUSION

True stories about real people are part of His-story. When God superintends their recording, these various accounts of biblical history reveal truth about personal relationships with God and others. They not only illustrate New Testament truth but are part of its foundation. The books of Joshua through Esther comprise a unit of Scripture—most of which requires an understanding of how the stories of historical narrative are structured.

The content of the Historical Books is generally arranged chronologically, from the theocracy of Israel to its monarchy and postexilic restoration. Each of the books by itself, and the sum of them all together, demonstrates God's faithfulness to bless or curse His people according to the provisions in the Mosaic covenant. As theological history, never present Old Testament narrative as a mere record of human experience without its theological meaning and practical significance. Likewise, never proclaim its spiritual lessons apart from their basis in history.

Analyze the literature of all biblical stories with respect to their *archetype, plot, point of view,* and *characters.* Archetypes refer to various plot patterns, such as *hero, epic, tragedy,* and *comedy.* The *plot,* or sequence of action, usually involves (1) an *exposition* that sets the stage, (2) a *crisis* that presents a problem, (3) the *resolution* that resolves the tension, and (4) a *conclusion* that summarizes the results. *Focalization* concerns whether the story is told from the perspective of the reader, characters, or narrator. Observing shifts in the point of view from which the story is told is essential to good understanding.

When a character is central to the story, he or she is classified as a *major character.* Stories generally have two or three kinds of major characters, the *protagonist,* who is the main subject of the action; the *foil,* whose character serves to heighten the effect of the central character; and the *antagonist,* who stands in opposition. *Minor characters* are not unimportant but are less prominent than major characters. In addition to observing each character's role in light of the factual information selected and arranged, always seek to understand what the story teaches about God. The story of Ruth is really about God's care of His people despite chaotic times in which they are unaware that He is acting to fulfill His plan and purpose.

DISCUSSION QUESTIONS

1. Do you agree that Bible stories tend to be neglected in expository preaching? If so, what do you believe is the main reason?
2. What is the point of the Historical Books, and what is the point of their *having* a point?
3. Why is it equally important to avoid preaching the stories of the Old Testament as mere history, and to avoid teaching spiritual lessons without reference to their basis in history?
4. Explain what is meant by an *archetype,* and tell why Ruth is a *comedy.*
5. Explain in your own words:
   a) plot:
   b) exposition:
   c) crisis:
   d) resolution:
   e) conclusion:

6. Explain the difference between internal and external *focalization*.
7. Explain the following:
   a) protagonist:
   b) antagonist:
   c) foil:
   d) minor character:
8. Why do you agree or disagree that Yahweh is the main character in the book of Ruth?

CHAPTER 11

Preaching the Poetic Books

THE BOOKS of Job, Psalms, Proverbs, Ecclesiastes, and the Song of Solomon are classified as the books of *poetry*, or the Poetic Books. Because of its poetic quality, Lamentations, traditionally grouped with the Major (longer) Prophets, is also included in this brief survey. These six books contain most of the Hebrew poetry of the Bible but also include *wisdom* and some *prophetic* literature. The primary distinction of these six books, five of which are appropriately located in the heart of the body of Scripture, is that their contents express the heights and depths of mental and emotional responses to God's greatness in the context of the toughness of life. For this reason their expository proclamation meets the needs of people who wonder how to process perplexity, persecution, and pain, as well as how to express prayer and praise to the sovereign God.

WISDOM LITERATURE

The Wisdom Literature of Job, Proverbs, and Ecclesiastes is "characterized . . . by the stance of a narrator who pictures himself as a wise man declaring his observations about human experience."[1] As a literary genre, it is distinguishable by its sustained argumentation for conclusions about spiritual, ethical, and moral issues. Whereas human wisdom says, "Know yourself," God's wisdom says, "Know God" (see James 3:17–18).

JOB

Overview

The author of the book of Job is unknown. Jewish tradition favored Mosaic authorship, but Job 32:16–17 seems to indicate that Elihu is the author. Other possible writers are Solomon and Job himself.[2] The events recorded in Job seem to be during the time of the patriarchs, Abraham, Isaac, and Jacob.[3] The setting is thought to be southeast of Israel, where good grazing made Job a wealthy man.

Job "is a comic narrative comprised of elements of wisdom, drama, lyric and tragedy."[4] As introduced in Chapter 10, *comedy* refers to its "U-shaped plot in which events begin in prosperity, descend into tragedy, and rise suddenly to a happy conclusion."[5] Though the story is told as if it were play, James refers to Job not as a fictitious character, but as a man who actually lived (5:11). The book bearing his name is known as a *theodicy*, "a work that attempts to reconcile God's goodness and sovereignty with the existence of evil and suffering in the world."[6] A literary analysis reveals Job 28:1–28 as the prominent center.[7] Its lesson is that God does not explain His ways to man (see Romans 11:33–36). Nowhere in the narrative is Job even told about the dialogue between God and Satan, in chapters 1 and 2. Without this knowledge, Job cursed the day of his birth, crying from his pain. This speech in chapter 3 serves as a foundation for God's discourse in chapters 38–41.

Job and his friends all shared the same philosophy of life, namely that God blesses the righteous and curses unrighteousness. They differed only in how they viewed Job! Job contended for his own righteousness. The book's writer, in fact, refers to him as "perfect" (1:1 KJV). (His "perfection" described not a sinless life, but his standing in right relationship with God.) His friends, however, judged him to be *un*righteous by the fact that he was suffering. Elihu defended God as greater (a correct but incomplete response). God does not explain.[8]

Figure 11-1 outlines the book.[9]

```
┌──────────────────────────────────────────────────────────────────┐
│                              Job                                   │
│                                                                    │
│                  God allows the righteous to suffer                │
│                     for His own good purposes                      │
│                                                                    │
│        I. The Prologue                                  1–2        │
│       II. The Dialogue                                  3–42:6     │
│           A. Dialogue-Dispute (3–27)                               │
│           B. Job's Discourses (28–31)                              │
│           C. Elihu's Defense of God (32–37)                        │
│           D. God's Rebuke and Challenge (38–42:6)                  │
│      III. The Epilogue                                  42:7–17    │
│                                                                    │
└──────────────────────────────────────────────────────────────────┘
```

Figure 11.1

Interpretive Notes

In producing the truth sheets on the book of Job, it is especially important to keep track of your answers to these questions: *Who* is speaking? *What* are the issues? *How* does it fit into the argument?[10] *What* is Yahweh's perspective? Then note other observations and lessons. For example, Job 1:7–12 indicates that Satan has access to the throne of God, where he accuses the "brethren" (Rev. 12:10 NKJV). This means that he has not yet been cast down to the earth. Like a dog on a leash held in God's hand, Satan can do no more harm than God allows for the accomplishment of His purpose, which is for the believer's ultimate good!

Job gives a unique view into the relationship of Satan to God and Satan's enmity toward men. It teaches the need for repentance on the part of even the most righteous of persons. It also shows that divine discipline of God's children is ultimately constructive, that He is worthy of implicit trust, and that He commands men apart from material rewards.

With regard to judging whether it is punishment or development, any trial should be evaluated on the basis of the character being tried. To assume that a person is being punished simply because he is enduring a trial is to miss a lesson from Job. (See Matthew 4:1 and James 5:11.)

On the subject of trusting, note that God's closing speech in chapters 38–41 is a response to Job's speech in chapter 3. It says, in effect, that there are no "mistakes" in this world. Everything is under God's good control. As Derickson once told a roomful of college students, "Trust is not in knowing answers, but confidence in the one who knows even though He has not told me. God is to be trusted without understanding His ways. God is worthy to be served apart from any 'perks' or external incentives. God does reward the righteous . . . in the end."[11]

Preaching Job

If Job is preached as a series of messages, be sure to maintain clarity on where the text is in relation to the drama as a whole. Job may be preached by stating questions raised in the story and then answering them by an inductive approach to the text.

PROVERBS

Title

The English word *proverbs* comes from two Latin words, *pro* ("instead of") and *verba* ("words"). A proverb is a short, catchy, memorable statement that summarizes a wise principle *in the place of many words*. The Hebrew word translated "proverb," *mashal*, conveys the idea of a governing life principle expressed by comparing two or more things.[12]

Authorship and Date

Solomon is mentioned as the author of most of the Proverbs (1:1; 10:1; 25:1). He either wrote or dictated chapters 1–25 and may be the one called "King Lemuel" in 31:1.[13] According to 1 Kings 4:32, Solomon spoke as many as three thousand proverbs that were probably recorded in the official records of the day. After God fulfilled His promise to give Solomon a wise heart (1 Kin. 3:12), Solomon became the most prominent among a class of sage men who sought and collected time-honored truisms about life during the Golden Age of Wisdom, 1000–700 BC.

Literary Forms

Proverbs appear in at least four forms: (1) individual units; (2) clusters of maxims on a particular theme; (3) expanded units, called *epigrams*; and (4) sonnets expressing the stages of a thought in progress.[14] The *motto*, or overarching principle, of the book of Proverbs is: "The fear of the LORD is the beginning of knowledge [or wisdom]" (1:7; 9:10 NKJV).

Argument

"Courtiers proclaim that Yahweh has established and upholds a righteous order in which a man lives."[15] It is the end or outcome that reveals the truth about a course of action, not the way it may appear at a moment in time.[16]

Structure

The collection is introduced so that the reader will appreciate the relevance and urgency of learning and implementing its wisdom.[17] The two-part introduction serves to "hook" the reader. And though the proverbs look disconnected, there appears to be an order to their arrangement.[18] (See figure 11-2.)

Interpretive Issues[19]

To properly understand Proverbs, at least six issues must be addressed. First, *proverbs* must be distinguished from *promises*. While some

Words concerning wisdom	1–9
Proverbs of Solomon	10–22
Sayings of the wise men	23–24
Proverbs of Solomon	25–29
Words concerning wisdom	30–31

Figure 11.2

promises are sprinkled among the proverbs (such as 3:5–6), proverbs are generalizations about life, to which there are notable exceptions. For example, though there is no better way to live a long life of prosperity on earth than to practice the principles of Proverbs 3:1–10, exceptions include John the Baptist and the Lord Jesus Christ. These men realized the principle only in a spiritual and eternal way not apparently envisioned by Solomon.

Second, "the fear of the LORD" must be understood. It includes both a willingness to obey His Word and a wholesome fear of the consequences of disobedience. It is not a beginning point beyond which a person progresses, but the foundational principle for understanding and applying all other principles. (See John 7:17.)

Third, *wisdom* and *folly* are personified as two kinds of women. There is a reason that Wisdom is exemplified by the industrious, faithful wife and mother of Proverbs 31. She nurtures the fear of Yahweh in her son's heart partly by honoring the authority of her husband. In stark contrast, Folly is portrayed as the immoral woman, who, by seducing the sons of others, asserts her fearless independence of the authority of God and man.

Fourth, Proverbs often compares or contrasts two aspects of two things, as in Proverbs 14:1. Not only is the wise woman compared/contrasted to the foolish, but their actions are compared as well. (See figure 11-3.)

Fifth, it is important to avoid the false distinction between the sacred and the secular. Proverbs generally describes "horizontal," human relationships, demonstrating that wisdom is ultimately behavioral (see James 3:13–18), and that civility, and all of life, is a concern to God.

Sixth, the characters of Proverbs must be understood in relation to one another.[20]

The wise woman builds her house,
But the foolish tears it down with her own hands.

Figure 11.3

The Simple: One who is gullible and easily misled. All start out untested, untaught, unlearned. The Simple "walk in the counsel of the wicked" (Ps. 1:1a NASU) and either become wise or foolish.

The Fool: One who is dull and obstinate. Ignores the pursuit of wisdom. Closed to reason but insists on making his views known publicly. He "stands in the path of sinners" (Ps. 1:1b NKJV). Without repentance, fools become mockers.

The Mocker: One who is contemptuous. Not only foolish and proud, but obstructs the way of wisdom for others. Mockers "sit in the seat of scoffers" (Psalm 1:1c NASU).

The Wise: Open and obedient heart toward God, eager to follow His instruction. The wise takes correction (see 15:31) and pays attention to biblical commands (see 10:8). The wise "delight . . . in the law of the LORD" (Ps. 1:2 NASU).

General Principles Underlying the Proverbs[21]

1. *Cause and Effect*. Obedience to God's moral law is generally beneficial, and disobedience is generally destructive (see Galatians 6:7).
2. *Good and Evil*. Redefining good and evil does not change what they are in the judgment of God (see Malachi 2:17).
3. *Worldly Influence*. The love for the Father and the lusts of the world are mutually exclusive (see 1 John 2:15).
4. *Self-deceit*. Self-centeredness and self-reliance are natural results of the fall of man into sin (see Jeremiah 17:9). It is consistent with fallen human nature to blame others, save oneself, determine truth on one's own, and demand the meeting of felt needs.
5. *Godly Minority*. The godly are often outnumbered, tempted by the rationale that "everybody's doing it," and in need of realizing their "majority" with God by living in the light of biblical standards. (See John 17:18–21.)

6. *Absolute Truth.* Truth is the same for all people in all places and at all times.[22]

Preaching the Proverbs

Proverbs can be preached in a topical-expository manner. This requires that every proverb and related passage of Scripture be identified, interpreted in its context, and its meaning related to the overarching theme by means of an outline. For example, the present writer (Dan) once preached a sermon on the proverbial sluggard, using an outline from a subject-study by Derek Kidner as a guide.[23] (See figure 11-4.) Such an approach is legitimate only if the passages are studied in their respective contexts and proper credit is given to the source of any organizational aid used.

The Proverbs can also be preached textually, as illustrated in figure 11-5.

The Sluggard
Proverbs
A Soft Way Leads to a Hard End

I. The Sluggard's Character
  A. He will not begin things (6:9–10)
      1. He does not even *commit* to refusal!
      2. He deceives himself
      3. His opportunities slip away
  B. He will not finish things (12:27; 19:24; 26:15)
  C. He will not face things
      1. He believes his own rationalizations (26:13–16)
      2. He avoids discomfort (20:4)
  D. He is restless
      1. He is dissatisfied (13:4; 21:25–26)
      2. He is helpless in the tangle of his life (15:19)
      3. He is wasteful (18:9)
      4. He is a worthless employee (10:26)
II. The Sluggard's Lessons
      1. Be a self-starter, like the ant (6:6–8; Heb. 4:11)
      2. Work when it is time to work (6:8; John 9:4)
      3. Putting things off catches up with you when it's too late (6:10–11, Luke 12:40)
      4. The soft way is harder in the end (12:24; Luke 16:19–25)
      5. Disorder can become irreversible (24:30–34, Rev. 20:15).

Figure 11.4

ECCLESIASTES

"Ecclesiastes" is the Latin form of the Greek word meaning "the preacher." The Hebrew title, *Quoheleth*, signifies the chair or teacher of an assembly. Ironically, "preachers" so often fail to preach the book of "the preacher," because they perceive it to be cynical, fatalistic, or existential. In reality, it puts human endeavor into proper perspective. It teaches us to enjoy life, since it is the gift of God, but to enjoy it *responsibly*, since we will give an account to Him.

Author

The phrase "son of David, king in Jerusalem" (1:1 NKJV) indicates that Solomon is the writer. He is thought to have written this near the end of his life after having strayed from the Lord and experienced the disillusionment of sinful pursuits.

Theme

"Satisfaction can be found only by fearing God and keeping His commandments."[24]

Wisdom Shouts Ignored
Proverbs 1:8–33

Individuals Are Responsible to Seek the Wisdom God Gives

I. The Enticement of Sinners	8–19
A. The bland benefits of parental guidance (8–9)	
B. The bitter bite of sinful adventure (10–19)	
II. Wisdom's Shouts of Warning	20–23
A. Why personified as a woman? (20)	
B. Why depicted as a city? (20–21)	
C. Why the negative response? (22)	
D. Why the generous offer? (23)	
III. The Foolish Neglect of Wisdom	24–33
A. Why wisdom laughs (24–27)	
B. Why wisdom hides (28–30)	
C. How waywardness is established (31–32)	
D. How wisdom is enjoyed (33)	

Figure 11.5

Outline

(See figure 11-6.)

Argument

Bruce Waltke states, "Although Quoheleth denies that one can observe a moral order in the creation, he affirms a wise, good, and just God rules over all."[25]

Key Phrases

"Vanity" refers not to what is bad, but to what is fleeting and incapable of being held on to. It is the word by which Abel was appropriately named, and means "vapor." "Under the sun" refers to all that makes up life but has no eternal significance in and of itself. "Striving after wind" amounts to wasting time.

Principles

Despite how life may seem, based on human experience, God is *wise*, *good*, and *just*. He is wise in that He has a plan (3:10; 7:14). God is good in having given creation to man as a gift to be enjoyed (2:24; 3:13–14). God is just in that there is a day of retribution and rewards (3:16–17; 11:9–10).

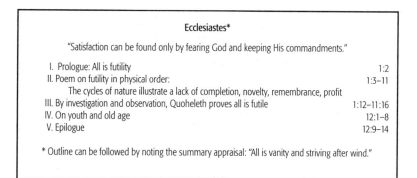

Ecclesiastes*

"Satisfaction can be found only by fearing God and keeping His commandments."

I. Prologue: All is futility	1:2
II. Poem on futility in physical order:	1:3–11
The cycles of nature illustrate a lack of completion, novelty, remembrance, profit	
III. By investigation and observation, Quoheleth proves all is futile	1:12–11:16
IV. On youth and old age	12:1–8
V. Epilogue	12:9–14

* Outline can be followed by noting the summary appraisal: "All is vanity and striving after wind."

Figure 11.6

Conclusion

The *didactic* wisdom literature, including the book of Job and Psalms 37 and 49, as well as the *reflective* wisdom literature of Job and Ecclesiastes, proclaim by faith that there is a just God upholding an ethical order. The reflective books, however, demonstrate that man cannot discover this order in the creation through observation and experience. The author-editor of Job, however, contends that there is sufficient evidence of God's greatness and sublimity to render man inexcusable for his arrogance against the Creator and his failure to walk humbly before Him.[26]

Psalms

The Psalms comprise prayers and poems collected from roughly 1500 to 500 BC. They were originally set to music accompanied by the plucking of stringed instruments. They lead the reader through the depths of despair to the heights of joy as Yahweh proves His faithfulness to provide, protect, deliver, sustain, and comfort His covenant people.

Authors of the Psalms

More than a dozen songwriters are represented in Israel's hymnal, sometimes called *The Psalter*. Ellisen's list in figure 11-7, based on inscriptions, indicates both the variety of composers and the preponderance of King David's contribution.[27]

Arrangement

Like the Pentateuch, the Psalms were written on five scrolls. Ezra is believed to have arranged the Psalms according to a progression of thought and by the usage of the names of God.[28] They were divided as follows. (See figure 11-8.)

Authorship of the Psalms

David wrote 73 psalms: 3–9; 11–32; 34–41; 51–65; 68–70; 86; 101; 103; 108–110; 122; 124; 131; 133; 138–145. Psalm 2 is attributed to David in Acts 4:25.

Asaph wrote 12 psalms: 50; 73–83.

Sons of Korah wrote 9 psalms: 42, 44–45; 47–49; 84–85; 87.

Solomon wrote two psalms: 72, 127.

Heman, Psalm 88

Ethan, Psalm 89

Moses, Psalm 90

Jeremiah, Psalm 137

Haggai and **Zechariah**: Psalms 146–147

Ezra: Psalm 119

Hezekiah: Psalms 120–134

The rest are called orphaned Psalms

Figure 11.7

The Five Books of Psalms

Book	Psalms	Author	Names of God
Book I	1–41	David	Yahweh
Book II	42–72	David	Elohim
Book III	73–89	Asaph	Yahweh-Elohim
Book IV	90–106	Anonymous	Yahweh
Book V	107–150	Various	Yahweh

Figure 11.8

According to Ellisen, "each Book of Psalms concludes with a doxology, an affirmation of praise to God found in the last verse or two of the concluding psalm."[29] "In the case of Book V the entire last poem, Psalm 150, is the concluding doxology."[30] Books I and II are composed primarily of Davidic psalms. Book III includes psalms of Asaph, Psalms 73–83, and of the sons of Korah,[31] Psalms 84–88. Books IV and V include anonymous psalms, along with a few by David and others.[32]

Types of Psalms[33]

The variety of biblical psalms include *songs of praise, royal psalms, thanksgiving* (national and individual), *lament* (national and individual), *imprecatory,* and *penitential.*

Songs of praise to God (or hymns) are generally structured with an introduction, body, and conclusion. The body usually gives the reason that God should be praised, typically introduced by words translated "for" ("because," e.g., 96:4; 106:1) or "who" (e.g., 103:3; 104:2). (See figures 11-9 and 11-10.)

Examples of *royal psalms* include 2:1–6; 5:2; 10; 18:1–4; 24:7–10; and 93. These psalms sometimes emphasize the universal and absolute reign of Yahweh, as does Psalm 93. Other times they proclaim the rule of Messiah, as does Psalm 24.

National psalms of thanksgiving typically celebrate Yahweh's deliverance of Israel. For example, Psalm 124:1–5 says:

> "If it had not been the LORD who was on our side,"
> Let Israel now say—
> "If it had not been the LORD who was on our side,
> When men rose up against us,

Psalm 103		
Intro:	1–5	Command to Praise
Body:	6–19	Reason we should praise Yahweh
Conclusion:	20–22	Command to Praise

Figure 11.9

Psalm 8		
Intro:	1	Praise
Body:	2–8	Rationale for Praise
Conclusion:	9	Praise

Figure 11.10

> *Then they would have swallowed us alive,*
>   *When their wrath was kindled against us;*
> *Then the waters would have overwhelmed us,*
>   *The stream would have gone over our soul;*
> *Then the swollen waters*
>   *Would have gone over our soul."* NKJV

The characteristic common to *individual psalms of thanksgiving* is the expression of gratitude for personal deliverance out of some calamity, for example, Psalm 30:2–3:

> *O LORD my God, I cried out to You,*
>   *And You healed me.*
> *O LORD, You brought my soul up from the grave;*
>   *You have kept me alive, that I should not go down to the*
> *pit.* NKJV

Psalms of lament express negative emotions either of the individual or nation. Such psalms often express a prayer of disorientation.[34] They are recognizable by expressions of grief, need, or complaint. They generally follow the pattern shown in figure 11-11.

In developing truth sheets, read psalms of lament in their literary and historical contexts. Ask *how* they reflect ancient Semitic expressions of grief and regret. Seek to understand the cause of the lament, asking *why? What* the psalm teaches about God is of utmost impor-

---

Patterns of Lament in Psalms 3, 5, 6, and 7

  I. Invocation (Pss. 3:1–2; 5:1–7; 6:1; 7:1a)
  II. Plea to God for help (Pss. 6:2–5; 7:1b)
  III. Complaints (Pss. 3:1–2; 5:8–10; 6:6–7; 7:2)
  IV. Confession of Sin or an Assertion of Innocence (Pss. 3:3–6; 6:8–9; 7:3–5)
  V. Curse of Enemies (imprecation) (Pss. 3:7–8; 6:10; 7:6–9)

Figure 11.11

tance to understand. Also, seek to discover *how* the lament appeals to the emotions.

National psalms of lament differ only in the sense that the complaints by God's people because of calamity and feeling forsaken by God are expressed corporately. Often these psalms contain lengthy descriptions of the people's affliction, as in Psalm 44.

Imprecatory psalms utter God's curses upon His enemies, as in Psalm 69:22–28. They express the justice in which God avenges Himself, thus giving both legitimate expression to the righteous indignation of believers today and freedom from the temptation to take one's own revenge. (See Romans 12:19–20.)

Penitential psalms express repentance of sin. The most well-known example is Psalm 51, in which David confesses his sin with Bathsheba.

Headings

Many of the psalms begin with a superscription (or inscription). In the Hebrew Bible, it is the first numbered verse. In most English translations the superscription is unnumbered, often in a contrasting font, and appears as the title. Most readers do not understand that superscriptions are part of the God-breathed text. Others simply don't agree. However, these introductory statements often provide helpful historical allusions that describe the setting. Often they give the names of biblical persons involved in the experience or writing of the psalm. They sometimes tell the reader what kind of psalm it is. This provides a tremendous clue into how the psalm should be interpreted. For example, when preaching Psalm 3, you should first study its historical setting in 2 Samuel 15–17, indicated in the superscription, and convey this to the audience in the introduction or body of the message.

Hebrew Structure

The psalms are structured in a variety of ways, including *recurring refrains, acrostics*, and *parallelism*.[35] Recurring refrains form what is called an *inclusio*, in which a central idea is enveloped within similar statements. For example, see Psalm 46:7–11 in figure 11-12.

The statement "The LORD of hosts is with us" clearly forms a refrain. The note in the *Nelson Study Bible* shows how recognizing an *inclusio* of this psalm suggests a theme or point of emphasis for the preacher: "The pairing of the words 'the Lord of hosts' with 'the God of Jacob' in both verses, praises the Almighty, the Commander of heaven's armies for choosing to live with the descendants of Jacob, His people. Who could protect His people better?"[36]

Other examples of *inclusio* include Psalm 49:12, 20. (See figure 11-13.)

An *acrostic* is accomplished when every line begins with the succession of letters of the alphabet, as in Proverbs 31:10–31. In the Bible's longest chapter, Psalm 119, each of eight lines in every paragraph begins with the same letter of the Hebrew alphabet, in succession. (See figure 11-14.)

Inclusio, Psalm 46:7–11

⁷**The LORD of hosts is with us; the God of Jacob is our refuge.** Selah ⁸Come, behold the works of the LORD, who has made desolations in the earth. ⁹He makes wars cease to the end of the earth; He breaks the bow and cuts the spear in two; He burns the chariot in the fire. ¹⁰Be still, and know that I am God; I will be exalted among the nations, I will be exalted in the earth! ¹¹**The LORD of hosts is with us; the God of Jacob is our refuge.** Selah (NKJV)

Figure 11.12

Inclusio, Psalm 49:12, 20

¹²Nevertheless man, though in honor, does not remain; he is like the beasts that perish.

> These similar statements *frame* the central idea developed within them, that human life is fleeting and dependent upon God for any sense of permanence.

²⁰A man who is in honor, yet does not understand, is like the beasts that perish.

Figure 11.13

As exciting as this may be to the serious Bible student, take care not to dwell on the mechanics of poetic structure, such as inclusio and acrostics. Derickson exhorts young preachers, "Don't stand up and preach on acrostics. But, in the midst of preaching, let people have insight into what God has chosen to do. Mention it in passing to praise God and motivate people to appreciate His character. Point out, as a tour-guide, what they could not otherwise see. People might otherwise be robbed of the riches of the medium as well as of the message. It has an aesthetic as well as utilitarian purpose."[37]

Parallelism refers to various ways in which the pairs of lines in Hebrew poetry (also called *couplets* or *cola*) work together to enhance the impact of their meaning. Parallelism can be complete, as in Psalm 103, or incomplete. Incomplete parallelism is an example of what is called *anacoluthon*. It sometimes signals an emotional state in which the writer is too excited, distracted, or simply forgetful to follow through on the structural scheme he began.

Parallelism also can be *internal* or *external*. Internal parallelism refers to how the second of two lines of poetry affects the first. Examples include *synonymous, antithetic, synthetic, emblematic, climactic,* and *inverted parallelism* known as *chiasmus*.

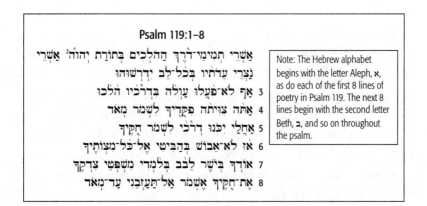

Psalm 119:1–8

אַשְׁרֵי תְמִימֵי־דָרֶךְ הַהֹלְכִים בְּתוֹרַת יְהוָֹה ²אַשְׁרֵי

נֹצְרֵי עֵדֹתָיו בְּכָל־לֵב יִדְרְשׁוּהוּ

3 אַף לֹא־פָעֲלוּ עַוְלָה בִּדְרָכָיו הָלָכוּ

4 אַתָּה צִוִּיתָה פִקֻּדֶיךָ לִשְׁמֹר מְאֹד

5 אַחֲלַי יִכֹּנוּ דְרָכָי לִשְׁמֹר חֻקֶּיךָ

6 אָז לֹא־אֵבוֹשׁ בְּהַבִּיטִי אֶל־כָּל־מִצְוֹתֶיךָ

7 אוֹדְךָ בְּיֹשֶׁר לֵבָב בְּלָמְדִי מִשְׁפְּטֵי צִדְקֶךָ

8 אֶת־חֻקֶּיךָ אֶשְׁמֹר אַל־תַּעַזְבֵנִי עַד־מְאֹד

Note: The Hebrew alphabet begins with the letter Aleph, א, as do each of the first 8 lines of poetry in Psalm 119. The next 8 lines begin with the second letter Beth, ב, and so on throughout the psalm.

Figure 11.14

Synonymous parallelism achieves amplification by repeating in a slightly different way in the second line what was stated in the first. Sometimes the first statement is general and the second more specific. Psalm 18:5 is an example:

> *The sorrows of Sheol surrounded me;*
> *The snares of death confronted me.* (NKJV)

In *antithetic* parallelism, the second line is a negative of the first line, not a contradiction. Look for an adversative conjunction, such as "but," as in Psalm 1:6.

> *For the LORD knows the way of the righteous,*
> *But the way of the ungodly shall perish.* (NKJV)

In *synthetic* parallelism the line or lines following the first line advances or completes the thought expressed in the first line. A good example is found in Psalm 1:1.

> *Blessed is the man who walks not in the counsel of the ungodly,*
> *Nor stands in the path of sinners,*
> *Nor sits in the seat of the scornful.* (NKJV)

Emblematic parallelism sets up a comparison by use of a simile often translated "like" or "as," or by use of a metaphor, which makes a comparison without these words. Psalm 1:3 is an example of emblematic parallelism with a simile: "He shall be like a tree planted by the rivers of water" (NKJV). "He" is compared, or paralleled, with "a tree" by the word translated "like." Another good example is found in Psalm 42:1, where David says "As the deer pants . . . so pants my soul" (NKJV).

Climactic parallelism, as its name implies, builds up to a climax, as in 92:9. (See figure 11-15.)

Inverted parallelism is also called *chiasmus,* because the order of comparison in the first line is reversed in the second line, creating a pattern that resembles the Greek letter χ (*chi*, pronounced "key"). The resulting pattern is a-b-b'-a'. (See figure 11-16.)

Psalm 91:14 (NKJV) is a good example of a chiasmus. (See figure 11-17.)

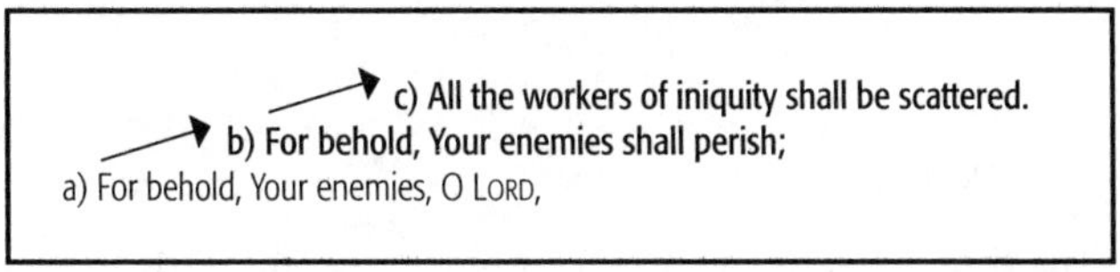

c) All the workers of iniquity shall be scattered.
b) For behold, Your enemies shall perish;
a) For behold, Your enemies, O LORD,

Figure 11.15

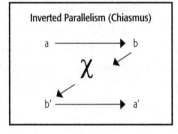

Inverted Parallelism (Chiasmus)

Figure 11.16

a Because he has set his love upon Me,
b therefore I will deliver him;
b' I will set him on high
a' because he has known My name.

Figure 11.17

It is clear from the chiastic structure of this verse that the Psalmist has narrowed the concept of loving God (a) to knowing His name (a').

External parallelism involves more than a single verse, providing both variety and an aid to memorization. A good example is Psalm 137: 5–6, which also illustrates the inverted parallelism (chiasmus) just discussed. (See figure 11-18.)

Preaching the Psalms

A sample sermon on Psalm 113 is outlined at the end of this chapter. The following outline by Gregory V. Trull, adapted and presented in figure 11-19, suggests a series of messages that could be entitled "Messiah in the Psalms."[38]

SONG OF SOLOMON

The Song of Solomon expresses the intensely passionate love between King Solomon and a young girl. Their mutual admiration and eager anticipation of consummating their relationship physically are stated with respect for the bonds of marriage within which human sexuality is properly celebrated.[39]

Background

In Hebrew the Song of Solomon was called "The Song of Songs Which Is Solomon's."[40] Jerome's Latin translation (Vulgate) named the book

---

External Parallelism, Psalm 137:5–6

a   If I forget you, O Jerusalem,
     b   Let my right hand forget its skill!
a'   If I do not remember you,
     b'   Let my tongue cling to the roof of my mouth—
a''   If I do not exalt Jerusalem above my chief joy.

Figure 11.18

"Canticles," Songs.[41] Both Jewish and Christian scholars generally agree that Solomon is the author.[42] Though the book is never mentioned by another biblical writer, it describes royal luxuries in keeping with Solomon's authorship indicated in 1:1 and by a total of seven mentions of his name.[43] The use of some Persian and Greek words may be explained by Solomon's acquaintance with other cultures.[44]

Literary Form

The introduction to the Song of Solomon in *The Nelson Study Bible* indicates several literary features of the poetry. First, the Song is a lyric *idyll*, a type of love song that is unique in the Bible.[45] Second, speeches and events do not necessarily follow in chronological order.[46] "At times

---

Messiah in the Psalms

Messiah the Son
- Ps. 2
  - –Coronation Song for Israel's kings
  - –Ultimately fulfilled in Jesus Christ

Messiah's Rejection
- Ps. 69:8–9 *Zeal of Messiah*
  - –Zeal of Messiah brought rejection to David
  - –Ultimate rejection in Christ
- Ps. 41:9 *Betrayal of a Friend*
  - –David betrayed by one at the royal table
  - –Christ betrayed by one at the Last Supper

Messiah's Death
- Ps. 34:19–20 *No bones broken*
  - –Image of Passover Lamb
  - –Literally fulfilled in Jesus (John 19:36)
- Ps. 22 *Agony of Crucifixion*
  - –Abandonment (v. 1)
  - –Water poured out (v. 14)
  - –Gambling for clothes (v. 18)
  - –Pierced hands and feet (v. 16)

Messiah's Resurrection
- Ps. 16:10 *Messiah Will Not Face Decay*
  - –Only Jesus did not decay in grave (Acts 2:31)

Messiah's Reign
- Ps. 72:11, 17 *Universal Reign of Blessing*
- Ps. 110:1–3, 5–7 *Messiah, the Warrior King*
- Ps. 110:4 *Messiah the King-Priest* (Heb. 7:13–14)

Figure 11.19

the story line remains suspended while the audience views scenes from earlier or yet untold incidents."[47] Third, "in addition to the two characters that carry the story line—the Shulamite and King Solomon, a group of women interrupt certain scenes with brief musical speeches or warnings. Solomon uses the chorus to make transitions from one scene to another, as well as to add emphasis to important themes."[48]

Interpretation

Perhaps because of its erotic language, with no mention of God, the Song of Solomon has been interpreted in a variety ways in an apparent attempt to discover a spiritual meaning. According to author Craig Glickman, this has resulted in the writing of more commentaries on the Song than on any other book of the Bible, with no view enjoying wide acceptance.[49] For example, it has been viewed by some as an allegory without an historical basis, "representing Jehovah's love for Israel in the Old Testament and Christ's love for His church in the New Testament."[50] Others, with respect for its historical basis, have seen it as a type of Christ's love for the Church, with limited points of similarity.[51] Still others have viewed Solomon's song as a drama, which was acted out.

Attempts to read spiritual meaning into the Song may stem from a low view of the material creation, including the human body and sexual love. Taken literally, however, the Song was held in high regard by the Jews. It was the first of the "rolls" (Megilloth) read in the synagogue on the eighth day of the Feast of Unleavened Bread.[52] That the Jews took a naturalistic view of the Song is evident from a tradition mentioned in the Nelson Study Bible: "Because of its explicit language, ancient and modern Jewish sages forbade men to read the book before they were thirty (and presumably kept women from reading it at all)."[53]

Theology

"The Song of Solomon provides an example of how God created male and female to live in happiness and fulfillment. People are created as sexual beings."[54] "God ordained marriage from the beginning of creation: Man and woman were to become one flesh (Gen. 2:25)."[55]

Message

The message of the Song is simple, says Derickson: "Human love and marriage are beautiful in their emotional and physical expressions."[56] He elaborates with four statements that put sex in divine perspective. This is a major contribution of the poem.

- Sex is a gift from God.
- Sex is God's design.
- Sex is most beautifully expressed within boundaries.
- Sex is holy, and should be treated as such.

Outline (See figure 11-20.)

Preaching the Song of Solomon[57]

The Jews' tradition of restricting access to the Song of Solomon shows that they understood its natural meaning. While this suggests due caution in proclaiming its message to a mixed audience of all ages, the book must not be abandoned in the pulpit. At least three aspects of its message are desperately needed today.

First, it represents a high view of woman as man's full equal, without blurring the important distinction of their respective roles. The

The Song of Solomon	
Exaltation of Married Love	
Courtship	1–2
Ceremony	3–4
Commitment	5–8

Figure 11.20

mutuality of the lovers' passion is demonstrated by the matching of re-
ciprocal speeches. Solomon and his bride are equally in love, ready to
initiate and enjoy physical intimacy.

Second, romantic love involves painful separation as well as the joy
of intimacy. Without interpreting the book as an allegory, it can be
used to illustrate the longing of the bride of Christ to be united with
Him when He comes for His Church.

Third, the message that sexual love is good in marriage, but not before, is needed more today than ever. The warning is sounded no less
than three times, "I charge you, O daughters of Jerusalem . . . do not
stir up nor awaken love until it pleases" (2:7; 3:5; and 8:4 NKJV).

LAMENTATIONS

Like the appendix of a book, Jeremiah's poetic Lamentations seems to
provide material that doesn't properly fit within his prophecy. Like the
appendix of the human body, Lamentations seems like a small, bitter
organ that the reader could live without. It has been called "the saddest
book in the Bible."[58] Who wants to listen to five movements of a funeral
dirge? And yet, the book of Lamentations displays hope in the midst of
heartbreak, which everyone needs at some point in life. Its record of,
and response to, Jerusalem's fall to Babylon in 586 BC (see Jeremiah 29
and 52) serves as a warning to return to God in faith and to trust Him
to restore them someday.

Structure and Message

Structured as a chiasm, the book takes the reader from grieving, to
confession, to trust. (See figure 11-21.) As an alphabetic acrostic, it
demonstrates order, even in the chaos of grief. Its overall lesson, says
Derickson, is: "When suffering, trust in God's faithfulness to demonstrate mercy."[59]

Preaching Lamentations

Lamentations lends itself to a *book sermon* in which chapters 1–2 and 4–5 may showcase the central poem in chapter 3. The key verses are 3:22–25, which shine all the brighter in the dark night of personal and national distress—politically and spiritually:

> Through the LORD's mercies we are not consumed, because His compassions fail not. They are new every morning; great is Your faithfulness. "The LORD is my portion," says my soul, "Therefore I hope in Him!" The LORD is good to those who wait for Him, to the soul who seeks Him. (NKJV)

Often referred to as "the weeping prophet," Jeremiah may be seen as a type of Christ, who wept over the same city centuries later (Matt. 23:37–38). As "a Man of sorrows and acquainted with grief" (Isa. 53:3 NKJV), Jesus is one from whom modern preachers and their listeners cannot afford to hide their faces. Lamentations, therefore, provides a needed reminder that God keeps His word in judging sin. It demonstrates that it is not ungodly to suffer as a consequence of the sins of others. In fact, ministers need to enter (and own) the suffering of those to whom they would minister. As one who wept bitterly, Jeremiah also teaches all men that it is not unmanly to show emotions. His book grants the believer "permission" to mourn, to outwardly express the

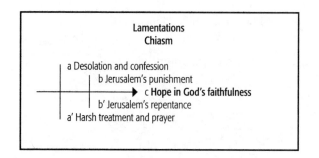

Figure 11.21

inward pain of loss. But the contrition it teaches is more than the bitter remorse of Judas Iscariot, recorded in Matthew 27:3. Confession of sin is an essential part of healing. (See 1 John 1:9.) Finally, the book illustrates the blessed comfort known only to those who mourn sin and its consequences. (See Matthew 5:4.) It illustrates the joy of the believer who sorrows not as those "who have no hope" (1 Thess. 4:13 NKJV).

PREACHING HEBREW POETRY OF SCRIPTURE

An important part of analysis is observing the author's literary arrangement of the text. In this way you can work to present the natural outline of the text rather than impose an artificial one upon it.

SAMPLE SERMON ON PSALM 113
TELLING THE GREATNESS OF GOD
PSALM 113

The Hallel, Psalms 113–118, all command the praise of Yahweh, "Hallel-u-jah"

1–3   Introductory statement of what is to be done by servants of Yahweh

        Command, not a request

        But what is praise?

            Praise must be done in community

            Thanksgiving can be done in private

            Saying the word *Praise* does not accomplish the task

            Praise is excited, public boasting

                We sometimes exaggerate when boasting

                    of grandchildren, etc.

                When extolling God's virtues, we can

                    never exaggerate

                You can never say enough

            The Name of Yahweh is to be praised.

                Name refers to reputation or character; His person and work

                  LORD in all caps stands in the place of the proper

name of God, Yahweh

Follows the Jewish tradition to avoid pronouncing
the name they were not to take in vain, by
substituting Adonai, correctly
translated "Lord."

Blessed be the name: now and perpetually

Servitude is a high or lowly honor depending on who is
served

Nothing is higher privilege than to be the servant of
Yahweh

From east of sun to the west, is every place; the
whole earth

4–9b Body

Sovereignty of Yahweh (transcendent)

High above all nations

Above the heavens

Incomparability of God

Tenderness of Yahweh (immanent)

Humbles Himself (Man naturally exalts himself)

God has to look "down" to look at what we regard as the
highest "up"

The combination of truth is unique to Hebrew/Christian
Monotheism

9c   Conclusion: Praise Yah

Mercy toward a barren woman (which was a cultural shame)

At our best, we should realize that we owe praise to God for
everything we are and have.

SUMMARY AND CONCLUSION

The books of Job, Psalms, Proverbs, Ecclesiastes, and Song of Solomon represent most of the Hebrew poetry in Scripture. Together, they express the heart and mind of man as he relates to God's greatness while experiencing the toughness of life.

Job demonstrates the need to trust and obey God even though He does not explain His ways.

Proverbs promotes the fear of God as the foundational principle of all others. The proverbs emphasize the sayings of wise men as generalizations to demonstrate God's maintenance of ethical order in a world made chaotic by sin. The simple need not become fools, and fools need not become mockers. By heeding the warnings of wisdom and yielding to her wooing, the simple may become wise.

Ecclesiastes stresses the inability of man to catch and keep a satisfying sense of purpose apart from the responsible enjoyment of life as a gift from God.

The Psalms generally lead the reader from the depths of despair to the heights of joy as Yahweh reveals His faithfulness to provide for, protect, deliver, sustain, comfort, and bless His covenant people. Different kinds of psalms express, through a variety of poetic structures, the praises, complaints, thanksgiving, lament, confession, and hope of God's covenant people. In addition, substantial hymnic literature, found in the book of Psalms alone, anticipates the sonship, rejection, death, resurrection, and reign of Messiah.

The Song of Solomon is an explicit love song about the courtship, ceremony, and commitment of King Solomon and a young Shulamite woman. It communicates important truths needed by youth and adults of both sexes. Among them are the equality of women and men, the pain of separation between lovers, and the appropriateness of arousing sexual passions only after a couple has married. While not an allegory, the love song does illustrate some aspects of the relationship between Christ and the Church as His bride.

Lamentations, while easy to neglect, reflects the bitter sorrows of sin and features God's faithfulness to His covenant people. It encourages the confession of sin and demonstrates the comfort and joy known only by those who mourn the effects of sin, as did Jeremiah and Jesus.

Sermons from scriptural Hebrew poetry should reflect the arrangement and structure of the text.

Discussion Questions

1. List the books of wisdom, and state in your own words what distinguishes Wisdom Literature.
2. Beside Hebrew poetry, describe in your own words what the poetic books all have in common.
3. What is one good way to preach Job, according to this chapter?
4. If preaching through the book of Job, what must the preacher be especially careful to do, and why?
5. Why do you agree or disagree that the book of Proverbs is compiled in an orderly fashion?
6. Explain your understanding of the motto of Proverbs given in 1:7. What does it mean . . . and not mean?
7. Describe two ways to preach the Proverbs according to this chapter.
8. According to this chapter, what does the phrase in Ecclesiastes "all is vanity" mean?
9. Describe each of the following kinds of Psalms:
   a. Songs of Praise
   b. Royal Psalms
   c. Thanksgiving (national/personal)
   d. Lament (national/personal)
   e. Imprecatory
   f. Penitential
10. Explain in your own words the meaning of these:
   a. Inclusio
   b. Acrostics
   c. Parallelism
      —Synonymous
      —Antithetic
      —Synthetic
      —Emblematic
      —Climactic
      —Inverted (Chiasmus)

11. What is the difference between *internal* and *external* parallelism?

12. Why would you preach from the Song of Solomon, and how?

13. Why would you preach from Lamentations, and how?

14. Identify three strengths in the sample sermon on Psalm 113, and three weaknesses, based on your understanding of the Whiting Method and this chapter.

CHAPTER 12

Preaching Old Testament Prophecy

THE NATURE OF OLD TESTAMENT PROPHECY

THE SEVENTEEN books of Isaiah through Malachi include most, but not all, of the prophetic literature of the Old Testament. Moses referred to himself as a prophet and predicted the coming of one (Christ) as a prophet like him, from among the people, to whom they must listen. (See Deuteronomy 18:15 and Acts 3:22 and 7:37.) As noted in Chapter 9, the Jews also regarded the books of Joshua, Judges, Samuel, and Kings as *former prophets*. Throughout the historical narrative of the Old Testament, some words of many of the speaking prophets have been recorded, including those of Nathan, Ahijah, Jehu, Elijah, Elisha, Shemaiah, Hanani, and Huldah.[1] In Acts 2:30, Peter refers to David as a prophet, having predicted the resurrection of Christ in Psalm 16:10. But even if "prophetic literature" was limited to the four major and twelve minor writing prophets, it would comprise no less than one quarter of the word Paul commanded Timothy (and the Church) to proclaim! (See 2 Timothy 4:2.)

THE PROPHETS

Speakers for God

The basic idea of a prophet is one who speaks for God. But, while modern preachers speak for God by declaring the meaning and relevance of revealed truth, they do not prophesy as direct recipients and communicators of divine revelation, as did the biblical prophets. Such spokesmen were divinely chosen and given God's message. Wilkinson and Boa list "dreams, visions, angels, nature, miracles, and audible voice"[2] as ways God used to reveal His will and words to them. Burdened with the word of Yahweh,[3] the prophets discharged their responsibility by telling it forth (*forthtelling*). Because they represented the covenant-keeping God of history, their message also involved *foretelling* future events. In Isaiah 41:21–23, the challenge issued to Israel serves to remind the nation of their dependence upon God's revelation:

> *"Present your case," says the* LORD.
> *"Bring forth your strong reasons," says the King of Jacob.*
> *"Let them bring forth and show us what will happen;*
> *let them show the former things, what they were,*
> *that we may consider them,*
> *and know the latter end of them;*
> *or declare to us things to come.*
> *Show the things that are to come hereafter,*
> *that we may know that you are gods;*
> *yes, do good or do evil,*
> *that we may be dismayed and see it together."* (NKJV)

In Daniel 2:28, Daniel declares the power of God to know and declare through His prophets things that are future and unseen: "But there is a God in heaven who reveals secrets, and He has made known to King Nebuchadnezzar what will be in the latter days. Your dream, and the visions of your head upon your bed, were these . . ." (NKJV).

Recipients of Revelation

British scholarship tends to regard the prophets as people of extraordinary human intuition or psychic gifts.[4] But according to Scripture, the prophets were ordinary people whom God called to be His mouthpieces (oracles) (see James 5:16–18 and 2 Peter 1:21). The Bible's denunciation of Balaam as a *false prophet* was made not on the basis that his predictions proved false, but that he led the people counter to God's will.[5]

Monitors of Covenant Responsibilities

The prophets simply announced what God would do, in keeping with His covenants with Israel, to provide universal blessing through one man. The consequences of obedience and disobedience spelled out in the Mosaic and land covenants (see chapter 9) were *predictable* based on both the general provisions of the covenants and specific revelation to the prophets concerning details and timing of God's judgment and restoration.

Because they spoke with divine authority primarily to the people with whom God had entered into covenant, the prophets served as watchmen for the nation. Their warnings and promises were also meant to motivate the holy living emphasized in the Pentateuch. The prophets also looked forward to the kingdom blessings of the coming Messiah.[6] Because God's warnings and promises related to material blessings and curses in the land, they are not to be explained away in favor of spiritual lessons. According to Ellisen, God's covenants are meant to: (1) reveal and guarantee God's redemptive purposes in His Eternal Covenant;[7] (2) reveal and guarantee God's Kingdom purposes through His chosen nation Israel; and (3) provide a faith basis for personal relationships with God.[8]

In addition to pronouncing judgments and consolation based on existing covenants, the new covenant is revealed in Jeremiah 31:33–34. As noted in chapter 8, the new covenant replaced the only temporary (Mosaic) covenant given by God, with one in which He graciously provided forgiveness of sin and inner guidance by the indwelling Holy Spirit. The Abrahamic covenant, which preceded the Mosaic covenant by five hundred years, is unilateral, unconditional, and still in force! Because the Church participates in the blessings of the *new* covenant, ratified by the blood of Christ, it is essential that preachers exposit the *old* covenant (Old Testament) prophecies in which it is rooted. (See Matthew 26:28 and Galatians 3:8.)

THE CHARACTER OF PROPHECY

The Prophetic Message

A proper understanding of six features of biblical prophecy will correct common misconceptions about it. First, it was given to be understood. Though one must be regenerate to truly appropriate the theological truth of Scripture and know it existentially (see 1 Corinthians 2:14–15), the unregenerate mind may comprehend it *intellectually*, because symbols used are often explained.[9]

Second, biblical prophecy often blends near and far things together. For example, the first and second comings of Christ are described as a single event in Isaiah 9:6. Jesus illustrated the necessity of discerning the partial fulfillment of a single statement of prophecy when, in the synagogue at Nazareth, He read from Isaiah 61. Stopping in the middle of verse 2, He said, "Today this Scripture is fulfilled in your hearing" (Luke 4:21 NKJV). The second half of verse 2, which Jesus did not read, pertained to the day of God's vengeance, which will not be fulfilled until He comes again.

Third, biblical prophecy is definite. Isaiah mentioned Cyrus 150 years in advance (44:28; 45:1). Josiah was named 300 years in advance (1 Kin. 13:2). Whereas sixteenth-century physician and astrologer Nostradamus[10] is celebrated for predictions thought to have come true only occasionally, God's prophets were accurate 100 percent of the time (see Deuteronomy 18:22).

Fourth, the speaker/writer of biblical prophecy was aware of the content and its implications. That they were not simply channeling information as a conduit is evident in their emotional involvement, reasoned explanations, and willingness to suffer for the truth they communicated. (For an example of this, see Jeremiah 1:17–19.)

Fifth, biblical predictions communicate knowledge of things that could only be known by revelation. For example, the seventy weeks of Daniel's prophecy (Dan. 9:24-27) reveal the length of time between the rebuilding of the temple in Jerusalem and the crucifixion of Israel's Messiah.[11]

Sixth, the predictions of biblical prophecy were relevant at the time that they were given. They were not merely forecasts that would eventually prove true, but warnings, judgments, and promises of restoration and of Messiah that met present needs.[12]

In view of these six features, a good working definition of biblical prophecy is: God's revelation of His eternal plan and purpose, provided in a written history of events before they occur in time and space.

Difficulties in Interpreting Prophecy

The literature of biblical prophecy in general, and apocalyptic literature[13] in particular, is rich in figurative language and symbolism that often challenge the interpreter's ability to understand and explain them.[14] For example, the description of Ezekiel's vision of wheels within wheels (Ezek. 1) may indicate that he saw the throne of God.[15] But it would be difficult to reach this conclusion based on the immediate context alone, and this interpretation neglects all of the details that would enable one to draw a picture of what Ezekiel saw.

The chronological gaps between what is often referred to as the *near* and *far* fulfillments of prophecies present another problem. For example, in His First Advent, Jesus fulfilled the prophecy of Isaiah 9:6 that a Child would be born and a Son given. But His shouldering of the mantle of government appears to refer to something yet in the future. However, the promise of Christ's reign was not irrelevant to those in whose time it was not fulfilled. Rather, it motivated holy living just as the anticipation of Christ's coming for His Church is meant to motivate holiness in the life of the New Testament believer. (See 1 John 3:1–3.)

Another challenge is understanding the geopolitical setting in which prophecies are given. The interpretation of Isaiah 6:1, for example, depends on the reader's awareness of the nature of King Uzziah's reign. Uzziah's death sets the stage for Isaiah's vision of the glory of the exalted, ever-living King, whose sovereignty is absolute, universal, and eternal.

Discerning *how* a prophecy is fulfilled also presents a challenge. Consider six scenarios: (1) Some Old Testament predictions, (e.g., Jeremiah 47) are clearly fulfilled in the Old Testament itself. But (2) others were not fulfilled until the New Testament. For example, the birth of Jesus in Bethlehem fulfilled Micah 5:2. (3) Old Testament prophecy may be fulfilled *partially*, or in one sense, but not fully, as it will be in the future. Isaiah 35, for example, refers to millennial glory, some miraculous aspects of which were fulfilled in the first coming of Christ. The resulting *tension* is sometimes referred to as the "already-not-yet" phenomenon. (4) Some Old Testament predictions *still* have not been fulfilled, in *any* sense, such as the creation of new heavens and a new earth, predicted in Isaiah 65:17–25. (5) Some New Testament predictions have been partially fulfilled. In Matthew 24 Jesus made predictions that have been accomplished "already-not-yet." Finally, (6) there are New Testament predictions that have yet to be fulfilled, such as 2 Peter 3.

Finally, the rabbinic method of interpreting the fulfillment of prophecy is important to understand. Arnold G. Fruchtenbaum explains that, in the rabbinic tradition of *Drash*, a prophecy was said to be fulfilled on the basis of only one point, or a few points, of resemblance among many points of nonresemblance. He cites, for example, Acts 2:16–21, where Peter referred to the outpouring of the Holy Spirit as *that* which Joel prophesied in Joel 2:28. In point of fact, *nothing* prophesied in Joel 2:28 occurred on the day of pentecost. There is no record that sons and daughters in Israel prophesied, that old men dreamed dreams, or that young men saw visions. In reality, the significant event of tongues-speaking that *did* occur on the day of pentecost is not even mentioned by Joel. The only point of connection is that Joel speaks of an outpouring of the Holy Spirit, an event that occurred on the day of pentecost, and the reason Peter quotes the Joel text.[16]

PRIMARY CONSIDERATIONS IN
PREACHING OLD TESTAMENT PROPHECY

In preparing to preach from the Prophetic Books of Scripture, you must pay careful attention to at least four areas: *historical background, literary analysis, theological understanding,* and *preaching points.*

Historical Background

The sermon on Isaiah 6:1–13, shown in figure 12-1, illustrates how important the setting of a passage can be to its proper exposition and proclamation. The sermon is entitled "Putting Our Worldview in Order." Based on the first four verses, the sermon begins by stressing the importance of "knowing who God is." The chapter begins with a statement of historical fact that is easy for the modern reader to breeze past while searching for some striking truth of spiritual depth and practical relevance. Yet, failure to understand this opening statement decimates the impact it would have had on its original readers. The phrase "In the year that King Uzziah died," does far more than date the vision that Isaiah goes on to describe. It provides the contrasting background against which the subject of Isaiah's vision must be understood and proclaimed.

In developing a truth sheet from this passage, you must apply the six interrogatives to Judah's long-time King Uzziah, as well as to Yahweh, whose glory Isaiah is allowed to see. *Who* was Uzziah? *What* distinguished him from other kings? *When* did he die? *Where* did Uzziah live and reign? *Why* was his death worth mentioning? While good commentaries can be helpful, and checking them *after* you have done your own analysis of the text is an important step, an exhaustive concordance[17] should be your primary source of biblical information about Uzziah. Consider the story of Uzziah as told in the historical literature of 2 Kings 15:1–5.

> In the twenty-seventh year of Jeroboam king of Israel, Azariah the son of Amaziah, king of Judah, became king. He was sixteen years old

when he became king, and he reigned fifty-two years in Jerusalem. His mother's name was Jecholiah of Jerusalem. And he did what was right in the sight of the LORD, according to all that his father Amaziah had done, except that the high places were not removed; the people still sacrificed and burned incense on the high places. Then the LORD struck the king, so that he was a leper until the day of his death; so he dwelt in an isolated house. And Jotham the king's son was over the royal house, judging the people of the land. (NKJV)

The names Azariah and Uzziah refer to the same king of Judah.[18] For no less than fifty-two years, he reigned in Jerusalem. In addition to enjoying an extraordinarily long reign, he did what was right in the sight of Yahweh. Yet, Yahweh struck him with leprosy for one sin. The account in 2 Chronicles 26:16–21, goes to the heart of the matter. In short, prosperity brought pride, which led to the king's sin in the temple (see figure 12-1, point I. A.).

But when he was strong his heart was lifted up, to his destruction, for he transgressed against the LORD his God by entering the temple of the LORD to burn incense on the altar of incense. So Azariah the priest went in after him, and with him were eighty priests of the LORD—valiant men. And they withstood King Uzziah, and said to him, "It is not for you, Uzziah, to burn incense to the LORD, but for the priests, the sons of Aaron, who are consecrated to burn incense. Get out of the sanctuary, for you have trespassed! You shall have no honor from the LORD God." (NKJV)

Then Uzziah became furious; and he had a censer in his hand to burn incense. And while he was angry with the priests, leprosy broke out on his forehead, before the priests in the house of the LORD, beside the incense altar. And Azariah the chief priest and all the priests looked at him, and there, on his forehead, he was leprous; so they thrust him out of that place. Indeed he also hurried to get out, because the LORD had struck him. King Uzziah was a leper until the day of his death. He dwelt in an isolated house, because he was a leper; for he was cut off from the house of the Lord. Then Jotham his son was over the king's house, judging the people of the land. (NKJV)

It is in stark, shocking contrast to the man the Judeans would have properly looked up to for generations that Yahweh is seen as the "indescribably Holy One" (see figure 12-1, point I. B). Isaiah continues:

I saw the Lord sitting on a throne, high and lifted up, and the train of His robe filled the temple. Above it stood seraphim; each one had six wings: with two he covered his face, with two he covered his feet, and with two he flew. And one cried to another and said: "Holy, holy, holy is the Lord of hosts; The whole earth is full of His glory!" And the posts of the door were shaken by the voice of him who cried out, and the house was filled with smoke. (6:1–4 NKJV)

The visible glory of the thrice-holy, ever-living, self-existent God (Yahweh) is to be appreciated against the dark backdrop of the king whose long reign of military, political, and domestic success ended

---

Putting Our Worldview in Order
Isaiah 6:1–13

I. Knowing Who God Is	1–4
A. The Importance of the Historical Setting to Isaiah's Vision	
(2 Kings 15:1–5; 2 Chronicles 26:16–21)	
• Prosperity Brought Pride	
• Uzziah's Sin in the Temple	
B. God the Indescribably Holy One	
II. Knowing Who We Are	5
A. Personal Reflection as We View God	
B. Personal Acceptance of Our Sinfulness	
III. Knowing Forgiveness Apart from Works	6–7
A. Recognition of Sin	
B. Undeserved Favor from God	
IV. Knowing Our Mission in View of Forgiveness	8
A. God's Desire to Interact with His People	
B. Our Need to Follow Forgiveness with Commitment	
V. Knowing That Judgment Often Precedes Redemption	(9b–13)

Figure 12.1

ingloriously. In the light of this breathtaking comparison, Isaiah realizes his own need of personal cleansing.

House's sermon outline in figure 12-1 emphasizes the passage's historical background:

Literary Analysis

Sidney Greidanus emphasizes the importance of the literary analysis of
prophetic texts in his book *The Modern Preacher and the Ancient Text*.
He says, "Anyone reading the latter Prophets will soon discover and be
frustrated by the lack of a chronological structure. This is not to say
that prophetic books have no structure at all but that they have a different structure from what we have come to expect in Western literature,
and even to some extent in Hebrew narrative."[19]

With regard to identifying the principle by which prophets organized their material, author Gene Tucker expresses a basic fact to bear in
mind: "The prophets, as all other creative individuals, were part of a
tradition, and they used the language and the forms of expression of
their own time and place."[20] Tucker contends that instead of looking
for a prophetic genre per se, we should be "looking for that continuity
which should aid us in understanding each individual."[21] He concludes
that most prophetic literature consists of accounts, prayers, or
speeches. An *account* refers to information the prophet reports—often
in first-person or third-person narrative.[22] According to Tucker, "relatively few *prayers*—words directed by man to God—are found in the
prophetic books."[23] "Most of the units within the prophetic books fall
under the general category of *speeches* in which the prophet himself addresses Israel, a group within Israel, an individual, or a foreign nation."
These speeches are usually "not long formal compositions," but "brief
and poetic utterances."[24] He identifies as *messenger speech* that which is
often introduced by the words "Thus says the LORD."[25] The content of
these speeches includes direct words from God, or *oracles*, and an-
nouncements (or pronouncements) of judgments and promises.[26]

Some prophetic material, such as the book of Ezekiel, is organized chronologically according to when the oracles were delivered. Haggai and Zechariah are also developed chronologically. The compilation of visions and oracles usually reflect a degree of topical arrangement as well, according to Greidanus, oracles of judgment being followed by oracles of salvation.[27]

Both prose and poetry are found in prophetic literature, but Von Rad states, "While there are exceptions, the prophets' own way of speaking is, as a rule, in poetry: that is to say, it is speech characterized by rhythm and parallelism. In contrast, passages in which they are not themselves speakers but are the subjects of report, are in prose."[28]

With regard to poetic forms, various kinds of parallelism were discussed in Chapter 10. An example of *external parallelism* is found in the book of Hosea. According to Dorsey, the content of Hosea is arranged as a chiasm.[29] (See figure 12-2.)

Recognizing the prominent center formed by this inverted parallelism will enable you to organize your sermon to communicate God's message. The rhetorical structures of *internal* parallelism, discussed in Chapter 10, also "reinforce, sharpen and extend the meaning of the passage."[30] Prophetic material is especially rich in metaphors (like Hosea's husband-wife picture of Yahweh and Israel), and deliberate overstatements called *hyperboles* (such as Amos's calling the rich women of Samaria "cows of Bashan" [4:1 NKJV]).

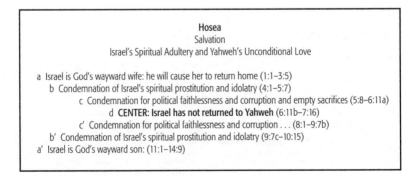

Figure 12.1

Theological Understanding

While paying attention to all of the historical background and literary structure of a prophetic text, don't forget that, as Greidanus puts it, "the primary concern of Scripture is to acquaint us with God, his word, his will, his acts."[31] Although "in prophetic literature, the theo-centric emphasis is so evident that it is hard to ignore," says Greidanus, "sometimes the central thrust is overlooked because preachers concentrate on the person of the prophet."[32] While it is possible to make a prophet such as Jonah the subject of a biographical sermon, this is not the viewpoint of the material itself.

Preachers can also become distracted by absorption with the details of apocalyptic predictions and their fulfillment in the distant future, thus missing the meaning of the prophecy to its immediate audience. Greidanus cautions, "When preaching on Old Testament prophecy, one ought not to move too quickly to the New Testament. For example, while Jesus Christ ultimately fulfills the type of Israel as a suffering servant of Yahweh, in Isaiah 53, to make the prophecy *only* about Him, and not about the nation, misses the point that the people associated with Christ have a servant-role to play.[33] The following diagram represents the servant of Yahweh as described by Delitzsch.[34] (See figure 12-3.)

The theological meaning of a passage is understood by using its various rings of context to answer what the text teaches about the char-

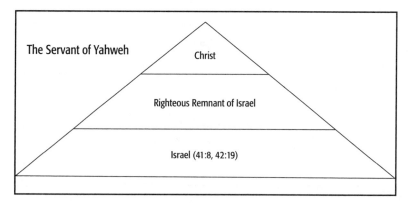

Figure 12.3

acter and work of God. It is the generalization about God that has timeless, universal application. In other words, it is a divine principle.

The theological meaning of Isaiah 6:1–13 might be stated as follows: Yahweh, in contrast to corruptible majesty of human kings, is glorious in absolute holiness and independent existence. The theological meaning of Hosea is that God is intolerant of spiritual adultery and yet faithful in extending His mercy to His undeserving people when they repent.

Preaching Points

Kaiser suggests four improper ways of preaching the prophetic texts of Scripture.[35] Each amounts to some form of taking the text out of context. One is directly applying a person's name or character in a prophetic text to a current social ill (e.g., applying 1 Kings 21 to "the Ahabs of our day"). Another is to select an action in the prophecy and use it as a launchpad to teach something unrelated to the context (e.g., "linking Ahab's aggrandizement with *institutional* systems like socialism, welfarism . . . and the government in general").[36] A third abuse is taking advantage of a statement that serves as a motto or springboard from which to bounce to numerous cross-references. For example, a preacher who sets out to preach against women's liberation might launch his salvos from the conveniently worded statement in 1 Kings 21:7, "I [Jezebel] will give you the vineyard of Naboth the Jezreelite" (NKJV). A fourth way to miss the author's intent is to treat a text's content as a parable (a fictitious story with a spiritual meaning), for example, treating the account of Jezebel's confiscation of Naboth's vineyard as if it were only a story told to *illustrate* the unlawful seizure of private property by the state, when, in fact, it is an historical example of it.

To help you avoid these abuses, Kaiser suggests that your sermon reflect the conditional aspect of prophecy. He states, "Preaching from the prophets can have a great contemporary appeal if we emphasize repentance as the condition for experiencing the favor of God."[37] While this is generally true in principle, be careful not to apply warnings and promises issued to Israel as if they were addressing the Church. Old Testament prophecy was written *for* us but not *to* us.

BOOKS OF PROPHECY

ISAIAH

Historical Background

Isaiah was the son of Amoz, who, according to Jewish tradition, was King Amaziah's brother.[38] If the tradition is true, Isaiah was the first cousin of King Uzziah.[39] Isaiah's wife was called a prophetess in Isaiah 8:3. The name of their son, Maher-shalal-hash-baz, means "Swift is booty, speedy is prey," and is thought to symbolize the imminent plunder of the Northern Kingdom by Assyria, as Isaiah prophesied in chapters 1–39.[40] The name of his second son, Shear-Jasub, means "A remnant shall return," and relates to the deliverance promised in chapters 40–66.[41]

The superscription (verse 1) of the book indicates that Isaiah prophesied mainly in Jerusalem in close connection with kings Ahaz and Hezekiah. He is called "the prince of Old Testament prophets," and "the evangelical prophet," because his writing provides the broadest scope of theology in the Old Testament and emphasizes the good news of Messiah.[42]

The date of writing is about 740–690 BC, after receiving his commission the year King Uzziah died (740 BC; see Isaiah 6). He probably spoke the prophecies of chapters 1–35 during the reigns of Uzziah, Ahaz, and Hezekiah, and the latter chapters (40–66) during the evil reign of Manasseh.[43] According to Freeman:

> The material prosperity of the two kingdoms produced the unusual
> social and moral evils, as well as religious declension, which inevitably
> results under such circumstances. The wealth and luxury which re-
> sulted from their economic prosperity, together with the spirit of opti-

mism created by their military successes, produced an attitude of carnal security in the two capitals, which was also rebuked by Isaiah's contemporary, Amos (760–753).[44]

Literary Analysis

As noted above, Isaiah is arranged with an emphasis on judgment in
the first thirty-nine chapters, and deliverance in the last twenty-seven
chapters. Chapters 36–39 have been described as an *historic interlude*[45]
forming the turning point of the book. With the threat of Assyria
averted in chapters 36–37, the threat of Babylon, predicted in chapters
38–39, was the result of Hezekiah's sinful treaty with them. But beginning with chapter 40, the emphasis changes to the deliverance God will
ultimately bring through His obedient, suffering Servant.

Theological Understanding

The prophet emphasizes both God's overall control of and His willingness to work through chosen servants, including the remnant of Jacob,
but even the Gentile king Cyrus, and ultimately, Messiah. In 7:14, the
prophecy of a virgin's conception was given as a sign to wicked King
Ahaz. In 9:6, the prophecy of Messiah was given both as judgment and
consolation when Israel had rejected God's Word. The events recorded
in chapters 13–23 are fulfilled during Manasseh's rule.

Preaching Points

The reader is confronted with the need to be part of a faithful remnant
that God will deliver. Hezekiah's sin of making a treaty with Babylon
explains the division of the book and was recorded in both Kings and
Chronicles because it was so critical. In a nutshell, one little sin cost the
nation its freedom.

Chapters 40–66 emphasize blessing with the return from captivity.
In this section, Persian king Cyrus is named 150 years in advance.

Called God's "anointed," in Isaiah 45:1 (NKJV), Cyrus is a type of the Messiah. Messiah, though made to suffer, would fulfill the type of Yahweh's servant, which national Israel had failed to be.[46] Of major importance is the fact that chapters 60–66 contain promises to Israel of restoration and blessing that prove that the Jews' rejection of Christ did not result in final rejection of Israel!

JEREMIAH

Historical Background[47]

The name Jeremiah means "whom Yahweh establishes," and fits the story of his prophetic calling and service to the Lord. Jeremiah's prophecies were compiled by an assistant named Baruch (36:4). Jeremiah was a priest, son of Hilkiah, and lived in the priestly town of Anathoth, about three miles north of Jerusalem (1 Chr. 6:60). He was chosen before he was born and received his call when quite young. Because of the threatening times, he was not allowed to marry (16:1–4). Jeremiah was appointed to stand against kings, princes, priests, and false prophets of Judah (1:18). He began his ministry in the thirteenth year of Josiah's reign (626 BC), during the early part of Josiah's reformation and about five years before the books of the Law were found in the temple by Hilkiah. His ministry continued through the eleventh year of Zedekiah, when the Southern Kingdom was taken into captivity in 586 BC.

With Babylon emerging as world empire over Egypt and Assyria, Jeremiah prophesied during the worst period of Jewish history. He lived through at least four national tragedies. First, Josiah's assassination at Megiddo (609 BC) brought national mourning similar to that for U.S. presidents Lincoln and Kennedy. (See Zechariah 12:11.) Second, Nebuchadnezzar's siege of Jerusalem began in 605 BC. Many captives, including Daniel, were taken, and Judah began to be destroyed by the Babylonians, Moabites, and Ammonites (2 Kin. 24:1–4). Third, Jerusalem fell to Nebuchadnezzar in 597. King Jehoiakim, Ezekiel, and many temple treasures were taken captive. Fourth, Jeremiah was imprisoned in 587, and Jerusalem was destroyed one year later. Religiously, Josiah's reforms came too late to spare the Southern Kingdom from rampant idolatry as a result of foreign alliances.

Literary Analysis

Arranged logically, not chronologically, most of Jeremiah is auto-biographical. Chapters 7–10 consist of a series of sermons.[48] Most famous is the *temple sermon*, in which God's destruction of the temple is stated as inevitable. Chapters 11–18 present Jeremiah's *covenant sermon*, which teaches that God keeps His covenant even though the people didn't keep theirs. (Compare 2 Timothy 2:13.)

Theological Understanding

Chapter 31 announces the new covenant, of which believers in Christ today enjoy a foretaste through the blessings of the indwelling Holy Spirit.[49] The provisions of the new covenant include forgiveness of sins, universal knowledge of Yahweh, and universal possession of the Holy Spirit. Jeremiah demonstrated faith in God's promise to restore a remnant to the land by buying a field there.

Preaching Points

Chapter 17 concerns idolatry, Sabbath breaking, and injustice. A society is measured partly by how it treats its dependent members.

Comfort is found in chapters 30–33. When the wicked prosper, as did Babylon, it is only a matter of time until God judges them.

God is faithful to honor those who honor Him. (See 1 Samuel 2:30.) When thirty-five despised Rechabites, whose father prohibited them from drinking wine, sowing seed, planting a vineyard, or building a house, obeyed their father's command, they were praised not for obeying the content of his command but for their steadfastness as an example to Judah. Likewise, the life of Ebed-Melech, an Ethiopian eunuch, was spared when others were slain, because he had rescued Jeremiah. God's faithfulness extends to His people even when they are under judgment, and He will bless those who wait patiently for His restoration.

Jeremiah himself was a type of Christ, who similarly predicted the destruction of Jerusalem by the Romans, and is called the "weeping prophet," foreshadowing Christ as the Man of Sorrows, who contended with the same religious hostility and also wept over Jerusalem (Luke 19:41).

EZEKIEL

Historical Background

The name Ezekiel means "God is strong," or "God strengthens." Though Ezekiel's name is not found elsewhere in Scripture, it is mentioned in 1:3 and 24:24, confirming his authorship of the book. A priest, the son of Buzi, Ezekiel was born about 622 BC and was taken captive with Jehoiachin in 597 BC. For five years he lived among the captives by the River Chebar before he began to prophesy at the age of thirty. Ezekiel was married, but his wife died when the siege of Jerusalem began, about 588 BC (24:1, 15–18). He ministered in his own hometown, where the elders came to hear him (14:1; 20:1, 3). His prophecy was written about 592–570 BC (see 1:2–3, 29:17). As Jeremiah prophesied in Jerusalem, and Daniel at the royal court in Babylon, Ezekiel spoke to the colony of captives.

Literary Analysis

Ezekiel is arranged according to the sequence in which he received and delivered his oracles, or words from the Lord. Following the call of Ezekiel in chapters 1–3, there are warnings for Judah in chapters 4–24 and prophecies against the nations in chapters 25–32. From chapters 32 on, the prophecies turn to Israel's restoration in the land with a glorious new temple.

Theological Understanding

Ezekiel spoke of God's willingness to restore His repentant people and be their Good Shepherd in a new Jerusalem, which would rise again with unparalleled splendor. As a priest, Ezekiel emphasized the new temple and its worship. His refrain is "'Then you shall know that I am the LORD'" (15:7 NKJV). Ezekiel is known for his use of signs and visions. He is the prophet of the "Spirit," whom he mentions more than twenty-four times. In Ezekiel 47:21–23, God's justice is evident in His refusal to dispossess the Gentiles assimilated into the tribes of Israel.

Preaching Points

Ezekiel's role as a watchman illustrates the principle that successful ministry is measured by faithfulness, not results.

DANIEL

Historical Background

The name Daniel means "God is my Judge." The Jews classed the book of Daniel among the *Writings* rather than with the *Prophets* because he was considered a statesman rather than a preacher.[50] Born about 625 BC, presumably of royal blood (see Daniel 1:3–6 and 2 Kings 20:18), he was brought to Babylon in 605 BC with the first deportees. Daniel was a contemporary of Jeremiah, having grown up during the reformation of Josiah. He ministered in the royal court of Babylon while Ezekiel ministered among the captives. Daniel prophesied from 603 (see Daniel 2:1) until about 535 BC (see 10:1), through the Babylonian reign into the Persian era. He served under four kings, including Nebuchadnezzar, Cyrus, and Darius, and was prime minister twice. At least one of the kings under whom Daniel served, Nebuchadnezzar, came to faith in Yahweh. Daniel would have known Zerubbabel and may have influenced Cyrus to allow the return of the captives to Jerusalem.[51]

Literary Analysis

Daniel is naturally divided between the accounts of personal triumphs that show God's control over people (chs. 1–6), and prophecies that demonstrate God's control over history (chs. 7–12). Interestingly, chapters 2 and 7, in which the time frame of Gentile world domination is outlined, were written in Aramaic, the language of the Gentiles.

Theological Understanding

Daniel was written to explain the *times of the Gentiles,* that is, God's sovereign tolerance of Israel's domination by Gentile world rulers.

Preaching Points

As a prophet, Daniel's personal deliverances illustrate God's sovereign control of events. Daniel and his friends were not the only young men taken captive. But they were the only ones who stayed true to God. Kidnapped, and possibly castrated, they were in dire straits from a human perspective. From God's standpoint, they were on assignment in a strategic position to fulfill God's purpose.

HOSEA

Historical Background

The name Hosea is a pronunciation of *Joshua,* which means "salvation" or "deliverance." The book is dated by the reigns of our four southern kings (Uzziah through Hezekiah), 755 to 725 BC. When Hosea prophesied against the Northern Kingdom, Israel was increasingly threatened by Assyria to the east and in political decline after its most prosperous period under Jeroboam II. Morally, the kingdom was approaching its lowest point. A band of priests committed murder (6:9), people were sacrificing their children, and worship had become polluted with prostitution! (See Hosea 4:11–14; 5:3–4; 6:10; 7:3–5; and 2 Kings 14–17.) Freeman notes that "the people confounded the worship of Yahweh with Baal, while calf worship was prevalent on every hand. The nation rejected God and trusted in foreign alliances (8:9–10)."[52]

Literary Analysis

The content of Hosea is arranged as a chiasm.[53] (See figure 12-2.) The prominent center emphasizes Israel's unfaithfulness to Yahweh.

Theological Understanding

Hosea's marriage to a wife he knew would be unfaithful to him symbolized Yahweh's rejection and subsequent restoration of Israel. Yahweh's covenant keeping is not dependent upon the faithfulness of His covenant people, but upon His faithfulness to His oath.

Preaching Points

The prophecy of Hosea illustrates God's unconditional love for those with whom He has entered into a covenant relationship. It also shows the devastating effects of sinning against God with the love of false gods, His intolerance of the idolatrous behavior, but also His commitment to His people.[54]

JOEL

Historical Background

The name Joel means "Yahweh is God." This lends emphasis to the statement in 2:27, "Then you shall know that . . . I am the LORD your God" (NKJV; 3:17 reads similarly). Joel, son of Pethuel (1:1), prophesied in Judah and Jerusalem. His frequent references to priests suggest that he, too, may have been a priest.

That Joel probably wrote around 835 BC is consistent with several facts: First, his attitude, writing style, and language are much like those of Amos rather than the prophets who wrote after the exile. Second, he is much quoted by Amos, Isaiah, and Micah. Third, in Joel, the enemies of Judah are Philistia, Egypt, Greece, and Edom, not Assyria or Babylon. The absence of any mention of a king or princes suggests the time when Josiah was the under-age king overseen by Jehoiada, the high priest.

Politically, the elders and priests seem to be dominating the scene (1:13–14). Internationally, Judah was being pestered by neighboring Tyre, Sidon, and Philistia, who raided the land and sold the people as slaves to Greece. Religiously, the sins were indifference and drunkenness. This suggests that Joel may have prophesied after Jehoiada and Joash had purged the land of Baal worship. If so, he would have been a contemporary of Elisha in Israel.

Literary Analysis

The book is naturally divided into two parts, chapters 1–2 predicting a plague of locusts as a foretaste of judgment, and chapters 3–4 promising future restoration and hope.

Theological Analysis

Joel emphasizes the outpouring of the Holy Spirit in the day of the LORD,[55] to which Peter compares Pentecost (Acts 2:16–20). The book teaches that judgment is to bring repentance (Joel 2:12–13) and that timely repentance brings assurance of restoration (vv. 25–26).

Preaching Points

Although God's judgment in the Day of Yahweh (Joel 1:15) could no more be averted than the devastating scourge of locusts (vv. 3–4), this judgment was to bring repentance. Joel's message was that a remnant would be delivered, including every individual who calls on the name of Yahweh (2:32) Today, as then, timely repentance assures restoration.

Amos

Historical Background

Amos was from the village of Tekoa, six miles south of Bethlehem, where he served not as a priest or trained prophet, but as a manager or owner of large herds of livestock (Amos 1:1; 7:14).[56] The meaning of his name, "burden" or "burdensome," also describes the heavy load of oracles God had given him to deliver against the Northern Kingdom and surrounding nations. Ellisen notes that Amos was the first prophet described as one who employed visions and predicted Israel's doom.[57] Freeman describes the political and moral setting in which Amos wrote:

> The nation's unprecedented prosperity and luxury, together with their sinful indulgences, ease and idleness were indicative of national decay and moral depravity.
>
> Israel's moral corruption is described by the prophet as: carnal security (6:1); scorn of judgment for sin (v. 3a); violence and oppression (v. 3b); indolence (v. 4a); wanton luxury and gluttony (vv. 4b, 6b); idle pleasures (v. 5); drunkenness (v. 6a; cf. 4:1); lack of compassion (v. 6b).[58]

Literary Analysis

Amos consists of three groups of oracles in nine chapters, arranged in a chiasm, with chapter 5 forming the prominent center for emphasis. (See figure 12-4.)[59] According to Tucker, "two basically different genres, superscription and motto, have been combined to serve together as the introduction of the Book of Amos."[60] Thus oracles against Judah, Israel, and the surrounding nations are unified under one title.[61]

Freeman observes:

The second section, chapters 3–6, consists of three sermons against Israel for her sins. The sermons of judgment are easily perceptible since each begins with the prophetic formula "Hear this word" which stands at the head of chapters 3, 4 and 5. Each of the three denunciations is concluded with an emphatic "therefore" (3:11; 4:12; 5:16; 6:7) which announces the nation of judgment to follow.[62]

The third cluster of judgments, in chapters 7–9, include five visions: the locusts (7:1), fire (7:4), a plumb line (7:7), a basket of summer fruit (8:1), and the altar (9:1).[63] The prophecy concludes with a promise of restoration and glory for Israel.

As for its placement in the canon and relation to the other prophecies, Amos's message amplifies Joel 3:16, which says, "The LORD also will roar from Zion" (NKJV).[64] Obadiah, in turn, builds on Amos 9:12, "that they may possess the remnant of Edom" (NKJV).[65] (See figure 12-4.)

Theological Understanding

Amos emphasizes and defends God's righteousness in judging Israel in view of her social injustices, moral degeneracy, and apostasy.[66] (See Amos 9:1 and Hebrews 10:26.) Amos is known for several classical passages, including 3:3 ("Can two walk together, unless they are agreed?" [NKJV]) and 7:7 ("Thus He showed me: Behold, the Lord stood on a

Amos The righteousness of God in Judging Israel	
a General Judgments on the Nations	1–2
b Destruction of Bethel's idolatry	3
c Condemnation of Decadent Women and False Worship	4
d **CENTER Call to repentance and lament**	5
c′ Condemnation of Decadent Men and False Worship	6
b′ Destruction of Bethel's Idolatry	7
a′ Symbolic Judgment on Nations	8–9

Figure 12.4

wall made with a plumb line, with a plumb line in His hand" [NKJV]. Eight times Amos says, "Thus says the LORD."

Preaching Points

Amos teaches that (1) there is a universal morality (chs. 1–2), (2) God delights to share His plans with His servants (3:7), and (3) insincere worship is an insult to God (4:4–5).

OBADIAH

Historical Background

Obadiah, a common Old Testament name, means "servant" or "worshipper of Yahweh." Nothing is known of the prophet Obadiah or the date of his writing. Because its content is the doom of Edom (descendants of Esau), it is believed to have been written in a time when Israel was oppressed by the Edomites. Several factors favor a date around 845 BC. First, the order in which Obadiah was placed in the Old Testament books suggests an early date of writing. It is also possible that Amos and Jeremiah quote Obadiah. It was during the reign of Jehoram and the ministry of Elisha that Edom revolted against her subjection to Judah and became her permanent enemy (2 Kin. 8:22). Arabia and Philistia raided Judah (2 Chr. 21:16–17). If the early date is accurate, Obadiah is (a) the first writing prophet and (b) the first to introduce the day of the LORD.[67]

Literary Analysis

According to Dorsey, "The structure of the Book of Obadiah serves to reinforce its message. The balancing of the portrayal of proud Edom's future fall (units a and b) with the declaration of fallen Israel's future rise and ascendancy over Edom (units b' and a') highlights the theme that Yahweh will right the wrongs that Edom has committed against Israel by reversing the fortunes of the two nations.[68] See figure 12-5.[69]

Obadiah
Servant of Yahweh
God Knows How to Humble the Proud

a Proud Edom will be defeated (1–4)
   b Edom will be completely plundered (5–7)
      c Edom's population will be slaughtered (8–11)
         d **CENTER: Indictment of Edom** (12–14)
      c' Edom and the nations will be judged (15–16)
   b' Israel will regain what it has lost (17–18)
a' Humbled Israel will be victorious (19–21)

Figure 12.5

Theological Understanding

The prophecy of Obadiah pictures the history of Israel. Edom's judgment typifies God's attitude toward all pride and His determination to destroy the enemies of Israel. Edom was built on the cliffs of Mount Seir, which was impregnable to men but vulnerable to God, who humbles the proud (cp. Obadiah 1:3–4, Amos 9:2). (See figure 12-6.)

Preaching Points

Obadiah was written to proclaim the doom of Edom for her pride, hatred, and mistreatment of the Jews, and the eventual glory of Israel (1:10, 15). The Israelites were commanded not to hate (show less esteem for) the Edomite, "for he is your brother," said Deuteronomy 23:7 (NKJV). Yet the Edomites' hatred of Jews became a symbol for all hostility against Jews. Herod, an Edomite, mistreated Christ. By AD 70, there was only a remnant of Edomites. God promised to tear down any attempts they make to rebuild (Mal. 1:3–4). In Obadiah 1:12–14, where God expresses displeasure with Edom for their maltreatment of their "brother Jacob" (v. 10 NKJV), the words translated "Do not" (NASB) suggest "You should not [have]," as expressed variously in the King James, New King James, and New International Versions.

Several lessons can be drawn from Obadiah. First, the struggle between Jacob and Esau began in the womb. It was fueled by favoritism

Figure 12.6

based on man's choice rather than God's choice. Second, pride is dangerous. As Proverbs 16:18 (NKJV) states, "Pride *goes* before destruction, and a haughty spirit before a fall."

JONAH

Historical Background

The name Jonah means "dove" and fits his mission as a messenger of peace. Jonah was the son of Amittai, from Gath Hepher in Zebulon (modern el-Meshad), four miles north of Nazareth. He was recognized as a prophet during the early reign of Jeroboam II, 793–753 (2 Kin. 14:23–25). If he wrote the book of Jonah later in life, a probable date is around 765 BC.[70]

Critics have rejected the historicity of Jonah because of their disbelief in the miraculous events recorded in the book. But conservative scholars believe in the historical nature of the book for at least three reasons. First, nothing in the book contradicts historical reality or suggests that the literature is a parable, legend, or allegory. Second, Jewish tradition has always regarded the book to be historically factual. Third, Christ referred to Jonah's being swallowed by the fish and Nineveh's repentance as historical fact[71] (Matt. 12:40–41; Luke 11:29–30).

Politically, Israel lived in constant fear of flash attacks from Syria and Assyria. Assyria was on the rise as a world power. Its capital city, Nineveh, had a population of 600,000 inside an outer wall some sixty miles in circumference. As the first foreign missionary, Jonah addresses the Northern Kingdom with the account of his mission to Nineveh, its archenemy.

Literary Analysis

On the structure of Jonah, Dorsey writes:

> Most people reading the Book of Jonah recognize that the book is composed of a series of episodes. There appear to be seven, each marked off for the audience by shifts in setting, genre and characters. These seven episodes are arranged in chronological order. But a secondary parallel arrangement scheme is also relatively conspicuous. The first three episodes (Jonah's first commission, his first experience with the pagans, and his first prayer) are matched by the second three episodes (his second commission, his second experience with the pagans, and his second prayer) in an a-b-c, a'-b'-c' configuration. Following these six episodes is Yahweh's lesson for Jonah, which concludes the book. The seven episodes of the book thus exhibit a parallel arrangement: a-b-c, a'-b'-c', d.[72] (See figure 12-7.)[73]

Theological Understanding

The book is an object lesson to show Israel God's concern for the lost in contrast to Israel's lack of compassion. Thus, while Obadiah empha-

Jonah
Dove

God's Concern for the Lost in Contrast to Israel's Lack of Concern

a Jonah's commissioning and flight (1:1–3)
　　b Jonah and the pagan sailors (1:4–16)
　　　　c Jonah's prayer (1:17–2:10)
a' Jonah's recommissioning and obedience (3:1–3a)
　　b' Jonah and the pagan Ninevites (3:3b–10)
　　　　c' Jonah's prayer (4:1–4)
d Yahweh's lesson for Jonah (4:5–11)

Figure 12.7

sizes God's vengeance, Jonah demonstrates His mercy. Jonah further serves to typify the death, burial, and resurrection of Jesus Christ from the dead in that both were in the place of death for parts of three days and nights (Matt. 12:40).

Preaching Points

Jonah teaches that convenient circumstances often attend the way of disobedience to God (1:3). People should willingly obey God, as do His other creatures, the storm, the great fish, the shade plant, and the worm. The story demonstrates once for all that missions is obedience in extending *God's* compassion for the lost, not one's own compassion. But He can work through a person in spite of himself. And God honors the genuine repentance of anybody. Nevertheless, God is as interested in the work He is doing *in* His servants as in what He is doing *through* them.

MICAH

Historical Background [74]

The name Micah means "Who is like Yahweh?" (see Micah 7:18). Micah was from Moresheth, twenty miles southwest of Jerusalem, on the border with Philistia. He is the only minor prophet whose writing ministry addressed both kingdoms, though he mainly prophesied to the Southern Kingdom of Judah. Hezekiah's memory of Micah's prophecy spared Jeremiah's life (Jer. 26:18). Micah prophesied around 725 BC, during the reigns of Jotham, Ahaz, and Hezekiah. To understand the nature of Micah's ministry, it is beneficial to compare and contrast him with his contemporary, Isaiah:

- Both warn of invasion.
- Both speak of Judah's deliverance from Assyria.
- Both speak of Judah's captivity in Babylon.
- Both foresee millennial blessings after regathering and national repentance.
- Both speak of Messiah, Isaiah foretelling His virgin conception, and Micah, His place of birth (5:2).

Differences between Isaiah and Micah include the facts that, whereas Isaiah spoke to the upper class, Micah wrote to the common people, with the touch of a "country preacher" (like Amos).[75] Isaiah concerned himself with the political life of Judah, but Micah wrote of religious and social issues. Finally, while Isaiah's prophecy includes surrounding nations, Micah's is confined to the people of Israel and Judah.

Literary Analysis

According to Dorsey, "Careful analysis of the book's layout reveals a seven-part symmetric arrangement . . . that is artful and at the same time highlights Micah's central themes, particularly (1) Israel's social sins, (2) the moral failure of its leadership, and (3) the ultimate establishment of Yahweh's own benevolent kingship over the land."[76]
(See figure 12-8.)[77]

Theological Understanding

In 6:8, the prophecy asks what Yahweh requires of a person. The answer emphasizes heart righteousness. Another classic question in 7:18,

Micah
Who Is Like Yahweh?

Both Kingdoms Will Be Judged and Delivered by Messiah

a Coming defeat and destruction (1:1–16)
    b Corruption of the people (2:1–13)
        c Corruption of the leaders (3:1–12)
            d **CENTER: Glorious Future Restoration**
        c′ Corruption of leaders (6:1–16)
    b′ Corruption of the people (7:1–7)
a′ Future reversal of defeat and destruction (7:8–20)

Figure 12.8

"Who *is* a God like You?" emphasizes Yahweh as a pardoning God like no other.

Preaching Points

Micah's purpose was to warn of approaching judgment on both kingdoms for their idolatry and injustice, and the eventual deliverance Messiah would bring. He prophesied Bethlehem as the birthplace of Jesus, seven hundred years before Caesar's decree for David's descendants to register there, resulting in its fulfillment (5:2; see Luke 2:1–4). When preaching the book of Micah, emphasize not only the precise fulfillment of predictive prophecies, but also the theological understanding stated under the previous heading.

NAHUM

Historical Background

The name Nahum means "consolation" and corresponds with the prophet's ministry. The town of Capernaum in Galilee is named *caper* ("town of") *naum* (Nahum), and is thought to have been named for the prophet who made his home there. Nahum may have escaped the northern captivity and fled to Judah, where he prophesied against Nineveh for the purpose of consoling Judah at a time of temporary reform.

Though there are two possible dates of writing, Nahum most likely wrote during the reign of Hezekiah, around 700 BC. Nahum prophesied against the same city of Nineveh that had repented seventy-five years earlier in response to Jonah's reluctant mission. The city was later destroyed by Nebopolassar in 612 BC. In keeping with the meaning of his name, Nahum writes as if the action was taking place at the time of writing, yet doesn't mention a single sin of Judah!

Literary Analysis

Because 1:2–10 reflect an incomplete acrostic, various theories seek to explain the composition of Nahum. John Paterson notes a suggestion that the book is a *prophetic liturgy* but doubts that it was written by the same person at the same time.[78] Dorsey, on the other hand, finds seven units arranged in a chiasm around a center that emphasizes "lament over fall of Nineveh, the lions' den" (2:11–13). He suggests that Nahum's use of a 4 + 3 pattern echoes a Hebrew dirge, "reinforcing the sense of eulogy over Nineveh's demise."[79] So viewed, the "opening vision is an effective attention-getting device, and it also introduces the issue of the cause of Nineveh's fall, to which Nahum will subsequently return." (See figure 12-9.)

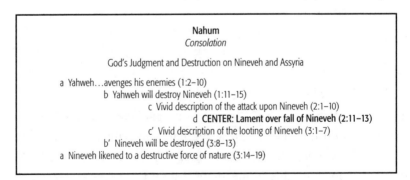

Nahum
Consolation

God's Judgment and Destruction on Nineveh and Assyria

a   Yahweh…avenges his enemies (1:2–10)
   b   Yahweh will destroy Nineveh (1:11–15)
      c   Vivid description of the attack upon Nineveh (2:1–10)
         d   **CENTER: Lament over fall of Nineveh (2:11–13)**
      c′   Vivid description of the looting of Nineveh (3:1–7)
   b′   Nineveh will be destroyed (3:8–13)
a   Nineveh likened to a destructive force of nature (3:14–19)

Figure 12.9

Theological Understanding

According to Nahum, Nineveh's destruction shows that delayed judgment of sin is not to be mistaken as divine approval of it. God's justice and omnipotence made His eventual obliteration of Nineveh inevitable. At the same time, God is intimately acquainted with those who seek refuge in Him (1:7). In chapter 2 the destruction and exile of Nineveh as the result of a flood is seen as divine judgment. Chapter 3 emphasizes Nineveh's cruelty by the absence of anyone to grieve her annihilation.

Preaching Points

As a basis for never taking their own revenge, believers need to know that they can count on God to take vengeance against His enemies (Rom. 12:19). They are not to think that God is slow about His promise (see 2 Peter 3:8–9).

HABAKKUK

Historical Background

According to Wilkinson and Boa, "The only explicit time reference in Habakkuk is to the Babylonian invasion as an imminent event (1:6; 2:1; 3:16)."[80] "The most likely date for the book is in the early part of Jehoiakim's reign (609–597 B.C.). Jehoiakim was a godless king who led the nation down the path of destruction (cf. 2 Kin. 23:34–25:5; Jer. 22:17)."[81] The name Habakkuk, meaning "to embrace," fits well his engagement of Yahweh in prayer with questions (1:2; 3:2). "He is concerned over the unchecked iniquity and widespread corruption in Judah which seems to go unpunished."[82] When he learns of Yahweh's intention to use the Babylonians to punish Judah, the prophet questions God's use of an executioner more wicked than Judah.

Literary Analysis

"The linear layout of the Book of Habakkuk, beginning with the negative and closing with the positive, suggests that the purpose of the book is to take the audience from confusion and despair to clarification and hope."[83] As Dorsey views it, the book is centered around 2:1–5, where the righteous are said to live by faith. (See figure 12-10.)[84]

Theological Understanding

Speaking to God about men sets Habakkuk apart from most of the prophets who spoke to people about God. The book shows the destruction of the enemies of the Southern Kingdom as the inevitable result of the holiness of God (1:13).

Preaching Points

Habakkuk's statement in 2:4, "But the just shall live by his faith" (NKJV) articulates a principle of physical survival in the coming Babylonian onslaught. The apostle Paul applied it to New Testament believers. (See Hebrews 10:38 and Paul's reference's to Habakkuk 2:4 in Romans 1:17 and Galatians 3:11). In Habakkuk 2:20, the prophet's reference to Yahweh in His holy temple calls for silence before Him as Judge. The great declaration of Habakkuk in 3:17–18, "Though the fig tree may not

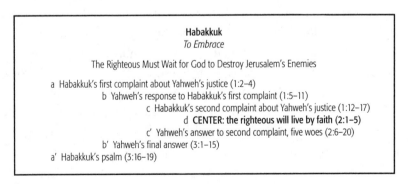

Habakkuk
To Embrace

The Righteous Must Wait for God to Destroy Jerusalem's Enemies

a Habakkuk's first complaint about Yahweh's justice (1:2–4)
　　b Yahweh's response to Habakkuk's first complaint (1:5–11)
　　　　c Habakkuk's second complaint about Yahweh's justice (1:12–17)
　　　　　　d CENTER: the righteous will live by faith (2:1–5)
　　　　c′ Yahweh's answer to second complaint, five woes (2:6–20)
　　b′ Yahweh's final answer (3:1–15)
a′ Habakkuk's psalm (3:16–19)

Figure 12.10

blossom . . . Yet I will rejoice in the LORD," emphasizes the fact that God Himself, not His material blessings, is the proper motivation for worship.

ZEPHANIAH

Historical Background

The great-great-grandson of King Hezekiah, Zephaniah was a distant cousin to King Josiah and probably had an influential role in Josiah's reforms (see Zephaniah 1:1). He is the only minor prophet with royal blood. He wrote around 625 BC.[85] The name Zephaniah means "Yahweh hides" and harmonizes with the statement in Zephaniah 2:3: "Seek the LORD, all you meek of the earth, who have upheld His justice. Seek righteousness, seek humility. It may be that you will be hidden in the day of the LORD's anger" (NKJV). At the time, Josiah's reforms are not connecting with the people. Jerusalem was deserving of judgment for rampant idolatry and adultery in which even the prophets and priests participated despite various punishments (3:7). Zephaniah wrote the most detailed genealogy in the Minor Prophets.

Literary Analysis

According to Dorsey, Zephaniah is usually divided into seven major units that exhibit a symmetrical pattern:

> The announcement of coming judgment in the first unit is balanced by the announcement of coming restoration in the final unit. The condemnation of Jerusalem's princes and wealthy people in the second unit is balanced by the condemnation of the wicked princes and leaders of Jerusalem in the next-to-last unit. The description of the terrible day of Yahweh in the third unit is balanced by the depiction of Yahweh's judgment against the nations in the third-to-last unit. The book's fourth, central unit, is Zephaniah's call to repentance.[86]

(See figure 12-11.)[87]

Theological Understanding

In 1:14, the prophet warns, "The great day of the LORD is near; it is near and hastens quickly" (NKJV). In 2:3, he urges the people to "seek the LORD." God always provides a way of escape from judgment if it is taken in time (Zeph. 2:1–3; 1 Cor. 10:13).

Preaching Points

Zephaniah encourages righteous living in view of God's judgment of the world and restoration of Judah. This book teaches that failure to maintain separation from the world leads to spiritual compromise and judgment (1:4–5; see 2 Kings 17:33). If a community is not missionary *minded*, it soon becomes a mission *field* (see Zephaniah 1:6).

HAGGAI

Historical Background

The name Haggai means "festive" and fits the prophet Haggai's promotion of building the temple and resuming the observances of Israel's

---

Zephaniah
Yahweh Hides

The Day of the LORD and the Judgment of Judah

a Coming judgment upon the wicked of Jerusalem (1:2–6)
  b Coming judgment of corrupt leaders (1:7–13)
    c Yahweh's judgment of all nations: (1:14–18)
      d **CENTER: Call to repentance (2:1–3)**
    c' Yahweh's judgment of all nations (2:4–15)
  b' Coming judgment of corrupt political leaders (3:1–7)
a' Coming restoration of Jerusalem and its fortunes (3:8–20)

Figure 12.11

feasts (Ezra 5:1, 6:14). Haggai is the first of three "restoration prophets," meaning that he, along with Zechariah and Malachi, ministered in Judah to those who returned from the Babylonian captivity. Haggai may have been born in Babylon and also been one of the first to return to Jerusalem with Zerubbabel. His prophecy is the most precisely dated, written in the second year of Darius's reign, between September 1 and December 24, 520 BC.

Zerubbabel was governor of Judah, and Joshua was the high priest. After nearly fifty thousand captives returned to Jerusalem from Babylon, the rebuilding of Jerusalem and the temple was halted by a decree by Artaxerxes (Cambyses) in 529 BC (Ezra 4:21). The people then began to accept the impossibility of observing temple worship and feasts and turned their attention to personal interests. At the urging of Haggai and Zechariah, however, the people resumed the work, which then won the support of Darius I.[88]

Having returned just seventy years after the first deportation (606), the temple was completed in 516 BC, just seventy years after its destruction in 586. Thus the prophecy of seventy years of captivity was fulfilled from two points of view.

Literary Analysis

This book is a collection of five dated messages, together with a narrative episode, which are arranged in chronological order. (See figure 12-12.)

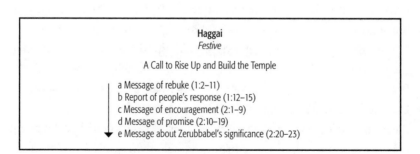

Haggai
Festive

A Call to Rise Up and Build the Temple

a Message of rebuke (1:2–11)
b Report of people's response (1:12–15)
c Message of encouragement (2:1–9)
d Message of promise (2:10–19)
e Message about Zerubbabel's significance (2:20–23)

Figure 12.12

Theological Understanding

Haggai teaches that there is no true prosperity out of God's will (1:6). Also, while contamination from sin comes by touch, the same is not true of holiness (2:13).

Preaching Points

Haggai's purpose in writing was to convict the people of neglecting the temple reconstruction in favor of their own interests, and to indicate that such neglect was the cause of their drought and economic depression. His resounding refrain is "Consider your ways" (1:5, 7 NKJV), because the people were saying, "The time has not come, the time that the LORD's house should be built" (1:2 NKJV). In 2:9, the people were to be motivated by God's promise that "the glory of [the] latter temple [would] be greater than the former" (NKJV). A preachable principle from 1:2 is that temptation to spiritual neglect is ever present.

MALACHI

Historical Background[89]

The name Malachi means "my messenger" and aptly describes the prophet himself, the priest of 2:7, the messenger of the covenant, and Messiah's forerunner in 3:1. Malachi was the last prophet before John the Baptist, whose coming he predicted. The burden of Malachi's revelation is so prominent in the book that the prophet himself remains in the shadows. Malachi wrote about 430 BC, after the temple had been rebuilt. Enough time had elapsed for worship to have become a formal, empty routine. Politically, the nation was under Artaxerxes I, the Persian king who allowed Ezra and Nehemiah to return to Jerusalem. Despite experiencing several revivals, including that of Ezra in 445 BC, the returned exiles were demoralized, certain that God had let them down by not ushering in the promised age of Messiah. They proudly and bitterly questioned God's love and commitment to justice.

Literary Analysis

Dorsey regards the arrangement of Malachi as effective in highlighting the book's main points:[90]

> The first and last units in the symmetry (positions of prominence) underscore the point that Yahweh rewards faithfulness and punishes wickedness . . . the two fold condemnation of the priests and people for cheating and robbing Yahweh with their inferior offerings, in the second and next-to-last units, draws attention to this theme. And the double coverage of the key role of the Levites in renewal, in the third and third-to-last units, highlights their importance in Israel's religious life. In addition, the placement of the call to repentance at the center of the book's symmetric arrangement emphasizes the key role that repentance must play if the people are to receive God's forgiveness and blessing.[91]

(See figure 12-13.)[92]

Theological Understanding

Malachi emphasizes the greatness of God in writing to correct the haughty attitude of his readers. Though he assures them of Yahweh's love, he also presents Yahweh's case against His people for their sinful attitudes and formal religion.

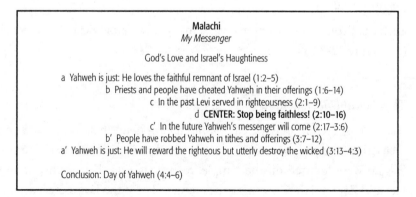

Figure 12.13

Preaching Points

According to Malachi, the pride and arrogance of the people's lifeless, formal worship was the result of their failure to love God in response to His love for them.

ZECHARIAH

Historical Background

Zechariah was one of the prophet-priests. His name means "Yahweh remembers," and complements the prophet's emphasis on Israel's future restoration and cleansing through the redeeming work of the Messiah. Zechariah was the son of Berechiah, a priest whose name means "Yahweh blesses." The name of his grandfather, Iddo, means "the appointed time." Thus, in order, the three names mean: "the appointed time . . . Yahweh blesses . . . Yahweh remembers.[93] Zechariah began to prophesy about two months after Haggai began, so the setting was the same. Chapters 1–8 were written between October 520 and November 518. Chapters 9–14 were written probably after 480 BC. According to Jewish tradition, Zechariah was slain in the sanctuary. His death was recalled by Jesus in Matthew 23:35 and Luke 11:51.

Literary Analysis

Zechariah consists of seven messages that are chronologically arranged. (See figure 12-14.)

Theological Understanding

Like Isaiah, Zechariah is a great *messianic* prophet. Whereas Daniel was focused on the prophecy of Gentile world domination, Zechariah and Haggai were focused on the temple, reemphasizing the prophecies of Joel and Zephaniah concerning the coming day of the LORD. Zechariah correlates all of the previous prophecies about the restoration of Israel in the land under the Messiah—including Messiah's work in both His first and second comings.

Preaching Points

Zechariah's prophecy is distinguished by the prevalence of visions, information about angels, and a detailed picture of Israel's future. He wrote to encourage those who had returned from exile to Babylon to trust in Yahweh, by painting a meticulous portrait of future restoration. In interpreting the eight night visions, understand that they form a chiasm emphasizing the power of the Holy Spirit. (See figure 12-14.)[94]

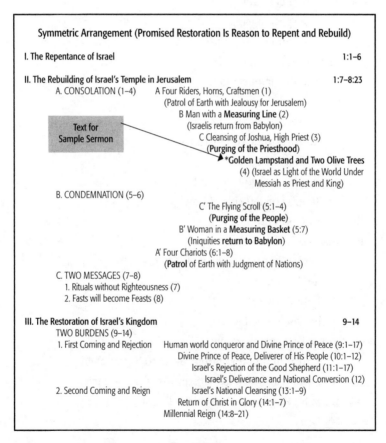

Figure 12.14

* This paragraph on the Golden Lampstand and two Olive trees is the text for the sample sermon that follows.

SAMPLE SERMON

GOD'S WORK, GOD'S POWER
ZECHARIAH 4:1–7
MAN DOES GOD'S WORK / ONLY BY GOD'S POWER

I. Revelation of God's Power   1–3

   A. The Prophet's Arousal

      1. by a speaking angel (1a)

      2. as if from sleep (1b)

   B. The Prophet's Description

      1. a golden lampstand (2)

         a. a bowl on top

         b. seven lamps

         c. forty-nine supply tubes

      2. two olive trees (3)

         a. one on right side of bowl

         b. one on left side of bowl

II. Request by God's Prophet   4–5

III. Reassurance for God's People   6–7

   A. Yahweh's Word to Zerubbabel (6)

      1. not by might

      2. not by power

      3. by God's Spirit

   B. Yahweh's Warning to Obstacles (7a)

      1. a great mountain of opposition to be flattened

      2. Zerubbabel to personally finish what he starts

   C. Yahweh's People to celebrate God's grace (7b)

Summary and Conclusion

Unlike modern preachers, who proclaim the message of established texts, the prophets received messages directly from God. But like today's ministers of the Word, they were ordinary people whom God chose and called to bear His message of judgment and hope in keeping with the stipulations of His covenants and His ability to predict the future in detail with absolute accuracy. The fulfillments of some of their predictions have already been recorded. Others are yet to be fulfilled. All were taken seriously by the New Testament writers and must not be dismissed, or spiritualized, by preachers today.

Among the challenges facing interpreters of prophetic literature are figurative language, understanding of the geopolitical situation, chronological gaps, and the various ways that predictions can be fulfilled. But the prophetic word is understandable and relevant. Even when the fulfillment of predictions would not occur in the lifetimes of those who heard them, they served to motivate repentance and provide the hope needed at the time.

In preparing to preach from Old Testament prophecy, give special consideration to the historical background, literary analysis, theological understanding, and preaching points of the particular book and passage under study. Familiarity with the basic message of each book will give you a framework within which to develop the message of a given text.

Isaiah urged his readers in the Southern Kingdom of Judah to trust in Yahweh rather than turn to other nations for help, because He promised to restore Judah after judging her.

Jeremiah's unpopular message that it was too late to ward off the Babylonian captivity by repentance is balanced by the promise of the new covenant, in whose spiritual blessings the Church is already participating.

As a priest, **Ezekiel** emphasized the new temple and its worship. While focused on the departure and return of God's glory, Ezekiel's role as a watchman illustrates the principle that successful ministry is measured by faithfulness, not results.

As a prophet, **Daniel's** personal deliverances illustrate God's sovereign control of events. The content of his prophecy demonstrates Yahweh's control over the domination of Israel and the world by Gentile nations.

Hosea's marriage to an unfaithful wife symbolized Yahweh's rejection and subsequent restoration of Israel. Yahweh's covenant keeping does not depend upon the faithfulness of His covenant people, but upon His faithfulness to His oath.

Joel compares the coming Day of Yahweh to the unstoppable onslaught of locusts. But he also predicts the future outpouring of the Holy Spirit, which was partially fulfilled at Pentecost. The book teaches that judgment is meant to inspire repentance, and that timely repentance brings assurance of restoration.

Amos vindicates the righteousness of God in judging His people. His prophecy emphasizes the existence of a moral plumb line by which God holds His people accountable.

Obadiah's prediction of the doom of Edom demonstrates God's ability to humble the proud.

Jonah records the phenomenal repentance of Nineveh in response to God's compassion and mercy for the lost, qualities not shared by the prophet or his people.

According to **Micah**, the ultimate cure for social injustice and idolatry is the coming of a deliverer "who is like Yahweh." This deliverer would be born in Bethlehem.

The book of **Nahum** reveals that Nineveh's destruction shows that delayed judgment of sin is not to be mistaken as divine approval of it.

Habakkuk teaches that the holy justice of Yahweh makes His punishment of Israel's enemies inevitable, and that He is to be worshipped for who He is, not what He bestows.

Zephaniah encourages righteous living in view of God's judgment of the world and restoration of Judah.

Haggai shows that neglecting the ministries of the Spirit can result in the loss of material blessings and bring God's discipline, which in turn leads to the blessings of a restored relationship.

Zechariah wrote to encourage those who had returned from the Babylonian exile to trust in Yahweh. He does this by giving a detailed picture of future restoration.

Malachi emphasized that the pride and arrogance of the people's lifeless, formal worship was the result of their failure to love God in response to His love for them.

A sample sermon from Zechariah shows how to develop a paragraph from a minor prophet for a modern audience. People today, as in the time of Zechariah, cannot do God's work without the power that He supplies by His Holy Spirit, portrayed in the vision of the candelabra supplied with oil from living olive trees.

Discussion Questions

1. Compare and contrast the ancient prophet and the modern preacher. Describe ways in which they are similar as well as different.
2. If the prophets primarily monitored the attitudes and behavior of the descendants of Jacob in relation to the old (Mosaic) covenant, by what rationale can their messages be applied to people living in the church age of grace?
3. What is meant by near and far fulfillments of prophecy, and what is one example?
4. What is meant by the "already-not-yet" tension in relation to prophecy?
5. In what sense was Joel 2:28 fulfilled at Pentecost?
6. How does the meaning of Isaiah 6:1 depend on an understanding of the historical background?
7. According to Von Rad, did the prophets usually speak in prose or poetry?
8. In preaching Old Testament prophecy, why is it important not to move too quickly to New Testament applications or fulfillment?

9. Identify and describe two or three improper ways of preaching prophetic texts of Scripture, as suggested by Walter Kaiser.

10. What sin, committed by King Hezekiah, explains the division of the book of Isaiah?

11. Which of the minor prophets predicted the birthplace of Christ?

12. Which book of the Major Prophets is known for his use of signs and visions?

13. In view of Daniel's emphasis upon the *times of the Gentiles*, what is significant about the language of chapters 2 and 7?

14. Whose prophecy taught that Yahweh's covenant keeping is not dependent upon the faithfulness of His covenant people, but upon His faithfulness to His oath?

15. Which of the minor prophets emphasizes the outpouring of the Holy Spirit in the day of the LORD?

16. Whose prophecy is distinguished by the prevalence of visions and a detailed picture of Israel's future?

17. How does a knowledge of the geography of Petra help a person understand the message of Obadiah?

18. Why do conservative scholars insist on the historicity of Jonah?

19. Describe the state of Jewish society at the time that Jeremiah wrote.

20. What attributes of God does the book of Nahum emphasize?

21. Whose prophecy emphasizes the fact that God Himself, not His material blessings, is the proper motivation for worship?

22. Who is the first of three restoration prophets?

23. Describe the times and message of Malachi.

24. Which of the minor prophets repeats, "Thus says the LORD," eight times?

25. Find two strengths and two weaknesses in the sample sermon on Zechariah 4:1–7.

CHAPTER 13

Preaching the Gospels and Acts

THROUGHOUT this book, much has been made of bridge building as an analogy for effective expository communication of God's Word. When your sermon is developed from one of the four Gospels or from the book of Acts, your very text is a like a plank from the bridge God has provided between the Old Testament prophecy and New Testament instruction for the Church. Using such *bridge material* to construct a sermon that communicates God's message will require you to think as a first-century Jew would in biblical times. In preaching the Gospels, you must put yourself in the place of those living under the Law in the presence of the promised Messiah, who spoke of the Church in the future. In preaching the Acts, you must be mindful of the transitional nature of the book. To treat the Gospels or Acts as other than the bridge they form is to confuse things that are, in reality, separate, or to deny the connection of things that are, in reality, related.

References to the kingdom must be carefully understood in terms of which aspect is being discussed. You must view historical facts through the lens of the writer's literary composition in order to discern his theological intent. Having discussed the Hebrew Scriptures in the last four chapters, a consideration of the Gospels and Acts must now begin with an introduction to the New Testament.

INTRODUCTION TO THE NEW TESTAMENT

The words *New Testament* refer to the new covenant ratified by the blood of the Messiah and put into effect by His death. (See Matthew 26:28; Mark 14:24; Luke 22:20; 1 Corinthians 11:25; and 2 Corinthians 3:6.) It is *new* in relation to the Mosaic covenant, which it replaced as the basis for fellowship with God (Jer. 31:31; Heb. 8:8, 13; 9:15–17; 12:24). Entrance into the new covenant with God by faith in His Son Jesus the Messiah has both redemptive and kingdom implications (1 Pet. 2:7–9). Twenty-seven books written in *Koine* (common) Greek, from about AD 45 to 95, are called the *New Testament*. Each book of the New Testament makes its own distinct contribution to the revelation of God's plan to reclaim lost sinners and reestablish His rule on the earth (see Genesis 3:15; 12:1–3; 2 Samuel 7:8–17; Jeremiah 31:31; Hebrews 2:5–9). Regarding their recognition as Scripture, authors Wilkinson and Boa say,

> The New Testament books were separately circulated and gradually collected together. Their inspiration and apostolic authority guaranteed them a place in the canon of Scripture as they were set apart from other writings in the early church. As these books were copied and distributed throughout the Roman Empire, they were eventually placed in a standard order (more logical than chronological).[1]

The New Testament is Christ-centered. It includes the historical books of Matthew, Mark, Luke, John, and Acts; the Epistles of Paul, Peter, John, James, Jude, and Hebrews; and the Revelation. The historical books concern the person and work of Christ as the fulfillment of Old Testament prophecy and the foundation of the church, as He continues His work through His Spirit-filled people. The Epistles instruct, correct, and encourage churches and individual believers in Christ to realize their freedom not only from the *penalty* of sin (Rom. 8:1, Titus 2:11), but also from the *power* of sin (Rom. 6–7; Titus 2:12) as they look forward to freedom from the very *presence* of sin at Christ's coming for His Church (Titus 2:13). The Revelation was written to promote the worship of Christ in view of His exaltation in glory, His authority in the church, and His coming again to finally destroy His enemies, redeem the faithful remnant of Israel, and reign on the earth.

In preaching the New Testament, keep in mind both its continuity with the Hebrew Scriptures and its revelation of the church as distinct from Israel.

THE GOSPELS

"Gospel"

The word *gospel* is from the Old English *godspel*,[2] translated from the Greek εὐαγγέλιον (euaggelion), which means "good news." Eventually the term was applied to the titles of the first four books of the New Testament because they are about Jesus, the subject of the Bible's good news.[3] In 1 Corinthians 15:1–5, the apostle Paul writes:

> Moreover, brethren, I declare to you *the gospel* which I preached to you, which also you received and in which you stand, by which also you are saved, if you hold fast that word which I preached to you—unless you believed in vain. For I delivered to you first of all that which I also received: that *Christ died for our sins according to the Scriptures, and that He was buried, and that He rose again the third day according to the Scriptures,* and that He was seen by Cephas, then by the twelve. [emphasis added] (NKJV)

Genre

The writers of the four accounts of the life of Christ—Matthew, Mark, Luke and John—have been called *evangelists*, though their writings addressed those who were already regenerate, not the lost. The four Gospels teach theology primarily through biographical narrative, sermons, sayings, parables, and apocalyptic literature.[4] Ryken, in explaining the importance of discovering the genre of a Gospel passage, says, "It usually provides the best descriptive framework for organizing a given unit. And sometimes the correct interpretation of a unit depends on identifying the precise genre of the passage."[5] According to Greidanus, the essential, distinguishing characteristic of the Gospel genre is information intended for declaration, to elicit faith in the listener/reader.[6] "Thus the gospel genre may be characterized as proclamation of the good news of the kingdom of God that has come in the person of Jesus Christ," he concludes.[7] Genre classification "sets the expectations of interpreters and determines the questions they ask of the text . . . Thus genre designation is an initial step in interpretation."[8] So, before considering the questions to ask of the text, briefly examine their basic proclamation.

Kerygma

The *kerygma* refers to the common content of the apostles' proclamations of the gospel. According to *Baker's Dictionary of Theology*, the common apostolic gospel included: "(1) a historical proclamation of the death, resurrection and exaltation of Jesus, set forth as the fulfillment of prophecy and involving man's responsibility; (2) a theological evaluation of the person of Jesus as both Lord and Christ; (3) a summons to repent and receive the forgiveness of sins."[9] In addition, Jesus' baptism by John, His miracles, and His sayings are mentioned often in the Gospels. The irreducible minimum of the content of the gospel, which Paul says he received from the Lord's disciples, is the deity, death, and resurrection of Christ (1 Cor. 15: 3–4).[10]

Not all have appreciated the kerygmatic character of the gospel genre as its distinguishing mark. When reduced to mere history or simple literature, the Gospels have failed to win critical acclaim.

Criticism

The Gospels have been subjected to scholarly examination on two levels, *higher criticism* and *textual* (or *lower*) *criticism*. Higher criticism concerns such issues as authorship, date, literary structure, origins, and content of Scripture. When used with caution, higher criticism can be helpful in interpreting Scripture.[11] When it subjects the Bible to the limitations of human understanding and subjective judgment of un-believers, however, higher criticism undermines faith in the historicity, authenticity, and authority of the Gospel accounts. Textual criticism, a necessary step of exegesis, attempts to establish the original text by comparing manuscript evidence. *Source criticism*, as a subset of higher criticism, contends with what is called the *synoptic problem*.[12] It seeks to answer two questions: (1) Why does a text in Matthew, Mark, or Luke appear to be duplicated in one or all of the others? and (2) Why are there differences in accounts of the same events?[13]

The *documentary hypothesis* assumes that Mark wrote first, fol-lowed by Matthew, Luke, and then John. It leads *redaction critics* (those who would *edit* the text) to assume that Matthew altered Mark's origi-nal, and that Luke used Matthew, plus an "L" document.[14] A conserva-tive view of Scripture rejects this assumption, based on the fact that all of the church fathers believed that Matthew was written first. They even quoted from it as authority for the Church. Further, Paul treated Luke's writing as being on par with Scripture, and taught that the Gospels were written with the authority of the apostles, who were given to the Church (Eph. 2:20; 4:11). Mark was informed by Peter. Luke was informed by Paul.

The apostle John himself indicates that the Gospel writers *selected* historical material from all that *could* have been said, then arranged and adapted it according to the particular purposes for which they wrote.[15] This explains both the similarities and differences in the con-tent of the Gospels. By no means must this lead to the conclusion reached by some critics, that the historical data was manufactured to support preconceived doctrines.

"Ultimately, the issue of reliability is a matter of faith in God's word,"[16] says Greidanus. Such faith is reasonable, because the facts pre-sented in the Gospels are reasonable and as well-established as any in history.[17] The historical accuracy of the Gospels is crucial to their purpose and was easily checked by those who first heard the kerygma. The historicity of the Gospels is believable on the bases that they were (a) written relatively soon after the events they record, (b) based on eyewitness accounts, (c) accepted by the apostles, and (d) ensured to have been accurately recorded by the Holy Spirit's superintendence.[18] Greidanus, summarizing how the Gospels were compiled and why they can be trusted, says, "They relate actual historical events to proclaim their good news. Even though they write their accounts in a special, kerygmatic style, the evidence for their historicity is sufficient for approaching the Gospels with confidence in their reliability."[19]

Yet to reduce the Gospels to history alone misses the purpose for which the writers chose, organized, and adapted their material. In completing truth sheets for sermons on the Gospels, you must ask yourself: "Why did the author relate this incident? Why did he include it in his Gospel? What did he intend to convey? What kind of response did he expect from his hearers?"[20]

Preaching the Gospels

Text Selection

Preaching texts (or *pericopes*) are recognized by observing the writer's use of rhetorical devices discussed earlier in this book, including repetition, inclusion, parallelism, and chiasm. The goal is to identify a literary unit. Whether a paragraph or a longer portion of Scripture, the text must convey a complete thought. Using a *synopsis* (meaning "see together") makes it is easy to compare and contrast the content of a given text with parallel accounts in other Gospels. This is helpful in discovering the particular purpose of the writer of the text under study.[21] But such analyses should never seek to import into the text something the writer deliberately left out.

When the material of the Gospels is rearranged and collated into a single chronological account, the product is sometimes called a *harmony* of the Gospels.[22] While harmonies aid in understanding where the events of a given text fit into a chronology of Jesus' life, remember that this is *not* how the Spirit of God directed any of the Gospel writers to present the material. The goal of the biblical text is not to produce a movielike, comprehensive mental image of the life and times of Christ as much as it is to emphasize one aspect at a time. But examining a Gospel text in light of parallel accounts or harmonies will answer the questions that will help you determine the writer's intent.

The Right Questions

Greidanus poses excellent questions that can be easily incorporated into the truth sheet–making process:

> Is [the preaching text] found in other Gospels? If not, does its inclusion in this Gospel . . . point to the author's interests and purposes? If it is found in another Gospel but in a different context, does the different arrangement of the preaching text shed light on the purpose of its author? Has the author "added or omitted anything? What verbal changes has he made? Are they merely stylistic? Are they more substantive?[23]

Using this approach with Matthew 8:18–27 provides a good example of its value. The emphasis of this passage is on *discipleship*, but Matthew contains intervening stories that Mark and Luke do not include. (See Mark 4:35–41 and Luke 8:22–25.) Why? How does adding these accounts serve Matthew's theological purpose? What purpose is served by Matthew's use of the words "Master," "Teacher," and "Lord"? The story of the wind and waves was given, following Matthew's accent on discipleship, to emphasize complete submission to the lordship of Christ. It stressed the worthiness of Jesus to be followed despite the surprising difficulty in doing so.

Interpretation

Gospel texts are properly interpreted in light of the life situations of both the characters *in* the story and the writer *of* the story. To accomplish this, you must carefully consider the historical background, literary analysis, and theological understanding of the passages.

HISTORICAL BACKGROUND

"Historical interpretation seeks to understand the text as it was understood by its original audience."[24] It provides "the only objective point of control against subjective and arbitrary interpretations."[25]

Literary Analysis

Literary analysis is concerned with how the text is structured to convey its message. How does the text fit into the argument of the book? If it is narrative, the scene, characters, dialogue, and plot must be understood. If the text is apocalyptic, or discourse, be alert to such figures of speech as repetition, inclusion, chiasm, parallelism, double entendre, irony, and the use of the passive voice in reference to the unseen hand of God.[26]

Theological Analysis

Since the Gospels are about the person and work of Jesus Christ, every passage should be interpreted in light of what the writer intended to say about Him. While many other colorful characters in the Gospels might be the subjects of a good biographical sermon, they are simply the supporting cast. If they are allowed to outshine the Star, more than the writer's intent is missed! For example, the parable of the good Samaritan (Luke 10:30–37), given by Jesus and recorded by Luke, was not written merely to promote human compassion on the horizontal plane. Jesus, who had earlier been derisively called a "Samaritan" (John 8:48), is the one who, unlike the uncompassionate priest and Levite (religious leaders of Israel), demonstrated the Father's concern. The parable is about who Jesus is, not just about being a good neighbor.

MATTHEW

Historical Background

"Matthew is the gospel written by a Jew to Jews about a Jew," say Wilkinson and Boa. "Matthew is the writer, his countrymen are the readers and Jesus Christ is the subject."[27] The writer, identified in the title, *Kata Matthaion* ("according to Matthew"), was also called Levi (Mark 2:14; Luke 5:27). Matthew's authorship and its early date of writing (before the fall of Jerusalem in AD 70) have been rejected by scholars who assume the priority of Mark's Gospel and the impossibility of Jesus predicting Jerusalem's ruin.[28] However, Guthrie concludes that "there is no conclusive reason for rejecting the strong external testimony regarding the authorship of Matthew.[29] Whether or not he originally wrote his Gospel (or notes for it) in Aramaic, as some have suggested, the Greek edition was most likely written in Antioch, Syria, between AD 58 and 68.[30] The son of Alphaeus, Matthew bore the social stigma of a publican, collecting taxes in Capernaum for the Roman government (Mark 2:14).

Literary Analysis

Greidanus identifies five teaching sections, all having to do with the kingdom of heaven:

1. The law of the kingdom (5–7)
2. Preachers of the kingdom (10:5–42)
3. Parables about the kingdom (13:1–52)
4. Life in the kingdom (18:1–35)
5. The consummation of the kingdom (24:1–25:46)[31]

The chiastic structure of Matthew places the parables of the kingdom of chapter 13 at the prominent center for emphasis.[32] (See figure 13-1.[33])

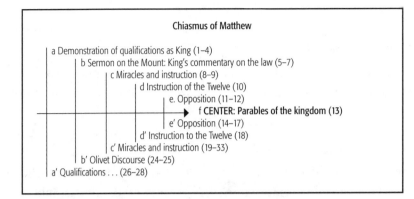

Figure 13.1

Theological Understanding

Matthew wrote to present Jesus as Israel's messianic King, beginning with David's son. He also explains to the followers of Jesus the postponement of His rule on David's throne as a result of His rejection by Israel's leaders, and describes the nature of His present rule in the hearts of those who receive Him.

There is a great emphasis on Gentiles in Matthew. He mentions the magi (2:1), Christ's church (16:18), church discipline (18), and "all the nations" (28:19 NKJV).[34] Tenney explains this frequent emphasis: "Matthew's Gospel is admirably suited to a church which was still closely related to Judaism, though becoming increasingly independent of it. It breathes the atmosphere of Messianism, yet it has a message for 'all the world.'"[35] He adds, "The Theme of the Gospel of Matthew is announced by its opening words: 'The book of the generation of Jesus Christ, the son of David, the son of Abraham' (Matt. 1:1)."[36] Even in the genealogy designed to show Jesus' descent from King David, Gentiles are prominent. Boaz, for example, was the son of a Canaanite prostitute, and Ruth was a descendant of Moab. The mention of Tamar and Bathsheba is also important to Matthew's purpose, as was his omission of the names of certain bad kings. Jesus is the King of Gentiles as well as of Jews, but entering and participating in His future Davidic (millennial) kingdom is conditional. It is the reward for the faithfulness of those who have received, by faith, the free gift of deliverance from the consequences of their sins.

MARK

Historical Background

Many writers believe that Mark is the earliest of the synoptic Gospels.[37] But whether or not it is the earliest, it is surely the shortest and simplest. The writer is John Mark, Barnabas's cousin (Col. 4:10), whose mother, Mary, opened her home in Jerusalem as a meeting place for believers (Acts 12:12). Based on Peter's greeting to Mark as "my son," in 1 Peter 5:13 (NKJV), Peter may have been the one to lead Mark to faith in Christ. If Mark was the "certain young man" in Gethsemane who followed Jesus wearing only a linen cloth (Mark 14:51–52 NKJV), then he was an eyewitness of some events about which he wrote. But it is generally assumed that Peter was the source of Mark's information, lending the Gospel his apostolic authority.[38]

Mark accompanied Saul and Barnabas on their missionary journeys but left early to return home to Jerusalem (Acts 13:13). Because Paul then refused to allow Mark to join him and Barnabas on their second journey, Barnabas took Mark and went to Cyprus, while Paul took Silas to Syria and Cilicia (Acts 15:36–41). About twelve years later, though, Mark was with Paul in his first imprisonment (Col. 4:10, Philem. 24). At the end of his life, Paul sent for Mark, commending him for his beneficial service (2 Tim. 4:11).

Mark's authorship of the Gospel that bears his name was accepted by the early church without exception. He is thought to have written before AD 70, since Jesus' prediction of the temple's destruction is treated as unfulfilled in Mark 13:2. The most likely date is sometime between AD 55 and 65.[39]

Early tradition indicates that Mark was written to a Roman audience, from Rome.[40] This would explain why he did not include the genealogy of Christ, references to the Law, Jewish customs, fulfilled prophecies, and other items that would not have been meaningful to Gentiles. He also explained several Aramaic words, the language of the Jews, and sometimes substituted Latin words in their place.[41]

Literary Analysis

Mark emphasizes the service and suffering of Jesus, punctuating his quick-moving, action-packed account with the word translated "immediately" some forty times.[42] His style is described as "*a popular literary style,* even though it does not rise to the literary standards of the highly educated."[43] The theme of Mark is stated in Mark 10:45: "For even the Son of Man did not come to be served, but to serve, and to give His life a ransom for many" (NKJV). Chapters 1–8 primarily concern Jesus' miracles in Galilee, with chapters 9–16 emphasizing His teaching on His way to the cross. Aune notes that "only once is a story-unit presented out of chronological sequence as a 'flashback': the story of John the Baptist's fate in Mark 6:17–29."[44]

At Caesarea Philippi, after Peter's great confession of faith, in answer to Jesus' question, "Who do you say that I am?" Jesus began to teach them that He would be betrayed into the hands of men and killed, but after three days He would rise again (9:31). The turning point is Jesus' transfiguration, recorded in the middle of the Gospel (9:1–8). Greidanus credits M. Philip Scott for the chiastic structure of Mark, adapted in figure 13-2.[45]

Theological Understanding

Mark's Gospel begins and ends with declarations of Jesus' deity. As noted in the literary analysis, the turning point begins with 8:27, where Jesus asks, "Who do men say that I am?" (NKJV). This leads to the Father's pronouncement at the Transfiguration, "This is My beloved Son. Hear Him!" (9:7 NKJV). Having demonstrated that He was the Son of God by His miracles (chs. 1–8), and having had that demonstration

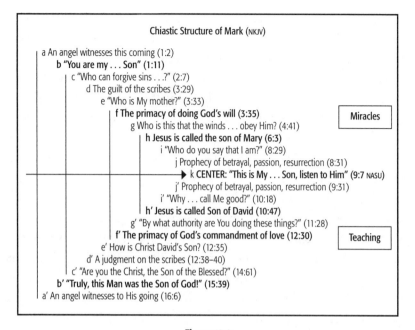

Figure 13.2

confirmed by the Father's declaration, Jesus teaches His way to the cross, where a *Roman* centurion would state the truth that Mark wrote his Gospel to establish: "Truly this Man was the Son of God!"

Jesus commanded people not to tell about His miracles for several possible reasons. First, He was not seeking publicity. Whenever it came, it made it more difficult for the people. Second, the timing of when He disseminated Church truth was critical. Also, when demons were testifying, their witness had a negative effect.

LUKE/ACTS

Historical Background

According to the opening statements of the third Gospel, its writer was not an eyewitness to the accounts he records. He was, instead, a well-

educated historian who certifies the accuracy of his documentation of
others' eyewitness accounts. His purpose was to establish the historical
facts on which the faith of a prominent young man named Theophilus
("Friend of God") might rest.[46] His orderly presentation of the evidence makes a convincing argument that the historical Jesus of oral
tradition is indeed the Son of the only true God, the Savior of all men,
and worthy of universal worship.

Luke's authorship of the third Gospel is deduced on the basis of two
connections: First, the "we sections" of the book of Acts identify its author as Luke the physician (Col. 4:10–14), who accompanied Paul on
some of His missionary journeys.[47] Second, the introduction to the
book of Acts indicates that it is part two of a two-part series.[48] Acts 1
takes up where Luke 24 leaves off. Writing to the same Theophilus, the
writer of Acts refers to the "former account," which almost certainly is
the third Gospel: "The former account I made, O Theophilus, of all
that Jesus began both to do and teach, until the day in which He was
taken up, after He through the Holy Spirit had given commandments
to the apostles whom He had chosen, to whom He also presented
Himself alive after His suffering by many infallible proofs, being seen
by them during forty days and speaking of the things pertaining to the
kingdom of God" (1:1–3 NKJV).

If Luke is the writer of both Luke and Acts, as has been traditionally
understood, then the date of his writing can be fixed at about AD 60
based on three reasonable assumptions. First, enough time must have
elapsed between the resurrection of Christ and the writing of Luke's
Gospel for the eyewitness accounts of others to have circulated and for
Theophilus, a Gentile, to have been attracted to Christianity.[49] Second,
the Gospel was written prior to Acts. Third, the fall of Jerusalem, which
Jesus prophesied in Luke 19:41–44 and 21:20–24, was not mentioned as
fulfilled. (It took place in AD 70.)[50]

If these assumptions are correct, then Luke is unique among the
Gospels in predicting the fall of Jerusalem,[51] and its author is the only
Gentile writer of a New Testament book.[52] His Gospel must be read as

the logically ordered work of a Gentile writing to a Gentile in order to provide a basis for his faith in Christ. Its profitability for teaching in the Church is, therefore, certified.

Literary Analysis

The "orderly account" Luke presents is arranged more logically than chronologically. The organizing principle is, in the words of Tenney, "the central concept of Jesus as a member of humanity who lived the perfect and representative life of the Son of man through the power of the Holy Spirit."[53] Luke's thesis is stated in 19:9–10: "And Jesus said to [Zacchaeus], 'Today salvation has come to this house, because he also is a son of Abraham; for the Son of Man has come to seek and to save that which was lost'" (NKJV). It suited this purpose of Luke to expand on Jesus' journey from Galilee to Jerusalem, to which Luke devotes the bulk of his writing (9:51–19:27).[54] As literature, Luke is highly praised for its artistic beauty and masterful use of the Greek language.[55]

Thompson follows Charles Talbert in observing in Luke-Acts "a definite chain of authority, with each successor imitating his predecessor: the sequence moves 'from the faithful among the Jewish people, symbolized by John the Baptist . . . , to Jesus, and from Jesus to the Twelve.' Then from the Twelve, who were sent out by Jesus, the chain of authority passes to Paul and the churches which he founds. Those who belong to that chain are given in Luke an exemplar character."[56]

Greidanus views the structure of both Luke and Acts as consisting of three major parts marked by changes in geography. This may be illustrated as follows. (See figure 13-3.[57])

Theological Understanding

The Gospel of Luke emphasizes the humanity of Christ; His birth; infancy; and compassion for women, children, and the disenfranchised of society. Referring to the Holy Spirit more times than Matthew and

Luke	Acts
What Jesus began to do and teach:	What Jesus continues to do through the people He indwells:
Introduction: Preparation for the Ministry of Jesus (1:5–2:52)	
I. The Ministry in **Galilee** (4:14–9:50)	I. The Ministry in **Jerusalem** (1:12–7:60)
II. The Ministry between **Galilee and Jerusalem** (9:51–19:27)	II. The Ministry in **Judea and Samaria** (8)
III. The Ministry in **Jerusalem** (19:28–23:56)	III. The Ministry to the **End of the Earth** (9:1–28:31)
Conclusion: Consummation of the Ministry of Jesus (24:1–53)	

Figure 13.3

Mark combined,[58] Luke provides the theological basis for how Gentiles, as well as Jews, can participate in the blessings of Abraham. Luke's own skills as an historian, physician, and writer of literature serve to emphasize the nobility of humanity when redeemed by the Son of Man. As Luke follows the movement of Christianity from Galilee to Jerusalem, and from Jerusalem to Rome and the end of the earth, he also stresses the personal progress of discipleship. Leon Morris states, "It is probably significant that Luke speaks a number of times of Christianity as 'the way' (A9:2; 19:9, 23; 22:4; 24:14, 22); sometimes also he refers to it as 'the way of the Lord' (A18:25) and 'the way of God' (A18:26) . . . It draws attention to Christianity as a whole way of life, not simply as a means of satisfying religious impulses."[59]

The book of Acts was written in Rome, probably before AD 64, since there is no mention of the Neronian persecution that occurred after the burning of Rome. Luke maintains his focus on the Spirit in which Christ continues His work through the people He indwells (see Acts 6:10).[60] Acts is a history of the birth and building of the church between AD 33 and 62. When interpreting the book, pay careful attention to where a given passage fits into the context of transition from the temporary to the permanent indwelling of the Spirit, and from a focus upon Israel to the equality of Gentiles as full participants in the church. Learn to ask and answer the question, "How was God working at this juncture?"

Not everything *described* in the book of Acts is necessarily *prescribed* for the Church to follow. A helpful guideline is given in the saying, "Apostolic practice points to apostolic principle." This means that the apostles did what they did for a reason. The reader must seek to understand the underlying principle that gave rise to a particular practice rather than dismiss the record of what was done as a mere description of a bygone era. For example, does Luke's record of the casting of lots to determine Judas's replacement (Acts 1:26) simply *describe* what the apostles did? Or does it *prescribe* the way in which matters must be decided today? The underlying theology is that the sovereign God met the apostles' need for direction in a decision that they were biblically responsible to make. The principle of prayerful obedience to Scripture is never outdated and can be honored without necessarily following the Jewish *custom* of casting lots. (Proverbs 16:33 states, "The lot is cast into the lap, but its every decision is from the LORD" [NKJV].) On the other hand, consider the apostolic practice of baptizing new believers. The fact that every baptism recorded in Acts is *described* as having been done immediately upon the person's confession of faith in Jesus Christ indicates an urgency to obey that is dishonored by unnecessary delays.

JOHN

Historical Background

The fourth Gospel was written by John the apostle after the synoptics, between AD 70 and 90. John was evidently a Galilean Jew who may have been one of the disciples of John the Baptist until he was called to follow Jesus at the outset of His public ministry (1:19–51).[61] After the ascension of Jesus, John is mentioned as a pillar of the church at Jerusalem (Gal. 2:9). According to tradition, he later went to Ephesus. He wrote his three epistles and Revelation while in exile on the island of Patmos (Rev. 1:9). John's purpose in writing his Gospel was to supplement the synoptic Gospels with a different emphasis.

Literary Analysis

In contrast to Matthew, Mark, and Luke, John structures his Gospel to emphasize the descent of the Word, who became flesh, and His ascent to glory[62] after having manifested the life that is in the Father, died for the sins of the world, and risen from the grave.

In the first part of John's Gospel, chapters 2–12, John records seven miracles that Christ performed publicly. Each one pointed to His deity as the Master of His creation and was associated with a discourse in which Jesus identified Himself with Yahweh (The I AM . . . Who Is). He says, for example, "I Am the Bread of life," "I Am the Light of the world," etc. In this way, John lays the basis for his reader's saving faith in Christ.

In chapters 13–20, John records the words and events that prepare Christ's people to live the abundant and fruitful lives of joy and unity in the Holy Spirit until He comes to take them home.

The following diagram represents another way to trace the development of John's Gospel. (See figure 13-4.[63])

Theological Understanding

John 1:1–18 emphasizes the deity of Christ. He is the uncreated Creator, yet He is distinct from the Father, whom He came into the world to *exegete*! The living Word became flesh to bring light, life, and love to all who receive Him by faith. The statement of John's purpose in 20:30–31 is usually misunderstood as a message of how sinners may be

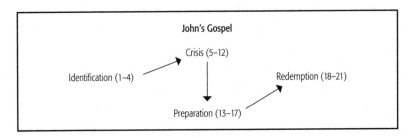

Figure 13.4

justified.[64] But John writes about eternal life—not in terms of how to get it, but how to be enjoying it now[65]: "And truly Jesus did many other signs in the presence of His disciples, which are not written in this book; but these are written that you may believe that Jesus is the Christ, the Son of God, and that believing you may have life in His name" (NKJV). John writes so that those of His readers who have, in fact, believed that Jesus is the Christ, the Son of God, might, "by [continually] believing," "keep on having [the quality of] life [that is] in His name."[66]

SAMPLE SERMON #1

WHY THE SON DESCENDED
JOHN 3:10–16
THE SON OF GOD CAME DOWN
TO LIFT MEN UP TO GLORY

I. The Witness of Heavenly Things (10–13)
  A. The Understanding of Spiritual Truth Is a Personal Responsibility (10)
  B. The Witness of Spiritual Truth Must Be Received (11)
  C. Christ is the Revealer of Heavenly Things (12–13)
II. The Gift of Eternal Life (14–16)
  A. Pictured in the Serpent
    1. Lifted up (14)
    2. Looked to with faith in God (15)
  B. Provided in the Son (16)
    1. Because the Father Loved the World
    2. Because the Son is Uniquely Begotten

SAMPLE SERMON #2

THE IMPORTANCE
OF OFFICIAL SERVICE IN THE CHURCH
ACTS 6:1–7
OFFICIAL SERVICE REFLECTS THE LORD
AND ADVANCES HIS MISSION

I. The Mission of the Church (1, 7)
  A. The Spread of God's Word (7)
  B. Increasing the Number of Disciples (1, 7)
  C. Obedience to the Faith (7)
II. The Management of the Church (1–6)
  A. Leaders Attack Problems (1b–3)
  B. Leaders Apply Principles (2)
  C. Leaders Establish Priorities (3–4)
  D. Leaders Delegate Power (3, 6)
  E. Congregations Participate (5–6)

SAMPLE SERMON #3

ACTION OR APATHY:
WHAT WE NEED TO LEARN FROM THE GOOD SAMARITAN STORY
LUKE 10:25–37 (NKJV)

Introduction:

Why I like this parable:

It concerns a lawyer, which, having been a law professor for a number of years, has interest for me in his method of argument and perspective.

It reveals how a person approaches the task of interpreting the Bible, whether in a normal sense or a spiritualizing sense.

It reveals the heart of humans, who are able to find so many ways to avoid the plain requirements of Christ.

It demonstrates that the task of the Christian does not end with traditional religious service but goes beyond our words to actions, similar to God.

I. Good Questions Can Have Bad Motives (v. 25)

Luke 10:25: And behold, a certain lawyer stood up and tested Him, saying, "Teacher, what shall I do to inherit eternal life?"

  A. The Example of the Lawyer

  "What must I do to inherit eternal life?" *Seeking to test Him.*

  B. Other Examples in the Bible

    1. "Why does He still find fault? For who has resisted His will?" (Rom. 9:19) *Seeking to place blame on God for man's condemnation.*

    2. "Why have you made me like this?" (Rom. 9:20) *Seeking to blame God for our own sinfulness.*

    3. "Why did I not die at birth? Why did I not perish when I came from the womb?" (Job 3:11) *Questioning God's goodness and direction in his life.*

  C. How and Why Have We Questioned God?

    1. Why did God let this happen to me?

    2. Why did God take my loved one?

    3. What are our motives?

II. Good Answers Can Have Inadequate Application (vv. 26–28)

Luke 10:26: He said to him, "What is written in the law? What is your reading of it?"

Luke 10:27: So he answered and said, "'You shall love the LORD your God with all your heart, with all your soul, with all your strength, and with all your mind,' and 'your neighbor as yourself.'"

Luke 10:28: And He said to him, "You have answered rightly; do this and you will live."

  A. The Lawyer's Response: A Great and Theologically Correct Answer

    1. This lawyer had his understanding of Old Testament theology down pat.

    2. He did not understand, however, the implications that arose from his theology.

B. How Do We Respond?

  1. Sometimes we fail to do what is right because we do not have our theology straight: this is ignorance.

    a. Not being baptized

  2. Sometimes we fail to do what is right in spite of having good theology: this is slothfulness, if not rebellion.

    a. Failing to see God's control in our lives when we have a flat tire

III. People Sometimes Have Improper Responses to God's Direction (v. 29)

Luke 10:29: But he, wanting to justify himself, said to Jesus, "And who is my neighbor?"

  A. The lawyer, after being confronted with his own understanding of truth, sought to alleviate his guilt.

  B. Our attempts:

    1. There's not enough time in the day.

    2. Somebody else will do it.

    3. Be warmed, and be fed.

    4. It won't make a difference.

    5. I would, but . . .

IV. God's Teaching on Fulfilling the Second Table of the Law: Love Your Neighbor as Yourself (vv. 30–35)

Luke 10:30: Then Jesus answered and said: "A certain man went down from Jerusalem to Jericho, and fell among thieves, who stripped him of his clothing, wounded him, and departed, leaving him half dead."

Luke 10:31: "Now by chance a certain priest came down that road. And when he saw him, he passed by on the other side."

Luke 10:32: "Likewise a Levite, when he arrived at the place, came and looked, and passed by on the other side."

Luke 10:33: "But a certain Samaritan, as he journeyed, came where he was. And when he saw him, he had compassion."

Luke 10:34: "So he went to him and bandaged his wounds, pouring on oil and wine; and he set him on his own animal, brought him to an inn, and took care of him."

Luke 10:35: "On the next day, when he departed, he took out two
denarii, gave them to the innkeeper, and said to him, 'Take care of him;
and whatever more you spend, when I come again, I will repay you.'"

A. How Not to Interpret a Parable, Particularly This One

"A **certain man** went down from Jerusalem to Jericho"; **Adam himself** is meant;

Jerusalem is the heavenly city of peace, from whose **blessedness Adam** fell;

Jericho means the moon, and signifies **our mortality,** because it is born, waxes, wanes, and dies.

Thieves are the **devil and his angels.**

"Who **stripped him,**" namely, of his immortality; and beat him, by persuading him to sin; and left him **half-dead,** because **insofar as man can understand and know God, he lives,** but **insofar as he is wasted and oppressed by sin, he is dead;** he is therefore called half-dead.

The **priest and Levite** who saw him and passed by, signify the **priesthood** and **ministry of the Old Testament,** which could profit nothing for salvation.

Samaritan means "Guardian," and therefore the Lord Himself is signified by this name.

The **binding** of the wounds is the **restraint of sin.**

Oil is the **comfort of good hope; wind** the **exhortation to work with fervent spirit.**

The **beast is the flesh in which He deigned to come** to us.

The **being set upon the beast is belief in the incarnation** of Christ.

The **inn** is the **Church,** where travelers returning to their heavenly country are refreshed after pilgrimage.

The **morrow is after the resurrection** of the Lord.

The **two pence** are either the **precepts of love or the promise of this life and of that which is to come.**

The **innkeeper** is the **apostle (Paul).** The supererogatory payment is either his counsel of celibacy or the fact that he worked with his own hands, lest he should be a burden to any of the weaker brethren when the Gospel was new, though it was lawful for him to live by the Gospel.

B. Possible Responses to the Wounded Man in the Story

   1. The wounded man made a bad decision: this road was treacherous.

      a. Do we hold that against him and use this as an excuse not to help?

      b. We are not talking about professional beggars who are making lots of money and simply too lazy to hold down a job. The beggars helped by Christ and the apostles were truly in need (usually blind or lame), with no one to help them.

   2. Should We Respond as the Priest and Levite? (people highly conscious of their religious responsibilities)

      a. Religiosity without compassion

      Too busy in doing God's work (the first table of the Law) to obey God's commands toward fellow humans (the second table of the Law): Are these really in conflict?

        This really is an illustration of what Christ sought to teach to the leaders and people throughout His whole ministry.

        1) The leaders especially saw themselves exempt from their need to have compassion on others and help them, because they were trying to center on God's detailed laws on purity, to the exclusion of helping one's neighbor.

        2) Christ's example:

        a) Sabbath versus caring for infirm

        b) Sabbath versus disciples being hungry

        c) Paying all the monetary requirements of the Law, but leaving responsibilities of other things (mercy, compassion, justice) undone

   3. The Samaritan interrupted his busy life to help someone who probably despised him.

      a. Samaritans and Jews did not get along well.

      b. The Samaritan not only saw and expressed concern but went the extra mile.

V. The Question Is Turned Around: From "Who is *my* neighbor?" to "Who is neighbor?" (v. 36)

Luke 10:36: "So which of these three do you think was neighbor to him who fell among the thieves?"

    A. You can find your neighbor when you are willing to be neighborly.

    B. You don't have to scour the forests to find a neighbor, but simply respond to those whom God reveals along your daily journey.

VI. Christ's command is short but unequivocal: Go and do the same as the good Samaritan (v. 37)

Luke 10:37: And he said, "He who showed mercy on him." Then Jesus said to him, "Go and do likewise."*

*Scriptures in this outline are from the New King James Version.

SUMMARY AND CONCLUSION

The Gospels and Acts are themselves *bridge material* in their role of linking the old and new covenants. Be careful to treat these historical books of the New Testament as connecting links that have continuity, while at the same time recognizing the things that must be kept separate. The Gospels teach theology through a variety of literary genre, but are distinguished by their contribution to what was proclaimed by the early church, the *kerygma*. If reduced either to mere historical accounts or stories, the Gospels are misunderstood. In reality they are historical stories, which must be understood by appreciating why their factual information was selected and arranged the way it was by a particular author.

When selecting sermon texts, be sure they express a *complete* thought, or literary unit. Comparing a text with parallel accounts in other Gospels will help you determine the given author's intent. Harmonies of the Gospels can also help establish a temporal framework within which to view a given text. Proper interpretation of a text depends on asking the right questions when completing a *truth sheet* as part of the Whiting Method. Put yourself in the life situations of both the characters of the narrative and the writer. To do this, you must carefully consider the historical background, literary analysis, and theological understanding of the writer and those about whom he is writing.

To preach from the Gospel of Matthew, pay attention to the kingdom emphasis of the book. How does the text fit into Matthew's purpose of explaining to Gentiles as well as Jews the nature of the kingdom during this time in which the King is not reigning on David's throne? The chiastic structure of the book focuses attention on the parables, which address this very issue of the inter-Advent kingdom.

Mark must be appreciated for its reflection of Peter's influence of the content, and the Roman audience which he addresses. It also has a chiastic structure centered in the Father's declaration of Jesus' sonship at the Transfiguration. The record of miracles leading up to this point demonstrates His supernatural character as God. The record of His teaching on the way to the cross emphasizes His servanthood.

Luke and Acts are best understood as two parts of a whole. The emphasis of his Gospel upon the perfect humanity of Christ suited his Greek audience (represented by Theophilus), who needed to know that Israel's Messiah also deserved the worship of Gentiles, since He "came to seek and to save that which was lost" (Luke 19:9–10 NKJV). Luke's Gospel and the book of Acts are both structured with three major parts marked by changes in geography. The concept of movement toward the goal of mature discipleship also seems to be reflected by Luke's emphasis upon Christianity as "the way." Acts traces the birth and building of the Church as the ongoing work of Christ, by His indwelling Holy Spirit. Always interpret texts in Acts in view of what God is doing at the time. The book is transitional, and what is *described* (practices) is not always *prescribed*, so wisely seek the *abiding principles* which underlay the apostles' *practices*.

John's Gospel, written later than the synoptics, is concerned with who Jesus is as the living Word who became flesh, to demonstrate the truth, life, and love of the Father. John emphasizes the enjoyment of eternal life through the continual exercise of faith in Jesus, whose worthiness of such trust was attested by the seven signs John records, and by the statements and discourses in which Jesus claims equality with Yahweh.

DISCUSSION QUESTIONS

1. Explain, in your own words, what is meant by *New Testament*. In relation to what is it new, and how so?
2. Explain the difference between the *gospel* and the *Gospels*.
3. What is meant by the following terms?
   a. Kerygma
   b. Higher criticism
   c. Textual criticism
   d. Source criticism
   e. Synoptic problem
4. What is the objective when selecting a text from the Gospels or Acts for preaching? (What determines its parameters?)
5. What are some of the interpretive questions that are particularly important to ask of Gospel texts?
6. Whose life situation must the preacher seek to understand when interpreting the Gospels, and why?
7. Describe the concerns of each of the following:
   a. Historical background
   b. Literary analysis
   c. Theological understanding
8. Explain the value of recognizing chiasmus in the structure of Matthew and Mark.

9. Give several reasons for concluding Lukan authorship of the third Gospel and Acts.

10. Describe several ways in which the Gospel of John differs from the synoptics.

11. Find two commendable qualities and two negative observations about each of the sample sermons provided in this chapter.

CHAPTER 14

Preaching the Epistles

INTRODUCTION

COMPARED to the gulf that separates the modern Bible student from the world of the Old Testament, the Gospels, and Acts, the New Testament Epistles are closer to home. They would seem to call for a verbal bridge that is simpler for the preacher to construct. The Epistles consist of letters sent to churches and individual Christians with whom we find it easier to identify. In many cases their recipients were Gentiles—sometimes even Europeans! Their contents address many of the same problems with which we are still dealing in this church age. If the recipients of John's first epistle were living in the "last hour" (1 John 2:18 NKJV), we are more so. So, less effort would seem to be required to demonstrate the relevance of their content. When interpreting the New Testament Epistles, we have only (what Greidanus calls) "one horizon," not two, on which to focus our attention.[1]

While all of these observations may be true, it would be easy to exaggerate the ease of preaching the Epistles. For one thing, they are more closely related to the Gospels than one might imagine.[2] Ryken says, "Everything considered, the New Testament epistles are an extension of the Gospels. Both were written by authoritative Christian leaders and both existed to explain the life and teachings of Jesus."[3] Also, while the narrative of much of the Old Testament, Gospels, and Acts presents its challenges to the interpreter, the Epistles present difficulties of their own.[4] They tend to be more didactic, technical, and abstract, if not less personable. Again, it is Ryken who states, "The personality of the writers is much less important than the religious content of their letters. The writers, indeed, do not write primarily as individual persons but in their roles as apostles—as the conveyors of divine truth in a manner reminiscent of the Hebrew prophets."[5] Of the Epistles, Greidanus writes, "They are full of detailed truth and careful shades of meaning. In them every single word is full of significance. Expounding them therefore calls for hard work by the preacher before he can even begin to put a message together."[6]

On the other hand, the Epistles have a quality that has been called "situational immediacy," meaning that they were written not as essays in systematic theology, but in response to specific people living in real places and struggling with common problems. For this reason, the amount of space given to an issue may be disproportional to its importance apart from a local controversy or specific question (e.g., the discussion of celibacy in 1 Corinthians 7, or tongues in 1 Corinthians 12–14).

Our goal again in this chapter is to survey the basic factors of historical background, literary analysis, and theological understanding so that the reader will have a handle on how to use the Whiting Method to prepare sermons to deliver God's message.

THE GENRE OF EPISTLE

Epistle

Most of the New Testament books (twenty-one of twenty-seven) are classified as *epistles*. The word *epistle* is a transliteration of the Greek word ἐπιστολη (*epistole*, pronounced *ep-is-tol-ay*), which means "a written message."[7] While the New Testament Epistles bear the marks of private letters occasioned by specific issues, they were evidently written with a consciousness of apostolic authority (see Romans 1:1; 1 Corinthians 1:1; 2 Corinthians 1:1; 2 Thessalonians 3:14, etc.) and intended for circulation (1 Thess. 5:27; Col. 4:16). That the Epistles were written in response to particular concerns, however, takes them out of the category of *theological treatises*.[8] In other words, they are not systematic, abstract, exhaustive treatments of the subjects they address. Rather, they are always focused on, and therefore somewhat limited by, their applicability to the situation either of the writer or his readers. According to Aune, "the overlap between letter and speech suggests two important dimensions for understanding the former. First, oratory was very important in the Greco-Roman world and rhetoric occupied a central role in ancient education."[9] In this way, the Epistles are more like sermons—especially those that were dictated to a scribe.[10] Ryken states, "Paul, moreover, composed most of his letters orally while dictating them to a secretary. As a result, New Testament epistles and oratories show great similarity in style."[11] Because this is true, when the Epistles are understood in the context of the historical situation of both writer and reader, their relevance for preaching today is often obvious.

Literary Devices

Like the Gospel genre, the Epistles include various other literary forms. According to Greidanus, "we find the narrative genre in Gal 1:13–2:21; apocalyptic in 1 Thess 4:13–5:11; a hymn in Phil 2:6–11; and wisdom in Gal 5:9; 6:7; 1 Cor 15:33; and 2 Cor 9:6."[12] In addition, Greidanus finds a liturgical formula in 1 Timothy 3:16, a creedal affirmation in Colossians 1:15–20, lists of vices and virtues in Romans 1:29–31 and Galatians 5:22–23, clusters of imperatives in Colossians 3, and reliance on figurative language.[13]

With regard to Paul's use of sources, Guthrie states that "the passages from the Epistles point to a primitive substratum on which the major Pauline doctrines were based . . . The most important passage is I Corinthians xv. 1–7 where the apostle clearly states that he preaches what had been delivered to him. The same emphasis is found in Romans i:4, viii. 34 . . . Dodd finds two other aspects of primitive preaching, eschatology (Rom. i.16; I Thes. i. 10) and the work of the Holy Spirit in the believer (Gal. iv. 6)."[14]

Paul may also have been influenced by early catechetical forms that appear in his writings as "faithful sayings," according to Guthrie,[15] who also observes the incorporation of hymnic literature into Paul's writing: "The apostle recognized the value of rhythmic expressions of Christian truth and would not have regarded these, as some scholars have tended to do, as steps away from the nobler heights of creative thinking towards a stereotyped formality. But hymns are more easily remembered than abstract statements of truth (e.g. I Cor. xiii.)."[16]

Virtually every rhetorical device discussed in this book appears in the Epistles. For examples, Greidanus observes Paul's use of *dialogue*, or *diatribe*, as he argues his points with an imaginary opponent who poses pertinent questions in passages such as 1 Corinthians 15:35–36). He notices Paul's sevenfold *repetition* of the word "one" in Ephesians 4:4–6 (see NKJV), and how it builds to the *climax* with his threefold repetition of the word "all" in verse 6.[17] "Grace and peace," are sometimes used to form an *inclusio*, unifying the text it encircles. An example of *chiasm* is found in 1 Corinthians 12, 13, and 14, in which chapter 13 forms the prominent center emphasizing love, between 12 and 14, which both discuss spiritual gifts.[18] Other examples include various kinds of parallelism,[19] antithesis,[20] and metaphor.[21] When recognized and understood, figures of speech not only enhance the interpretation of a passage but provide the preacher with an abundance of illustrative material to enlighten his listeners.

Form

According to Greidanus, letters at the time of the apostles typically consisted of an introduction, a body, and a conclusion. Wilkinson and Boa comment on the New Testament adaptation of this simple form:

> This shell was filled with the richness of revelation, and a transformation took place that makes it appropriate to call these writings epistles as well as letters. Their literary quality and length distinguished them from ordinary letters. Even Philemon (335 words) is considerably longer than the usual letters of Paul's day which easily fit on one sheet

of papyrus. Paul's epistles required a number of these sheets to be joined and rolled into scrolls.[22]

In addition to being greater in length and spiritual depth, Paul's epistles added the elements of thanksgiving and exhortation.[23] Observing the resulting pattern helps the interpreter outline the argument of the book to see where the parts fit into the whole, and where an element may have been omitted, added, or changed for some reason.[24] (See figure 14-1.[25])

EPISTLE OF JAMES

Historical Background

The Lord's half-brother James (see Galatians 1:19) wrote the earliest epistle, around AD 44–46, not long before the Jerusalem Council, over which he presided (see Acts 15:13). Tenney establishes that "the church was still within the general circle of Judaism before it [became] an independent movement."[26] This was during the phase in which the Church was reaching out to Gentiles (Acts 11:19–15:35), and probably before Paul's first missionary journey.

Literary Analysis

James has been compared to the book of Proverbs and to the Sermon on the Mount because it deals with the practical application of super-

Typical First-Century Letter	Typical Pauline Epistle
Introduction: (sender, addressee, greeting)	Opening: (sender, addressee, greeting)
	Thanksgiving
Body	Body
	Exhortation
Conclusion: (Greetings, prayer sentence, sometimes a date)	Closing: (Peace wish, greetings, warning, benediction)

Figure 14.1

natural wisdom to ethical behavior. Wilkinson and Boa's describe the writing:

> James writes with a very concise, authoritative, and unvarnished style. Combining pithy maxims of Wisdom Literature with the impassioned rhetoric of Amos, James' pointed barbs are born out of an uncompromising ethical stance. His Greek is of a good quality and he communicates his thoughts effectively by means of vivid imagery (especially from nature), illustrations, and figures of speech. This is a formal and sometimes severe epistle, authoritatively written and full of imperatives (54 in 108 verses).[27]

Theological Understanding

When James asserts that faith by itself is dead, he does not mean that it is nonexistent or that his readers, whom he calls "my beloved brethren," (James 1:16; 1:19; 2:5) are not justified. He rather urges his readers to demonstrate the reality of their faith by performing the good works it produces. "James wrote this incisive and practical catalog of the characteristics of true faith to exhort his Hebrew-Christian readers to examine the reality of their own faith . . . James also rebukes those who succumb to the pursuit of worldly pleasure and wealth rather than God, and encourages patient endurance in light of the coming of the Lord."[28]

EPISTLES OF PAUL BEFORE HIS IMPRISONMENT

GALATIANS

Historical Background

If "the churches of Galatia" (1:2 NKJV) refers to those of Lystra, Iconium, and Pisidian Antioch, planted by the apostle Paul on his first missionary journey, then the epistle may have been written as early as AD 48. This would explain why no mention is made of the decision of the Jerusalem Council which dealt with the same issue of Judaizers attempting to mix the gospel of grace with works of the Law.[29] Paul seems to have written from Syrian Antioch.

Literary Analysis

Paul develops his argument beginning with personal vindication, in chapters 1–2, and moves to his polemical presentation in 3–4, before concluding with practical application in 5–6.

Theological Understanding

Tenney views Paul's epistle to the Galatians as "a protest against corruption of the gospel of Christ."[30] The theological impact of this "Magna Charta of spiritual emancipation,"[31] as it has been called, can hardly be overstated. According to Radmacher, Allen, and House, "in the whole Bible, there is no more passionate, comprehensive, yet concise statement of the truth of the gospel than Galatians. Salvation through faith in Jesus Christ alone (2:16; 3:11, 12). No work can earn salvation. Paul's succinct refutation of the Judaizers in this letter has transformed the lives of many—from Martin Luther to John Wesley."[32]

The Christian life is lived not by keeping rules, suppressing the flesh, eradicating the sin nature, or by *self*-crucifixion, but by realizing one's *co*crucifixion with Christ.

1 AND 2 THESSALONIANS

Historical Background

Paul is thought to have written both of his epistles to the church at Thessalonica, from Corinth, within a few months of each other, in AD 50–52. Launstein explains the apostle's movement as follows:

> Following the Macedonian vision at Troas, Paul went to Philippi where the Gospel met with some success. This success resulted in persecution

and imprisonment. After their release from prison they went through Amphipolis and Apollonia (Acts 17:1) and came to Thessalonica, where they stayed at least for three Sabbaths, and maybe up to six weeks. While Paul was in Athens he sent Timothy back to Thessalonica to check on their spiritual welfare (1 Thess. 3:1–2). Paul went to Corinth (Acts 18:1) where Timothy and Silas joined him (Acts 18:5). Timothy reported to Paul concerning the Thessalonian believers and Paul then wrote the first epistle.[33]

Literary Analysis

Tenney describes the content of 1 Thessalonians as twofold: "praise for the steadfastness of the Thessalonians under persecution by the Jews and the correction of certain errors and misunderstandings that had grown up among them."[34]

Second Thessalonians communicates Paul's consolation concerning the Lord's return in chapter 1, correction concerning the Second Coming in chapter 2, and commands in view of the Second Coming in chapter 3.[35]

Theological Understanding

Whereas Galatians addressed the problem with Jewish Christians, 1 Thessalonians deals with Gentile converts to Christianity who need correction and instruction regarding sexual morality, social conduct, the state of dead believers, and church discipline. Though James had mentioned the Lord's coming in James 5:7–8, the Thessalonian epistles have the earliest full discussion of the coming of the Lord for His Church.[36] Paul's purpose is primarily to comfort his readers with instruction of Christ's coming *for* His saints.

The second epistle was written to correct some misunderstandings regarding the day of the Lord. Some in the church had stopped working for a living. Paul's remedial instruction informs the church about the Antichrist and tells of Christ's coming *with* His saints.

1 and 2 Corinthians

Historical Background

Without any training in the Hebrew Scriptures, the church at Corinth presented Paul with nagging problems that stemmed from their pagan background.[37] Located on the narrow isthmus that connected the main part of Greece with the island of Achaia, Corinth was a crossroads city of some 700,000 people at the time when Paul wrote.[38] It was known for the Isthmian games, its love of philosophy, and for the sexual immorality that was fostered by the worship of Aphrodite.[39] Having planted the church on his first missionary journey, Paul's concern for their spiritual maturity became the occasion for writing to them while staying in Ephesus in AD 55. In his first letter he commends Apollos for having had a good ministry there. (See Acts 18:24; 19:1; and 1 Corinthians 1:12; 3:4–6, 22; 4:6; and 16:12.) The church must have had a visit from Peter as well, or it is unlikely that they would have formed a Cephas party, as is indicated in 1 Corinthians 1:12.

In 1 Corinthians 5, Paul refers to having written an earlier letter concerning the church's need to separate themselves from professing believers who continued in immorality.[40] Having heard rumors of their unsatisfactory response to the first letter, and also wanting to thank them for the gift they had sent to him in Ephesus by Stephanas, Fortunatus, and Achaicus, Paul writes what has survived as 1 Corinthians.

Second Corinthians was written from Macedonia around AD 57, partly to express Paul's relief upon Titus's good report of their response to the letter we call 1 Corinthians, and to defend his apostleship against opponents in the church.[41] Paul also urges the Corinthians to follow through on their commitment to contribute to the needs of the saints in Jerusalem, and to prepare them for a third visit during which he hopes there will no longer be a need to speak to them with the severity required in his letters.

Literary Analysis

The content of 1 Corinthians is arranged in the order in which Paul addressed the problems reported to him. Chapters 1–4 concern division in the church. Chapters 5–6 deal with the resulting disorder. Chapters 7–14 are devoted to various difficulties the church is facing. Paul concludes his epistle by clarifying the doctrine of the resurrection of Christ.

Harvey cites Charles Talbert's work on the Corinthian correspondence in noting that chiasmus, inclusion, ring-composition, and the ABA' pattern "alert us to expect numerous examples of oral patterning in 1 Corinthians."[42]

The unevenness and rugged style of 2 Corinthians reflects the emotional interaction of Paul with his readers.[43] It is personal to the point of being almost autobiographical. The very factors that make 2 Corinthians difficult to outline or arrange under a single theme also account for its great value as a commentary on the nature of a minister and his ministry. Paul's defends his ministry in chapters 1–7. He upholds his collection for the saints in chapters 8–9. He defends his apostolic authority in chapters 10–13.

Theological Understanding

First Corinthians is about the life and problems of a carnal local church. Paul's purpose is to deliver the church from division and disorder. Paul skillfully addresses people proud of their wisdom, oratory, and liberty. He shows the practical implications of the centrality of Christ for their concepts of wisdom, sexual morality, discipline, marriage, worship, spiritual gifts, love, and the resurrection.

Second Corinthians reveals the nature of the ministry and the authority of the minister. If Paul had not experienced opposition and conflict, and then felt the need to speak of it from his heart, we would not have the record of God's self-disclosure of the God of all comfort (1:3–4), the fragrance of Christ (2:15), the letter written on human hearts (3:3), the believer's transformation from glory to glory (3:18), the believer's treasure in earthen vessels (4:7–10), the Christian's new creation (5:17), the ministry of reconciliation (5:18–20), the importance of spiritual separation from unbelievers (6:14), the ministry of giving as Christ gave (8:9; 9:7), and the sufficiency of God's grace (12:9).

ROMANS

Historical Background

Written by Paul from Corinth in AD 57, the Epistle to the Romans was occasioned by Paul's plan to visit the church at Rome (Acts 19:21).[44] He wrote partly to solicit support for his plans to take the gospel to Spain (Rom. 15:24), but primarily to firmly establish the Roman believers in the apostolic teaching of God's plan of salvation for Gentiles as well as for Jews (1:16). It is evident from Romans 1:13 and 15:22, that Paul had been hindered on more than one occasion from visiting Rome, where he had several friends. How the church in Rome was established is unknown.[45]

Literary Analysis

Romans is mostly didactic material, but rich in a variety of literary devices, including dialogue and parallelism, to which the preacher must be alert. Greidanus says, "Rom 3:27–31 provides a compact example of this Hellenistic debating style: 'Then what becomes of our boasting? It is excluded. On what principle? On the principle of works? No, but on the principle of faith . . . Do we then overthrow the law by this faith? By no means! On the contrary, we uphold the law' (cf. Rom 2–3, 1 Cor 9, Jas 2)."[46] He further observes that Romans 4:25 is a good example of antithetic parallelism: "Who was *put to death for our trespasses* and *raised for our justification*."[47]

Antithesis, prominent in the Epistles, is exemplified in Romans

5:12–21 and 8:18–39.[48] Other literary and rhetorical devices should be analyzed with the caution suggested by Harvey's comment: "Welch thinks that Romans contains little in the way of chiastic structure. On the other hand, Jouette Bassler identifies instances of ring-composition in her analysis of Romans 1:16–2:29; and Peter Ellis analyzes the entire letter using ABA' and 'chiastic' formats."[49]

Theological Understanding

Romans is clearly and carefully laid out to set forth the good news of how the righteousness of God is needed by all kinds of men, imputed through faith, imparted by the Holy Spirit, consistent with God's program for Israel (past, present, and future), and lived out in service. Douglas Moo, while calling the book a "treatise," or "tractate," states that "Romans is far from being a comprehensive summary of Paul's theology."[50] He concludes, "Romans, then, is a tractate letter and has at its heart a general theological argument, or series of arguments."[51] It emphasizes the power of the gospel (1:16–17); the depravity of man (1:18–32); the universal need of God's righteousness (2–3); the importance and adequacy of faith in appropriating God's righteousness (4–5); the principles, problems, and power of holy living, (6–8); God's sovereignty over Israel's temporary rejection and future restoration (9–11); and the practice of righteousness (12–15).

EPISTLES OF PAUL FROM PRISON (ACTS 21:17–28:31)

In four of Paul's epistles, Philemon, Ephesians, Colossians, and Philippians, he makes reference to his bonds or chains. The traditional view is that Paul wrote these letters from prison in Rome, between the mid-to-late 50s and the early 60s, though some say he wrote them from Caesarea Martima, where he was held before being shipped to Rome.[52] References to "Caesar's household" (Phil. 4:22 NKJV) and the praetorian guard (Phil. 1:13), as well as the freedom with which he was visited by friends, tilt the balance in favor of the traditional view. Ellisen notes:

Though in prison, [Paul] had a measure of liberty, living in "his own hired house, and received all that came in unto him" (Acts 28:30). His opposition at this time was not from the Roman government but from the Jews. Eight workers were present with Paul at this time: Tychicus, Onesimus, Aristarchus, Mark, Jesus Justus (of the circumcision); Gentiles were Epaphras, Luke and Demas (Col. 4:7–14).[53]

PHILEMON

Historical Background

Onesimus, Philemon's escaped slave, had stolen from his master and run away to Rome, where somehow he met Paul and was won to faith in Christ (Philem. 10). According to Colossians 4:9, he was a native of Colosse. Paul sent him back to Philemon with a request that he be welcomed and forgiven. Paul promised to pay whatever Onesimus owed to Philemon. According to Guthrie, "it has traditionally been supposed that Philemon was a member of the Colossian church, who had in some way been converted to Christianity through the agency of Paul (cf. verse 19)."[54]

Literary Analysis

The letter, though brief and "intensely personal," is also quite theological in its illustration of the doctrine of Christian forgiveness.[55] This observation lends weight to the suggestion by U. Wicket that this is "not so much a private letter, but ... an apostolic letter about a personal matter."[56] Ellisen outlines the epistle with three divisions: Paul's plea for Philemon (1–7), Paul's plea for Onesimus (8–21), and Paul's plan for himself (22–25).[57]

Harvey notes that the repetition of the word translated "refresh," in verses 7 and 20, "frames the letter-body of Philemon." The repetition of the word "appeal" in verses 8–10, and of "owe" in verses 18–19, form word chains that heighten emphasis.[58]

Theological Understanding

Tenney finds in Philemon "all the elements of forgiveness: the offense (11, 18), compassion (10), intercession (10, 18, 19), substitution (18, 19), restoration to favor (15), and elevation to a new relationship (16)."[59] Not only does Paul illustrate what Christ has done for the believer, but he exemplifies the way Christians should treat one another in turn. (See Colossians 3:12–17.) On the matter of slavery, Guthrie's comment is insightful:

> This Epistle brings into vivid focus the whole problem of slavery in the Christian Church. There is no thought of denunciation even in principle. The apostle deals with the situation as it then exists. He takes it for granted that Philemon has a claim of ownership on Onesimus and leaves the position unchallenged. Yet in one significant phrase Paul transforms the character of the master-slave relationship. Onesimus is returning no longer as a slave but as a brother beloved (verse 16). It is clearly incongruous for a Christian master to "own" a brother in Christ in the contemporary sense of the word, and although the existing order of society could not be immediately changed by Christianity without a revolution . . . , the Christian master-slave relationship was so transformed from within that it was bound to lead ultimately to the abolition of the system.[60]

Finally, there is a model for Christian diplomacy in Philemon. Paul appeals to a man whom he could simply order with the authority of his office as an apostle.

EPHESIANS

Historical Background

Paul took advantage of Onesimus's return to write other letters, which were sent with him and a messenger named Tychicus (Eph. 6:21; Col.

4:7–9) to churches in other cities in Asia, namely Ephesus, Colossae, and Philippi. The writing of these letters was probably in AD 60–61.[61] Guthrie describes Ephesians as a circular letter, sent to Laodicea, Paul's spiritual testament, an introduction to Paul's body of writing, intended as a philosophy of religion for the whole Christian world, and as a general safeguard against the spread of the Colossian heresy.[62]

Literary Analysis

Developmentally, Ephesians divides in half, with chapters 1–3 establishing the believer's position in God's sight, and chapters 4–6 emphasizing the believer's walk on earth. As mentioned earlier in this chapter, Ephesians 4:4–6 exemplifies the rhetorical devices of repetition and climax, and Ephesians 6:11–17 is an extended metaphor, in which the armor of a Roman soldier is used to picture the implements of spiritual warfare provided to the believer in Christ.[63] In tone, Ephesians is calm and thoughtful (like Romans), in contrast to Colossians, which expresses strong emotion (like Galatians).[64] Wilkinson and Boa state, "Ephesians abounds with sublime thought and rich vocabulary, especially in chapters 1–3, where theology and worship are intertwined. Many regard it as the most profound book in the New Testament."[65]

Theological Understanding

Ephesians addresses the Church as the universal body of believers rather than responding to a local church issue.[66] The emphasis is on the power of God, the unity of all who are positioned "in Christ," and the need to behave in accordance with what is true of the believer as a result of God's gracious work in his behalf. There is a relatively cool development of such profound doctrines as election, predestination, salvation by grace, eternal security, the church, unity, spiritual gifts, being filled with the Holy Spirit, marriage and family relationships, and spiritual warfare.

COLOSSIANS

Historical Background

Colosse, located about one hundred miles east of Ephesus, was a minor city at the time of Paul. Though it had little influence on others, it was greatly influenced by Oriental merchants from the East who passed through the city on their way to Rome.[67] Tenney describes the Colossians as "Phrygian Gentiles (1:27), whose religious antecedents were highly emotional and mystical."[68] Paul had never visited the church that Epaphras founded there.[69] The letter appears to have been prompted by a report brought to Paul by Epaphroditus. Guthrie describes the heresy threatening the Colossian church. "It advocated a rigid observance of the Jewish law together with severe asceticism. There may also have been some form of sun-worship linked with an esoteric doctrine of angels."[70] He surmises that the Colossian error was more like that of the Essenes than the Gnostics.[71]

Literary Analysis

Critics have doubted that Paul wrote Colossians based on differences in its style and theological emphasis from his so-called *main* letters.[72] The argument for his authorship is maintained by others, however, because the specific falsehoods taught in Colosse evoked a stronger tone in response than he used in Ephesians.[73]

Theological Understanding

Colossians is Christological, positively presenting an accurate knowledge of the person and work of Christ as the antidote to error.[74] Guthrie notes the emphasis on the headship of Christ as Paul's basis for strongly opposing the ascetic tendencies in Colosse:

> The Christian is rather to hold to the Head (ii. 19). He is risen with
> Christ (ii. 12, iii. 1 ff) and should therefore live the risen life. It requires

self-mortification (iii. 5), but Paul recognizes the clear distinction between this and rigid asceticism. The Christian is called upon to "put on" the new man (iii. 10) as well as to "put off" the old; positive action is linked with prohibition, in contrast with rigid asceticism which always tends to overstress the negative to the neglect of the positive.[75]

PHILIPPIANS

Historical Background

Marshall notes that "Philippi was the first major town in ancient Macedonia to be visited by Paul and Silas when they crossed over into Europe from Asia (Acts 16:11–40)."[76] Paul's letter of friendship, fellowship, and thanks is thought to have been penned some ten years later. During this time since the conversions of Lydia and her household (Acts 16:14–15) and the Philippian jailer and his family (Acts 16:31–34), there had been a good response to the gospel. Paul writes in response to the church's loyalty and financial gift.

Literary Analysis

Paul's epistle to Philippi was written more like Romans than Ephesians, perhaps because Philippi was European, not Asian.[77] The most personal letter of Paul not addressed to specific individuals, it is replete with first-personal pronouns.[78] Greidanus observes that Philippians 2:1–11 is a textual unit that contains an ancient hymn.[79] It should not be broken up, but understood as a whole.

Theological Understanding

Philippians is about the joy and responsibility of sharing in the gospel of Christ. Sharing in prayer is the focus of 1:1–11. Sharing in persecution is the concern of 1:12–2:11. Sharing in people's lives is the issue in 2:19–30. Sharing in proper goals is the emphasis of chapter 3; and sharing in practical needs is the subject of chapter 4. Marshall says, "In the main part of the letter that begins in Philippians 1:12 . . . Paul relates his experiences in such a way as to provide encouragement for the readers in their trying circumstances."[80]

PASTORAL EPISTLES

According to Homer Kent, "the designation 'Pastoral Epistles' is appropriate for the letters to Timothy and Titus because they contain instruction for pastoral work in churches."[81] But the title is relatively recent,[82] and it is worth noting that Timothy and Titus are never called *pastors* or *elders* (who are charged with the responsibility of shepherding God's flock [1 Pet 5:1–3]).[83] They appear to have functioned as apostolic representatives with authority delegated to them by Paul. Tenney, commenting on the circumstances under which these relationships were developed, says, "Within the range of the Pastoral Epistles there was probably some lapse of time. I Timothy pictures Paul as traveling and active, counseling his young lieutenant concerning his pastoral duties. Titus is quite similar in its outlook. II Timothy, however, is definitely a terminus, for Paul evidently was confident that he would not survive the winter."[84]

1 TIMOTHY

Historical Background

Hendriksen describes the circumstances under which Paul wrote his first epistle to Timothy. "Hence, about the year 63 Paul, having recently departed from Ephesus where he had left Timothy, and being now in Macedonia (I Tim. 1:3), tells Timothy *how to administer the affairs of the church*."[85] According to Tenney, "the organization of the church had increased in complexity. Offices had become fixed and were sought by some as affording desirable eminence, so that the prestige of the office rather than its usefulness became the chief objective."[86]

Of Timothy, the *Nelson Study Bible* says,

Timothy was a native of Lystra in Phrygia (Acts 16:1–3). His father was Greek, and his mother, Eunice, and grandmother, Lois, were godly Jewish women (2 Tim. 1:5; 3:14, 15). It was through the influence of these women that Timothy learned the Hebrew Scriptures as a child. Paul calls Timothy a "true son in the faith" (1:2), suggesting that he was converted during Paul's first missionary visit to Lystra (Acts 14:6, 19).[87]

Literary Analysis

Because of the very personal style and conversational tone of 1 Timothy, it is not easy to outline. If organized under the general theme or heading "The Work of the Ministry,"[88] however, the three-point outline suggested by Radmacher, Allen, and House serves to trace its development. First Timothy 1:1–20 provides *reminders* in ministry. *Regulations* in ministry are the concern of 2:1–3:16. The remainder of the book, 4:1–6:21, deal with *responsibilities* of the ministry.[89]

Theological Understanding

First Timothy 3:15 summarizes the main purpose of the letter: "I write so that you may know how you ought to conduct yourself in the house of God, which is the church of the living God, the pillar and ground of the truth" (NKJV). "The church is God's primary vehicle for accomplishing His work on earth (Matt. 16:18–20)."[90]

TITUS

Historical Background

After Paul left Ephesus, he went to Macedonia, and may have sailed from there to Crete. Having spent some time in Crete, Paul left Titus to organize the unruly church, which reflected the careless, lazy, greedy, and divisive culture for which the islanders were known (Titus 1:12). Titus was a Gentile convert to Christianity from the days of Paul's first missionary journey. When Paul and Barnabas attended the Jerusalem Council, Titus was used as an example of a Greek who did not need circumcision (Gal. 2:1, 3). He is commended as Paul's representative to the church at Corinth (2 Cor. 7:6–16), and for his effectiveness in raising funds in Macedonia (2 Cor. 8:16, 19, 23).

Literary Analysis

Titus is known for its summary of New Testament doctrine stated almost as a formulated creed. "The word 'sound' implies that a recognized standard of doctrine had been acknowledged, to which correct life and teaching must conform."[91]

Theological Understanding

In the greeting, Titus 1:1–4, Paul "puts all that follows into a spiritual context. The practical and ethical instructions that follow must be understood in its light, and the author continually reminds us of this."[92] The central themes of Christian salvation are compacted into what Tenney calls "a veritable doctrinal digest."[93] Yet Marshall is correct in his assertion that "the letter has a limited purpose, and it will not cover the whole of Christian life and experience. It is slanted in a particular direction to deal with particular problems, and therefore we are not to expect a full exposition of Christian theology from it."[94]

2 TIMOTHY

Historical Background

The circumstances under which Paul wrote his final epistle, 2 Timothy, are quite different from those of the other "pastoral epistles." He is in prison, charging his understudy with the sobering responsibility of withstanding false teachers as a gentle warrior.

Literary Analysis

"The apostle uses everyday illustrations from army life, athletics and agriculture to show that service requires self-discipline, and Timothy must therefore be prepared for some hardship (ii. 3–6)."[95]

Theological Understanding

In view of his own years of faithfully serving the Lord, and seeing the increasing apostasy and persecution on the horizon, Paul instructs Timothy in areas of both his personal and his public life. If 1 Timothy was about the work *of* the ministry, and if Titus was about the work *in* the ministry, then 2 Timothy is about the work *of* the *minister.*[96] Chapter 2 presents a successful ministry as one that is reproducing (2:1–2), enduring (2:3–13), studious (2:14–18), and holy (2:19–26).[97] Not surprisingly, Paul emphasizes Christ and His work to prepare the way for the believer to follow Him to glory. Wilkinson and Boa summarize this emphasis as follows: "Christ Jesus appeared on earth, 'abolished death and brought life and immortality to light through the gospel' (1:10). He rose from the dead (2:8) and provides salvation and 'eternal glory' (2:10); for if believers 'died with *Him*' they will 'also live with *Him*' (2:11). All who love His appearing will receive the 'crown of righteousness' (4:8) and 'reign with *Him*' (2:12)."[98]

EPISTLES OF THE SUFFERING CHURCH

1 PETER

Historical Background

Peter wrote his first epistle in about AD 65–67, a few years after Rome began persecuting Christians. His readers in the provinces of Asia Minor had not yet felt the full effects of this threatening violence but were in need of a crash course in how to face it. They are formed in elder-led congregations (5:1) whose ministries are carried out by the members who are gifted to serve and speak (4:10–11).

Literary Analysis

First Peter is structured with the use of imperatives (thirty-four of them between 1:13 and 5:9),[99] which express a sense of informality and urgency on the part of a man convinced that Christians have a faith worth suffering for! Marshall notes that the word translated *suffer* occurs no less than twelve times, "more than any other book in the New Testament."[100] The epistle breaks down into a twofold outline in which the believer's position is emphasized in 1:1–2:10, and the believer's conduct is emphasized in 2:11–5:14.

Theological Understanding

Peter speaks of the sufferings of Christ in 2:23, 3:18, 4:1, 4:13, and 5:1. He speaks as an eyewitness who knew his own failure until he was impacted by the Resurrection he mentions in 1:3. He speaks of the love of Christ in 1:8 as one who had been asked, "Simon, son of Jonah, do you love Me?" (see John 21:15–19). He exhorts the elders to tend the flock of God, having been told by Christ, "Shepherd my sheep" (see John 21:16–17). He commands his readers to gird themselves with humility (5:5), having watched Jesus wrap the towel around Himself before washing the disciples' feet—including his! (John 13:5–17).[101]

Throughout the epistle, the sufficiency of God's grace (cf. 2 Cor. 12:9) is also emphasized, as Tenney explains:

> In addition to the theme of suffering that pervades the epistle there is the counter-theme of "the true grace of God" (5:12). Suffering should be met with grace and should develop grace in the individual. The term appears in the greeting (1:2), as the summary of the message of the prophets (1:10), as the expectation of the future (1:13), as the pattern for conduct under abuse (2:19, 20; Greek text), as the fullness of the blessings that come in answer to prayer (3:7), as the equipment for spiritual service (4:10), and as the favor which God shows to those who wait on Him humbly (5:5).[102]

Hebrews

Historical Background

Hebrews was written before AD 70, since the temple sacrifices are spoken of in 10:11 in the present tense. If the writer's identity had to be known in order to understand his writing, God would have revealed it, but such is not the case. More important to the interpretation of the text is the fact that it was written to second-generation Jewish Christians, who, under the threat of persecution, were tempted to return to the sacrificial system under the Mosaic Law.

By the time the epistle was written, its readers had been Christians long enough to become teachers (5:12), to lose their leaders to death (13:7), and to have forgotten "former days" in which they had been more faithful (10:32 NKJV). With the danger of persecution imminent (Heb. 10:32–36; 12:4), the writer's purpose is to demonstrate the superiority of Christ and the Christian faith to those shadowy types of Christ which He fulfilled. The epistle assumes a knowledge of the Old Testament in Greek (Septuagint), without which it cannot be understood.

Literary Analysis

Though written in polished Greek, with quotations from the Septuagint, the epistle is written like the oration of one who is steeped in the Old Testament Scriptures. Ellisen's outline of Hebrews is adequate to demonstrate the organization of the writer's argumentation. The author's opening statement concerns "the glory and sufficiency of Christ's person," in 1:1–4:13. Next, he sets forth "the glory and sufficiency of Christ's priesthood," in 4:14–10:18. Finally, in 10:19–13:25, he shows "the glory and sufficiency of Christ's program."[103]

Theological Understanding

In demonstrating the supremacy of Jesus Christ over all of the elemental laws, institutions, and ceremonies that point to Him, the writer confirms the temporary nature of the Mosaic covenant. Like scaffolding used in erecting a building, the Law had served its covenantal purpose. The end, to which the Jewish sacrificial system was a means, is Jesus! Those who know Him have no good alternative to moving on to maturity, by faith, as did their Hebrew ancestors. Hebrews not only gives the reader better understanding of the Old Testament, but also a critical message for all who are in need of greater endurance of faith.

Epistles to Combat Heresies

The final five epistles of the New Testament were all written to correct false teaching that had arisen from within the church as well as from without.

2 Peter

Historical Background

In his farewell to the Ephesian elders, recorded in Acts 20, Paul predicted the very thing that was happening when Peter wrote his second epistle: "For I know this, that after my departure savage wolves will come in among you, not sparing the flock. Also from among yourselves men will rise up, speaking perverse things, to draw away the disciples after themselves" (vv. 29–30 NKJV). The operative words, in relation to 2 Peter, are "from among yourselves." Peter begins his second chapter saying, "But there were also false prophets among the people, even as there will be false teachers among you, who will secretly bring in destructive heresies, even denying the Lord who bought them, and bring on themselves swift destruction" (2:1 NKJV).

While Jude speaks of outsiders who sneaked undetected into the fellowship of believers (1: 4), the false teachers in 2 Peter are described as apostate believers (2:1, 20–22). Though their specific errors are not identified per se, the text itself indicates that a low view of Scripture led to a denial of Christ's return and resulted in a permissive, immoral lifestyle. (See 1:4; 2:1–3; 3:3–4.)[104] Peter's readers seem to be the same as those identified in his first epistle, since he refers to this letter as his second (3:1).

Second Peter was written just before the apostle's death, about AD 67 or 68, probably from Rome.[105] The dark, cold environment of a jail cell, without the assistance of an amanuensis, accounts for the rougher style of Greek than that found in 1 Peter.

Literary Analysis

"There is a decided difference of vocabulary and style between I and II Peter. The second epistle is written in a more labored and awkward Greek. Perhaps a different amanuensis was employed, or possibly Peter transcribed it himself."[106] The letter can be outlined with these three points: the reminder to grow (1), the reminder of false teachers (2), and the reminder of the day of the Lord (3).

Theological Understanding

If, in contrast to Jude, Peter is addressing the problem of *regenerate* heretics, whose judgment for false teaching leaves them worse off (in this life) than when they believed (2 Pet. 2:21–22), the epistle contributes to the doctrine of salvation by grace alone. At the same time, it stresses the importance of true, experiential knowledge of the truth for a rich entrance into the eternal kingdom of the Lord (1:5–11). Knowing the truth, revealed by God to men set apart for the purpose of recording it, is the antidote to false teaching (1:19–21). Realizing the faithfulness with which God keeps His promises to rescue the righteous and judge the wicked is the key to holy living (2:9; 3:11).

JUDE

Historical Background

Whoever the audience to whom Jude wrote, and whatever their ethnic composition may have been, their progress in the faith was being threatened by false teaching introduced by unbelievers. The error Jude addresses seems to be "an antinomian version of Gnosticism."[107] The Lord's half-brother, Jude did not believe in Jesus until after the Resurrection (John 7:5; see Acts 1:14).

Literary Analysis

George Lawlor notes Jude's love of the triad, or speaking in triplets. He states, "The author seems to miss scarcely a single opportunity to express himself in this unique threefold manner."[108] In verse 1, for example, "Jude," "servant," and "brother" make up a triad, as do the words "called," "beloved," and "kept."[109] In verse 2, Jude joins "mercy, peace, and love" (NKJV). Lawlor cites no fewer than eighteen instances of this technique, which he says "has no parallel anywhere else in the New Testament Scriptures."[110]

Also noteworthy is the unreserved language with which Jude denounces the false teachers. This is indicative of the intolerance with which Jesus rebuked the scribes and Pharisees (see Matthew 15:1–14 and 23:1–26). This serves as a warning to modern Christians tempted to embrace the political correctness of our pluralistic society.

Regarding Jude's quotation of noncanonical sources, Tenney says, "The apocryphal works were sometimes used to illustrate certain principles for those who regarded them with reverence."[111] That truth was found in such sources in no way implies that they were considered inspired. The same is true of Paul's quotation of the poet Aretas in Acts 17:28, and of the Cretan prophet quoted in Titus 1:12.

Theological Understanding

Jude's reference to "the faith which was once for all delivered to the saints," in verse 3 (NKJV), identifies a completed body of truth.[112] No new content of the Christian faith was needed or is possible. It is a faith worth fighting for!

Jude strikes the crucial balance in emphases between the believer's *responsibility* to contend for the faith (v. 3) and keep himself in the love of God, looking for His mercy (v. 21), on the one hand, and the believer's *preservation* by Jesus Christ (v. 1), who is able to present him faultless before God (v. 24), on the other.

A careful examination of Jude indicates significantly different wording regarding the nature and destiny of the false teachers he describes. In contrast to those of Peter's second epistle, they are clearly unregenerate and destined for eternal damnation (v. 13).

1, 2, AND 3 JOHN

Historical Background

In reference to 1 John, Guthrie states, "It is impossible to grasp the purpose of the Epistle until something has been said about the background of thought to which it belonged."[113] First John was probably written in Ephesus after the Gospel of John but before the persecution that began in Rome under Domitian in AD 95,[114] since nothing is said about persecution. Most likely, it was sent to the Asian churches surrounding Ephesus over which John had some oversight.[115] From what he says in 2:7, 18–27; and 3:11, John's readers were well-established believers. Their enjoyment of fellowship with God and with one another, however, was threatened by those who denied the reality of the incarnation of Christ. The Gnostic belief that spirit and matter can have no real connection led to the false conclusion that fellowship with God is independent of how one behaves in his body. John writes to denounce this error by assuring his readers of the truth by which they could also know with certainty that they were having fellowship with God, i.e., enjoying eternal life.

Second and Third John were purportedly written at about the same time, but were addressed differently. The "elect lady" of 2 John seems to refer to a church, but its identity is impossible to ascertain.[116] Third John was addressed to a man named Gaius, whose identity remains a mystery. Guthrie says, "It is not possible to be any more specific than this, but as it has already been shown that this Epistle is closely related both to 1 John and 2 John and as these Epistles are fairly reasonably assigned to an Asian destination, it may be supposed that Gaius' church was one of the circuit of Asiatic churches under the general supervision of the apostle John."[117]

Literary Analysis

The structure of 1 John is difficult to outline but may be best pictured as a triangular spiral in which he moves from doctrine (a), to morality (b), to community (c), to doctrine (a'), to morality (b'), to community (c'), to doctrine (a"), to morality (b"), to community (c"), and so forth.

Theological Understanding

First John contributes greatly to the understanding of fellowship in the family of God.

Doctrine: Fellowship in the family of God depends on the incarnational facts that Christ is real (1:1–4), that Jesus is the Christ (2:18–29), and that eternal life is in God's Son (5:1–12).

Morality: The practice of righteousness is walking in the light (1:5–10), which is obedience to God (2:3–6), which is proven by love for fellow believers (2:7–11), and results in a hope leading to purity in this life (3:1–10). This is an objective basis for knowing that one has (is enjoying) eternal life (5:13–21).

Community: It is impossible to love God and the world (system) at the same time (2:12–17). Love for God is demonstrated by the believer's compassion (3:11–18), which produces confidence before God (3:19–24), and is shown by obedience to God (5:1–12).

Second John stresses that love cannot be separated from truth. Truth binds believers together in love (1–3). Truth governs believers' walk in love (4–6). Truth makes believers' love discriminating (7–13).

Third John stresses that by faithful love, believers show they are of the truth.

SAMPLE SERMON

THE EXCELLENCE OF LOVE

1 CORINTHIANS 13:1–13

LOVE EXCELS GIFTED MINISTRIES IN PRIORITY, PERFORMANCE, AND PERMANENCE

I. The Priority of Love in Relation to Gifted Ministries (1–3)
   A. Tongues
   B. Prophecy
   C. Merciful Deeds
II. The Performance of Love in Relation to People (4–7)
   A. How "Love is"
   B. What "Love does not" do
   C. What Love Does
III. The Permanence of Love in Relation to Faith and Hope (8–13)
   A. Lasting (8)
   B. Complete (9–11)
   C. Consummate (12–13)

SUMMARY AND CONCLUSION

While less "bridge work" may be required for you to convey God's message from the New Testament epistles to the contemporary listener, the Epistles present their own challenges. An epistle is a letter written with apostolic authority in response to a particular concern, which determines the scope of its theological development. Epistles include other genre and employ most of the rhetorical devices found in other biblical literature. In form, New Testament epistles tend to follow the pattern of an adaptation of the typical first-century letter.

James was written first, probably before Paul's first missionary journey. James confronts churches at a time when most Christians were Jewish. He employs many imperatives in his application of divine wisdom to his listeners' need to demonstrate the reality of their faith.

Next came the epistles that Paul wrote before his imprisonment. These include Galatians, 1 and 2 Thessalonians, 1 and 2 Corinthians, and Romans. Galatians is a protest against the Judaizers' attempts to corrupt the pure gospel of grace. Sanctification is the result of realizing the believer's crucifixion with Christ, not of keeping rules. The letters to the Thessalonians were written to clarify misunderstandings about the coming of the Lord *for* His saints, and of His return to earth *with* them. The epistles to the Corinthians were written to deliver a carnal local church from division and disorder by addressing the practical implications of the centrality of Christ (in 1 Corinthians), and defending Paul's apostleship (in 2 Corinthians).

Romans explains how the righteousness of God, needed by all men, is appropriated by faith, demonstrated practically by the power of the indwelling Holy Spirit, and evident in God's program for Israel.

From prison in Rome, Paul wrote Philemon, Ephesians, Colossians, and Philippians. In his personal letter to Philemon, Paul shows how Christians are to forgive as they have been forgiven in Christ. Ephesians presents Christ as the head of His body, the Church, and exhorts the believer to behave in keeping with his position "in Christ." Colossians is much like Ephesians, but emphasizes the headship of Christ over all things as a basis to combat asceticism. Philippians is about the joy and responsibility of sharing in the gospel of Christ.

The so-called *Pastoral Epistles* include 1 Timothy, Titus, and 2 Timothy, and deal with the conduct of church life. First Timothy shows that the church is the primary agency through which God is working in the world today. Titus summarizes Christian doctrine for a young man charged to establish order in the churches of Crete. In his final epistle, 2 Timothy, Paul gives the reader a look into the heart of a minister as he charges Timothy.

The epistles of the suffering church include 1 Peter and Hebrews. First Peter encourages churches of Asia Minor to realize the grace of suffering. Hebrews prods Jewish Christians to go on to maturity in Christ in view of His glory and sufficiency.

The last five epistles of the New Testament were written to combat heresies: 2 Peter, Jude, and 1, 2, and 3 John. While 2 Peter addresses the problem of believing false teachers, Jude denounces those who are unbelievers. Both books, however, promote the truth as the antidote to error. John's epistles confront the error of Gnosticism with the implications of the Incarnation.

A sample sermon on 1 Corinthians 13 provides an example of how a chapter from the Epistles can be prepared using the Whiting Method.

DISCUSSION QUESTIONS

1. What factors make the verbal *bridge* between the New Testament Epistles and the modern audience easier to *construct* than that between other biblical literature and today's audience?

2. What bridge-building challenges do the Epistles pose compared to other biblical literature?

3. What are the marks of a New Testament Epistle that distinguish it from a personal letter?

4. How does an understanding of the background and literature of James affect the way you would preach it?

5. If Paul wrote letters to the Corinthian church that have been lost, can we say that the canon of Scripture is complete? If so, how?

6. What ministry needs might motivate you to preach from 2 Corinthians on the basis of its content?

7. Why do you agree or disagree with Douglas Moo that Romans is far from being a comprehensive summary of Paul's theology?

8. Why do you agree or disagree with the assertion that Paul's *intention* in writing Philemon was to teach principles of forgiveness?

9. Describe important similarities and differences between Ephesians and Colossians.

10. Why would it be proper or improper to preach a sermon using Philippians 2:5–8 as your text?

11. Which of the Pastoral Epistles would be especially appropriate for teaching doctrine to a new members class, and why?

12. Which of the Epistles would provide preaching texts that are especially appropriate for those who are suffering, and why?

13. Why do you agree or disagree that Peter and Jude address false teachers with different eternal destinies?

14. Explain your understanding of the Gnostic problem against which John's first epistle was written.

15. List two strengths and two weaknesses in the sample sermon outline of 1 Corinthians 13.

CHAPTER 15

Preaching the Revelation

THE UNIQUE importance of final words is often mentioned by way of introduction to the Great Commission passages of Matthew 28:19–20, Mark 16:15–18, Luke 24:44–50, and Acts 1:8. However, the last recorded words of Jesus are not found in the Gospels or Acts. They are found in the Revelation of Jesus Christ, who says, "Surely, I am coming quickly" (Rev. 22:20 NKJV). Nothing is more urgently needed today than the obedient worship and hope that depend on a vision of Christ as He is in glory.

Yet the Bible's last book is often neglected in the pulpit ministry because of uncertainty about its nature and purpose. For the untaught, to understand the meaning of its symbols and Old Testament references is a daunting task. The responsibility of choosing between vastly different systems of interpretation is intimidating. Horrific descriptions of cataclysmic destruction and human carnage are abhorrent to the imagination. The sensationalism of preachers who have abused the Revelation to draw crowds and impress them with their ingenuity is repulsive. But none of these is a valid reason to ignore God's latest Word. So this chapter is dedicated to encouraging you to preach the book of Revelation with appropriate confidence and humility.

INTRODUCTION TO THE BOOK OF REVELATION

Title

The editors of our English translations have generally entitled the book
The Revelation of John. But the Greek text simply begins with the
words translated "The Revelation of Jesus Christ." The first word,
translated "revelation," is ἀποκαλύψις, transliterated "apocalypse."[1] In
modern vernacular, it is sometimes used to refer to the cataclysmic destruction of the world. But the word simply means "to uncover or dis-
close." The content of the revelation is centered on Jesus Christ. It
comes from the Father to the Son, and from the Son to John, by an
angel. (Note for the preacher: This chain of communication is instructive. God chooses to mediate a message He could have delivered more
directly. In communicating His messages, God is pleased to work
through personal agencies, including you!)

The book begins: "The Revelation of Jesus Christ, which God gave
Him to show His servants—things which must shortly take place. And
He sent and signified it by His angel to His servant John, who bore witness to the word of God, and to the testimony of Jesus Christ, to all
things that he saw" (1:1–2 NKJV).

The "things" John saw, "things which must shortly take place," refer
to events that will occur quickly or in rapid succession once they begin.
This is the meaning of the word translated "shortly." Verse 3 promises a
special blessing for those who read and heed the things John wrote, because they could begin to occur at any moment. Verse 4 reiterates that
John is the channel.

Historical Background

With regard to authorship, Guthrie writes, "Although the author calls
himself only 'John', it was traditionally assumed that this John was the
apostle."[2] After a lengthy discussion of objections to the authorship of
the apostle John,[3] Guthrie concludes that the traditional view is better
than the alternatives.[4]

Addressed to seven churches in the Roman province of Asia (1:4), the Revelation was written during a time of Roman persecution of Christians (1:9; 2:10, 13), probably near the end of the reign of Domitian (AD 81–96). This was the testimony of Irenaeus, disciple of Polycarp, disciple of John.[5]

Radmacher, Allen and House state:

> Reliable historical sources dating from the second century A. D. place the apostle John in Ephesus and ministering throughout the province of Asia from about A. D. 70–100 . . . John was undoubtedly placed on the island of Patmos because of his Christian testimony. He was released after eighteen months by Emperor Nerva (A.D. 96–98), after which the apostle returned to Ephesus to resume his leadership role there.[6]

Genre

In *Preaching Old Testament Prophecy,* Robert Thomas views the Revelation as a genuinely prophetic document, which has apocalyptic elements, i.e., "when the message was passed on to the prophet in the form of visions." He further states, "The literary genre of inspired writings was not the choice of the human author, but was an inevitable result of the manner in which God chose to reveal his message to the prophet."[7]

The Revelation certainly meets Greidanus's criteria for identifying prophetic literature. First, it is from God and about God.[8] As we have seen, it is not ultimately *from* John or ultimately *about* the future. Second, as prophecy was generally addressed by the writer to his contemporaries, John writes to the seven churches of Asia Minor.[9] The message of prophecy is never just to satisfy curiosity or fuel speculation. It always has immediate application to those who hear it (e.g., "Worship God! For the testimony of Jesus is the spirit of prophecy" [Rev. 19:10 NKJV]). Third, as prophetic literature is generally about the kingdom,[10] the book of Revelation concerns the kingdom in its universal aspect

(1:5; 17:14; 19:6; 20:11), "continuity with the past" (1:5, 19; 4:11; 5:9, 12; 12:1), the "coming King" (19:7), and "progressive fulfillment"(20:4).[11]

The Revelation has the apocalyptic elements identified by Leland Ryken, which include: contrast of good and evil; an angelic interpreter; prose, not poetry; looking to end times; use of symbolism (concrete images to represent something else); animal characters (living creatures, lamb, horses, etc.); and colors (white versus red).[12]

At the same time, the Revelation has characteristics in common with the Epistles. It was addressed to churches by an apostle to meet their needs at the time.

Interpretation[13]

Walvoord outlines the basic approaches that have been taken in interpreting the Revelation. The *allegorical approach* spiritualizes the text, denying a literal millennial reign of Christ or any historical relevance. *Preterists* view the Revelation as a symbolic history of events completed in the past.[14] The *historical approach* views the Revelation as a symbolic representation of Church history, culminating with the return of Christ. *Futurists* view Revelation 4–22 as predictive of "things which will take place after these things" (1:19 NKJV) (i.e., subsequent to the things Jesus describes as occurring at the time).

Literary Analysis

More than perhaps any other biblical book, understanding the literary structure of the Revelation is crucial to its interpretation. According to Leland Ryken, "the book of Revelation is the most carefully structured long work in the Bible."[15] This does not mean that scholars agree on the principle by which it is organized.

Guthrie surveys no fewer than seven theories that have been presented to explain the arrangement of John's material.[16] They range from the assumption that it is the "patchwork" of editors, to a supposition that the Revelation is an impressionistic work of poetry. Others find the symbolism itself to furnish the key to understanding the book's meaning. According to this theory, "the number seven, Jewish liturgy, and astrology (the signs of the Zodiac),"[17] provide clues that the reader must use to find a meaning beyond the normal use of words. Still others view the writing as a drama, a song with seven choruses, a series of visions that must be rearranged, or a liturgy moving the reader from one focus of attention to another in a progression of worship.

In our judgment, each of these views errs by its preoccupation with form. John's use of the number seven in structuring his material is obvious, but it is a means to the end that the urgent message he has to communicate might be more easily understood and remembered. The literal approach to interpreting Scripture, discussed in chapter 2, assumes that the meaning of John's message is one that he understood and expected his readers to understand—not in isolation from the context of the entire Bible, but as the culmination of its message.

John appears to have organized his material according to several literary devices or techniques. First is a system of contrasts between good and evil. To paraphrase Ryken:

> Satan is opposed to God and Christ. The followers of the beast are set against the saints. The whore of Babylon is seen in opposition to Israel and the virginal bride of Christ. The dragon is against the Lamb. The unholy trinity (the dragon, the beast from the sea, and the beast from the earth) oppose the Trinity. The dragon's angels oppose Michael's angels. Heaven is seen in contrast to the bottomless pit, and the New Jerusalem, in contrast to Babylon. Time is opposed to eternity, and the deliverance of believers is contrasted with the destruction of God's enemies.[18]

Second, John organizes the myriad details of his content into groups of seven and lists them in a series. Again quoting Ryken, "There is a prologue, a series of six sevenfold units, and an epilogue, as the following outline demonstrates."[19] (See figure 15-1.[20]) Ryken notes: "An awareness of this structural principle makes the work as a whole easy to remember and allows the reader to pick up the flow of action at any point and have a general grasp of what is happening."[21]

Third, instead of ordering his record of events chronologically, John moves in a line through a variety of things toward an ultimate destination or goal. In a way that fascinates the careful observer, John follows the same sequence of events that Jesus presented in His Olivet Discourse, Matthew 24. The following table shows this relationship in connection to Revelation 6. (See figure 15-2.[22])

Fourth, John makes more use of archetypes than any other biblical writer. Many terms for elemental, human experiences are used, including *life, death, blood, lamb, dragon, beast, light, darkness, earth, heaven, water, sea, sun, war, harvest, white, scarlet, bride, throne, jewels,* and *gold.*[23] Ryken further notes John's references to rising, associated with

---

John's Six Series of Sevens

Prologue (1)
1. Seven Churches (2–4)
2. Seven Seals (5–8)
3. Seven Trumpets (8–11)
4. Seven Signs (12–14)
5. Seven Bowls (15–16)
6. Seven Events of Final Judgment (17–22:5)
Epilogue (22:6–21)

Figure 15.1

Matthew 24	Revelation 6
(1) Wars and rumors of war (vv. 4–8)	4 Seals: Conqueror, war, famine, death (vv. 1–8)
(2) Persecution of Christ's followers (vv. 9–10)	5th Seal, martyrs (vv. 9–11)
(3) Appearances of false prophets and false messiahs (vv. 11–28)	
(4) Great natural disasters (v. 29)	6th Seal, terror (vv. 12–14)
(5) A final judgment (vv. 29–31)	Wrath of the Lamb (vv. 15–17)

Figure 15.2

spiritual goodness, and falling, associated with spiritual evil; heaven is high and light; the bottomless pit is low and dark.[24]

Fifth, several type patterns are prominent in the Revelation, including the damsel in distress, delivered by the hero who kills the dragon (cf. ch. 12); the wicked witch, who is finally exposed; the marriage of the triumphant hero to his bride (cf. ch. 18); the celebration of the wedding feast (cf. ch. 19); a place glittering with jewels, in which the hero and his bride live happily ever after (cf. ch. 21); and the journey of the narrator to supernatural realms, where he encounters spiritual beings and returns to human life newly equipped (cf. 22:10–21). One could argue that these motifs are represented not because life is imitating art, but because John is describing the saga of cosmic history from which literary motifs are taken.

Recognizing each of these methods for what it is enhances an understanding of *how* John was superintended by the Holy Spirit to communicate with maximum impact and memorable quality. However, the actual outline John follows is given in Revelation 1:19, where he is told, "Write the things which you have seen, and the things which are, and the things which will take place after this" (NKJV). Walvoord comments:

> The things referred to as having already been seen are those contained in chapter 1 where John had his preliminary vision. This vision, of course, introduces the main subject of the entire book, Jesus Christ the glorious coming King. The second division, "the things which are," most naturally includes chapters 2 and 3 with the seven messages Christ delivered to the churches. This contemporary situation gives the historical context for the revelation which follows. The third division, "the things which shall be hereafter," would naturally include the bulk of the book which was to be prophetic as anticipated in 1:3 in the expression "the words of this prophecy."[25]

Theological Understanding

Leon Morris's description of the content of the Revelation as communicating "a theology of power" reflects the futurist view of one who interprets Scripture literally. Says Morris, "The writer is saying, in effect: 'You are seeing only part of the picture. If you could look behind the scenes, you would see that God is working his purpose out and that in his own good time he will completely overthrow all evil. The salvation he worked out at Calvary will not fail to achieve its final aim.'"[26]

In view of increasing persecution of Christians, John assured his readers that the Lord Jesus is bringing history to a glorious, purposeful climax. Jesus is seen in glory, directing the churches, judging the world, and bringing righteousness to the earth in fulfillment of biblical prophecies. The believer is thus given every reason to worship God and serve Him faithfully.

With regard to the present and future work of Christ, He is seen as the Head, giving direction to the local manifestations of His body, the Church, in chapters 2–3. His righteous judgment is described as "the wrath of the Lamb" in 6:16 (NKJV). It encompasses the sinful world in chapters 6, 8, 9, 14, and 16–18. He is coming for His bride, with whom He will rule the earth for a thousand years, according to 20:2–6.

The person and work of Christ, as viewed in John's present and future, are grounded in His past, completed works of creation and redemption. These include: His death and resurrection (1:5); His ascension (12:5); His gracious offer of eternal life to all who will repent (2:5 and 9:20–21), based on the shed "blood of the Lamb" (12:11 NKJV); His worthiness of worship based on His creation of all things (4:11); and His redemption of all kinds of people (5:9).

The power of the Holy Spirit is prominent in John's reception of visions and in the ultimate victory of Christ and His saints over Satan, demons, and the people they control. The royal priesthood of believers is prominent in their worship around the throne of God in heaven (4:10–11); in their prayers, which are ever before the throne of God (5:8; 8:3–4); and by their share in Christ's reign (20:4–6).

The closure of the canon of Scripture is another important theological consideration. Thomas writes, "This is a canonizing of the book of Revelation parallel to the way the Deuteronomy passage [4:1] came to apply to the whole OT canon. Use of the canonical model is equivalent to saying that there was no more room for inspired messages."[27]

Preaching the Revelation

In view of the peculiarities of the Revelation, several cautionary notes are in order when preparing to preach it.[28]

First, make sure that you choose a text on the basis of its communication of a complete thought.

Second, always ask what a given symbol typically means in the literature accessible to the original readers—particularly the Old Testament, to which the Revelation makes hundreds of allusions, and of which the Revelation is the climactic conclusion.

Third, ask what the passage teaches about God, His attributes, His plan, and His purpose. What is made known about the person and work of the Lord Jesus Christ? How does the text shed light on the nature of man and his purpose, role, and responsibilities? How is the passage related to messianic prophecies and their fulfillment?

Fourth, in developing the theme, ask what the prophet is asserting. In stating the principle that expresses the text's main thrust, reflect the form and tone of the text. If the text is confrontational, demanding, picturesque, comforting, and so forth, so should be the sermon. Restate the textual theme in terms of the "here and now." How is the textual theme confirmed, contrasted, fulfilled, balanced, deepened or expanded, etc., by the whole of Scripture?

Fifth, in applying the message, ask how the needs of the contemporary audience differ from those of the original audience.

Sixth, in delivering the message, maintain humility, objectivity, compassion, and reverence. If John fell as a dead man at the feet of Christ in glory (1:17), you, too, should exhibit appropriate fear as you nevertheless faithfully proclaim His message with boldness (1:19). Maintain objectivity. Avoid sensationalism, speculation, dogmatism, and disrespect for those with opposing views. And be careful not to exhibit callous indifference—let alone glee—in response to graphic descriptions of God's punishment of the wicked. The human toll, environmental impact, and eternal consequences of natural disasters and divine judgments recorded in the Revelation should make us sensitive to our listeners' needs for the comfort of salvation.

Seventh, preach worshipfully—but *preach it!* The Revelation is given to exalt the Lord Jesus Christ and move the reader to glorify Him in the heartfelt worship of the redeemed.

SAMPLE SERMON

THE REVELATION OF JESUS CHRIST

REVELATION 1:1–8

THE RULER OF EARTH'S KINGS IS COMING!

  I. The Introduction to the Book and Its Blessings (1–3)

     A. The Revelation of Jesus Christ Is Designed to Make Secrets Known (1)

     B. The Revelation of Jesus Christ Is for His Bondservants

     C. The Revelation of Jesus Christ Is from the Father

     D. The Revelation of Jesus Christ Is a Blessing

 II. The Introduction to the Subject and His Sovereignty (4–8)

     A. Christ Is the Source of Peace-Producing Grace

       1. Faithful witness

       2. Firstborn from the dead

       3. Ruler of the kings of the earth

       4. Him who loves us

       5. Him who released us from our sins by His blood

       6. Him who made us a kingdom of priests

       7. To whom be eternal glory

     B. Christ Is Coming with the Clouds

       1. His Fulfillment of Messianic Prophecy (Zech. 12:10)

       2. His Majesty as Eternal God

SUMMARY AND CONCLUSION

In spite of its unique importance as God's final word, the Revelation has been neglected by many preachers, partly as a result of its abuse by some. However, having come, as it did, from the Father to the Son, and from the Son to John, by way of His angel, the book promises a special blessing to those who hear and heed its message of events that will unfold rapidly.

As prophecy, with both epistolary and apocalyptic elements, the Revelation was addressed by the apostle John to churches expected to understand its meaning and current relevance to them.

Of several approaches that have been taken to interpreting the Revelation, the futuristic view is the only one that takes literally the things that are promised and have not yet taken place.

Many attempts to explain the rationale for how John's material is arranged have failed to *see the forest for the trees!* The literal approach does not dismiss the importance of literary analysis, but regards it as a means to the end of enhancing the reader's understanding and memory of the content of the Revelation. John himself gives the outline for his work in 1:19, which orients the reader to its movement from the past to the present, and to the future.

Since the content of the book is centered in Jesus Christ, it is not surprising that it provides a wealth of Christological understanding, from His person and work to His gracious inclusion of faithful believers in His rule.

Preaching the Revelation calls for courage and for special care in selecting the text, interpreting symbols, and dealing with Old Testament references. Focus on what your passage teaches about God, Christ, man, and the kingdom. Make sure your theme reflects the form and tone of the sermon. Adapt your applications carefully to your contemporary listeners, and deliver your sermon with humility, objectivity, compassion, and reverence.

DISCUSSION QUESTIONS

1. Explain the reasons that you agree or disagree with the assertions made in this chapter for both the importance and neglect of the Revelation.

2. Why is it important to understand the correct title of the book?

3. In what ways is the Revelation prophetic, apocalyptic, and epistolary?

4. Which principle of organization do you believe best explains the arrangement of John's material, and why?

5. How can symbolism be adequately recognized for its value without eclipsing the understandable meaning of the text?

6. List several aspects of the present and future work of Christ that are unveiled in the Revelation.

7. Which of the guidelines for preaching the Revelation do you think will be most beneficial to you personally, and why?

Appendix:

Outlining from the Nestle-Aland *Novum Testamentum Graece*[1]

The *section*, consisting of any number of paragraphs, is indicated by an extrawide spacing from the preceding text, e.g. between Romans 4:25 and 5:1, and Acts 21:14 and 21:15.

The *paragraph*, which is indicated by indentation, begins with a majescule (capital letter). It may consist of one or more sentences.

The *subparagraph*, which is a division within a paragraph, also begins with a majuscule (e.g. Romans 5:15, 18). Where there is one subparagraph, there will always be another, and each may consist of one or more sentences.

The *sentence* usually begins with a miniscule (small letter), unless, of course, it happens to be the first sentence of a paragraph or subparagraph. All sentences end with a full stop (American "period"). CAUTION: a sentence beginning with a proper name will naturally be capitalized but may or may not commence a new subparagraph.

The *colon*: The parallel (grammatically and therefore logically) clauses (cola) within a sentence are separated by a raised dot (·). See Romans 6:5–7 for a sentence of three parallel clauses separated by two raised dots, or colon marks. CAUTION: The colon also introduces certain direct quotations, which are often subordinate (not parallel).

The *comma* separates the subordinate clauses and lesser phrases within a sentence or clause. These are more for easy reading than for logical division and can be neglected in analysis.

SAMPLE TEXTUAL-EXPOSITORY (PARAGRAPH) SERMON
(MANUSCRIPT STYLE)
CHRIST OUR ADVOCATE
1 JOHN 2:1–2

Courtroom drama is a staple of American entertainment. Questions of justice seem to captivate the imagination of TV viewers. But mention the phrase *defense attorney* and the name that jumps to mind may not be Perry Mason or Matlock, but Johnnie Cochran. Cochran led the "dream team" that successfully won the acquittal of celebrity O. J. Simpson in 1995. Simpson, a famous football player, sports commentator, and actor, had been charged with murdering two people, including his wife. When the longest jury trial in California history ended, involving 150 witnesses and costing $15 million, everyone seemed to have his own opinion.

People have a God-given capacity to make judgments. As a result of sin, they are also subject to the judgment of God. For Christians, sin raises tough questions. On one hand, how can one who sins stand before the God of absolute justice? On the other hand, if the blood of Jesus has cleansed them, why should it matter that they sin? The answer to these questions involves a greater courtroom drama than any on earth. It begins with:

I. The Problem of Sinning Christians, found in 1 John 2:1

"My little children, I am writing these things to you so that you may not sin." [NASU]

John was believed to be about ninety when he penned these words. The word translated "little children" indicates that John regarded himself as the spiritual father of people who were still trustfully looking up to him and learning from him. John is the only New Testament writer to use this diminutive form of the word for children, and of his eight uses of this word, this is the only time he attaches the pronoun *my* to it. This indicates the personal affection he feels for his readers and his sense of responsibility for their spiritual well-being.

In the original language, the words *these things* are pushed forward in the sentence for emphasis. Referring to his act of *writing* in the present tense, John announces his current awareness of the reason he has taken pen in hand and expressed the thoughts found in chapter 1. His purpose is that his readers *may not sin*. The clause could be translated *that you may never sin.*

Here's a news flash! Believers need not *ever* sin. Contrary to popular opinion among many Christians, sin is not a necessity. Being human does not require that we sin. Satan would love to have us all think that sin in the life of a believer is normal, natural, usual, to be expected, and therefore acceptable behavior. But it isn't. Even though "everybody does it," it's not OK.

Of the several words used for "sin" in the New Testament, this is the one that means "to fall short of the mark." The devil would like for us to think that sin is just a part of what it means to be human. But that's not what our baptisms portrayed. Our baptisms told everyone who observed them, or who would later hear about them, that we are now able to operate by the supernatural power in which Jesus lives, and is alive in us!

Where did we ever get the idea that we're being true to ourselves when we sin? Where in the Bible does it say that our weaknesses, faults, and failures are the common denominator of Christians, the basis for our bond in men's groups, ladies' groups, and youth groups? Nowhere! The fact is, every believer is a saint, and what we have in common is Christ, by His indwelling Spirit and the Word of God.

The words *these things* could refer to the content of the entire epistle. More likely, they are the statements just made in chapter 1. There, John addressed those who deny a principle of sin within them. In 1:8, he says, "If we say that we have no sin, we are deceiving ourselves and the truth is not in us" [NASU]. The fact is, every believer on earth lives in an unredeemed body. Even John himself contended with a principle of sin that Paul called "the flesh." Having a body of sin does not mean that the body itself is evil or that we who are living in our old bodies *have* to slip into these old ruts of our presalvation days. It *does* mean that those ruts are there, and that we are fully capable of behaving like the people we were as the children of Adam. This is one of the "these things" that John has written to his readers.

Another of the "these things" is found in 1:10, where he says, "If we say that we have not sinned, we make Him a liar and His word is not in us" [NASU]. In verse 8, the issue was denying the presence of a sinful tendency in our bodies.

But here, in verse 10, the issue is denying ever having given in to that tendency. In other words, John is talking about people who deny ever having committed an act of sin.

John's point is that there is a principle of sin operating in the physical body of every Christian, and that every last one of us has chosen to obey it on occasion. We didn't *have to,* but we *did.*

Now, between verse 8, which speaks of our sinful *tendency,* and verse 10, which speaks about our *acts* of sin, John tells the benefit of agreeing with God about our sins when we commit them. He says, "If we confess our sins, He is faithful and righteous to forgive us our sins and to cleanse us from all unrighteousness" [NASU]. At this point, we modern readers may be saying to ourselves, "If *everyone* has a principle of sin operating in his unredeemed body; and if *everybody* occasionally slips and acts like the person he was before God made him new; and if all you've got to do to enjoy restored fellowship with God when you sin is to agree with Him that your pride, or lust, or theft, or outburst of anger was wrong, then what is the big problem when we sin?" We may be especially prone to think this way when we read those Scriptures that describe our secure position before God. Ephesians 1:7, for example says, "In Him we have redemption through His blood, the forgiveness of our trespasses" [NASU].

Many years ago I attended some meetings at which the main speakers were teaching that 1 John 1:9 refers to a person's initial confession of sin, and not to a spiritual discipline to observe throughout one's Christian life. It seemed as if they were saying that to be constantly vigilant about sin in your life is a negative preoccupation that actually leads to a vicious cycle of sin. Their solution to the pesky problem of sinning Christians was simply to rest in the positional truth that we stand forgiven by Christ's finished work on the cross. In other words, don't worry about the acts of sin that we all commit as Christians, because they can't affect our relationship with God.

Many of us seem to have adopted a similar attitude. But there is an important difference between our relationship with God, which *is* secured by Christ's finished work on the cross, and our enjoyment of that relationship, which must be maintained by walking in the light, as He Himself is in the light. There's a difference between position and fellowship. The apostle John is talking about fellowship, and he's addressing people like most of us, who already have a relationship with God, in which we are children in His Forever Family, but who often forfeit the joy of reveling in the abundant spiritual life.

John was combating that religious error called Gnosticism. The Gnostics were infected with the false idea that spirit and matter have no real connection. They denied that the eternal Word of God had ever actually come to earth as a physical human being. This is why John, in the first four verses of 1 John, goes to such lengths to emphasize that he and the other apostles heard, saw, gazed at, and handled the Word of God.

Those who denied that God actually took a physical body also denied that anything they might do in their physical bodies had any effect on their spiritual lives. To the Gnostic, a person had fellowship with God through exclusive, experiential knowledge of mysterious truth, not by how they conducted themselves in their bodies.

But John said, in verses 5–7 of chapter 1, "This is the message we have heard from Him and announce to you, that God is Light, and in Him there is no darkness at all. If we say that we have fellowship with Him and yet walk in the darkness, we lie and do not practice the truth; but if we walk in the Light as He Himself is in the Light, we have fellowship with one another, and the blood of Jesus His Son cleanses us from all sin." [NASU]

According to John, fellowship with God has everything to do with how we are behaving in our bodies. It is precisely because we all still *tend* to sin, and have all committed *acts* of sin, that we must be careful *not* to sin. We dare not downplay the importance of our deeds, as the Gnostics did.

The second part of 2:1 begins by saying, "And if anyone sins" [NASU]. This is essentially an admission that believers do sin. We don't have to, but we do. John wrote the "these things" of chapter 1 so that his readers, including us, might never enter into sin. But knowing that we all do, he prepares to tell us the solution to our problem.

Notice, he does not dismiss the issue as *no big deal* . . . nor does he tell us that we can clean up our own messes by just mending our ways. No. Our sinning as Christians is *such* a big deal that we need help that only God Himself can provide! John says in effect, *when believers sin, Christ is their righteous Advocate.*

The ministry of the risen Savior on our behalf should not lead us to make light of sin, but to realize how seriously God takes it.

The last part of verse 1, along with verse 2, tells us four important things about . . .

II. The Solution of Christ's Advocacy

"And if anyone sins, we have an Advocate with the Father, Jesus Christ the righteous" [NASU].

The word translated "Advocate" in the New King James and New American Standard is the Greek word from which we get the English word *paraklete*. In some contexts it has the idea of one who is called to the side of another to render whatever aid is needed. But here it describes Jesus as a defense attorney in a court of law.

The New King James and New American Standard Versions actually capitalize Advocate as an official title. Other versions render the word by describing what an advocate *does* so that their readers will not have to learn a new word. But the original language implies what Jesus *does* by emphasizing who He *is* in relation to the believer who sins. Jesus is the One who intercedes for the believer and pleads his case, appealing to the Father on his behalf.

The words "we have" are in the present tense: *we are having*. Every Christian—including you and me—has a court-appointed legal counsel who is *for* him, on his side, making his case and winning it!

To say in response, "Well then, that settles it. My sins really *aren't* an issue. I can do whatever I want to, and my Daddy's lawyer will get me off," is to completely miss the point. Just consider how seriously the triune God takes our sins: that each of us *needs* legal representation, and that it is *provided* by the risen Savior, should bring us to our knees in humble repentance and thanksgiving.

There are four things about the believer's Advocate, in verse 2, that are very significant. First we're told that He is *with* the Father. In other words, having accomplished His purpose in coming to earth, Jesus who died, was buried, and rose again has ascended and is exalted in glory, at the Father's right hand. None of this would be true if He were not the Father's full equal as God the Son, or if His mission had not been successful.

Could we possibly have representation with the Father that was more apt to win our case? No, but more is said about Him!

Second, He is "Jesus Christ righteous." The absence of the article, translated "the" in the original language, stresses the quality or character of righteousness. It describes the exalted Lord as qualified to stand His ground before the Father because, as a Man, He fulfilled the Law of God on behalf of everyone who trusts in Him.

Third, verse 2 says, "And He Himself is the propitiation for our sins" [NASU]. Not only is Christ our defender, with legal standing in the Father's presence, but He is also the propitiation for our sins. This means that His intercession on our behalf is based on a satisfactory payment, also made on our behalf—which consisted of His own sacrificial death.

Defense attorneys don't normally take the place of the clients they represent and pay the penalty they owe. But Jesus did. The only human being who fulfilled the Law (not only by not breaking it, but by fulfilling its positive demands) also paid the penalty for those who, by breaking one commandment one time, were guilty of all.

Fourth, in addition to His being with the Father, being righteous, and being the One who personally satisfied the Father's just requirement by enduring the essence of eternal hell in our place, He did so in the place of every man, woman, young person, and child of Silverton, Oregon; the U.S.; and the world.

At the end of verse 2, John adds: "and not for ours only, but also for those of the whole world" [NASU]. Our Advocate satisfied the Father's just demands on behalf of the sins of every human being. This doesn't make everybody "saved," but it makes them savable by faith. Christ's death will not secure anyone's salvation apart from the faith that every person of mental competence is responsible for putting in Christ. This is why missionaries are sent all over the world. For people to hear the good news, other people must be sent to tell them. But it makes little sense to run around and tell everyone about the good news of Jesus Christ, or to support those who do, if, at the moment, you and I are in denial about the toll sin is taking in our own lives. Look up at verse 3 of chapter 1. Speaking for himself and all of the apostles—*sent ones*—John says, "what we have seen and heard we proclaim to you also, so that you too may have fellowship with us; and indeed our fellowship is with the Father, and with His Son Jesus Christ" [NASU].

Fellowship with the Father, and with everyone else who is having fellowship with the Father, is why the Father sent His Son and why our Lord's "sent ones" told us about Him. It is why we must tell others. But we won't share what we aren't enjoying. That is one reason that John wants his readers, who are already saved from the penalty of sin, never to sin as Christians. That is why God has made a provision for us when we do. Just think about how seriously He takes our sins. According to this text, *when believers sin, Christ is their righteous Advocate.* If you have not yet believed in Christ, you have an opportunity right now that you cannot count on having this afternoon, tomorrow, or next week. I urge you to receive forgiveness of your sins and eternal life by believing on the Lord Jesus Christ as having died for your sins and risen again.

If you already believe in Him but have not been baptized as He commanded, that is an issue of fellowship, whether you realize it or not. I urge you to take this important first step of biblical discipleship.

If you are a baptized believer who has been living a careless life, not taking your sins as seriously as God does, think not only about the work Christ has done, but what He *is doing* to stand before the Father in your defense! Can you really continue with *business as usual?*

Finally, if you are a baptized believer who, though imperfect, is enjoying fellowship with God, confessing your sins, and confident of the cleansing of His Son's blood, will you join me in thanking Him for Christ our Advocate?

Gracious Father, thank You for Jesus Christ the righteous, who is representing us. Thank You for the life He lived, the death He died, and for the efficacy of His blood to cleanse us from all unrighteousness. As we walk in the light of Your fellowship, may we also have fellowship with one another, and may that include those You have sent us to win with the good news of Christ. In His Name, we pray. Amen.

Sample Textual-Topical Expository Sermon
(Manuscript Style)
Judas's Real Estate
Matthew 27:6–10, Acts 1:15–20

One of the most effective lenses through which God allows us to see something of His magnificence is that of human rebellion and failure. It is like the dark glass that allows a person to observe the dazzling corona of the sun without damage to the eyes. For example, in the international war against terrorism, it may seem that the enemies of peace are like pieces of the puzzle of God's plan and purpose that seem to have been malformed, ill conceived. But whether you're talking about tyrants or traitors, the Antichrist or Judas, even Satan and his demons, these persons—no less than we—are under the control of God for His ultimate glory. As Psalm 76:10 says in effect, *God causes the wrath of man to praise Him.*

This does not mean that we should celebrate the wrath of man. But we should rest in the fact that the worst men and devils can do is just as useful a thread in the tapestry God is weaving as the genuine worship of men and angels! Nowhere is this important principle better demonstrated than in the story of Judas's real estate. And, as we get involved in it, ask yourself, what is *my* real estate? What is the true condition of my soul?

With respect to the piece of property associated with Judas Iscariot, the Bible refers to it in three ways. The first is as:

I. The Field of Blood
Beginning with Matthew 27:6 in the New King James Version, we read:

> But the chief priests took the silver pieces and said, "It is not lawful to put them into the treasury, because they are the price of blood." And they consulted together and bought with them the potter's field, to bury strangers in. Therefore that field has been called the Field of Blood to this day. Then was fulfilled what was spoken by Jeremiah the prophet, saying, "And they took the thirty pieces of silver, the value of Him who was priced, whom they of the children of Israel priced."

This is one of two traditions that explain the naming *of the Field of Blood.* The price of the parcel was the blood money of the Prince of glory. What is especially interesting about this is the priests' sudden conscience. These are the same religious leaders who offered Judas thirty pieces of silver. I'm sure they carefully weighed it out so as not to be more or less than the amount they had set. Somehow these Bible teachers were blind to the fact that the price they put on Jesus' head was exactly the amount prophesied centuries earlier in Zechariah. And somehow, they had no scruples about the use of God's money to hire a snitch and condemn an innocent man. That did nothing to offend their sense of honor.

If you say it is because they sincerely thought they were serving God in expediting the arrest of one they believed to be making false claims to deity, then you have to account for another detail. Up in verse 4, when confronted with Judas's own admission that he had "sinned by betraying innocent blood" [NKJV], they neither denied that he was right nor launched an investigation into the facts. Instead, as if they agreed with him, they said, "What is that to us? You see to it!" [NKJV].

After Judas threw down the coins in the temple, the next scene in the story is pathetic: Learned, grown men, down on their hands and knees, looking for, and picking up, each of the same thirty pieces of silver that they had so carefully weighed out to buy the death of Jesus. "Oh, here's one! Here's another!" But now, all of a sudden, they regarded this money as tainted—not by *them* or by *their* actions, of course, but by Judas's betrayal of Jesus, who was crucified. Now they must sanitize it by some pious act of generosity.

You and I do not have to be into money laundering to do a similar thing. Instead of repenting of some wrong that we know, or should know, we have committed, we simply try to do something religious, thinking that our devotion will make up for it. Like the chief priests, we may also try to balance our guilt by placing the blame on someone else, as they did with Judas. There is nothing like ministry to anesthetize a nagging conscience. Many people have entered the ministry or gone to the mission field in order to offer God some service in the place of needed repentance of sin. But, as Samuel exhorted Saul in 1 Samuel 15:22, *to obey is better than sacrifice.* So beware of yourself and of others when you see great and meticulous attention being given to the letter of the law. Straining at a gnat while swallowing a camel often signals a vain at-tempt to redeem oneself and salve a guilty conscience. Be sure you are always constrained by the love of Christ, and that your ministry is never to work off a guilt complex.

The other note I make is from verse 7 and has to do with the purchase of a strangers' cemetery. We're told that the priests "consulted together and bought with [the coins] the potter's field, to bury strangers in" [NKJV].

One of the reasons I believe that the apostles appointed elders in the churches they established is that there is generally safety in the counsel of many. But there is no safety in the counsel of unqualified elders! The fact that the unrepentant architects of Jesus' murder were able to agree on a plan for His blood money shows that the value of a consensus depends on the charac-ter of those who are consenting!

The word *strangers* is thought to refer at least to Jews from outside of Jerusalem who happened to die there, and probably includes Gentiles. Burial was an issue because the Pharisees believed in a bodily resurrection. The burn-ing of bodies, and spreading of ashes, was considered one of the worst ways to desecrate the remains of another human being.

A possible reason that a potter's field was considered a desirable location for a cemetery is that holes had probably been dug to get clay to make pottery. Ironically, the apostle Paul refers to our bodies as earthen vessels, or clay pots, in 2 Corinthians 4:7. (In fact, you may have known a few *crackpots* over the years!) But there is a more significant reason that the potter's field was chosen for a graveyard.

The second tradition that explains the naming of the field of blood is found in Acts 1, verses 18–19. There, it is clear that this same piece of real es-tate was named for Judas's spilt blood! Beginning with verse 18, and reading through verse 19, we have the following statements of the apostle Peter when he met with the 120 in Jerusalem, just before the Day of Pentecost: "Now this man purchased a field with the wages of iniquity; and falling headlong, he burst open in the middle and all his entrails gushed out. And it became known to all those dwelling in Jerusalem; so that field is called in their own language, Akel Dama, that is, Field of Blood" [NKJV].

It is stated in Matthew 27:5 that Judas hung himself. Although it is not actually said that he did it in the vicinity of the Potter's Field that the religious leaders purchased, or that his body was found there, it is strongly implied by the fact that this became another explanation of how the field of blood got its name.

By the way, it is often speculated that when Judas hung himself, either the rope or the tree branch to which it was tied, broke. Later, his disemboweled body was found on what we can imagine were the rocks below, the very picture of perdition, which means "destruction," or "damnation."

With regard to the suicide, to die at one's own hands graphically demonstrates that sin is naturally self-destructive. Proverbs 14:12 says, "There is a way that seems right to a man, but its end is the way of death" [NKJV]. Regarding the symbolism, it seems highly significant that Judas's own blood was spilled on the very real estate that Jesus' blood money went to purchase. This illustrates the principle of the harvest that Paul wrote in Galatians 6:7–9: "Do not be deceived, God is not mocked; for whatever a man sows, that he will also reap. For he who sows to his flesh will of the flesh reap corruption, but he who sows to the Spirit will of the Spirit reap everlasting life. And let us not grow weary while doing good, for in due season we shall reap if we do not lose heart" [NKJV].

That there is poetic justice in Judas's end, in contrast to the empty tomb of Jesus, is not meant to make us giddily happy. But it does provide reassuring evidence of a moral order. God does judge sin and reward righteousness, whether in this life or in the life to come.

The second way in which Judas's real estate is discussed in Scripture is in terms of . . .

II. The Potter's Field

Beginning again with Matthew 27:7, we read:

And they consulted together and bought with them the potter's field, to bury strangers in. Therefore that field has been called the Field of Blood to this day. Then was fulfilled what was spoken by Jeremiah the prophet, saying, "And they took the thirty pieces of silver, the value of Him who was priced, whom they of the children of Israel priced, and gave them for the potter's field, as the LORD directed me." [NKJV]

The phrase *potter's field* was first used in Jeremiah 18. The prophet was told that Israel was like clay in the hand of a potter. In chapter 19, Jeremiah was instructed to buy an earthenware jar and take it out to the Valley of Hinnom, which was at the entrance of the dump where they threw the broken jars. There Jeremiah prophesied against the nation. This was the very place where the Israelites had offered up their baby boys as burnt offerings to the false gods Baal and Molech. God directed Jeremiah to use the potter as a picture of God Himself, who can do what He pleases with the nations—including Israel—which are like clay jars.

The second time we read of the potter's field is in Zechariah 11:12–13, where God speaks through Zechariah: "Then I said to them, 'If it is agreeable to you, give me my wages; and if not, refrain.' So they weighed out for my wages thirty pieces of silver. And the LORD said to me, 'Throw it to the potter'—that princely price they set on me. So I took the thirty pieces of silver and threw them into the house of the LORD for the potter" [NKJV].

Zechariah prophesied the rejection of Christ right down to the price of His betrayal! Because he uses the imagery of Jeremiah's prophecy, Matthew attributes his words to the better-known prophet. He sees the priests' purchase of the field, using Jesus' blood money, as fulfilling God's command of Zechariah. That command, to throw the ridiculous payment to the potter, was a vivid demonstration of God's utter displeasure with their estimate of His Son! In other words, when the priests bought the land that was both *the field of blood* and *the potter's field*, they were unknowingly showing *God's* contempt for their contempt for His Son, Jesus! It was as if God was saying, *To hell with your money!* and even used their hands to put it there!

Judas's real estate, then, was *the field of blood* that shows how the wicked get caught in their own trap. It was also *the potter's field*, which reveals God's ability to use His enemies to doom themselves. And there is one more aspect of Judas's real estate that we cannot afford to ignore. As we noted from Jeremiah 19:2, it was also . . .

III. The Valley of Hinnom (or Gehenna)

The location of Judas's real estate is associated with the ravine southwest of Jerusalem, where King Ahaz had led the people in burning their children in the worship of false gods. It became the garbage dump, where the bodies of criminals were thrown without burial. It is where the precious body of our Lord Jesus would have been discarded had God not provided the tomb from which He arose in victory.

As far back as Isaiah, this valley had been a word picture for the actual punishment of the wicked. Isaiah 30:33 speaks of it as being set on fire by the breath of Yahweh, like a torrent of brimstone. Isaiah described the torment of that awful place with words that look beyond the physical real estate of Judas, to the real estate of everyone who dies in unbelief. In Isaiah 66:24, Yahweh describes the demise of the wicked dead with words Jesus applied to Gehenna: "Their worm does not die, and their fire is not quenched. They shall be an abhorrence to all flesh" [NKJV]. The book of Mark repeats most of these words in chapter 9, verses 44, 46, and 48.

The Lord Jesus referred to the eternal lake of fire as *Gehenna,* into which, Revelation 20:14 says, death and Hades will ultimately be thrown. So Judas's real estate, at the entrance of the Valley of Hinnom, is in the area that pictures hell.

There are at least five ways we can apply the overarching principle of these accounts, that *God causes the wrath of man to praise Him.*

1. At the very least, it ought to fortify our respect for the Word of God, whose sixty-six books are one. With regard to its Old and New Testaments, Dr. Henrietta Mears liked to say, "The New is in the Old contained; the Old is in the New explained."[2]

The Bible is one book with one author and one theme. How else could more than forty writers from all walks of life, over a period of sixteen centuries and in three different languages, predict with such precision the acts performed by rebellious people, and have it fulfill a single purpose?

2. At the sight of hell—even the brief and poetic glimpse from the texts we've considered—we ought to thank God for loving us in such a way that He gave His one-of-a-kind Son, that whoever believes in Him will not follow Judas into the pit of eternal destruction but will instead realize His merciful deliverance and eternal dwelling in the presence of God. By the grace of God, you can know that your real estate is in heaven, where Christ is preparing a place for you, and from which He is going to come, anytime now, and take us

home. As Paul and Silas told the Philippian jailer, "Believe on the Lord Jesus Christ, and you will be saved, you and your household" [Acts 16:31 NKJV].

3. Our brief tour of these cursed grounds should make sin less of an attractive nuisance. I'm much more likely to toy with sin if I think of it as a potent weapon that empowers me, like a .44 Magnum pistol, than if I realize it is powerless against God's purpose.

As the Lord told Saul from heaven, "It is hard for you to kick against the goads" [Acts 26:14 NKJV]. The Bible also says that the way of the transgressor is hard. Since God causes even the vengeful anger and spiteful rebellion of man to result in His praise, ultimately—since the day is coming when every knee will bow and every tongue confess that Jesus is Lord, to the glory of God the Father—why settle for calling Him "Rabbi" now, as Judas did? In view of the futility of thwarting God's purpose, why not surrender the members of our bodies like captured weapons, and commit ourselves to live for Him?

4. The lessons of Judas's real estate should make us bow before our Maker and confess: "Thou art the Potter; I am the clay." It ought to lead each of us to yield to Him with an attitude that says, *"Have Thine own way, Lord."* If you have been struggling with a particular area of obedience to the will of God, I invite you to surrender to Him now. In the quiet of your heart, just say, *Not my will, but Thine be done.* Those are the words that Jesus said on your behalf, and God saved Him out of the death that is worse than any prospect you may be dreading in the will of God.

5. Instead of fretting over the events of this life that you *don't* control—the performance of your retirement funds, a loved one's illness, the threat of terrorism—make sure you're honoring the Lord in the things you *do* control. If the actions of God's enemies are under His control to the degree indicated in these passages, without any coercion of people against their will, don't you think the same is true of your unsaved spouse or boss, and of whoever seems to be standing in the way of your progress toward proper goals? Even the heads of terrorist organizations and rogue states are like clay in the hands of their Potter, and *God causes the wrath of man to praise Him.*

SAMPLE DOCTRINAL SERMON
AUTHORITY IN THE CHURCH
CHRIST GOVERNS HIS CHURCH AS CONGREGATIONS
YIELD TO THE SPIRITUAL GUIDES THEY AFFIRM

I. All Authority Resides in Christ *Exclusively*

    A. He has been given all authority in heaven and on earth (Matt. 28:18).

    B. He is the Head of the Church, His body (Col. 1:18; Eph. 5:22–24).

    C. He is the Shepherd of the Church, God's flock (John 10:11–16; Heb. 13:20).

    D. He is the High Priest of the Church, a priesthood (1 Pet. 2:9; Heb. 2:17–31).

    E. He is the Vine upon whom the branches depend (John 15).

II. Christ Resides in All Believers *Equally*

    A. He indwells the Church, His temple (1 Cor. 3:16–17).

    B. He indwells believers individually (Rom. 8:9; 1 Cor. 6:19).

        1. All believers are members of one another in the body of Christ (Rom. 12:4–5; 1 Cor. 12:12–13).

        2. All believers have a capacity for understanding the Word of Christ (1 John 2:20, 27; 1 Cor. 2:15; Col. 3:16).

        3. All believers are empowered to minister as priests (1 Pet. 2:5, 9; Rom 12:1; James 5:16).

        4. All believers are gifted to serve one another (Rom. 12:6–8).

        5. All believers are to participate in the selection and affirmation of biblical officers (Acts 6:1–6; 1 Thess. 5:12–13; 1 Tim. 3:10; Heb. 13:17).

        6. All believers are to participate in the discipline of erring members and elders (Matt. 18:15–20; 1 Cor. 5:12–13; 1 Thess. 5:14; 2 Thess. 3:14; 1 Tim. 5:19).

III. Qualified Officers Serve as Christ's *Executives*

    A. Only those recognized by the congregation for their spiritual maturity and exemplary character are charged with the responsibility to shepherd the flock of God (Acts 20:17, 28; 1 Tim. 3:1–7; Titus 1:5–9; 1 Peter 5:1–4; Heb. 13:7, 17).

B. The authority of elders

1. Managers of God's household (1 Tim. 3:5)
2. In charge of those allotted to their care (1 Pet. 5:3)
3. Possess authority, that must not be abused (1 Pet. 5:3)
4. Authorized to "let no one despise" their exhortation and rebuke (Titus 2:15)
5. Accountable to Christ for those responsible to submit to them (Heb. 13:17)

Sample Biographical Sermon (Manuscript Style)
A Man Called Andrew
John 1:35–42

Meet Andrew. He's not a big-name Christian, like Peter, Paul, or Mary. He's like most of us, whose ministries are little celebrated and mostly behind the scenes. Yet, by identifying with Andrew we are motivated in four areas: our priorities, our preparation for ministry, our pursuit of Jesus Christ, and our personal relationships with others.

Andrew is a Greek name that means "manly." Manliness can be thought of not only as maleness, but as describing the maturity of a faithful follower of Christ regardless of sex.[3] In this sense, the subject of our study lived up to the meaning of his name, and so can every one of us who will.

The fact that he had a Greek name is interesting, since John 1:44 indicates that he was from Bethsaida, the fishing village on the northern shore of the lake called Galilee, and the brother of Simon (Peter), a Jew. This may indicate that Andrew and his family were not in isolation from the world in their day, but rubbed shoulders with unbelievers, like we know at school and work.

Andrew lived in the shadow of his brother, Peter. Both were fishermen by trade. The brothers apparently formed a partnership with James and John. Fishing was physically demanding. If Andrew shook your hand, you would have felt his calluses and strength from long hours of rowing and handling fish nets. He worked hard for a living, like most of us.

Mark 1:29 refers to the house of Simon and Andrew, near the synagogue in Capernaum. The reference to Peter's mother-in-law, in the next verse, indicates that Peter was married. Living with his married brother, who would become the lead disciple and spokesman for the twelve apostles, Andrew seems to have been overshadowed.

Though less prominent than Peter, Andrew was his own man, a disciple of John the Baptist. This observation leads us to consider the first way in which Andrew challenges us:

I. Our Priorities

Beginning with John 1:35, we read:

> Again, the next day, John stood with two of his disciples. And looking at Jesus as He walked, he said, "Behold the Lamb of God!" The two disciples heard him speak, and they followed Jesus. Then Jesus turned, and seeing them following, said to them, "What do you seek?" They said to Him, "Rabbi" (which is to say, when translated, Teacher), "where are You staying?" He said to them, "Come and see." They came and saw where He was staying, and remained with Him that day (now it was about the tenth hour). One of the two who heard John speak, and followed Him, was Andrew, Simon Peter's brother.

To have been a disciple of John, Andrew would have had to sacrifice lots of hours and potential income from his fishing business. He would have put spiritual concerns ahead of material interests. From what we have read, there is reason to believe that if Andrew were living today, he would be an active member of a local church—something any believer can be. You and I do not have to be a Peter, Paul, or Mary to be faithful, available, and teachable! You simply have to put first things first.

The second hallmark of Andrew's character is that he was a prepared man. And his readiness to act in response to divine direction challenges us in the area of . . .

II. Our Preparation

Andrew would have been baptized by John, indicating his repentance of sin and identification with John's message of the kingdom. He was committed to receiving Messiah on His terms. He was living up to the light (truth) that he had. You don't have to be a prominent leader to do that. And yet, having become a faithful follower in response to divine revelation is the most important quality of a godly leader. It qualified Andrew to lead a man to Christ who would far outshine Andrew in greatness. The first step in bringing others to Jesus is to make sure we are practicing all that we know to be true. You and I cannot expect to lead others into receptivity to spiritual things that we do not have ourselves. *Faithful followers of Christ bring others to Him.*

A third principle we can draw from the life of Andrew is found in verses 35–37. Here we are told that he and another of John's disciples followed Jesus. Consider, then . . .

III. Our Pursuit of Jesus

John the Baptist got the attention of the religious leaders of Israel. A delegation of priests and Levites were sent from Jerusalem to ascertain whether he claimed to be the Christ, Elijah, or *the Prophet*. In John 1:23, the Baptist indicated his role as the Messiah's forerunner, and the next day he identified Jesus as the Lamb of God, who takes away the sin of the world. In John 1:34, John says of Jesus, "I have seen and testified that this is the Son of God" [NKJV].

Andrew was one of two men who acted in response to John's identification of Jesus as the Lamb of God. When asked, "What do you seek?" Andrew was the one who asked where Jesus was staying. When invited to come and see, Andrew and his companion (probably John the Evangelist) came and saw. He was not a mere hearer of the prophetic word, but one who acted on it with a proper sense of self-interest. Andrew sought to know Jesus personally. In a similar way, you and I need to pursue Christ for our own benefit before attempting to introduce others to Him. The personal pursuit of God logically follows hearts that have been prepared on the basis of the right priorities. Acting with a sense of desperate personal need logically precedes the invitation of others to join us.

One reason that our witnessing is often weak, sporadic, or nonexistent, is that our own experiences of God are weak, sporadic, or nonexistent. If we are letting the Lord Jesus meet our deepest longings for truth and grace, we will not hesitate to bring others to meet Him. *Faithful followers of Christ bring others to Him.* Andrew didn't hesitate. He ran and got Peter, and this brings us to the fourth area of challenge:

IV. Our Personal Relationships

In verses 41–42, we read, "He first found his own brother Simon, and said to him, 'We have found the Messiah' (which is translated, the Christ). 42 And he brought him to Jesus. Now when Jesus looked at him, He said, 'You are Simon the son of Jonah. You shall be called Cephas' (which is translated, A Stone)" [NKJV].

Andrew did what any one of us can do. He began with the person nearest to him who did not know Christ. The words translated "found" and "brought" imply that Andrew went to some effort. Whether Peter was wary, reluctant, or quite willing, we aren't told. But having expended the time and energy to look for Peter and to locate him, Andrew also did whatever may have been necessary to help Peter overcome any reticence to come with him to Jesus.

In the same way, to bring your family member, friend, or acquaintance to Jesus may take some persistent effort. And in the same way, your friend could be the next Billy Graham, D. L. Moody, Charles Spurgeon, Martin Luther, or Mother Teresa! Your friend could be another Andrew, Priscilla, or Dorcas. God used Andrew to make introductions between Jesus Christ and Peter, who would later express the confession of faith on which Christ would build His Church! It would be Peter, not Andrew, who walked on the water. Peter was first to enter the empty tomb of Jesus. It was Peter whose sermon at Pentecost was used to gather in three thousand people on one day. And it was Peter who used the keys of the kingdom to open the doors of evangelism to every ethnic group. But where would Peter have been without the faithful witness of his less flamboyant brother, Andrew?

Bible students have noticed that each time Andrew is mentioned in this Gospel, he is bringing someone to Jesus. In chapter 6, it is Andrew who brings the boy with the loaves and fish to the Lord. In 12:22, it is Andrew again who goes to Jesus with a request on the part of some Greeks who wanted an interview with Him. No wonder Andrew was made the patron saint of both Russia and Greece. But as the Scripture paints his portrait, he is a manly man, and he challenges each of us in the areas of our priorities, preparation, pursuits, and personal contacts.

I first got acquainted with Andrew in 1982, when the Billy Graham Crusade came to Boise, Idaho, and our small church participated in that effort. We learned that as big a name as Billy has, eight out of every ten persons who respond to his invitation to trust Jesus Christ were brought to the crusade, not by his name, but by a Christian friend who cared about them.

Even Andrew may be a big-name Christian in contrast to you and me. But his willingness to introduce those near him to Jesus Christ gives us an example that we can follow, if only we will. If you have not yet come to Christ, you can do so today. Simply believe in the Lord Jesus Christ and you will be saved [Acts 16:31]. To believe *in* Him is to trust Him as the Son of God who came as a man, lived a sinless life, offered Himself as the sacrifice and died in your place, to pay the penalty of your sins, and who rose again.

If you know the Lord Jesus as your Savior today, it is probably because someone was willing to be an "Andrew" to you. In any case, God confronts us in this passage with the life of a man who serves as an example to us. *Faithful followers of Christ bring others to Him.*

Sample Gospel Sermon
(Manuscript Style)
From Death to Life
John 5:24–29

About 1930, the Communist leader Bukharin journeyed from Moscow to Kiev. His mission was to address a huge assembly. His subject, atheism. For a solid hour he aimed his heavy artillery at Christianity, hurling argument and ridicule. At last he was finished and viewed what seemed to be the smoldering ashes of men's faith. "Are there any questions?" Bukharin demanded. A solitary man arose and asked permission to speak. He mounted the platform and moved close to the Communist. The audience was breathlessly silent as the man surveyed them first to the right, then to the left. At last he shouted the ancient Orthodox greeting, "CHRIST IS RISEN!" The vast assembly arose as one man, and the response came crashing like the sound of an avalanche, "HE IS RISEN INDEED!"[4]

Today, hundreds of people pass by Lenin's mausoleum in Moscow's Red Square and view the corpse of a father of Communism. The nation has a body on its hands and is not quite sure what to do with it. Such is not the case with Christians—once committed to mental asylums in the former Soviet Union, for their belief in God. While Lenin has obviously passed from the state of life to death, the believer in Jesus Christ has passed from death to life.

Beginning with John 5:24, and concluding with verse 29, our Lord speaks of life as freedom from judgment. He says in effect that

I. Believers are Spiritually Free from God's Judgment Now

"Most assuredly, I say to you, he who hears My word and believes in Him who sent Me has everlasting life, and shall not come into judgment, but has passed from death into life." [NKJV]

The "death" Jesus is talking about at the end of verse 24 is spiritual death. Spiritual death is separation from the love of God. It is the consequence of our choice, in Adam, to disobey God. Romans 5:12 explains: "Therefore, just as through one man sin entered the world, and death through sin, and thus death spread to all men, because all sinned" [NKJV].

According to history, I was born in the state of California. But according to Scripture, I was also born in the state of death. Ephesians 2:1–2 tells us: "And you He made alive, who were dead in trespasses and sins, in which you once walked according to the course of this world, according to the prince of the power of the air, the spirit who now works in the sons of disobedience." [NKJV]

The Bible's good news is that a person can move from one state to another. Just as definitely as I moved out of California and crossed the state line into Oregon in 1973, I also passed out of the state where I was subject to the death penalty and into the state where "there is therefore now no condemnation for those who are in Christ Jesus" [Rom. 8:1 NKJV].

How do I know? I know it because God's Word assures me that Jesus and His words are absolutely trustworthy. John 5:24, in the New American

Standard Version, begins with the words "Truly, truly." This signals the great importance and reliability of what follows. And the first thing I'm told about my new state is that I passed into it permanently. It happened when I heeded the message of Jesus Christ, recorded in the Bible. I believed the Father who sent Him. I began depending on God the Father as having loved the world of people—including me—in such a way that He gave His unique Son, Jesus, that whoever believes in Him should not perish but have eternal life.

Eternal life is not just natural life that never ends. It is a relationship with God in which I am no longer subject to judgment, because He punished Jesus His Son for my sins, in my place. Isaiah 53:6 describes the believer when it states, "All we like sheep have gone astray; we have turned, every one, to his own way; and the LORD has laid on Him the iniquity of us all" [NKJV]. But not only did Jesus take the punishment for my sins; His own righteousness was put to my account so that God the Father relates to me as He relates to Jesus! Second Corinthians 5:21 says of the Father, "For He made [Christ] who knew no sin to be sin for us, that we might become the righteousness of God in Him" [NKJV].

When John 5:24 says of me, "has passed," it translates the perfect tense, which speaks of action that was completed in the past, with a result that continues to present. The result is life free from judgment—permanently. *Spiritual life is freedom from judgment.*

My possession of this life is not only *permanently* but also *presently.* In verse 25, Jesus goes on to say, "Most assuredly, I say to you, the hour is coming, and now is, when the dead will hear the voice of the Son of God; and those who hear will live" [NKJV]. The "hour" that "now is" refers to the present, when those still under God's judgment "hear the voice of the Son of God" in the sense of heeding the Bible's good news. This could include you, this very moment. Perhaps you are finally able to understand, and willing to receive, the work God has accomplished for you through His Son. God's promise is that "those who hear will live." In other words, you, too, will pass out of the state of condemnation and into the state of freedom from God's judgment already poured out on Jesus in your place!

This spiritual relocation takes place *permanently, presently,* and also *personally.* Verses 26–27 tell us that it all depends on the Son's relationship to the Father, and upon our relationship to the Son.

"For as the Father has life in Himself, so He has granted the Son to have life in Himself, and has given Him authority to execute judgment also, because He is the Son of Man." [NKJV]

"The Son of Man" is Jesus' favorite title. It identifies Him not only as a fellow human being, but as the Messiah who is God the Son in human form. His coming was anticipated with this title in Daniel 7:13–14, where He is said to be given dominion, glory, and a kingdom.

Since the believer was judged in union with Him at Calvary, and has already been raised spiritually with Him in glory, he or she has received life very *personally*, because *life is freedom from judgment.* No wonder the Lord says, in John 8:36, "Therefore if the Son makes you free, you shall be free indeed" [NKJV].

Verses 28–29 of our text advance the thought from the believer's spiritual freedom from God's judgment *now,* to the fact that . . .

II. Believers Will Be Physically Free from God's Judgment Later

"Do not marvel at this; for the hour is coming in which all who are in the graves will hear His voice and come forth." [NKJV]

If you have already crossed over the border from the state of death into the state of spiritual life, *permanently*, *presently*, and *personally*, then it should not be particularly marvelous or hard to accept the concept of a resurrection *physically*. In fact, verse 28 teaches resurrection for all the dead—including unbelievers—even Lenin! But the prospect of mere resurrection is no reason to be encouraged, because there are two kinds of resurrection, and only one is good. Verse 29 states, "those who have done good, to the resurrection of life, and those who have done evil, to the resurrection of condemnation" [NKJV]. The "good" is to have heard Jesus' words and believed Him who sent Him. It may include all of the deeds that give evidence of having believed. The "evil" is to have rejected Jesus. It may include the deeds that confirm a person's unbelief. But the issue is whether or not a person has believed in Christ.

Physical freedom from God's judgment, then, is simply the result of spiritual freedom from His judgment, which already belongs to anyone who simply trusts in Jesus. The question is whether you are spiritually dead or alive. Do you possess permanently, presently, and personally the spiritual freedom from judgment that results in the physical freedom from judgment? If you're not sure, you can make certain right now. Simply believe on the Lord Jesus Christ, and you will be saved. You will receive as a free gift the *life* that *is freedom from judgment.*

Sample Textual-Expository Sermon
(Example of preaching a chapter, a psalm, and prophetic literature)
Springs of Thanksgiving
Isaiah 12:1–6
Remembering Our Redemption Produces Praise and Proclamation

I. Praise (1–3)

    A. Thanks for comfort in place of anger (1)

    B. Trust in response to God's powerful deliverance

        1. The believer's song of salvation (2)

        2. The believer's source of joy (3)

II. Proclamation (4–6)

    A. Telling every people group about Yahweh

        1. His name (4a)

        2. His deeds (4b)

        3. His majesty (4c)

    B. Trumpeting the Lord's triumph

        1. Singing of His glory (5a)

        2. Spreading His reputation (5b)

        3. Shouting His greatness (6)

SAMPLE EXPOSITORY BOOK SERMON
THE BOOK OF JUDE
BELIEVERS ARE TO CONTEND FOR THE FAITH
IN LIGHT OF UNGODLY MEN IN THE CHURCH
INTRODUCTION

I. The Reason for Contending

    A. Because they are the elect of God (1)

        1. Loved in God (1a)

        2. Kept for Jesus Christ (1b)

    B. Because ungodly men crept in (4)

    C. Because of the tendency to defect (5–11)

        1. A reminder of general occurrences of apostasy (5–7)

Illustration

            a. Exodus (5)

            b. Flood (6)

            c. Sodom and Gomorrah (7)

        2. An account of specific apostasy (11)

            a. Like the way of Cain (11a)

            b. Like the way of Balaam (11b)

            c. Like the rebellion of Korah (11c)

Transition Sentence:

Believers are to contend for the faith in light
of ungodly men in the Church.

II. Ungodly Men in the Church

    A. Their deeds revealed (4, 8–10)

        1. They changed the grace of God (8a)

        2. They rejected authority (8b)

        3. They reviled heavenly beings (8c, 9)

        4. They reviled like raging animals (10a)

    B. Their character revealed (12, 13, 16)

Illustration

        1. Pride (12a)

        2. Death (12b)

  3. Shame (13a)

  4. Darkness (13b)

  5. Dissatisfaction (16a)

  6. Arrogance (16b)

  7. Deceit

C. Their Judgment Foretold (14–15)

  1. Occurs at the Lord's return (14)

  2. Purpose to judge ungodliness (15)

Application:

"How does *a believer contend for the faith in light of ungodly men in the church?*"

III.

A. Remember the words of the apostles (17–19)

  1. Based on knowledge of Christ (17)

  2. Warn of mockers in the end time (18)

  3. Warn of godless men (19)

B. Keep one another in the love of God (20–21)

  1. By building one another (20a)

  2. By praying in the Holy Spirit (20b)

  3. By waiting for eternal life (21)

C. Have mercy on those perishing (22–23)

  1. Those who are wavering (22)

  2. Those who are being destroyed (23a)

  3. Those who are defiled (23b)

    a. In fear of defilement (23ba)

    b. In hate toward defilement (bb)

D. Be assured of victory (24–25)

  1. The protecting God (24)

  2. The saving God (25a, b)

  3. The eternal God (25c)

Conclusion:

Principles:

  1. The elect are loved in God.

  2. The elect are kept for Jesus Christ.

3. Believers are to contend for Christian doctrine.

4. Ungodly men infiltrate the church.

5. Ungodly men can be a danger to believers.

6. Believers are to be reminded of the apostles' words

Theme:

Believers are to contend for the faith in light of ungodly men in the Church.

Introduction:

The book of Jude has been slighted considerably in Christian circles in these latter days, and yet no book in the New Testament speaks more to our generation than this small letter. It may be slighted by some because they feel that the importance of a book is determined by its length. Others may feel that because of its negative character, having stern warnings and rebukes, other New Testament books are to be preferred for reading and study, but Jude possesses a quality of life and concern throughout. Those who are tolerant to perverters of the faith will find the book of Jude distasteful, for its warnings are severe and uncompromising against defectors from the truth of Jesus Christ. To those of us, though, who approach the book of Jude with receptive hearts and the mind of the Spirit, Jude's words will be as clear and helpful as they were two thousand years ago. Jude teaches that *believers are to contend for the faith in the light of ungodly men in the Church.*

Conclusion:

If believers will be careful to recognize those who sow discord among them, and if they will rely on God, they will be doing the will of God, for *believers are to contend for the faith in the light of ungodly men in the Church.*

Notes

1. Source unknown.
2. The Second Helvetic Confession of 1566, initiated in 1561 by Swiss reformer Heinrich Bullinger (1504–1575), asserts that "the preaching of the Word of God is the Word of God." The explanation, "when this Word of God is now preached in the church by preachers lawfully called, we believe that the very Word of God is proclaimed," seems to confuse the absolute authority of Scripture itself with a questionable concept of ecclesiastical authority. In our view, whether or not one's sermon communicates God's message depends upon the proper development and delivery of the textual principles. (John M. Cromarty, "Bullinger and the Second Helvetic Confession," *Our Banner* [June 1976], http://www.pcea.asn.au/bullingr.html.)
3. Haddon W. Robinson, *Biblical Preaching* (Grand Rapids: Baker, 1980), 30.
4. Lawrence O. Richards and Gary J. Bredfeldt, *Creative Bible Teaching* (Chicago: Moody, 1998), 61ff.
5. Richards and Bredfeldt's well-known model for structuring lessons for creative Bible teaching involves "Hook, Book, Look, Took," and promotes the stating of lesson aims, based on the generalized meaning of the text, that are *cognitive, affective,* and *behavioral.* (Richards and Bredfeldt, *Creative Bible Teaching,* 160, 138ff).
6. R. E. O. White said, "Only when preaching is made an act of worship, in which divine truth is explored and shared from faith to faith, in the power of the Holy Spirit, with a view to persuasion and decision, then indeed divine things can happen and the Word of God be glorified." (R. E. O. White, *A Guide to Preaching* [Grand Rapids: Eerdmans, 1973], 11.)
7. See Walter L. Liefeld, *New Testament Exposition* (Grand Rapids: Zondervan, 1984), 3–24.
8. In the words of Merrill F. Unger, expository preaching is "preaching that

expounds the Scriptures as a coherent and coordinated body of revealed truth." (Unger, *Principles of Expository Preaching* [Grand Rapids: Zondervan, 1955].), 48.

9. White, *A Guide to Preaching*, 3.

10. Richards and Bredfeldt, *Creative Bible Teaching*, 195.

11. *Exegesis* is "leading out" of a text what is in the text.

12. *Eisegesis* is "leading into" the text what is not there.

13. See Benjamin B. Warfield, *The Inspiration and Authority of the Bible* (Philadelphia: Presbyterian and Reformed Publishing, 1970); and Clark H. Pinnock, *Biblical Revelation* (Chicago: Moody, 1971).

14. Recommended Bible software includes Logos, Bible Works, QuickVerse, and Accordance.

CHAPTER 2

1. Though a variety of texts will be used to elucidate or illustrate various components of sermon preparation, 1 John 2:1–2 will serve as the text for a model sermon throughout the introductory chapters.

2. Richards and Bredfeldt, *Creative Bible Teaching*, 25.

3. J. I. Packer, *Knowing God* (Downers Grove, IL: InterVarsity Press, 1973), 33.

4. Richards and Bredfeldt, *Creative Bible Teaching*, 25.

5. Ibid.

6. Paul tells Timothy that it is the sacred writings that are able to give him the wisdom that leads to salvation through faith, which is in Christ Jesus (2 Tim. 3:13–15). In Romans 1:16, the gospel is said to be the "power of God to salvation for everyone who believes" (NKJV). God's Word never fails to accomplish the purpose for which He sends it (Isa. 55:11).

7. Richards and Bredfeldt, *Creative Bible Teaching*, 33, 35.

8. In Colossians 1:28 the presentation of every man complete in Christ is declared as the purpose for which Paul and the other apostles proclaimed Christ, "teaching every man and admonishing every man."

9. "In fact, the more committed we are to the authority of Scripture, the more dangerous it is to read the narratives incorrectly. There is no greater abuse of the Bible than to proclaim in God's name what God is not saying. God commands us not to bear false witness." (Robinson, quoted by Steven D. Mathewson, *The Art of Preaching Old Testament Narrative* [Grand Rapids: Baker, 2002], 12.)

10. Richards and Bredfeldt, *Creative Bible Teaching*, 62, quoting John H. Walton, Laurie Bailey, and Craig Williford, "Bible-Based Curricula and the Crisis of Scriptural Authority," *Christian Education Journal* 13, no. 3 (1993): 85.

11. Walter C. Kaiser Jr., *Toward an Exegetical Theology: Biblical Exegesis for Preaching and Teaching* (Grand Rapids: Baker, 1981), 70.

12. Nothing in Scripture indicates that the Lord's Sermon on the Mount in

Matthew 5–7 (or the sermons of Peter, Stephen, and Paul, recorded in the book of Acts) includes every word that was spoken or was intended to be repeated verbatim to modern audiences.

13. When Paul tells Timothy to give attention to reading (1 Tim. 4:13), he also mentions exhortation and doctrine, implying the ministry of the public reading of Scripture, as indicated in the New International Version, and by italics in the New American Standard Bible and New American Standard Bible, Updated Edition.

14. Memorization, meditation, recitation, singing, prayer, and exhortation represent biblical uses of Scripture apart from the authoritative declaration of its meaning from the original context to people in a different context (Ps. 1:2; 119:11).

15. See Leland Ryken, *The Word of God in English* (Wheaton, IL: Crossway, 2002).

16. "The Second great need for a science of hermeneutics is *to bridge the gap between our minds and the minds of the Biblical writers.*" (Bernard Ramm, *Protestant Biblical Interpretation* [Grand Rapids: Baker, 1980], 4)

17. See Roy B. Zuck, *Basic Bible Interpretation* (Wheaton: Victor, 1991), 16–18.

18. That the Old Testament was the "Bible" of Jesus and His apostles is often forgotten, according to Halvor Ronning, tour guide and founder of the Home for Bible Translators in Jerusalem, Israel.

19. For example, the early date of the Exodus and conquest of Canaan (1446–1406 BC), indicated by the biblical chronology, is supported by the discovery of remnants of the collapsed wall of Jericho in the destruction layer dated with pottery that Garstang concluded was not found after 1400 BC. (Bryant G. Wood, "The Walls of Jericho," *Bible and Spade* [Spring 1999]: 35–42.)

20. See the relationship between Paul's personal testimony and the passion and purity of his motivation to preach (1 Cor. 15:9–11; Gal 1:11–23).

21. See Leland Ryken, *How to Read the Bible as Literature* (Grand Rapids: Zondervan, 1984).

22. In John 3:3–8, 16 the word *a[nwqen* may best be translated as "above," as in this context, rather than as "again" or "anew," as it is sometimes translated.

23. In Galatians 1:10, Paul contrasts striving to please men with being a "bondservant" of Christ (NKJV).

24. Scriptural evidence that God's Word needed to be explained in order for the writers' contemporaries to understand it includes the fact that Ezra and other priests helped the people understand the Law after it was publicly read. Nehemiah 8:8 says they "gave the sense" and "helped them to understand the reading" (NKJV). In Matthew 13:10–11, Jesus indicated that one reason He spoke in parables is that the ability to know the mysteries of the kingdom of heaven was not granted to all. The writer of Hebrews 5:12 refers to readers who remained in need of teaching on the elementary principles of the oracles of God, even after the time when they should have become teachers. Also, Peter

refers to Paul's writings as containing "some things hard to understand" (2 Pet. 3:16 NKJV).

25. See Ronald B. Mayers, *Balanced Apologetics* (Grand Rapids: Kregel, 1984), 52–53.

26. Ramm, *Protestant Biblical Interpretation*, 101–2.

27. Robert Traina, *Methodological Bible Study* (Wilmore, KY: Asbury Theological Seminary, 1952), 156.

28. Stanley A. Ellisen, *3 Worlds in Conflict* (Sisters, OR: Multnomah, 1998), 24.

29. The "seed" of "the woman" was to be bruised on the heel, according to Genesis 3:15, an apparent reference to the temporary death of Christ, who, as the Suffering Servant of Isaiah 53, fulfilled Yahweh's promise to Abraham in Genesis 12:3: "In you all the families of the earth shall be blessed" (NKJV). (See Galatians 3:7–9, 26–29.)

30. Ellisen, *3 Worlds in Conflict*, 23.

31. A clear example of changes in the administration of God's kingdom program on earth is found in His instruction to Peter to kill and eat creatures formerly forbidden for the sake of ceremonial cleanliness (Acts 10:13–15).

32. See Lewis Sperry Chafer, *Salvation* (Grand Rapids: Zondervan, 1917), 31–39; and Earl D. Radmacher, *Salvation* (Nashville: Word, 2000), 113–28.

33. The doctrines of justification, sanctification, and glorification are related but distinct, and not to be confused. (See 1 Thessalonians 1:9–10 and Titus 2:11–14.) Confusing justification and sanctification leads to misunderstanding both grace and works (Rom. 11:6).

34. "The right attitude or approach to the Bible is not all that is necessary for understanding its meaning . . . There is a right and a wrong way to build. Furthermore, certain skills must be developed before a person, through using the right method, can build properly. So it is with understanding the Bible." (J. Robertson McQuilkin, *Understanding and Applying the Bible* [Chicago: Moody, 1984], 14.)

35. Ramm, *Protestant Biblical Interpretation*, 1.

36. Ibid.

37. "To determine the single meaning is the objective of biblical interpretation. Otherwise, the fancy of the interpreter, or the preconceptions he imposes on the text, becomes the authority." (McQuilkin, *Understanding and Applying the Bible*, 66)

38. E. D. Hirsch makes a helpful distinction between *meaning* and *significance*. Meaning, or implication, is *in* what the author wrote, and doesn't change, while significance speaks of the relationship of meaning *to* things, and does change. (E. D. Hirsch, *Validity in Interpretation* [New Haven and London: Yale, 1967], 63.) Even Old Testament types exemplify the single meaning of Scripture in that they epitomize the truth fulfilled in the New Testament.

39. "The historical and grammatical principle. This is inseparable from the literal

principle. The interpreter must give attention to *grammar*; to *times, circum-stances, and conditions* of the writer of the biblical book; and to the *context* of the passage." (Ramm, *Protestant Biblical Interpretation*, 55.)

40. For a fuller explanation of these principles, see Ramm, *Protestant Biblical Interpretation*, 97ff.; Zuck, *Basic Bible Interpretation*, 9–26; and Elliot E. Johnson, *Expository Hermeneutics: An Introduction* (Grand Rapids: Zondervan, 1990), 31–53.

41. Ramm, *Protestant Biblical Interpretation*, 98.

42. Ibid.

43. Henrietta C. Mears, *What the Bible Is All About* (Ventura, CA: Regal, 1999), 23.

44. Ramm, *Protestant Biblical Interpretation*, 105.

45. See ibid., 107ff, for a good discussion of how this principle relates to various theories regarding the unity of Scripture.

46. Ibid., 197ff.

47. Ramm, on ibid., pages 111ff, discusses the unity of Scripture as a corrective to interpretation methods that assert a plurality in the meaning of Scripture, in-cluding allegory, cults, and Protestant Pietism.

48. Ibid., 113.

49. David Neff, "Hermeneutics, Anyone?" *Christianity Today* 49, no. 11 (2005): 92.

50. See Zuck, *Basic Bible Interpretation*, 44–45.

51. Ramm, *Protestant Biblical Interpretation*, 115.

52. William Ames, *The Marrow of Theology*, ed. and trans. John D. Eusden (Boston: Pilgrim, 1968), 188.

53. "The word 'inductive' means to go from specific details to a general principle." (Richards and Bredfeldt, *Creative Bible Teaching*, 63.)

54. Ibid., 30. The authors distinguish the conservative view of Scripture from the liberal view, which treats the Bible as a record of human attempts to find God in the normal events of life; and from the neo-orthodox view, which asserts that the Bible becomes the Word of God to those who encounter Him through it.

55. *Connotation* is "a meaning in addition to or apart from the thing explicitly named or described by a word." *Denotation*, by contrast, refers to that which is marked out plainly. (*Webster's New American Dictionary*)

56. In Galatians 4:24–31, Paul states that he is speaking allegorically in his reference to Hagar and Sarah as representatives of Mount Sinai and Jerusalem. Interpreting this allegory is not to be confused with the allegorical interpreta-tion of Scripture in general. For a good discussion of allegorical interpretation, see Traina, *Methodological Bible Study*, 172–74. Also see Zuck, *Basic Bible Interpretation*, 143–68.

57. W. E. Vine, *Expository Dictionary of New Testament Words*, 4 vols. (Old Tappan, NJ: Revell, 1940), 1:208.

58. See the work of Arnold Fruchtenbaum, who sets forth the four ways in which New Testament writers quote the Old Testament, including the Rabbinic

method of *drash*, which applies a passage to only one point of similarity. (Arnold G. Fruchtenbaum, "Rabbinic Quotations of the Old Testament and How It Relates to Joel 2 and Acts 2," www.pre-trib.org/article-view.php?id=2.)

59. Source unknown.

60. Ramm, *Protestant Biblical Interpretation*, 115; Zuck, *Basic Bible Interpretation*, 20.

61. Ramm, *Protestant Biblical Interpretation*, 115.

62. Note: More complete, "working definitions" for these terms will be given in Chapter 4. Also see Zuck, *Basic Bible Interpretation*, 279–92; and Walter C. Kaiser and Moisès Silva, *An Introduction to Biblical Hermeneutics* (Grand Rapids: Zondervan, 1994), 271–83. For a good discussion of the basis of valid applications, see Johnson, *Expository Hermeneutics*, 224–64.

63. Arthur B. Whiting, as quoted by William Milton Jones, Professor of Homiletics (class handout, Western Conservative Baptist Seminary, 1971–1975).

64. This table by S. F. Logsdon was taken from Richard Parke, unpublished "Complete Class Notes for PTH 201" (Western Conservative Baptist Seminary, 1972), 2.

65. Kaiser, *Toward an Exegetical Theology*, 19.

66. John R. W. Stott, *The Preacher's Portrait* (Grand Rapids: William B. Eerdmans Publishing Co., 1961), 17.

67. Ibid., 32.

68. Howard Hendricks, *Teaching to Change Lives: Seven Proven Ways to Make Your Teaching Come Alive* (Sisters, OR: Multnomah, 1987), 39.

69. Richards and Bredfeldt, *Creative Bible Teaching*, 321.

70. Ibid., 153.

71. Ibid., 94–95.

72. Hendricks, *Teaching to Change Lives*, 93.

73. Richards and Bredfeldt, *Creative Bible Teaching*, 93.

74. Hendricks, *Teaching to Change Lives*, 94.

75. Richards and Bredfeldt, *Creative Bible Teaching*, 64.

76. Robinson, *Biblical Preaching*, 27.

CHAPTER 3

1. Whiting, as quoted by Jones (class handout, 1974).

2. Donald Macleod, *The Problem of Preaching*, (Philadelphia: Fortress, 1987), 23.

3. "Others may perceive the preacher as a thinker, quiet man of prayer, avid reader, a heavenly minded man, a spiritual psychiatrist, strong leader, good mixer, one who understands finances, and a good communicator. But his usefulness as a reliable steward (1 Cor. 4:1–2), trusted ambassador (2 Cor. 5:19–20) and credible witness (Acts 1:8; 26:16) depends on his integrity as a man of God." (Jones, class handout, 1974).

4. Hendricks, *Teaching to Change Lives*, 74.

5. Ibid.

6. Ibid.

7. The first foreign missionary, Jonah, was used, in spite of himself, to show God's concern for Gentiles, in contrast to Israel's lack of concern.

8. "The Oracles of Balaam" refers to Balaam's prophecies found in Numbers 23–24.

9. Hendricks, *Teaching to Change Lives*, 35.

10. Ibid., 17.

11. Andrew W. Blackwood, *The Fine Art of Preaching* (Grand Rapids: Baker, 1976), introduction by Ralph G. Turnbull.

12. James 3:1 warns that not many should be teachers due to the stricter judgment they will incur.

13. For discussion on the differences between ministries and offices, see Alexander Strauch, *Biblical Eldership* (Littleton: Lewis and Roth, 1995), 101–17; 175–80; Earl D. Radmacher, *The Nature of the Church* (Portland: Western Baptist Press, 1972), 269–99; Robert L. Saucy, *The Church in God's Program* (Chicago: Moody, 1972), 127–65; and Jay E. Adams, *Shepherding God's Flock* (Grand Rapids: Zondervan, 1986).

14. See Unger, *Principles of Expository Preaching*, 56–63.

15. Remo P. Fausti and Edward L. McGlone, *Understanding Oral Communication* (Menlo Park, CA: Cummings, 1972), 176.

16. Hendricks, *Teaching to Change Lives*, 84.

17. Ibid., 86.

18. Ibid.

19. Ibid., 95.

20. Ibid., 87.

21. Ibid., 76.

22. Richards and Bredfeldt, *Creative Bible Teaching*, 109.

23. The attributes of God are commonly differentiated as *communicable* and *noncommunicable*. Noncommunicable attributes include His omniscience, omnipotence, omnipresence, and eternality, which man will never manifest. God's communicable attributes, however, describe the divine nature that believers *can* manifest, including grace, mercy, peace, love, patience, kindness, etc. (W. Robert Cook, *Systematic Theology in Outline Form*, vol. 1 [Portland: Western Baptist Seminary Press, 1970], 54–58. Also see Stephen Charnock, *The Existence and Attributes of God* [Minneapolis: Central Baptist Theological Seminary, 1797; repr., Minneapolis: Klock & Klock, 1977], and A. W. Tozer, *The Knowledge of the Holy* [New York: Harper Collins, 1961].)

24. See www.reformed.org/documents/wcf_with_proofs/.

25. See Acts 11:15–18 for evidence of Gentiles believing and being baptized in the Holy Spirit with the apostles' indwelling at Pentecost.

26. Consider Moses in Exodus 4:11–12, and Jeremiah in Jeremiah 1:5–10.
27. Hendricks, *Teaching to Change Lives*, 25.
28. As Hendricks asserts, "If you stop growing today, you stop teaching tomorrow." (Ibid., 60.)
29. Hendricks made the following statement relative to the Seven Laws of the Teacher (Teacher, Education, Activity, Communication, Heart, Encouragement, and Readiness): "If you boil them down, these seven laws essentially call for a passion to communicate." (Ibid, 15.)
30. Whiting, as quoted by Jones (class handout, 1974).

CHAPTER 4

1. Jones, lecture, 1974.
2. After seven years of unfruitful preaching, British-born Samuel Chadwick (1860–1932) reportedly burned all of the sermons he had prepared over that period. Turning to prayer to revitalize his ministry, Chadwick began to see remarkable conversions, which he later attributed to the "gift of Pentecost." He concluded, "Destitute of the Fire of God, nothing else counts: possessing Fire, nothing else matters." (www.homestead.com/ephesusfwb/files/fire2.doc) It was as principal of Cliff College, a Methodist training school for preachers, that Chadwick wrote his famous book *The Way to Pentecost* (Fort Washington, PA: Christian Literature Crusade, 2001), published after his death in 1932. It is not necessary to adopt Chadwick's nineteenth-century Wesleyan Pentecostalism to agree that effective preaching must be both Spirit filled and true to Scripture. Indeed, one cannot truly have one without the other.
3. Jones, "An Investigation and Explanation of the Whiting System of Homiletics as a Practical Approach to Preaching," (master's thesis, Western Conservative Baptist Seminary, 1965), 12.
4. Undoubtedly, refinements have been made by virtually every student who has implemented the system and adapted it based on personal abilities and style. Ron Allen, Duane Dunham, Dennis Wretlind, H. Wayne House, Rev. Ron Harper, and Rev. Norm Carlson have all taught the Whiting Method and contributed to its development.
5. Jones, lecture, 1970.
6. Jones, "An Investigation and Explanation of the Whiting System," 34.
7. As sample sermons from various literary genres are developed in chapters 8–15, indicators of where a text begins and ends will be identified by various markers.
8. As was illustrated in Figure 2-3, the context of a biblical passage may be thought of as concentric circles beginning with words and extending to clauses, sentences, immediate context, argument of the book, dispensation, culture, and history.

9. Whiting, as quoted by Jones, "An Investigation and Explanation of the Whiting System," 5.

10. According to Whiting, "The textual-expository sermon is one in which the message is prepared within the confines and order of a given text." (Ibid., 48.)

11. Ibid.

12. Ibid., 36.

13. Ibid.

14. "An *Essentially Literal* translation 'strives to translate the exact words of the original-language text in a translation, but not in such a rigid way as to violate the normal rules of language and syntax' of the translation language." (Ryken, *The Word of God in English*, 19.)

15. For help on diagramming see Lee L. Kantenwein, *Diagrammatical Analysis* (Winona Lake, IN: BMH Books, 1979).

16. For example, the word translated "spirit," in Romans 8 recurs.

17. Suggested resources for word studies for non-language users include, for word studies: Kenneth Wuest, *Word Studies in the Greek New Testament*, vol. 1–3 (Grand Rapids: Eerdmans, 1973); A. T. Robertson, *Word Pictures in the New Testament*, vol. 1–6 (Nashville: Broadman, 1930); Donald J. Wiseman, ed., *Tyndale Old Testament Commentaries* (Downers Grove, IL: Intervarsity Press, 1976); Hershel H. Hobbs, *Preaching Values from the Papyri* (Grand Rapids: Baker, 1964); F. F. Bruce, *The New International Commentary on the New Testament* (Grand Rapids: Eerdmans, 1971). For grammatical help, see Nigel Turner, *Grammatical Insights into the New Testament* (Edinburgh: T & T Clark, 1965); Ronald A. Ward, *Hidden Meaning in the New Testament* (Old Tappan, NJ: Revell, 1969).

18. Helpful Bible software includes Libronix, BibleWorks, Accordance, and QuickVerse.

19. See explanation in the introduction.

20. Without the ability to read the text in its original language, a preacher forfeits a wealth of information, including (in the Greek New Testament) emphasis based on word order, the presence or absence of the article, figures of speech, synonyms not used, Hebraisms, etc.

21. Jones, "The Relation of Exegesis to Homiletics" (supplementary review sheet, Western Conservative Baptist Seminary, September 21, 1972).

22. Ibid.

23. Dennis O. Wretlind, "Greek Exegesis and The Whiting System of Homiletics: The Preacher's Preparation" (paper presented to Dr. W. Robert Cook, Western Conservative Baptist Seminary, December 10, 1973).

24. Ibid., 7.

25. Ibid.

26. Ibid., 7–8.

27. Wretlind, "Principles of Exegesis in the Greek New Testament" (class syllabus for NT 201, Western Conservative Baptist Seminary, 1973).

28. Adapted from Wretlind, "Greek Exegesis," 11–14.

29. Jones, "An Investigation and Explanation of the Whiting System," 7, 31.

30. Brevard S. Childs all but dismisses the explanation of biblical material on the basis of timeless, universal ideas, describing this approach as an "idealistic philosophy." This would be true if the principles were imposed upon the text rather than exegetically induced from it. So we agree with Childs's statement, "In sum, the thematic approach to Biblical Theology cannot be dismissed categorically, but its success depends largely on how critically and skillfully it is employed." See Brevard S. Childs, *Biblical Theology of the Old and New Testaments* (Minneapolis: Fortress Press, 1992), 15–16.

31. Josh McDowell, *Right from Wrong* (Dallas: Word, 1994), 17.

32. Jones, "An Investigation and Explanation of the Whiting System," 31.

33. Ibid.

34. H. Wayne House, syllabus for Expository Preaching, Faith Evangelical Seminary, 2004.

35. Jones, "An Investigation and Explanation of the Whiting System," 32.

36. Adapted from ibid.

37. Ibid., 6, 33.

38. Robinson, *Biblical Preaching*, 31.

39. Richards and Bredfeldt, *Creative Bible Teaching*, 86.

40. Ibid., 133.

41. Jones, "An Investigation and Explanation of the Whiting System," 37.

CHAPTER 5

1. Richards and Bredfeldt, *Creative Bible Teaching*, 152.

2. www.ketchum.org/tacomacollapse.html.

3. http://en.wikipedia.org/wiki/Galloping_Gertie.

4. Richards and Bredfeldt, *Creative Bible Teaching*, 155–56.

5. Robinson, *Biblical Preaching*, 156.

6. Ibid., 125–33.

7. Ibid.

8. Jones, "An Investigation and Explanation of the Whiting System," 39.

9. http://en.wikipedia.org/wiki/Assonance.

10. There may be exceptions, when it makes sense to start at the end of a text and work backward to the beginning, but this is unnatural and would require a good, easily explainable reason.

11. Jones, "An Investigation and Explanation of the Whiting System," 49.

12. Ibid.

13. Ibid., 24.

14. Stephen Farris asserts, "There is a fundamental analogy between Bible and contemporary world that gives life to sermons of vastly different styles." He views

the preacher's creativity in discovering such analogies as connecting the relevance of a passage to the audience. See Stephen Farris, *Preaching That Matters* (Louisville: Westminister John Knox Press, 1998), 24.

15. Ibid. Also see Kaiser, *Toward an Exegetical Theology*, 123–24, for a concise listing and description of figures of speech.

16. Jones, "An Investigation and Explanation of the Whiting System," 51.

17. Richards and Bredfeldt, *Creative Bible Teaching*, 157.

18. Ibid.

19. Ibid., 157, 150.

20. Ibid., 157, 159.

21. This diagram is an adaptation of one that appears in ibid., 160.

22. See figure 3-1 for an illustration of the concept of incarnating the truth.

23. The introduction of formal invitations is generally attributed to Charles Grandison Finney (1792–1875), often assailed by some Christians for his overemphasis on man's free will and his Palagian interpretation of man's nature. Around 1835, Finney took the *mourner's seat* practice that Eleazar Wheelock had used in 1741 and called it the *anxious seat*. The anxious seat was "a front pew left vacant where at the end of the meeting 'the anxious may come and be addressed particularly . . . and sometimes be conversed with individually."(J. I. Packer, "Puritan Evangelism," www.apuritansmind.com/Puritan%20 Evangelism/JIPackerPuritanEvangelism.htm.) In about 1815, however, Asahel Nettleton, (1783–1844), a Calvinist, introduced the *prayer room*, which later became known as the *inquiry room*, and home visitation to counsel those concerned about their souls. For a good defense of Finney against alleged attacks by Calvinists, see Jim Stewart, "No Uncertain Sound," www.gospeltruth.net/ nouncertain.htm. For a good analysis of how both Nettleton and Finney have affected modern evangelism, see Rick Nelson, "How Does Doctrine Affect Evangelism? The Divergent Paths of Asahel Nettleton and Charles Finney," www.founders.org/FJ33/article1.html.

24. Example of an invitation in Scripture: God to man: "Where are you?" (Gen. 3:9). Other examples include Exodus 32:26; Joshua 24:15; 2 Chronicles 34:30–32; Nehemiah 9:38; Matthew 4:19; Luke 19:5; Acts 2:40; 19:8, 26; and 26:28; and Revelation 22:17.

25. Richards and Bredfeldt, *Creative Bible Teaching*, 149.

26. Jones, "An Investigation and Explanation of the Whiting System," 55–56.

27. Ibid.

28. James S. Hewett, ed., *Illustrations Unlimited* (Wheaton: Tyndale, 1988), 452.

CHAPTER 6

1. See Appendix for a sample Paragraph Sermon.

2. See Appendix, Galen Currah, "Outlining from the Nestle-Aland *Novum*

Testamentum Graece" (handout, Western Conservative Baptist Seminary, ca. 1973). Used by permission.

3. Kurt Aland's *Synopsis Quattuor Evangeliorum* (New York: American Bible Society), which places side by side the Greek texts of parallel Gospel accounts, is a useful tool in understanding passages from the synoptic Gospels.

4. In what sense Christ went in the Spirit and proclaimed to the spirits in prison who were disobedient in the days of Noah; and how Noah's delivery by the ark relates to a saving effect of baptism, have been described as among the most difficult passages to interpret in the entire Bible. (William Barclay, *The Letters of James and Peter* [Edinburgh: St. Andrew Press, 1958], 275) For a careful analysis of various views, see Wayne Grudem, "Christ Preaching Through Noah: 1 Peter 3:19–20 in the Light of Dominant Themes in Jewish Literature," *Trinity Journal* 7 (1986): 2.

5. The number and description of paragraph sermons discussed here are taken from Jones, "Supplement to Notes" (handout, ca. 1975).

6. See Appendix for a sample chapter sermon.

7. See G. Campbell Morgan, *Great Chapters of the Bible* (Old Tappan, NJ: Fleming H. Revell, 1935) and Tom Carter, *Spurgeon's Commentary on Great Chapters of the Bible* (Grand Rapids: Kregel), 1998.

8. See page 175 for a sample sermon on the book of Ruth, and page 354 for a sample sermon on Jude.

9. Jones, "An Investigation and Explanation of the Whiting System," 69.

10. See Appendix for a sample doctrinal sermon.

11. Original source unknown.

12. For a sample biographical sermon, see page 345 of the Appendix.

13. For example, there are eight Judases mentioned in Scripture.

14. For a sample sermon on a parable, see page 276. For a good discussion of "The Expositor and the Interpretation of Parables," see Unger, *Principles of Expository Preaching*, 186–200.

15. Zuck, *Basic Bible Interpretation*, 194.

16. Ibid.

17. Ibid.

18. Hence the familiar refrain in such passages as Luke 8:8, "He who has ears to hear, let him hear!" (NKJV)

19. Leonard L. Thompson, *Introducing Biblical Literature: A More Fantastic Country* (Englewood Cliffs, NJ: Prentice-Hall, 1978), 256.

20. See the list "The Parables of Jesus" in Zuck, *Basic Bible Interpretation*, 198.

21. Zuck, *Basic Bible Interpretation*, 204, 210.

22. Ibid., 211–19.

23. Stanley A. Ellisen (class handout, Western Conservative Baptist Seminary).

24. Ibid.

25. For example, Childs refers to N. A. Dahl's "The Parables of Growth." He says,

"Dahl attempts to recover an apologetical dimension of these parables which are offered in specific criticism of Jesus' ministry. How could this be the kingdom when the signs are so insignificant? How could his kingdom succeed when so many followers have fallen away? The parables of growth seek to contrast the secret beginnings, small and insignificant as the mustard seed and leaven, with the richness of the final harvest or the grandeur of the mighty tree." (*Biblical Theology of the Old and New Testaments*, 639.)

26. Ellisen, class handout.

27. Ibid.

28. Ibid.

29. From a dispensational point of view, the parables do *not* teach the doctrines of justification by faith, forgiveness, the Church, or the millennial reign of Christ. They *do* teach the reason for Messiah's rejection at His first coming; the fruitfulness of the Word in receptive hearts; the postponement of the Davidic kingdom during the absence of the King; the role of the King now as Shepherd leading His own out of the fold of Israel; the kingdom of darkness; the responsibility and rewards of those faithful in the stewardship of the King's business, etc. For an alternate view of the parables, see Simon Kistemaker, *The Parables of Jesus* (Grand Rapids: Baker, 1980).

30. Ellisen, "Lesson 6: Guidelines for Preaching the Parables" (class handout, 1976), 3.

31. Much of the material under this heading was adapted from unpublished class notes taken from James Devine, a teaching assistant at Western Conservative Baptist Seminary in the area of Homiletics, 1976–1977. See Appendix for a sample Gospel sermon.

32. Compare Paul's approach to evangelism in Athens, in Acts 17, to his testimony before the Jews in Acts 22, and before King Agrippa, in Acts 26.

33. For a Sample Sermon on a type, see page 120. For a good discussion of "The Expositor and Scriptural Typology," see Unger, *Principles of Expository Preaching*, 201–16.

34. Zuck, *Basic Bible Interpretation*, 176.

35. Ellisen, class handout. Also, see Zuck, *Basic Bible Interpretation*, 177–182.

36. Of James Barr, Childs states: "Barr was at pains to demonstrate that in terms of method there was no basic difference between allegory and typology. Both derive from a 'resultant system' in which the text is construed from the perspective of an outside system brought to bear upon it, and that the difference between allegory and typology depends largely on the resultant system being applied . . . In sum, Barr characterized the New Testament's use of the Old as a different sort of operation from exegesis, and no modern approach such as typology could bridge the discrepancy." (*Biblical Theology of the Old and New Testaments*, 14) Barr's opinion seems to ignore distinctions between *types* and *allegories* (such as their physicality) and, more importantly, the unity of Scripture itself.

37. Compare the list of symbols in Zuck, *Basic Bible Interpretation*, 187–93.

38. Historical schools of excessive typology include the Rabbinic (pre-Christian) Period; the Middle Ages (Dark Age) (500–1400), in which the allegorism of Origen won over the literalism of Antioch; the school of Johannes Cocceius (1603–69), though he made an attempt to study types systematically, dividing them into "innate" and "inferred" classifications; and the school of John Hutchinson (1784), who reacted to the extreme rationalism of his day by finding typical significance in virtually everything in the Old Testament. (Ellisen, class handout)

39. Historical schools of neglect include Reformers Luther and Calvin, whose reaction to the long-entrenched allegorism of the dark ages, and desire to return to the literalism of the Antiochan school, led them to dismiss the validity of typology. The Rationalistic school denied the supernatural and assumes that New Testament writers simply accommodated their material to Old Testament material for pedagogical purposes. The school of Bishop Marsh (1757–1839), recognized only those types "declared to be so by the New Testament." (Ellisen, class handout.)

40. Patrick Fairbairn, *The Typology of Scripture or the Doctrine of Types*, 2 vols. (Philadelphia: Daniels and Smith, 1852). "The most exhaustive and definite work on the history and principles of the interpretation of Bible types. Old and laborious, but still unsurpassed." (Ellisen, class handout)

41. St. Augustine, as cited by Mears, *What the Bible Is All About*, 23.

42. Ellisen, class handout.

43. Also helpful are Zuck's nine principles for interpreting symbols, which recognize the elements of object (the symbol), referent (what the symbol refers to) and the meaning (the resemblance between the symbol and the referent). Zuck, *Basic Bible Interpretation*, 185–86.

44. Ellisen, class handout.

45. Childs refers to the observation of Stanley Walters, that key words in Genesis 22 have "peculiar resonance within the larger canonical collection." The words *ram, burnt-offering* and *appear*, found in the same cluster only in Leviticus 8–9 and 16, link "Abraham's uniquely private experience to Israel's public worship, and conversely Israel's sacrifice is drawn into the theological orbit of Abraham's offering: 'God will provide his own sacrifice.'" (*Biblical Theology of the Old and New Testaments*, 327–28.)

46. Childs complains about the typological interpretation of Genesis 22, referring to "an uncritical Christian tendency to fasten on to an external similarity between such features as Isaac's carrying the wood and Jesus' carrying the cross which obscured the true witness of the text itself. Again, the attempt to relate each biblical witness mimetically badly blurs the radical discontinuities of the text. It belongs to the basic theological task to pursue exegetically how the uniqueness of each text is preserved along with a frequently broadened theological application for ongoing Christian faith." (Ibid., 335–36.)

47. Ellisen, class handout.
48. Ibid.
49. Ibid.

CHAPTER 7

1. Note the similar list of attributes given by Charles Koller: "In order to be well received, the sermon must have unity, structure, aim and progression; it must be sustained by Biblical authority, and must be intelligently presented. There is no doubt that expository preaching would be far more popular than it is, if it were more generally well done." (Charles W. Koller, *Expository Preaching Without Notes* [Grand Rapids: Baker, 1962], 28.) For "six sermonic characteristics" thought essential to effective communication, see Macleod, *The Problem of Preaching*, 75–88. His suggestions are: be personal, be pictorial, be propulsive, be pastoral, be persuasive, and be prophetic.
2. John Gray, *I and II Kings: A Commentary* (Old Testament Library) (Philadelphia: Westminster, 1970), 522. Josephus, however, relates that during the Roman siege of Jerusalem, people ate dung. (*Antiquities*, 9.4.4)
3. M. G. Easton, *Easton's Bible Dictionary* (Oak Harbor, WA: Logos Research Systems, Inc., 1996, c1897).
4. Kaiser, *Toward an Exegetical Theology*, 113.
5. Richards and Bredfeldt, *Creative Bible Teaching*, 115.
6. Illustrations should not introduce extraneous material or a new subject. They should be related to the audience and limited to the facts that are needed.
7. Sue Nichols, *Words on Target* (Richmond: John Knox Press, 1973), 17.
8. White, *A Guide to Preaching*, 219.
9. Hendricks, *Teaching to Change Lives*, 15.
10. Ibid., 17–36.
11. Koller, *Expository Preaching Without Notes*, 35, quoting Blackwood, *The Fine Art of Preaching*, 159.
12. "There are, as there always have been, ministers who preach effectively from manuscript or copious notes in the pulpit, as well as some who read their sermons in full; but the same preachers would be even more effective if they could stand note free in the pulpit. This seems clearly to be the verdict of history." (Koller, *Expository Preaching Without Notes*, 24. Also see Blackwood, *The Fine Art of Preaching*, 153.)

CHAPTER 8

1. Donald E. Demaray, *Pulpit Giants* (Chicago: Moody, 1973), 57–58.
2. Ibid.,166.
3. In 1 Corinthians 15:9–10, Paul states, "I am the least of the apostles, who am not worthy to be called an apostle, because I persecuted the church of God. But

by the grace of God I am what I am, and His grace toward me was not in vain; but I labored more abundantly than they all, yet not I, but the grace of God which was with me" (NKJV).

4. Richards and Bredfeldt, *Creative Bible Teaching*, 213–14.

5. Ibid., 222.

6. Learn to adapt the manner of a sermon's delivery to the culture of the audience being addressed. This may call for radical adjustment of what seems most natural to you, but it communicates sensitivity to, and acceptance of, the audience. This is essential to good communication.

7. Some speakers conclude their messages by taking questions from the listeners. Others offer their personal e-mail addresses for follow-up discussions with those who have questions or comments.

8. Source unknown.

9. Hendricks, *Teaching to Change Lives*, 72.

10. Lynn R. Wessell, "Great Awakening: The First American Revolution," *Christianity Today* 17 (August 1973): 23.

CHAPTER 9

1. The books of Moses are referred to as the *Pentateuch* because they were originally written on five scrolls (*penta*), or books (*teuchos*). These same books are often referred to as the *Law* because they contain the revelation of God's moral and civil code. They are also called the *Torah*, a term that has the idea of giving direction for a right relationship with God and which is sometimes used of the entire Hebrew Bible.

2. Gleason Archer, *A Survey of Old Testament Introduction* (Chicago: Moody, 1964), 17.

3. Ibid.

4. Ellisen, "Part I: The Pentateuch," in *Western Baptist Seminary Bible Workbook* (Portland: Western, ca. 1973), 2.

5. Ellisen, *3 Worlds in Conflict*, 16.

6. Ellisen, "Part I: The Pentateuch," *Western Baptist Seminary Bible Workbook*, 3.

7. Ibid.

8. Welhausen's Documentary Hypothesis (1866) was based on the assumption that Israel was first a pastoral people; then more organized; then obsessed with holy living; then had a highly developed priesthood. JEDP: Jehovahistic, Elohistic, Deuteronomic, Priestly. For an evaluation of the JEDP Theory, see Umberto Cassuto, *The Documentary Hypothesis* (Jerusalem: Magnes, 1961).

9. Bruce Wilkinson and Kenneth Boa, *Talk Thru the Old Testament* (Nashville: Thomas Nelson, 1983), 3.

10. David Dorsey, *The Literary Structure of the Old Testament* (Grand Rapids: Baker, 1999), 30.

11. Gary Derickson (lecture, Faith Evangelical Seminary, Tacoma, WA, 2004).

12. Ibid.

13. Adapted from Ellisen, *Western Baptist Seminary Bible Workbook*, 4.

14. For a more complete treatment of the biblical covenants and how they are related, see Ellisen, *3 Worlds in Conflict*, 31–44.

15. Derickson (handout, Faith Evangelical Seminary).

16. Ellisen, *Western Baptist Seminary Bible Workbook*.

17. Von Rads observes another unifying feature in his comments "Over all this multitude of commands, regulations and ordinances, stands the authority of the First Commandment," and "We must study the first commandment at considerable length, because it is the head and chief of all the commandments." (Gerhard von Rad, *Moses* [London: Lutterworth Press, 1960], 49, 39.)

18. For more on the chiasmus and other literary devices, see Dorsey, *The Literary Structure of the Old Testament*; and Kaiser, *Toward an Exegetical Theology*.

19. The following observations may be made of the Ten Commandments: (1) Man's relations with God are *balanced* by man's relations with man. (2) Man's relations with God come *first* in priority. (3) God's Law deals with *how we think* in our hearts, as well as how we act. (4) The theme of God's Law is *holiness*. (5) The Law is addressed to *individuals*. (6) The Law is a *whole*. (7) The Law was *verbally dictated* by God Himself. (8) Eight of the Ten Commands are *negative*. (9) God's Law was meant to be *kept*, not worshipped. (10) The Law *never justified sinners*. (11) The Law provided God's covenant people with the conditions for enjoying His *blessings* in the land. (12) As God's standard of right behavior, the Law *continues* to serve its purpose of convicting sinners (1 Tim. 1:8).

20. Archetypes include: (1) *hero stories* such as that of Joseph; (2) the *journey*, as in the case of Jacob; (3) the *comedy*, which begins happily and ends happily after encountering a degree of sorrow or loss; (4) the *tragedy*, in which the sequence of events led from prosperity to disaster; (5) the *revelation*, as with Abraham, who was taken from ignorance to hope of a glorious future. See Mathewson, *The Art of Preaching Old Testament Narrative*; and Ryken, *How to Read the Bible as Literature*.

21. *Apodictic* refers to law that necessarily follows from grounds. (Clarence L. Barnhard and Robert K. Barnhard [eds.], *The World Book Dictionary* [Chicago: Doubleday, 1984], 97.)

22. Ibid., 323.

23. K. A. Kitchen, *Ancient Orient and Old Testament* (Chicago: IVP, 1966), 90–102.

24. Ibid.

25. Ibid.

26. Earl D. Radmacher, Ronald B. Allen, and H. Wayne House, eds., *The Nelson Study Bible, New King James Version* (Nashville: Thomas Nelson, 1997), 134.

CHAPTER 10

1. Mathewson, *The Art of Preaching Old Testament Narrative*, 21–23.
2. Ibid., 26.
3. Wilkinson and Boa, *Talk Thru the Old Testament*, 47.
4. Ibid., 47–48.
5. Derickson, class handout.
6. Notice that the books of Samuel, the Kings, and the Chronicles are summarized without reference to the fact that they were each written on two scrolls due to their length, resulting in 1 and 2 Samuel, etc.
7. According to Thompson, "the separation of Ezra-Nehemiah into two books, Ezra and Nehemiah, can only be viewed as artificial." (*Introducing Biblical Literature*, 135.)
8. Kaiser designates as the *syntactical-theological* method of exegesis the "pointing out of the abiding meanings and continuing significance for all believers of all times." (*Toward an Exegetical Theology*, 197.)
9. Kaiser calls the emphasis on historical facts for their own sake, leaving the lessons in the past, *Ebionite,* since Ebionism viewed Jesus as a merely historical human being, and not as divine also. (Ibid., 203 [footnote])
10. Ibid., 203. Kaiser calls the emphasis on spiritual lessons without reference to their historical context a *docetic* approach to Bible study, because the Docetists tried to separate the nature of Christ from the historicity of His life.
11. Ibid., 209.
12. Ibid., 78.
13. Ibid. In light of Kaiser's observations about narrative, Thompson's comments are worth noting: "In the Bible nothing is described which does not contribute to the action. Description of character, scenery, inner feelings, and objects extraneous to the action never distracts the narrator from bringing his story to a rapid climax . . . The suppression of description, rather than giving an effect of incompleteness, gives to biblical stories an air of mystery. The emptiness and silence in the narrative become 'fraught with background' (Auerbach) like a Japanese painting." (*Introducing Biblical Literature*, 32–33.)
14. Mathewson, *The Art of Preaching Old Testament Narrative*, 47.
15. Ibid.
16. Ryken, *How to Read the Bible as Literature*, 75.
17. Ibid.
18. Ibid., 77.
19. It is also true that Old Testament characters are not to be judged on the basis of revelation they didn't have.
20. Ryken, *How to Read the Bible as Literature*, 79–81.
21. Ibid.
22. Ibid., 83.
23. Ibid., 84.

24. Ibid.
25. Ibid.
26. Ibid, 82.
27. Ibid.
28. Ibid, 83.
29. Ibid.
30. Mathewson, *The Art of Preaching Old Testament Narrative*, 43.
31. Ibid.
32. Thompson, *Introducing Biblical Literature*, 42.
33. Ibid.
34. Mathewson, *The Art of Preaching Old Testament Narrative*, 44.
35. Ibid.
36. Ibid.
37. Ibid., 45.
38. Ibid.
39. Stanley A. Ellisen, *Interpretive Outline of the Whole Bible* (Portland: Western Baptist Seminary, c 1974).
40. Gregory Trull, Survey of Biblical Literature [class] (lecture, Corban College, Salem, OR, 2005).
41. Mathewson, *The Art of Preaching Old Testament Narrative*, 58–59.
42. Ibid.
43. Ibid.
44. Ronald M. Hals, *The Theology of the Book of Ruth* (Philadelphia: Fortress, 1969), 3–19.
45. Kaiser, *Toward an Exegetical Theology*, 78.
46. Hals as cited by Kaiser, *Toward an Exegetical Theology*, 79.
47. Kaiser, *Toward an Exegetical Theology*, 78–79.
48. Mathewson, *The Art of Preaching Old Testament Narrative*, 73. Thompson's reference to the "editorial point of view" is a different matter, not to be confused with focalization of the storyteller. Thompson seems to hold a low view of Scripture when he says, "The editorial point of view establishes the Christian believer as the partner superseding all others in the line of God's covenanting with man." He further states, "The placement of the Christian books after the Jewish books has stamped the Christian point of view on the whole Bible." (*Introducing Biblical Literature*, 44) While revelation was given progressively, and its narrative patterns, symbols, images, character types, etc., reflect a forward relatedness, the inspired text is not ultimately the product of editors.
49. Mathewson, *The Art of Preaching Old Testament Narrative*, 73.
50. Ibid.
51. Ibid.
52. Ibid.
53. For example, "And the LORD smelled a soothing aroma. Then the LORD said in

His heart, 'I will never again curse the ground for man's sake, although the imagination of man's heart is evil from his youth'" (Gen. 8:21 NKJV). Mathewson, *The Art of Preaching Old Testament Narrative*, 73.

54. Ibid.
55. Ibid., 74.
56. House based his analysis on Hals, *The Theology of the Book of Ruth*.

CHAPTER 11

1. Ryken, *The Literature of the Bible*, 243.
2. Adapted from Stanley Ellisen, *Western Baptist Seminary Workbook*, 6ff.
3. This is based on the pattern of sacrifices offered by Job as priest of his household; his longevity (about two hundred years; see 42:16); and the lack of reference to Israel, the miraculous Exodus, or Mosaic Law. Eliphaz the Temanite may have descended from Esau through his son Eliphaz and his son Teman (Gen. 36:15). (Ibid.)
4. Ryken, *The Literature of the Bible*, 109.
5. Ibid.
6. Ibid., 110.
7. Dorsey, *The Literary Structure of the Old Testament*, 170.
8. See Francis I. Anderson, *Job* (London: IVP, 1976).
9. Arthur B. Whiting outlined the book of Job as follows: Distress, 1–2; Discussion, 3–41; Deliverance, 42. (Ellisen, *Western Bible Workbook*, lecture, 1974)
10. "One of the tragedies of topical, eisegetical preaching is that it refers to portions of Scripture without reference to where they come in the argument of the book. Job had highs and lows in the process of having his skewed view of life corrected, as it was in the end." (Derickson, lecture)
11. Ibid.
12. Ellisen, *Western Bible Workbook*, 43; Thompson, *Introducing Biblical Literature*, 251.
13. Radmacher, Allen, and House, *Nelson Study Bible*, 1076.
14. Ellisen, *Western Bible Workbook*, 44.
15. Bruce Waltke, "Do Quoheleth and Job Contradict Proverbs?" (an unpublished syllabus).
16. Ibid.
17. Dorsey, *The Literary Structure of the Old Testament*, 187.
18. Ibid., 189.
19. See Derek Kidner, *Proverbs* (London: IVP, 1976); H. Wayne House and Kenneth M Durham, *Living Wisely in a Foolish World* (Grand Rapids: Kregel, 1992); J. Carl Laney, *Balancing Your Act Without Losing It* (Wheaton: Tyndale, 1988); and Bob Deffinbaugh, *Wisdom Literature, Proverbs* (www.Bible.org).

20. Kidner, *Proverbs*, 31–43.

21. For further study, see House and Durham, *Living Wisely in a Foolish World*, 198–214.

22. McDowell, *Right from Wrong*.

23. This outline was adapted from Kidner's subject-study of "the Sluggard." (Kidner, *Proverbs*, 42–43.)

24. Radmacher, Allen, and House, *Nelson Study Bible*, 1082.

25. Waltke, "Do Quoheleth and Job Contradict Proverbs?," 5.

26. Ibid., 7.

27. Ellisen, *Western Bible Workbook*, 27.

28. Ibid., 30.

29. Ibid.

30. Ibid.

31. Korah rebelled against God (Num. 16:1-35) , but his sons rebelled against their father's rebellion by remaining faithful. God then used them to compose the kinds of songs that should be used in the worship of the local church.

32. Radmacher, Allen, and House, *Nelson Study Bible*, 873.

33. See Claus Westermann, *The Praise of God in the Psalms* (Richmond: John Knox, 1965); Ronald B. Allen, *Praise! A Matter of Life and Breath* (Nashville: Nelson, 1980); *When Song Is New* (Nashville: Thomas Nelson, 1983); and *Lord of Song: The Messiah Revealed in the Song* (Portland: Multnomah, 1985); and Derek Kidner, *Psalms,* 2 vols. (London: IVP, 1975).

34. Thompson refers to two human situations that determine the perspective of the psalmist when he writes in first person. Either he is *off-center* (distressed) or *at-center* (enjoying a right relationship with God). The movement is generally "toward, not away from, the center" as man partners with God—sometimes as the Creator and sometimes as the Covenanter. (*Introducing Biblical Literature*, 72.)

35. "The basic unit in biblical poetry consists of two, sometimes three, parallel lines. A two-line unit is called a couplet or a distich; a three-line unit, a tristich" (Ibid., 25.)

36. Radmacher, Allen, and House, *Nelson Study Bible*, 925.

37. Derickson, lecture.

38. Trull, handout.

39. Radmacher, Allen, and House, *Nelson Study Bible*, 873.

40. Ellisen, *Western Bible Workbook*, 84.

41. Ibid.

42. Ibid.

43. Ibid.

44. Ibid.

45. Radmacher, Allen, and House, *Nelson Study Bible*, 1097.

46. Ibid.

47. Ibid.

48. Ibid.
49. Craig S. Glickman, *A Song for Lovers* (Downers Grove, IL: IVP, 1977), 173.
50. Ibid.
51. Ibid.
52. Ellisen, *Western Bible Workbook*, 84.
53. Radmacher, Allen, and House, *Nelson Study Bible*, 1098.
54. Ibid.
55. Ibid.
56. Derickson, lecture.
57. See Glickman, *A Song for Lovers*.
58. Wilkinson and Boa, *Talk Thru the Old Testament*, 206.
59. Derickson, lecture.

CHAPTER 12

1. Wilkinson and Boa, *Talk Thru the Old Testament*, 185.
2. Ibid.
3. For examples of the phrase "The burden of the word of the LORD," see Zechariah 9:1; 12:1; and Malachi 1:1.
4. For an example, see Roland K. Harrison, *Introduction to the Old Testament* (Grand Rapids: Eerdmans, 1969), 757–58. In a similar vein, Von Rad regarded revelation as given to the prophet "to equip him for his office" with a special endowment of the spirit that was not normative for other people. (Von Rad, *Old Testament Theology*, 63) However, it was the revelation itself, not the prophet, who carried divine authority.
5. See 2 Peter 2:15; Judges 1:11; and Revelation 2:14.
6. In Luke 24:27, Luke writes of Jesus: "And beginning at Moses and *all the Prophets*, He expounded to them in all the Scriptures the things concerning Himself" (NKJV, emphasis added). In Acts 10:43, Peter said, "To [Jesus] *all the prophets* witness that, through His name, whoever believes in Him will receive remission of sins" (NKJV, emphasis added).
7. For biblical references to the Eternal Covenant, see Hebrews 9:15 and 13:20.
8. Ellisen, *Three Worlds in Conflict*, 29.
9. For example, the image of Nebuchadnezzar's dream in Daniel 2.
10. "Nostradamus is the Latinized name of Michel de Nostradamus, a physician and astrologer who lived in 16th-century France . . . Nostradamus has been credited with prophesying dozens of pivotal episodes in recent history, including the rise of Adolf Hitler, the assassination of John F. Kennedy and, most recently, the destruction of the World Trade Center towers . . . The most compelling argument against Nostradamus' powers is that his apparent 'hits' are the result of random chance and creative interpretation. There are about a thousand quatrains, most containing more than one prediction and all but a few described in vague, ob-

scure terms. Over the course of hundreds of years, it's certainly possible that some events would line up with some predictions, simply by coincidence." (Tom Harris, "How Nostradamus Works," http://science.howstuffworks.com/nostradamus.htm.)

11. "One commonly held interpretation maintains that the sixty-two weeks can be added to the seven weeks of v. 25, resulting in a total of sixty-nine weeks, or 483 years. If these years are added to the date of the decree of Artaxerxes in Neh. 2, 445 B.C., with an adjustment to allow for the use of a 360-day year, the end of the sixty-nine weeks coincides with the date of the crucifixion of Jesus." (Radmacher, Allen, and House, *Nelson Study Bible*, 1437.)

12. Since the whole of Scripture is God-breathed and profitable (2 Tim. 3:16), the relevance of biblical prophecies cannot be limited to the original addressees. However, Von Rad's contention that the prophet's own understanding was "only one possible way among many of understanding an oracle" seems to confuse the single intended meaning (interpretation) of biblical texts with their many possible applications. Von Rad states, "By being referred to subsequent generations and the situations confronting them, fresh possible ways of taking the prophet's oracles were opened up, and this process continued right down to the time when, in the New Testament, the prophets' preaching was for the last time reinterpreted in the light of present events." (*Old Testament Theology*, 49)

13. Apocalyptic literature is distinguished by the facts that it usually involves an angelic interpreter; is written in prose, not poetry; looks to the conclusion of history; and is highly symbolic.

14. Rather than draw a sharp distinction between prophetic and apocalyptic literature, Robert Thomas views the Revelation as a genuinely prophetic document that has apocalyptic elements, i.e., "when the message was passed on to the prophet in the form of visions." He further states, "The literary genre of inspired writings was not the choice of the human author, but was an inevitable result of the manner in which God chose to reveal his message to the prophet." (Robert Thomas, *Revelation 1–7, An Exegetical Commentary*, vol. 1, ed. Kenneth Barker [Chicago: Moody, 1992], 29)

15. Daniel 7:9 seems to support this. In this verse Daniel describes God's throne as having wheels of "burning fire" (NKJV). Archaeological evidence indicates that ancient thrones also had wheels.

16. Fruchtenbaum, "Rabbinic Quotations of the Old Testament."

17. An *exhaustive* concordance lists every word used in a particular version of the Bible. See James Strong, *Strong's Exhaustive Concordance of the Bible* (New York: Abingdon, 1890), or search in Bible software such as Libronix.

18. Bible dictionaries, such as *Harpers Bible Dictionary*, *Easton's Bible Dictionary*, and *New Bible Dictionary*, show that Uzziah and Azariah are alternate names for the same individual.

19. Sidney Greidanus, *The Modern Preacher and the Ancient Text* (Grand Rapids: IVP, 1988), 239.

20. Gene Tucker, *Form Criticism of the Old Testament* (Philadelphia: Fortress, 1971), 54.

21. Ibid., 55.

22. Ibid., 57.

23. Ibid., 58.

24. Ibid.

25. Ibid., 59.

26. Ibid., 60–70.

27. Greidanus, *The Modern Preacher*, 239.

28. Von Rad, *Old Testament Theology*, 33.

29. Dorsey, *The Literary Structure of the Old Testament*, 266. (Note: Not all scholars find chiasm everywhere Dorsey does. You must analyze the literary structure of Scripture with objectivity.)

30. Greidanus, *The Modern Preacher*, 252.

31. Ibid., 256.

32. Ibid.

33. Ibid., 258.

34. C. F. Keil and F. Delitzsch, *Commentary on the Old Testament* (Grand Rapids: Eerdmans, 1973) 7:303. Also see Archer, *A Survey of Old Testament Introduction*, 348.

35. Kaiser, *Toward an Exegetical Theology*, 188.

36. Ibid.

37. Ibid., 194.

38. Hobart Freeman, *An Introduction to the Old Testament Prophets* (Chicago: Moody, 1968), 195.

39. Ibid.

40. See Strong, *Strong's Exhaustive Concordance of the Bible, Hebrew and Chaldee Dictionary*, 62.

41. Freeman, *An Introduction to the Old Testament Prophets*, 111.

42. Ellisen, *Western Bible Workbook*, 3–4.

43. Ibid.

44. Freeman, *An Introduction to the Old Testament Prophets*, 195.

45. Ellisen, *Western Bible Workbook*, 5.

46. "The Jews abandoned the traditional Messianic interpretation of the servant due to the Christian testimony of the identification of the servant with Jesus of Nazareth, and applied the prophecies to certain ones of the prophets, or to the nation of Israel itself. Beginning with the nineteenth century, critical scholars have adopted one or another of the Jewish interpretations either categorically or with certain modifications." (Freeman, *An Introduction to the Old Testament Prophets*, 209)

47. Ellisen, *Western Bible Workbook*, 27–28.

48. See Von Rad, *Old Testament Theology,* vol 2, 196ff.

49. In a lecture given at Faith Evangelical Seminary, Gary Derickson compared New Testament believers to the Israelites during their wilderness wandering. They received the covenant before they had the land in which they could fully experience its blessings.

50. Matthew Henry, *Matthew Henry's Commentary on the Whole Bible* (Peabody, MA: Hendrickson, 1996).

51. Ellisen, *Western Bible Workbook*, 61–62.

52. Freeman, *An Introduction to the Old Testament Prophets*, 178.

53. Dorsey, *The Literary Structure of the New Testament*, 266.

54. Compare 2 Timothy 2:13.

55. Note: Peter's reference to Joel 2:28 in Acts 2:17 meant not that Joel's prophecy was then being fulfilled, but that the coming of the Holy Spirit at the Feast of Pentecost resembled one aspect of Joel's prophecy.

56. The word used for "shepherds" in 1:1 is not the usual Hebrew word *ro'eh*, but the rare word *noqe*, suggesting instead "sheepbreeders," as seen in the New King James Version. The only other Old Testament occurrence of *noqe* is in 2 Kings 3:4, where Mesha, king of Moab, is said to have engaged in sheep breeding on such a scale that he was able to supply the king of Israel with one hundred thousand lambs and the wool of a hundred thousand rams. Amos evidently managed or owned large herds of sheep and goats and was in charge of other shepherds. (John F. Walvoord, Roy B. Zuck, and Dallas Theological Seminary, *The Bible Knowledge Commentary* [Wheaton: Victor Books, 1983], 1425.)

57. Ellisen, *Western Bible Workbook*, 14.

58. Freeman, *An Introduction to the Old Testament Prophets*, 184.

59. Adapted from Dorsey, *The Literary Structure of the New Testament*, 278.

60. Tucker, *Form Criticism of the Old Testament*, 73.

61. Freeman, *An Introduction to the Old Testament Prophets*, 184.

62. Ibid.

63. Ibid.

64. Keil and Delitzsch, *Commentary on the Old Testament*, 239.

65. Freeman, *An Introduction to the Old Testament Prophets*, 139.

66. Ibid, 184.

67. Ellisen, *Western Bible Workbook*, 21.

68. Dorsey, *The Literary Structure of the New Testament*, 289.

69. Adapted from ibid.

70. Ellisen, *Western Bible Workbook*, 23–24.

71. Ibid.

72. Dorsey, *The Literary Structure of the New Testament*, 290.

73. Adapted from ibid., 291.

74. Ellisen, *Western Bible Workbook*, 14ff.

75. "He spoke as a man of the people, whose sympathy was with the country folk, and he sought to protect them against the greedy rich and the nobles of the capital cities." (Charles F. Pfeiffer, *The Wycliffe Bible Commentary: Old Testament* [Chicago: Moody Press, 1962])

76. Dorsey, *The Literary Structure of the New Testament*, 296.

77. Ibid., 297.

78. John Paterson, *The Goodly Fellowship of the Prophets* (New York: Scribner's, 1948), 111.

79. Dorsey, *The Literary Structure of the New Testament*, 304.

80. Wilkinson and Boa, *Talk Thru the Old Testament*, 273.

81. Ibid.

82. Freeman, *An Introduction to the Old Testament Prophets*, 251.

83. Dorsey, *The Literary Structure of the New Testament*, 309.

84. Ibid., 306.

85. We know that Josiah reigned from 640 to 609, and his reform began in the twelfth year of his rule. Zephaniah wrote sometime after 628 BC, when the revival began, and before Nineveh was destroyed. Thus, Zephaniah wrote sometime before 612 BC.

86. Dorsey, *The Literary Structure of the New Testament*, 313.

87. Ibid., 311.

88. Ellisen, *Western Bible Workbook*, 46.

89. Ibid., 59.

90. Dorsey, *The Literary Structure of the New Testament*, 321.

91. Ibid., 324.

92. Ibid.

93. Ellisen, *Western Bible Workbook, Part V, Minor Prophets*, 49.

94. See also Dorsey, *The Literary Structure of the New Testament*, 318.

CHAPTER 13

1. Wilkinson and Boa, *Talk Thru the Old Testament*, 301.

2. *Webster's New American Dictionary*, s.v. "Gospel."

3. "1. Paul claimed that he received this creedal material from others (1 Cor. 15:3), probably from Peter and James in Jerusalem, ca. 33 to 38 AD (Galatians 1:18–20; especially 1:18: historeo). 2. Paul is himself an eye-witness to a resurrection appearance of Jesus (1 Cor. 15:8; cf. 1 Cor. 9:1; Gal. 1:16). 3. Paul's message was 'checked out' by the Jerusalem apostles (Gal. 2:1–10) and specifically approved (vvs. 6–10). 4. Paul said the apostles were preaching the same message he was concerning the resurrection appearances of Jesus (1 Cor. 15:11; cf. vs. 12, 14, 15)." (Gary R. Habermas, "Who Is the Real Jesus?" [lecture, Morning Star Church, February 25, 2006])

4. David E. Aune, *The New Testament in Its Literary Environment* (Philadelphia: Westminster Press, 1987), 46–54.

5. Ryken, *How to Read the Bible as Literature*, 136.

6. Greidanus, *The Modern Preacher*, 267.

7. Ibid, 268.

8. Ibid, 264.

9. Everett F. Harrison, Geoffrey W. Bromiley, and Carl F. H. Henry, eds., *Baker's Dictionary of Theology* (Grand Rapids: Baker, 1978), 257.

10. Habermas, "Who is the Real Jesus?"

11. Good examples of the constructive application of higher criticism are found in the works of Ryken cited in previous chapters.

12. See Donald Guthrie, *New Testament Introduction* (Downers Grove, IL: IVP, 1970), 121–236.

13. See Merrill C. Tenney, *New Testament Survey* (Grand Rapids: Eerdmans, 1961), 133.

14. Ibid., 136.

15. In John 20:30–31, John said, "Many other signs Jesus also performed . . . which are not written in this book; but these have been written so that you may believe" (NASU).

16. Greidanus, *The Modern Preacher*, 276.

17. According to Habermas, only four sources support the existence of Caesar Tiberius, and three of the four were written later than the Gospel of John. (Habermas, *"Who is the Real Jesus?"*)

18. Ibid. Also, see 2 Peter 1:16–21 and 2 Timothy 3:16–17.

19. Greidanus, *The Modern Preacher*, 277.

20. Ibid.

21. Language users will find an indispensable tool in Aland, *Synopsis Quattor Evangeliorum* (Stuttgart, Germany: Würtembergische, 1967).

22. An excellent resource is R. A. Meltebeke and S. Meltebeke, *Jesus Christ, the Greatest Life Ever Lived*, a revision of *The Greatest Story* (Portland: Western Seminary, 1994), a revision of Johnston M. Cheney, *The Life of Christ in Stereo*, eds. Stanley A. Ellisen and Earl D. Radmacher (Portland: Western Seminary, 1969). Also see Alfred Edersheim, *The Life and Times of Jesus the Messiah* (Grand Rapids: Eerdmans, 1971).

23. Greidanus, *The Modern Preacher*, 298–99.

24. Ibid., 299.

25. Ibid.

26. Ibid., 285–95.

27. Wilkinson and Boa, *Talk Thru the Old Testament*, 308.

28. Guthrie, *New Testament Introduction*, 34–44.

29. Ibid.

30. Wilkinson and Boa, *Talk Thru the Old Testament*, 309.

31. Greidanus, *The Modern Preacher*, 281.

32. For a review of how to preach the parables, see chapter 6.

33. Derickson, "Preaching the Gospels and Acts" (lecture).

34. Preachers should read Matthew 28 from the standpoint of who is speaking and who is being spoken about. Jesus commanded His disciples to baptize the Gentiles in the name of the Triune God. Jews never used the word ἔθνη, nation, of themselves. They were *ha 'am,* the people. Having gone first to the House of Israel (Matt. 10), they were now to go to the *nations.* This may explain the Trinitarian baptismal formula in contrast to the baptism of Jewish converts to Christianity, in the name of Jesus.

35. Tenney, *New Testament Survey,* 143.

36. Ibid.

37. Greidanus, *The Modern Preacher,* 279.

38. Wilkinson and Boa, *Talk Thru the Old Testament,* 319.

39. Ibid.

40. Ibid., 320.

41. Ibid.

42. Greidanus, *The Modern Preacher,* 279.

43. Aune, *The New Testament in Its Literary Environment,* 47.

44. Ibid.

45. Greidanus, *The Modern Preacher,* 280.

46. Wilkinson and Boa, *Talk Thru the Old Testament,* 328.

47. See the "we sections" in which the author of Acts speaks in first person, along with Paul: Acts 16:10–17, 20:5–15, 21:11–18; 27:1–28:16.

48. "The Gospel of Luke is part of a two-volume work composed by the same author." (Childs, *Biblical Theology of the Old and New Testaments,* 276.)

49. Tenney, *New Testament Survey,* 175.

50. Radmacher, Allen, and House, *Nelson Study Bible,* 134.

51. Ibid.

52. Ibid., 1682.

53. Tenney, *New Testament Survey,* 176.

54. Greidanus, *The Modern Preacher,* 283.

55. Aune states: "Jerome (ca. A.D. 327–420) described Luke as the Evangelist most learned in the Greek language (*Letter* 20:4)." (*The New Testament in Its Literary Environment,* 116)

56. Thompson, *Introducing Biblical Literature,* 278.

57. Greidanus, *The Modern Preacher,* 283.

58. Tenney, *New Testament Survey,* 181.

59. Leon Morris, *New Testament Theology* (Grand Rapids: Zondervan, 1986), 196.

60. The Holy Spirit is identified as the Spirit of Jesus in Romans 8:9.

61. Wilkinson and Boa, *Talk Thru the Old Testament,* 336.

62. Greidanus, *The Modern Preacher,* 284.

63. See Morris, *New Testament Theology,* 266–68.

64. Ibid.

65. Ibid.

66. In the purpose clause, ἵνα πιστεύοντες ζωὴν ἔχητε ἐν τῷ ὀνόματι αὐτοῦ, the word πιστεύοντες is the present active participle, nominative, masculine, plural of πιστεύω, "believe." John writes that those of his readers who have entered into belief that Jesus is the Christ, the Son of God, might, "by [continually] believing," "keep on having," ἔχητε, "[the quality of] life [that is] in His name."

CHAPTER 14

1. Greidanus, *The Modern Preacher*, 311.

2. "The Synoptic Gospels, John and Paul share a common basic theological perspective, which stands in continuity to Old Testament theology in contrast to Greek dualism . . . The Synoptic Gospels picture this Old Testament hope in process of fulfillment. In the person and mission of Jesus of Nazareth, the Kingdom of God has come to men in history, bringing to them many of the blessings of God's kingly rule. The God of heaven has visited men on earth to redeem them in fulfillment of the Old Testament hope." (George Eldon Ladd, *The Pattern of New Testament Truth* [Grand Rapids: Eerdmans, 1968], 109)

3. Ryken, *The Literature of the Bible*, 317.

4. Aune states, "The 'letter' was the most popular literary form in early Christianity. It is also the most problematic since it exhibits more variety and flexibility than any other literary form." (*The New Testament in Its Literary Environment*, 159.)

5. Ibid.

6. Greidanus, *The Modern Preacher*, 311.

7. Strong, *Strong's Exhaustive Concordance of the Bible: Greek Dictionary of the New Testament*, 32.

8. Greidanus, *The Modern Preacher*, 313.

9. Aune, *The New Testament in Its Literary Environment*, 158.

10. The use of a scribe, or *amanuensis*, to pen all but the concluding lines and signature of an epistle was apparently common, according to Romans 16:22, 1 Corinthians 16:21, Colossians 4:18, and 2 Thessalonians 3:17. "The popular culture of the first century was, technically, a rhetorical culture . . . The normal mode of writing is by dictation, and that which is written down is intended to be read aloud to a group rather than silently by the individual . . . Clues to the organization of thought are, of necessity, based on sound rather than on sight." (John D. Harvey, *Listening to the Text* [Grand Rapids: Baker, 1998], xv.)

11. Ryken, *The Literature of the Bible*, 327.

12. Greidanus, *The Modern Preacher*, 311.

13. Ibid.

14. Guthrie, *New Testament Introduction*, 658.

15. Ibid., 660.

16. Ibid., 661.

17. Greidanus, *The Modern Preacher*, 319, 321.

18. Ibid., 320–21.

19. See 1 Corinthians 15:55 for a good example of synonymous parallelism; 1 Peter 2:22 for inverted parallelism; and Romans 4:25 for antithetic parallelism. (Greidanus, *The Modern Preacher*, 322.)

20. Adam and Christ are contrasted in Romans 5:12–21; present and future suffering are opposed to one another in Romans 8:18–39 and throughout Paul's discussion in 2 Corinthians 4:16–18. (Ibid.)

21. Examples of metaphors include the armor of God in Ephesians 6:11–17, and the tongue as a fire in James 3:6. (Ibid., 323)

22. Wilkinson and Boa, *Talk Thru the Old Testament*, 367.

23. Greidanus, *The Modern Preacher*, 316.

24. Ibid., 316–17.

25. Adapted from ibid., 315–17.

26. Tenney, *New Testament Survey*, 261.

27. Wilkinson and Boa, *Talk Thru the Old Testament*, 466.

28. Ibid., 450.

29. Radmacher, Allen, and House, *Nelson Study Bible*, 1515–16.

30. Tenney, *New Testament Survey*, 265

31. Ibid.

32. Radmacher, Allen, and House, *Nelson Study Bible*, 1514.

33. Donald H. Launstein, handout, Western Baptist Seminary, 115.

34. Tenney, *New Testament Survey*, 279.

35. Ellisen, *Western Bible Workbook*, 99.

36. Tenney, *New Testament Survey*, 279.

37. Ibid.

38. Launstein, handout, 120.

39. Guthrie, *New Testament Introduction*, 421.

40. For a good discussion of Paul's possible visits and letters to the Corinthians, see ibid., 424–38.

41. Ibid., 438.

42. See Harvey, *Listening to the Text,* 156.

43. Launstein, handout, 129.

44. Aune notes: "Romans is the only letter of Paul written to a Christian community he had neither founded nor visited" (*The New Testament in Its Literary Environment*, 219)

45. For a good discussion of the origin and composition of the church in Rome, see Guthrie, *New Testament Introduction*, 393–96.

46. Greidanus, *The Modern Preacher*, 321.

47. Ibid., 322 (emphasis added).

48. Ibid.

49. Harvey, *Listening to the Text*, 120.

50. Douglas J. Moo, *The Epistle to the Romans* (Grand Rapids: Eerdmans, 1996), 24.

51. Moo, *The Epistle to the Romans*, 24.

52. Tenney, *New Testament Survey*, 314.

53. Ellisen, *Western Bible Workbook*, 7.

54. Guthrie, *New Testament Introduction*, 635.

55. Tenney, *New Testament Survey*, 316.

56. Guthrie, *New Testament Introduction*, 642, quoting U. Wickett (ZNTW, 52, 1961), 230–38.

57. Ellisen, *Western Bible Workbook*, 165.

58. Harvey, *Listening to the Text*, 279.

59. Tenney, *New Testament Survey*, 317.

60. Guthrie, *New Testament Introduction*, 640.

61. Tenney, *New Testament Survey*, 317.

62. Guthrie, *New Testament Introduction*, 509–14.

63. Greidanus, *The Modern Preacher*, 319–23.

64. Ellisen, *Western Bible Workbook*, 8.

65. Wilkinson and Boa, *Talk Thru the Old Testament*, 302.

66. See I. Howard Marshall, *New Testament Theology* (Downers Grove, IL: InterVarsity Press, 2004), 389.

67. Tenney, *New Testament Survey*, 321.

68. Ibid.

69. Wilkinson and Boa, *Talk Thru the Old Testament*, 411. See Colossians 1:4–8 and 2:1.

70. Guthrie, *New Testament Introduction*, 549.

71. Ibid., 550.

72. See Marshall, *New Testament Theology*, 366.

73. Earl Radmacher, Ronald B. Allen, and H. Wayne House, *Nelson's New Illustrated Bible Commentary* (Nashville: Thomas Nelson, 1999), 1559.

74. Marshall, *New Testament Theology*, 367.

75. Guthrie, *New Testament Introduction*, 551.

76. Marshall, *New Testament Theology*, 344.

77. Tenney, *New Testament Survey*, 324.

78. Ibid., 323.

79. Greidanus, *The Modern Preacher*, 324.

80. Marshall, *New Testament Theology*, 345.

81. Homer A. Kent, *The Pastoral Epistles* (Chicago: Moody, 1958), 20.

82. "It was not until 1703 that D. N. Berdot, followed later by Paul Anton in 1726, who popularized it, used the term 'Pastoral' to describe them." (Donald Guthrie, *The Pastoral Epistles* [Grand Rapids: Eerdmans, 1957], 11.)

83. This does not take anything away from the relevance of these epistles to those who function as shepherds, but these men should not be cited as New

Testament examples of solo or senior pastors of a church.

84. Tenney, *New Testament Survey*, 333.

85. William Hendriksen, *New Testament Commentary: Exposition of the Pastoral Epistles* (Grand Rapids: Baker, 1957), 41.

86. Tenney, *New Testament Survey*, 333.

87. Radmacher, Allen, and House, *Nelson Study Bible*, 1592.

88. Launstein, handout, 179.

89. Radmacher, Allen, and House, *Nelson Study Bible*, 1594.

90. Ibid, 1592.

91. Tenney, *New Testament Survey*, 338.

92. Marshall, *New Testament Theology*, 399.

93. Tenney lists the following doctrines addressed in the epistle to Titus: "1. The personality of God (2:11, 3:6). 2. The qualities of His love and grace (2:11, 3:4). 3. His title of Savior (2:10, 3:4). 4. The saviorhood of Christ (2:13, 3:6). 5. The Holy Spirit (3:5). 6. The implication of the triune being of God (3:5, 6). 7. The essential deity of Christ (2:13). 8. The vicarious atonement of Christ (2:14). 9. The universality of salvation (2:11). 10. Salvation by grace, not by works (3:5). 11. The incoming of the Holy Spirit (3:5). 12. Justification by faith (3:7). 13. Sanctification (purification) of His own people (2:14). 14. Separation from evil (2:12). 15. Inheritance of eternal life (3:7). 16. The return of Christ (2:13)." (*New Testament Survey*, 338)

94. Marshall, *New Testament Theology*, 401.

95. Guthrie, *New Testament Introduction*, 628.

96. Launstein, handout, 179.

97. Wilkinson and Boa, *Talk Thru the Old Testament*, 435.

98. Ibid.

99. Tenney, *New Testament Survey*, 351–52.

100. Marshall, *New Testament Theology*, 642.

101. Tenney, *New Testament Survey*, 350.

102. Ibid, 349–50.

103. Ellisen, *Western Bible Workbook*, 173.

104. So Marshall states, "Peter's main concern is to rehabilitate the expectation of the future coming (parousia) of Jesus." (*New Testament Theology*, 672.)

105. Guthrie, *New Testament Introduction*, 850.

106. Tenney, *New Testament Survey*, 367.

107. Wilkinson and Boa, *Talk Thru the Old Testament*, 502.

108. George Lawrence Lawlor, *Translation and Exposition of the Epistle of Jude* (Phillipsburg, NJ: Presbyterian and Reformed Publishing Co., 1972), 14.

109. Ibid.

110. Ibid.

111. Tenney, *New Testament Survey*, 374.

112. Ibid.

113. Guthrie, *New Testament Introduction*, 869

114. Wilkinson and Boa, *Talk Thru the Old Testament*, 485.

115. B. F. Westcott, *The Epistles of John*, (Grand Rapids: Eerdmans, 1966), xxxii.

116. Guthrie, *New Testament Introduction*, 893.

117. Ibid., 896.

CHAPTER 15

1. Aune notes that Revelation 1:1–2 marks "the first occurrence of the term [apoc-alypse] in apocalyptic literature, a sentence intended to function as a title." (*The New Testament in Its Literary Environment*, 226.)

2. Guthrie, *New Testament Introduction*, 934.

3. Dionysius charged inconsistencies of Greek grammar, vocabulary, expressions, theological content, and use of the author's name. There are, however, remark-able similarities between the Revelation and the Gospel of John. Apparent dif-ferences in style can be explained by the unusual circumstances under which it was written, including exile on the Isle of Patmos, startling visions, the nature of apocalyptic literature, and possible use of a secretary. (Radmacher, Allen, and House, *Nelson Study Bible*.)

4. Guthrie, *New Testament Introduction*, 949.

5. Ibid., 949–60.

6. Radmacher, Allen, and House, *Nelson Study Bible*, 2162.

7. Thomas, *Revelation 1–7*, 29.

8. Greidanus, *The Modern Preacher*, 229.

9. Ibid.

10. Ibid., 236–38.

11. Ibid.

12. Ryken, *How to Read the Bible as Literature*, 335.

13. John Walvoord, *The Revelation of Jesus Christ* (Chicago: Moody, 1966), 16–20.

14. Childs, for example, states of the apostle John, "The whole apocalyptic scenario which he inherited has now been reinterpreted as completed action. It does not lie in the future, but in every apocalyptic cycle described, God now rules his universe and the kingdom has come (7:10; 11; 15:19:6). Satan has been defeated by the Lamb and cast out of heaven. The Anti-Christ has been conquered and salvation is realized." (*Biblical Theology of the Old and New Testaments*, 321.)

15. Ryken, *The Literature of the Bible*, 335.

16. Guthrie, *New Testament Introduction*, 969–74.

17. Guthrie, *New Testament Introduction*, 971. In a footnote, Guthrie states that "Farrar was the first to connect the twelve houses of Israel with the signs of the Zodiac."

18. Ryken, *The Literature of the Bible*, 335.

19. Ibid., 336.

20. Adapted from Ryken, *The Literature of the Bible*, 337.
21. See Ryken, *The Literature of the Bible*, 337.
22. Charted on the basis of Ryken's observations and personal comparison to Revelation 6. (Ryken, *The Literature of the Bible*, 338.)
23. Ibid.
24. Ibid.
25. Walvoord, *The Revelation of Jesus Christ*, 48.
26. Morris, *New Testament Theology*, 292.
27. Thomas, *Revelation 1–7*, 517.
28. See Greidanus, *The Modern Preacher*, 250–62, for a fuller discussion of these and other guidelines.

APPENDIX

1. Currah, "Outlining from the Nestle-Aland *Novum Testamentum Graece*."
2. Mears, *What the Bible Is All About*, 23.
3. With reference to age, and to distinguish an adult man from a boy, see Matthew 14:21 and 15:38 (where ἄνδρες, γυναῖκες and παιδία are discriminated); with the added notion also of intelligence and virtue, see 1 Corinthians 13:11 (opposed to νήπιος); Ephesians 4:13; and James 3:2 (in the last two passages, τέλειος ἀνήρ).
4. James S. Hewett, ed., *Illustrations Unlimited*, 167.

Bibliography

Adams, Jay E. *Shepherding God's Flock.* Chestnut Hill: Presbyterian and Reformed Publishing Co., 1975.

Aland, Kurt. *Synopsis Quattor Evangeliorum.* Stuttgart: Wütembergische, 1967.

Allen, Ronald B. *Praise! A Matter of Life and Breath.* Nashville: Thomas Nelson, 1980.

———. *Lord of Song.* Portland: Multnomah, 1985.

———. *When Song Is New.* Nashville: Thomas Nelson, 1983.

Ames, William. *The Marrow of Theology.* Translated by John D. Eusden, ed. Boston: Pilgrim, 1968.

Anderson, Francis I. *Job.* London: InterVarsity, 1976.

Archer, Gleason. *A Survey of Old Testament Introduction.* Chicago: Moody, 1964.

Aune, David E. *The New Testament in Its Literary Environment.* Philadelphia: Westminster, 1987.

Barclay, William. *The Letters of James and Peter.* Edinburgh: St. Andrew, 1958.

Barnhard, Clarence L., and Robert K. Barnhard, eds. *The World Book Dictionary.* Chicago: Doubleday, 1984.

Blackwood, Andrew W. *The Fine Art of Preaching.* Grand Rapids: Baker, 1976.

Brown, Colin. *The New International Dictionary of New Testament Theology,* vol 1. Grand Rapids: Zondervan, 1967.

Bruce, F. F., ed. *The New International Commentary on the New Testament.* Grand Rapids: Eerdmans, 1971.

Carter, Tom. *Spurgeon's Commentary on Great Chapters of the Bible.* Grand Rapids: Kregel, 1998.

Cassuto, Umberto. *The Documentary Hypothesis.* Jerusalem: Magnes, 1961.

Chafer, Lewis Sperry. *Salvation.* Grand Rapids: Zondervan, 1917.

Charnock, Stephen. *The Existence and Attributes of God.* Reprint. Minneapolis: Klock & Klock, 1977.

Childs, Brevard S. *Biblical Theology of the Old and New Testaments.* Minneapolis: Fortress Press, 1992.

Cook, W. Robert. *Systematic Theology in Outline Form.* Portland: Western Baptist Seminary Press, 1970.

Cromarty, John M. "Bullinger and the Second Helvetic Confession." *Our Banner,* June 1976.

Currah, Galen. "Outlining from the Nestle-Aland *Novum Testamentum Graece.*" Portland: Western Conservative Baptist Seminary, [1973].

Deffinbaugh, Bob. *Wisdom Literature, Proverbs.* www.Bible.org.

Demaray, Donald E. *Pulpit Giants.* Chicago: Moody, 1973.

Dorsey, David A. *The Literary Structure of the Old Testament.* Grand Rapids: Baker, 1999.

Easton, M. G. *Easton's Bible Dictionary.* 1897. Oak Harbor: Logos Research Systems, Inc., 1996.

Edersheim, Alfred. *The Life and Times of Jesus the Messiah.* Grand Rapids: Eerdmans, 1971.

Ellisen, Stanley A. *3 Worlds in Conflict.* Sisters: Multnomah, 1998.

Eichrodt, Walter. "Is Typological Exegesis an Appropriate Method?" In *Essays on Old Testament Hermeneutics.* Edited by Claus Westermann. Translated by James Luther Mays. Atlanta: John Knox Press, 1960, 1979.

Fairbairn, Patrick. *The Typology of Scripture or the Doctrine of Types.* 2 vols. Philadelphia: Daniels and Smith, 1852.

Farris, Stephen. *Preaching that Matters.* Louisville: Westminster John Knox Press, 1998.

Freeman, Hobart. *An Introduction to the Old Testament Prophets.* Chicago: Moody, 1968.

Fruchtenbaum, Arnold G. "Rabbinic Quotations of the Old Testament And How It Relates To Joel 2 and Acts 2." *Ariel Ministries.* http://www.ariel.org.

Fausti, Remo P. and Edward L. McGlone. *Understanding Oral Communication.* Menlo Park: Cummings, 1972.

Glickman, Craig S. *A Song for Lovers.* Downers Grove: InterVarsity, 1977.

Gray, John. *I & II Kings* in "The Old Testament Library." Philadelphia: Westminster, 1970.

Greidanus, Sidney. *The Modern Preacher and The Ancient Text.* Grand Rapids: InterVarsity, 1988.

Grudem, Wayne. *Evangelical Feminism & Biblical Truth.* Sisters: Multnomah, 2004.

———. "Christ Preaching Through Noah: 1 Peter 3:19-20 In The Light Of Dominant Themes In Jewish Literature," *Trinity Journal* 7, 1986.

Guthrie, Donald. *New Testament Introduction.* Downers Grove: InterVarsity, 1970.

———. *The Pastoral Epistles.* Grand Rapids: Eerdmans, 1977.

Harrison, Everett F., Geoffrey W. Bromiley, and Carl F. H. Henry, eds. *Baker's Dictionary of Theology.* Grand Rapids: Baker, 1978.

Harrison, Roland K. *Introduction to the Old Testament.* Grand Rapids: Eerdmans, 1969.

Harvey, John D. *Listening to the Text.* Grand Rapids: Baker, 1998.

Hendricks, Howard. *Teaching to Change Lives.* Sisters: Multnomah, 1989.

Hendriksen, William. *New Testament Commentary: Exposition of The Pastoral Epistles.* Grand Rapids: Baker, 1957.

Hirsch, E. D. *Validity in Interpretation.* New Haven: Yale, 1967.

Hobbs, Hershel H. *Preaching Values from the Papyri.* Grand Rapids: Baker, 1964.

House, H. Wayne. *The Role of Women in Ministry Today.* Grand Rapids: Baker, 1995.

House, H. Wayne, and Kenneth M., Durham. *Living Wisely in a Foolish World.* Grand Rapids: Kregel, 1992.

Johnson, Elliot E. *Expository Hermeneutics: An Introduction.* Grand Rapids: Zondervan, 1990.

Jones, Milton, "An Investigation and Explanation of the Whiting System of Homiletics as a Practical Approach to Preaching." Th. M. thesis, Western Conservative Baptist Seminary, 1965.

Kaiser, Walter C., Jr. *Toward an Exegetical Theology.* Grand Rapids: Baker, 1981.

Kaiser, Walter C., Jr. and Moisès Silva. *An Introduction to Biblical Hermeneutics.* Grand Rapids: Zondervan, 1994.

Kantenwein, Lee L. *Diagrammatical Analysis.* Winona Lake: BMH Books, 1979.

Keil, C. F. and F. Delitzsch. *Commentary on the Old Testament.* 10 vols. Grand Rapids: Eerdmans, 1973.

Kent, Homer A. *The Pastoral Epistles.* Chicago: Moody, 1958.

Kostenberger, Andreas J. and Thomas R. Schreiner, eds. *Women In The Church.* 2nd ed. Grand Rapids: Baker Academic, 1995, 2005.

Kidner, Derek, *Proverbs.* London: InterVarsity, 1976.

———. *Psalms,* 2 vols. London: InterVarsity, 1975.

Kistemaker, Simon. *The Parables of Jesus.* Grand Rapids: Baker, [1980].

Kitchen, K. A. *Ancient Orient and Old Testament.* Chicago: InterVarsity, 1966.

Koller, Charles W. *Expository Preaching Without Notes.* Grand Rapids: Baker, 1962.

Ladd, George Eldon. *The Pattern of New Testament Truth.* Grand Rapids: Eerdmans, 1968.

Laney, J. Carl. *Balancing Your Act Without Losing It.* Wheaton: Tyndale, 1988.

Lawlor, George Lawrence. *Translation and Exposition of the Epistle of Jude.* Presbyterian and Reformed Publishing Co., 1972.

Liefeld, Walter L. *New Testament Exposition.* Grand Rapids: Zondervan, 1984.

Maier, Paul L. *In the Fullness of Time.* San Francisco: Harper San Francisco, 1991.

Macleod, Donald. *The Problem of Preaching.* Philadelphia: Fortress, 1987.

Marshall, I. Howard. *New Testament Theology.* Downers Grove: InterVarsity, 2004.

Mathewson, Steven D. *The Art of Preaching Old Testament Narrative.* Grand Rapids: Baker, 2002.

McQuilkin, J. Robertson. *Understanding and Applying the Bible.* Chicago: Moody, 1984

McDowell, Josh. *Right from Wrong.* Dallas: Word, 1994.

Mayers, Ronald B. *Balanced Apologetics.* Grand Rapids: Kregel, 1984.

Mears, Henrietta C. *What the Bible Is All About.* Ventura: Regal, 1999.

Moo, Douglas J. *The Epistle to the Romans.* Grand Rapids: Eerdmans, 1996.

Morris, Leon. *New Testament Theology.* Grand Rapids: Zondervan, 1986.

Nichols, Sue. *Words On Target.* Richmond: John Knox Press, 1973.

Packer, J. I. *Knowing God.* Downers Grove: InterVarsity, 1973.

———. "Puritan Evangelism." www.apuritansmind.com.

Paterson, John. *The Goodly Fellowship of the Prophets.* New York: Scribner's, 1948.

Pfeiffer, Charles F. *The Wycliffe Bible Commentary: Old Testament.* Chicago: Moody Press, 1962.

Pinnock, Clark H. *Biblical Revelation.* Chicago: Moody, 1971.

Piper, John and Wayne Grudem, eds. *Recovering Biblical Manhood and Womanhood.* Wheaton: Crossway, 1991.

Radmacher, Earl D. *The Nature of the Church.* Portland: Western Baptist Press, 1972.

———. *Salvation.* Nashville: Word, 2000.

Ramm, Bernard. *Protestant Biblical Interpretation.* Grand Rapids: Baker, 1970.

Richards, Lawrence O. and Gary J Bredfeldt. *Creative Bible Teaching.* Chicago: Moody, 1998.

Robertson, A. T. *Word Pictures in the New Testament.* 6 vols. Nashville: Broadman, 1930.

Robinson, Haddon W. *Biblical Preaching.* Grand Rapids: Baker, 1980.

Ryken, Leland. *The Literature of the Bible.* Grand Rapids: Zondervan, 1974.

———. *How to Read the Bible as Literature.* Grand Rapids: Zondervan, 1984.

———. *The Word of God in English.* Wheaton: Crossway, 2002.

Saucy, Robert L. *The Church in God's Program.* Chicago: Moody, 1972.

Stott, John R. W. *The Preacher's Portrait.* Grand Rapids: Eerdmans, 1961.

Strauch, Alexander. *Biblical Eldership.* Littleton: Lewis and Roth, 1995.

Tenney, Merrill C. *New Testament Survey.* Grand Rapids: Eerdmans, 1961.

Thomas, Robert. *Revelation 1-7, An Exegetical Commentary.* Kenneth Barker, ed. Chicago: Moody, 1992.

Thompson, Leonard L. *Introducing Biblical Literature: A More Fantastic Country.* Englewood Cliffs: Prentice-Hall, 1978.

Tozer, A. W. *The Knowledge of the Holy.* New York: HarperCollins, 1961.

Traina, Robert. *Methodological Bible Study.* Wilmore: Asbury Theological Seminary, 1952.

Tucker, Gene. *Form Criticism of the Old Testament.* Philadelphia: Fortress, 1971.

Turner, Nigel. *Grammatical Insights Into the New Testament.* Edinburgh: T & T Clark, 1965.

Unger, Merrill F. *Principles of Expository Preaching.* Grand Rapids: Zondervan, 1955.

Von Rad, Gerhard. *Moses.* London: Lutterworth Press, 1960.

———. *Old Testament Theology,* 2 vols. Translated by D. M. G. Stalker. New York: Harper & Row. 1960.

Walvoord, John. *The Revelation of Jesus Christ.* Chicago: Moody, 1966.

Walvoord, John F. and Roy B. Zuck. *The Bible Knowledge Commentary.* Wheaton: Victor, 1983–1985.

Ward, Ronald A. *Hidden Meaning in the New Testament.* Old Tappan: Revell, 1969.

Warfield, Benjamin B. *The Inspiration and Authority of the Bible.* Philadelphia: Presbyterian and Reformed Publishing Co., 1970.

Westcott, B. F. *The Epistles of John.* Grand Rapids: Eerdmans, 1966.

Westermann, Claus. *The Praise of God in the Psalms.* Richmond: John Knox Press, 1965.

White, R. E. O.. *A Guide to Preaching.* Grand Rapids: Eerdmans, 1973.

Wilkinson, Bruce and Boa. Kenneth. *Talk Thru the Bible.* Nashville: Thomas Nelson, 2004.

Wiseman, D. J., ed. *Tyndale Old Testament Commentaries.* Leicester: InterVarsity, 1974.

Wood, Bryant G. "The Walls of Jericho," *Bible and Spade.* Spring, 1999.

Wuest, Kenneth. *Word Studies in the Greek New Testament.* 3 vols. Grand Rapids: Eerdmans, 1973.

Zuck, Roy B. *Basic Bible Interpretation.* Wheaton: Victor, 1991.

Index